Marguerite Duras

Marguerite Duras

A LIFE

~

Laure Adler

Translated by
Anne-Marie Glasheen

THE UNIVERSITY OF CHICAGO PRESS

The University of Chicago Press, Chicago 60637
Victor Gollancz
An imprint of Orion Books Ltd

All rights reserved. Published 2000
Printed in the United States of America

09 08 07 06 05 04 03 02 01 00   1 2 3 4 5
ISBN: 0-226-00758-8 (cloth)

Library of Congress Cataloging-in-Publication Data

Adler, Laure.
    [Marguerite Duras. English]
    Marguerite Duras : a life / Laure Adler ; translated by Anne-Marie Glasheen.
        p. cm.
    Includes bibliographical references.
    ISBN 0-226-00758-8 (alk. paper)
        1. Duras, Marguerite. 2. Authors, French—20th century—Biography. I. Title.
PQ2607.U8245 Z5313 2000
843'.912—dc21
[B]

00-033773

CONTENTS

~

ILLUSTRATIONS

⌇

1. Marguerite Duras in Saigon with Max Bergier, one of her mother's pupils, 25 April 1933.
2. The Donnadieu family in 1920.
3. and 4. Madame Donnadieu and her son Paul.
5. The river crossing, where the first meeting with 'The Lover' took place.
6. Jean Lagrolet around the time he met Marguerite Duras.
7. Duras and Jean Lagrolet in the early thirties, © private collection.
8. Duras in the rue Saint-Benoît, © International Press.
9. Robert Antelme around the time he first met Marguerite Duras.
10. Duras in militant gear ready to go and sell *l'Humanité-Dimanche*.
11. Duras in the rue Saint-Benoît, in 1955, © Lipnitzki-Viollet.
12. Marguerite and her son Jean, nicknamed Outa.
13. Duras in Trouville, in 1963.
14. Film shoot for *India Song* in the Trianon Palace, Versailles. Marguerite Duras with Bruno Nuytten, to whom she dedicated *The Lover*, © Erica Lennard.
15. Elio Vittorini and Ginetta Vittorini, together with Albert Steiner and Duras.
16. Rehearsing *Shaga* with Marie-Ange Duteil and Claire de Luca, © Bernand.
17. Duras and Jules Dassin in 1967, working on the screen adaptation of *Ten-Thirty on a Summer Night*, © Cahiers du Cinéma.
18 & 20. Duras and *India Song*, Cannes Film Festival, 1974; photograph of Duras © Elizabeth Lennard.
19. Typed manuscript of the beginning of chapter III of *Ten-Thirty on a Summer Night* (1967) with handwritten corrections, © Marguerite Duras Foundation, IMEC.
21 & 22. Marguerite Duras at Les Roches Noires, Trouville, in 1990, © Erik Poulet and Henri Chatelain.
23. Duras and Yann Andréa in Neauphle, in the early nineties.

24. Neauphle, © Michèle Laverdac.
25. Marguerite's writing table.
26. Marguerite Duras, © Julio Donoso/Sygma.
27. Marguerite Duras, © Sichov/Sipa Press.

Photographs 1, 3, 4 and 5 © Max Bergier Collection.
Photographs 2, 10, 12, 13, 15 and 25 © Jean Mascolo Collection.
Photographs 6 and 9 © Jean-Louis Jacquet Collection.

I feel like a sleepwalker, as though fiction and life were merging. By writing so much, my life has become the life of a shadow; I feel as though I am no longer moving over the earth but floating weightless through an atmosphere made not of air but of darkness. And if the light were to penetrate this darkness, I should fall, crushed.

August Strindberg,
Correspondence

PREFACE

~

I first came across *The Sea Wall* in a collection of tired books in a house I was renting. It had shared the same fate as the airport novels that were lying around, either scorched by the sun on the beach or washed by sudden showers during nights spent under the stars. Needless to say it was the obvious choice, but I always had the feeling it had been lying there waiting for me.

That summer I'd had one of those experiences you think at the time you'll never get over. Yet by replacing my time with its time, the chaos of my life with the sequence of its story, *The Sea Wall* helped me take stock of the past and envisage a future. The fierce determination and understanding love of the young girl in the novel had a lot to do with it and on my return to Paris I wrote to Marguerite Duras and told her so.

Two days after I'd delivered my letter to her apartment in the rue Saint-Benoît, Duras called me. She wanted to see me. To talk, she said.

I have to admit I hesitated before taking the plunge and going to meet her. What a book can give, can – it is a well-known fact – often be taken away once you get to know the author. And I was aware that the name of Marguerite Duras had attracted a small circle of devoted admirers, for whom truth had undoubtedly been replaced by a self-perpetuating self-satisfied hagiography.

I wasn't feeling particularly relaxed as I rang at the door of the rue Saint-Benoît. Duras intimidated me. Her voice, her style, her outbursts, all had contributed to creating a Duras legend where a rather unhealthy interest in the person vied with admiration for the writer. I soon realized I had been quite wrong. The famous author opened the door, led me into the kitchen and made coffee. The first thing that struck me about her was the sparkle in her eyes and her tremendous laughing energy. That first impression was to stay with me. Her closest friends from her different lives (for she had had

3

several along the way) all said, when they talked about her, that what they most remembered of Marguerite was her laughter. That mischievous, childish laughter, that communicative laughter of friendship, that mocking, indeed sometimes spiteful laughter. Marguerite laughed at everything, at everyone and occasionally at herself. That day too she laughed a lot as she talked to me about her childhood, her younger brother, the photographs hanging near the mirror. She also spoke of her mother and of the adventures she'd had with her son.

For a while we continued to see one another. We often talked on the phone. Marguerite's speciality was phone calls in the middle of the night. Each time a book came out she'd panic like a child and clumsily or peremptorily entreat my advice. Then we became separated by illness. She cut herself off, was cared for and protected by a man who loved her. I was never her friend, just someone she said she 'liked a lot', someone she liked to chat to every now and then, not just about cinema, literature, fashion, events in the news and politics, but cooking too, in an unpretentious way, allowing our conversations to flow pleasantly.

She loved children. The day after her book *Blue Eyes Black Hair* was published, my daughter Léa was born. She had black hair and blue eyes. Marguerite said it was an omen. And then as time went by we drifted apart, though not away. Duras was caught up in the fame *The Lover* had brought her. Never again did she talk to me as she had done before; she became a parody of herself, referring to herself in the third person, unaware that she was supplying her critics with their most effective ammunition. After the adulation came the time when it was fashionable to hold Duras up to public ridicule.

Often Duras speaks secretly in us – but on occasion for us. At any rate, that's the impression I get. In Duras – in both her books and her films – the reader-voyeur is king. She is able to give us emotions drawn from the darkest and most hidden areas of the psyche. She has been accused of egoism, narcissism and all-consuming self-love. From the moment her first book was published, Marguerite Duras believed in her own talent. Very soon she saw herself as a genius. During the last twenty years of her life, she'd refer to herself as 'Duras', yet she no longer had a clear picture of who she was, of who this writing Duras was. Having to reread herself not long before her death, she wrote in the margin of an unpublished notebook, in her elegant cramped handwriting, 'Is this Duras?' 'It doesn't look like Duras.'

So who was Duras really? Mischievous Duras who wore so many masks, who delighted in clouding the issue, in hiding particular episodes of her life? Or the one so expert at autobiography, so adept at confession, who had us believing her lies. In the last years of her life, Marguerite Duras believed more in the existence of her fictional characters than in the lovers and friends who had accompanied her along the way. To her, the very word 'truth' was open to doubt and reality so touching she moved out of its reach. Only when she was writing was she one with herself. 'I know that when I write, something happens. I let something inside me, probably the product of femininity, take over ... and then it's as though I were returning to rugged terrain.'[1]

There is, on the one hand, the life Marguerite Duras lived, and, on the other, the one she recounted. How is it possible to untangle fact from fiction, from lies? As the years went by she wanted through writing to recreate her life and to make the biography her own. This book endeavours to separate out and compare the various versions, although it cannot claim to be a truthful account of a person who so loved to conceal herself. It will attempt to shed light on the shadowy areas she so skilfully described: her relationship in adolescence with a Chinese man, her behaviour during the Second World War and Liberation, her emotional, literary and political passions. Marguerite Duras was a child of the twentieth century; her life was that of a woman deeply involved in her time and wholly committed to the principal struggles of the era.

In a personal journal that came to light after her death, she had written on a torn-out sheet of paper, 'People who say they don't like their own books, if such people exist, do so because they haven't learned to resist the attraction of humiliation ... I love my books. They interest me. The people in my books are the people of my life.'

Marguerite Duras couldn't remember when she decided she wanted to become a writer. 'It's lost in the mists of time,' she used to say, but it was probably towards the end of her childhood. 'I've never written, though I thought I wrote, never loved, though I thought I loved, never done anything but wait outside the closed door,' she writes in *The Lover.*

And closed the doors would stay to the biographer. When in the autumn of 1992 I asked Marguerite Duras if she would allow me to write her biography, she shrugged her shoulders, referred me back to her books, offered me a cup of coffee and changed the subject: that day it was politics. At the time she was trying to postpone publication of a book about her.[2] Only later did I understand the aggression and anger that drove her. Duras hated people delving into her life, loathed on principle the idea that someone other than herself should write about her. It was not by accident that she had so skilfully hidden certain events in her life. So, no entry. Duras had so painstakingly created her own character that I could see it was pointless to expect her to give her consent.

I followed her advice and bought her early books. Reading her *oeuvre* in chronological order prompted numerous questions, biographical as well as literary. I went back to see her. Inside me, there were so many questions tripping over each other that I couldn't say a word. She was the one who started to talk that afternoon. She showed me a photograph of her younger brother pinned to the wall above her desk and then she was off ... In her inimitable husky voice and that disjointed way she had of speaking, she talked of Indo-China, her childhood, how throughout her life people had betrayed her, and above all of the fear, the fear that never left her.

All through her childhood and adolescence Marguerite Duras had suffered badly. This suffering may well explain why she was such a rebel. She was always an indignant *pasionaria* of freedom: not just political but sexual freedom too. Throughout her life she was a great lover, always advocating the right to pleasure. She loved making love and knew how to glorify the power of love, the pleasure, the indulgence, the rapture of love. She explored its extremes and sucked out its energies: the pursuit of pleasure was a search for the absolute. She said she couldn't help herself, she'd been made for that. 'At the age of fifteen I had the face of pleasure,' she said in *The Lover,* 'and yet I had no knowledge of pleasure.' Duras was to remain at the mercy of pleasure all her life. Desire was her line of conduct. She would never let it escape, even if it meant rejection, even if it meant great pain. 'You didn't have to attract desire. Either it was in the woman who aroused it or it didn't exist. Either it was at first glance or else it had never been. It was instant knowledge of the sexual relationship or it was nothing.'[3]

When work began on this book, Marguerite Duras and I met a few times but already her memory was beginning to go. Some days it was there, others it wasn't. There were days filled with her childhood or memories of her student days in the Latin Quarter of Paris. There were days spent analysing her books – the ones she still liked (she'd started to reject her work). Then there were the sad days, when smugness, narcissism and brooding over a grudge got in the way of conversation. But there was also good humour, Marguerite's tremendous good humour; she would occasionally burst out laughing and this laughter would brush everything aside, remove ill will and make her charming once more.

I soon came to realize that she wasn't the archivist of herself. I would have to search elsewhere. In the archives of colonial libraries, certain landscapes and places she'd lived in, a shared past recollected by former travelling companions, the unpublished texts, the personal journals found abandoned among the cookery books, whole days spent listening to those who had shared her life, her loves, her illusions.

There were many willing, for her sake, to play the truth game. Some became friends along the way. To you, thank you from the bottom of my heart. This book would never have been finished without the invaluable help of four people in particular: Jean Mascolo, Marguerite's son, who allowed me access to unpublished archives; Dionys Mascolo, his father and Marguerite's former partner, who lent me notebooks and correspondence; Monique Antelme, who was a great help and support all the time I was working on the book; and finally Yann Andréa, who was a conscientious messenger between Marguerite and myself. It was he who wrote down everything she said during those last few months; for example, the answers to questions I asked about writing. In one, the last I received, she said that no book was a mystery, that no life had secrets.

And yet secrets there are still. Some, I hope, will be disclosed, though there remains a hint of a shadow, a touch of mystery. Maybe it's better that way. There are times when the biographer can only make suppositions. It's for the reader to find the truth. In life as in her books, where pieces of the jigsaw were always missing, there are still holes, still gaps.

A biography of Marguerite Duras? She had sounded the warning: what is in the books is more real than what the author experienced. She also said, 'The story of my life doesn't exist. Does not exist. There's never any centre to it. No path, no line. There are great spaces where you pretend there used to be someone, but it's not true, there was no one.'[4]

Before she died, she authorized the transfer of all her personal archives to the Institut de la mémoire de l'édition contemporaine (IMEC). She claimed that little had been kept back. Like the wilted flowers she'd dried and preserved, Marguerite Duras had collected from here and there the traces of her past. Sixteen boxes arrived at IMEC, in the rue de Lille! Not only publications, corrected proofs and newspaper cuttings from all over the world, but scripts, screenplays, the different drafts of her books, sketches, her son's school notebooks, art books taken from local dustbins, recipes rewritten, reinvented, unpublished work, photographs with comments on the back, unfinished projects, the manuscripts of *The Lover*, the blue exercise books of *La Douleur*, personal journals, loose sheets torn out at night. One of these, undated, resounds like a warning: 'I say nothing to no one. Nothing about what goes through my life, the anger, the wild movements of my body towards that dark, hidden word "pleasure". I am modesty, I am silence itself. I say nothing. I express nothing. About what is important, nothing. It is there, unnamed, untouched.'

CHAPTER I

A Child of Indo-China

～

Marguerite Duras's country, her land of origin, the actual place in which her being was rooted would to the end of her days remain colonial Indo-China. It has even become a cliché. She was charmed by the poisonous splendours of Saigon, the forbidden vices of the Chinese town, the tamarind-lined avenues with their sumptuous carpet of old-rose flowers, white women wearied by the heat, saving their sexual zeal for their holidays in the West, the ravishing *congaïs* (local women) wooed by white men, despised by white women. Over the years Marguerite Duras became the ambassador of a forgotten Indo-China.

She once told me, 'You won't find anything in Vietnam. Get Yann to take you to the banks of the Seine, thirty kilometres outside Paris, where the river loops, where the leaves make a bed on the banks and where the earth has grown spongy. It isn't *like* the Mekong. It *is* the Mekong.'

I know, Marguerite, everything is everywhere. I went to the banks of the Seine. I shut my eyes. Nothing happened. It was autumn, the drizzle was blocking out the light and the refuse frustrated any attempt to imagine an elsewhere.

Summer 1996, Saigon – Ho Chi Minh City. From a wooden crate, opposite the Continental Hotel, a small boy was selling faded and badly stuck-together photocopies of *The Lover*. Hat battered, gaze nostalgic, Marguerite's photograph appeared on the counterfeit cover. But something didn't quite tally. You had to buy the book to see that no, it wasn't her, it was the actress from the film *The Lover*. It had been screened in Vietnam the previous year with the so-called erotic scenes cut out. Since then, supposedly uncut video versions have sold by the thousand on the black market.

Down from what used to be rue Catinat, the Champs-Elysées of the twenties, glittering with cafés and luxury boutiques, young people now sell Japanese computers. They're dressed like the sporty Americans you see on television – faded trainers, baggy jeans, baseball caps stuck backwards on their heads. Each morning they tip into the gutters the small rats that wander into the bamboo cages set up at night in shops to trap them.

Marguerite said that when she was little – eight or nine – her mother used to take her to the Eden Cinema. At that time the huge Saigon cinema was situated down an alley, next to the local theatre. Today, the former auditorium has been converted into a parking lot for mopeds. The cinema screens only pornographic films from Taiwan. Lovers go there in the afternoon to kiss and cuddle on the badly sagging leather seats. The film is shown in the auditorium itself, as there is no projection room. Cassettes of Jamaican rap are played to cover the din. Once night has fallen, girls from the red-light districts take their clients there. The music is played full blast to muffle their activities.

Much has remained unchanged: the avenues lined with trees so tall they block out the sky, the tropical splendour of a lush but judiciously ordered vegetation, in what used to be the fashionable area of Saigon; sumptuous colonial mansions, the scent of frangipani trees when the sun goes down, the cheery shouts of children selling soup, the intense noon light, the humidity of the precocious nights.

'Marguerite Duras was born in Indo-China where her father was a maths teacher and her mother a primary-school teacher. Apart from a brief stay in France when she was a child, she did not leave Saigon until she was eighteen.' This laconic biographical note, which the author supplied for her early books, would not change over the years.

Throughout her work, it was, we know, the theme of the mother that obsessed Marguerite Duras. Strict, authoritarian, courageous, feet firmly planted on the ground, hair pulled into a tight bun, chin resolute, gazing straight ahead: this is how she appears in photographs, frozen in the painful depiction of motherhood, more mother than woman, more rigid than affectionate. In the family album, she rarely smiles, her features are drawn. Physically she's close to her children but they're never seen held in her arms or sitting on her lap; all she does is touch them lightly.[1] The father looks exhausted, sad, his eyes staring vacantly into space. Marguerite said her mother used to force her children to pose for photographs. They were evidence of their existence and sent to the family in France. From these family photographs emanates an enduring impression of melancholy, of a destiny to be conquered.

'She was above all a peasant, she was in effect of peasant stock and had been a peasant', Marguerite told Michelle Porte, an admirer of her work who became a collaborator. Her mother's family was poor, extremely poor, she told me, stressing the fact. Mothers always tell their daughters that life was much harder when they were young. Marie Adeline Augustine Josèphe Legrand was born on 9 April 1877 in Fruges, in the Pas-de-Calais, northwestern France. This is stated on her birth certificate. Her parents, Alexandre and Julie, had also married in Fruges, when Julie was twenty-one and Alexandre twenty-eight. The two witnesses to their marriage were local people. One of them was Julie's brother Augustin Dumont, a merchant. Marie was the first child of many. At the time Alexandre was a wholesaler, but soon after Marie's birth he lost his job, so the family left Fruges and moved to Bonnières. The mother looked after the children, the father remained unemployed.

Marie would speak to her daughter Marguerite about the numerous siblings, about how hard it was at the end of the month, about her dreams and her lifelong passion for education. Education was the key word; it was the ideal from which she would never deviate, a model by which to live and a way to change the course of her destiny. Marie loved learning. She loved learning so much that she decided to become a primary-school teacher. She enrolled at Douai training college and then became a student teacher. Her first teaching post was at the school in Rexpoede and next in Dunkirk. On 10 March 1905 she was appointed temporary teacher at the Saigon school for young ladies.

Why go to Indo-China? There is a clue in the certificate of her second marriage, to Marguerite's father: one of the two witnesses, a doctor and major with the colonial artillery, Gustave André Cadet, aged thirty-eight and a cousin of the bride, was living in Cochin

China, the southern part of present-day Vietnam. Cochin China had been a French protectorate since 1867, and since 1887 part of the French Indo-Chinese union with Annam and Tonkin (central and northern Vietnam), Laos and Cambodia.[2] Was it Gustave who suggested Marie go there? Or was it her own decision to leave her native soil to start a new life in a faraway land, to start again from scratch?

Marie Legrand had married a young man from her village, Firmin Augustin Marie Obscur, in Fruges on 24 November 1904. Six months later she was in Saigon. Why? How? All we know is that she left her husband and never saw him again; he died two years later in France. Later she would joke about having been Widow Dark. The daughter refers to this in her most widely read book, *The Lover*: 'When she saw the diamond she said in a small voice: "It reminds me of the little solitaire I had when I got engaged to my first husband." I say, "Mr Dark." We laugh. "That was his name," she says, "it really was."' Literary critics can sometimes wilfully complicate or 'obscure' a writer's motives: such was the case with the eminent literary analyst who saw Marguerite's invention of the name *Obscur*, which he thought was ridiculous, as the absolute denial of parent-child relationships in her work.[3] And that is all we shall ever known about Monsieur Obscur. All that is left is a name in the records office and photographs of the mother taken when her name was Marie Obscur. She's extremely pretty and looks very happy, very cheerful, with a mischievous mouth and curly hair. She is certainly an attractive and appealing young woman.

The first white settlers arrived in Saigon in 1875 and planted coffee trees. They never left. Five years later, a lieutenant from the appropriately named ship *Espérance* (Hope) planted indigo and vanilla trees. He too stayed. On Sundays, the men would meet at dawn. They'd hunt the tiger, panther and wild boar with dogs, nets, bows and arrows, or poisoned darts from astride an ox or from a hide. On Sunday afternoons, as the sun sank down to the horizon of coffee trees, so that the dazzling light was less likely to make you screw up your eyes, the women would gather to take tea. 'Some of them are very beautiful, very white, they take enormous care of their beauty here, especially up-country. . . . They wait, these women. They dress just for the sake of dressing. They look at themselves.'[4]

There was a sense of adventure. The whites saw themselves as belonging to an élite that had not only cut itself off from the old world, but also took risks – financial and physical too, for dysentery and malaria were prevalent. Some hoped to do well. They were flagrantly encouraged by the authorities who gave these new colonists land; at the time all you had to do was clear a piece of land to own it. Cochin China became the new Wild West. But civil servants, the largest of the social groups, were not only at the bottom of the ladder, they were also the most poorly paid and the least respected.

It took France twenty years to complete the takeover of Indo-China. As early as 1900, the region was seen as a kind of colonizing college for France. 'It was where, one after another, every system and every policy was tried out.'[5] Cochin China, an 'annexed' colony and French territory with parliamentary representation, always considered itself to be superior to the other regions of Indo-China.[6] Any Frenchman who went there automatically had the moral authority of his race.[7] Every Frenchman represented an élite, 'whether of character, intelligence, energy, knowledge or benevolence.'[8] A colonist was believed to be a superior being, with a highly developed brain and a better physique than the local population – man at his most highly cultivated.[9] It was the duty of civilized people to shoulder the task of orderly colonization and gradually train the natives.[10] Contemporary ideologists, politicians, commentators, economists were all agreed on this.[11] Indo-China was the future granary of France, a virgin territory waiting to be opened up.

And so it was a woman on her own, not divorced, approaching forty, who landed in Indo-China to take up a teaching post.

The young principal, Henri Donnadieu, dashing, handsome and decent in every respect, fell madly in love with Marie Obscur shortly after she arrived in Saigon. Or had they met before? There is no way of knowing. There are inhabitants in Donnadieu's home village of Duras who maintain that Marie Legrand visited the region before she left for Saigon; they say the two met when Marie was there as a supply teacher and that she left surreptitiously to go and join him. But Henri was already married to his childhood sweetheart Alice, mother of his two children, with no profession.

When did the new relationship begin? Fairly quickly, judging by the letters of denunciation on file in the French Colonial Office. Was

Marie Alice's friend or Alice's husband's lover? Alice soon became seriously ill, and Marie was at her bedside until her death. Around this time, a letter in the post notified Marie that she was a widow. Imagine the snide remarks, the fierce disapproval and the unequivocal condemnation of the new couple who scandalized Saigon's nice white lower-middle classes. For Marie and Henri moved in together. They decided to get married as quickly as possible.

The second marriage took place very soon; for some, too soon after Alice's death. The groom was still in black. Five months was all that separated Alice's funeral from the marriage of Henri Donnadieu, aged thirty-seven, head of Gia Dinh training college in Cochin China, to Marie Legrand.

In a photograph of Marie and Henri taken when they were first married, they look a close couple as they gaze – like lovers – in the same direction. Marie still has her mop of frizzy hair, her eyes are made up and she's wearing lipstick and a lace collar. She has the look of all captive women, in love and yearning for marital bliss.

Henri was a handsome man. There's very little documentary evidence on him: the record card of the medical he had prior to going into the army in 1915 states 'light brown hair, brown eyes, high forehead, long nose, oval face'. One photograph, owned by Marguerite, was for a long time pinned up in the lobby of her apartment in rue Saint-Benoît. 'I never knew my father. He died when I was four. He wrote a mathematics book on exponential functions that I've lost. All I have left is this photo and a postcard he sent his children just before he died.'[12]

Marguerite adored her father, she often talked about him, claiming – and we know she liked to exaggerate and sensationalize – that he was a mathematical genius. At the end of her life she admitted to having missed him a great deal. She used to say she had inherited his fondness for seduction, his humour and the elegant nonchalance with which he yearned to be loved. In boxes kept in the Overseas Archives library are numerous administrative and military documents that help reconstruct the father's career. He was a student at Agen training college. In 1893 he took up a teaching post in Le Mas-d'Agenais, then in Marmande and finally in Mézin. On 15 September 1904, he gave up teaching in France, and in 1905 he and Alice arrived in Cochin China with their two children, both of whom had been born in Mézin, Jean in 1899, Jacques in 1904. From family correspondence we know that Jacques was in Saigon when his mother fell ill, and that he stayed with his father until after the birth of Marie's first son, Pierre.

Marguerite Duras deliberately omitted her two half-brothers from her fictional world and from her life. After the father's death, relations between Marguerite and the Donnadieu family would take a turn for the worse. In the village of Duras, they still tell the story today of how Marguerite, one summer at the beginning of the sixties, turned up in a convertible and stopped to fill up at the petrol station owned by her half-brother Jean. She is supposed to have said to the employee who went to fetch him from the next village, 'I don't have time to wait.' Elegant, influential Jean, president of the National Hunt Federation, a wealthy dealer, affable and generous, left his mark on the Duras region. The women certainly remembered him, and said of him that he had a princely bearing and was extremely proud of his half-sister. As for the younger, Jacques, he had also owned a garage in his father's birthplace before moving south. When Marguerite published her first novel, *Les impudents*, she dedicated it to 'my brother Jacques D. whom I never knew'.

While the Donnadieu side of the family loved mechanics, the Legrands revered education. Perhaps it was the conjunction of the two family cultures that made Marguerite Duras see writing from a material and intellectual point of view, not as a gift or inspiration but as a job, a labour, a banal activity that consisted of assembling words.

How and why did first Henri Donnadieu and then Marie Legrand go to Indo-China? Marguerite would tell a story about posters that sang the praises of the colony, the call of the wild, the yearning for adventure, the promise of a better way of life. 'There were Sundays at the town hall, when she'd find herself gazing dreamily at the propaganda posters for the colonies, "Join the Colonial Army." "Young people, fortune awaits you in the colonies." '[13] Around the end of the nineteenth century, it was the custom in Henri's predominantly commercial region for the young and fit to try their luck in the colonies. For Henri the move meant a promotion: from being an ordinary teacher at Marmande school he became principal of the Gia Dinh training college. He had in his charge four French teachers and five local ones.

When Henri landed in Indo-China, it wasn't yet a beautiful colony, and Saigon wasn't the pearl of the Far East. It would become so, but not until after the First World War. Had Henri, in 1900, visited the wonderful Indo-Chinese Exhibition in Paris that flaunted the charms of the colony? Did friends encourage him to go? There is no archive evidence or family story to explain his departure.[14] Marguerite had her own fictional, literary version: 'She married a teacher who, like herself, couldn't wait to leave his northern village, having, like herself, fallen prey to the mysterious writings of Pierre Loti.[15] Soon after they were married they applied to become teachers in the colonies and were posted to the large colony then referred to as French Indo-China.'[16]

It really doesn't matter why they left. In her imagination Marguerite Duras constantly reinvented the reasons for their departure and eventually created what became a veritable family myth. They left, and, in so doing, cut themselves off from Europe and from family traditions, escaped a life where everything was mapped out and a future that had nothing to offer them. But they left separately.

Henri Donnadieu arrived in Indo-China towards the end of 1905, at a time when the educational system was being modernized to include the Confucian method of acquiring knowledge. A new curriculum for Indo-China was being drawn up and the minister for colonies, through circulars and posters, informed the whole of the teaching profession that there were numerous posts that needed to be filled urgently. Six months later, a contingent of youth workers, teachers and civil servants arrived in Saigon. Henri was among them.

The white community could be divided into various categories: extremely wealthy planters who soon amassed a fortune from 'green gold', rubber trees mainly; affluent and unscrupulous entrepreneurs, come to make money from trafficking; high-ranking civil servants, who headed the colonial administration; whites of average means, shopkeepers and teachers; and the poor lower-class whites who formed a kind of lumpenproletariat.[17] Henri belonged to the majority group of civil servants, attracted no doubt by a desire for adventure and a change of scene. Teachers did not come out to seek their fortunes, for the contractual conditions laid down by the state were not what you would call advantageous. There was no special allowance that went with the job and no guarantee they would be found a job in metropolitan France in the event of tropical illness or depression.

In short, they received a single ticket, and had a statutory requirement to stay for a minimum of three years. The six-month holiday in France on full pay was carefully monitored. Extending the contract beyond the three years gave them the right to extra leave in France. Paid in francs, salaries were unaffected by the exchange rate between the piastre and the franc, thus allowing certain traffickers to accumulate vast sums of money. A teacher's starting salary was 3,000 francs, rising to no more than 7,000 by the end of their career, while an inspector or headmaster could earn between 3,200 and 7,200 francs. Compensation was available for those teaching in less salubrious areas, but officials required proof so difficult to obtain that neither Marguerite's father nor her mother was ever paid any, although both became seriously ill as a result of the climate and working conditions.

And so the ships of the Messageries Maritimes, sailing from Marseille to Saigon, carried not only civil servants, but also young couples from underprivileged areas seeking their fortunes. Among them were many from Corsica (Saigon soon became a Corsican colony), Auvergne and Brittany; shopkeepers with dreams of founding manufacturing empires; pretty young women looking for a protector and, why not, a husband; tourists en route for Angkor; opium smugglers; authors starved of exoticism come to see for themselves whether the Chinese ladies of Cholon did indeed wear metal plates over their nails to protect their talons, and whether the nipples of young Cochin Chinese women were indeed nineteen centimetres long.[18]

As for Henri Donnadieu, he had arrived with his head ringing with the fine words that had been drummed into him before he left: to be the head of a school is to represent France, to be the guardian of traditions and souls. Ideologues repeated it at every possible opportunity: the real, gradual and day-to-day colonization of a country is done through the school. The teacher must become a lay missionary. 'These beacons of civilization lit one by one throughout the Union are the only guarantee of the future of France in these the furthermost reaches of the Orient.'[19] To the majority of colonizers, school was, above all else, the way to conquer hearts and the most effective weapon in France's civilizing mission,[20] even though it had to be acknowledged that, in a country with an ancient civilization where intellectual culture had always been greatly valued, traditional teaching methods were already firmly established throughout the territory as a whole.[21] There was a critical period when the French wondered what they should do. Should they recognize and accept the trad-itional – stable and accepted – Confucian school or should they enforce the French system of education and the requirement to learn the language? Henri would live through an era of pedagogic experimentation, conducted by officials who praised the merits of assimilation while surrounded by colleagues who recognized the authority of the Vietnamese schoolteachers.[22]

In Ho Chi Minh City's small library of human sciences, not far from the fashionable rue Catinat, young Vietnamese students spend their breaks between classes practising foreign languages such as English and Japanese, but, alas, no longer French. The head librarian goes home at lunchtime. If you go to the library every day, you may be considered a regular and discreetly given to understand that if you really need to work at lunchtime, an exception can be made. The librarian locks you in, posts a dog at the entrance and shuts the gate. When it's siesta time, some of the young women, lulled by the hum of the wheezy ventilators, lie down on wooden benches strangely reminiscent of old school furniture and drop off to sleep with a smile on their faces. It is the ideal time to explore the library. There at the end of a small corridor, slowly easing open the drawers of the filing cabinet so as not to disturb the slumbering young ladies, I found the colony's carefully filed archives and monographs, meticulously written out by punctilious civil servants, mindful of administrative truths, and containing inventories of people and goods. In this way I was able to reconstruct the conditions. When Marguerite's father moved into his living quarters in Gia Dinh, there were eight white married couples, twenty white bachelors, and twelve white children living there. As to the 'others', all the others, the 'non-whites', that is, the report makes no mention of how many they were. Of course there were also Annamese, Chinese and 'other Asians' living there, but only the whites existed as individuals.

The Donnadieu family was part of the small, middle-class, white community of Gia Dinh, a suburb of Saigon. In Vietnamese Gia Dinh means 'perfect tranquillity'. Gia Dinh stretches from the Saigon River to the Mekong. Alluvial soil, vast expanses of soft green rice paddies crisscrossed by the darker green of the coconut palms. Here people

wonder where the earth begins. Under a limpid white sky, fields
shimmer in the sun. In small dykes between the rivers, running water
sometimes turns to mud, then to sludge that bakes and becomes earth
to which pathetic shrubs cling. 'Outside, rice paddies as far as the eye
can see. Empty sky. Pale heat. Veiled sun. And little roads all around
for the ox-carts the children guide.'[23]

Here nature is in a perpetual state of becoming. The river can silt,
the sea recede and the earth turn to reddish mud. The banks are
edged with mangroves whose intricate networks of roots are covered
and uncovered by the tide. It seems a land of toil, with its depleting
climate and the uniformity of its landscape – the red of the mud and
the green of the rice paddies. There are splashes of colour – purplish
flowers hiding under the foliage of the flame trees, vast blue stretches
of Japanese hyacinths. And all around this sea-land forests grow, huge,
unhealthy, riotous forests, inhabited by packs of monkeys, wild boar,
tigers, leopards, tiger-cats and Malayan bears. Not forgetting the
legions of rats and other smaller animals. Although the elephant is
seldom seen and the rhinoceros began to disappear from the region
at the start of the century, the crocodile abounds, and grilled crocodile
tail is an extremely popular dish.

Gia Dinh nowadays has barracks and botanical gardens, an orphan-
age run by the Sisters of St Paul of Chartres, highway number two
which skirts the Canavaggio concession, and the steam tram, which,
stopping four times only, will take you all the way to Saigon, through
badly stocked markets, scattered villages and remote houses screened
by tall mango trees or shielded by fortresslike bamboo plantations.
The villages here have names that mean Quiet Water, Pacification,
Perfect Beauty. In Vo Vap market, they sell powdered vulture bones
to protect against venereal diseases and amulets for pregnant women
containing fragments of monkey tibia. You can get anything in Gia
Dinh; the best French wines, spirits from all over Europe, brown
sugar, wheat flour, Italian rice and Greek olives.

The white community did not like the new Madame Donnadieu,
unlike the first, who had been kind and gentle. Henri Donnadieu had
a good position, indeed an enviable position, and she had hardly set
foot in the place before she was married to him, without waiting for
the period of mourning to be over and without playing the role of
the grief-stricken stepmother.

Marmande, 21 April 1914

Dear Sir,

How is it possible for an infamous man like Donnadieu with his terrible reputation to remain principal of Saigon College? A man whose wife died in mysterious circumstances whilst being cared for by his mistress in Saigon; and there was a scandal, the mistress was pregnant, the wife had to go and a few days after her death the mother became Donnadieu to ward off the threats of exposure.

How humiliating for the brave teachers who have to take orders from such a dreadful person.

Here in Marmande, he kept very bad company, a midwife in the family who specialized in abortions, he had her go to Saigon. Keep a very watchful eye on that lot.

Yours very faithfully.

The minister for colonies kept the letter, signed by a woman from the Duras region, and passed it on to personnel for filing. An embittered woman after revenge? A denunciation? Marie's first child wasn't in fact born until eleven months after they were married, so on this occasion conventions were respected. He was registered as 'a male child born on Wednesday 7 September 1910 at 1 a.m. in the administrative centre of Gia Dinh, in the village of Binh Haoxa, canton of Binh Tri Thuang. The parents had named him Pierre.' Pierre would feature large in all the stories of Marguerite's unhappy childhood and adolescence.

A teacher of fourth-year students, Marie did not give up work when she became a mother; but it was when Pierre was born that the couple's problems first started. Henri was having problems with his health. Several medical reports state that he regularly suffered from headaches and that he had lost weight as a result of persistent stomach pains. He was examined but nothing was found. A year later another son, Paul, was born. Henri continued to grow weaker and more depressed. Did he panic? Whatever the reason, he suddenly left Saigon with his wife and two small boys and went home to France. The Donnadieu family landed in Marseille in April 1912, and did not return to Indo-China on the day they had planned to, Henri having found an administrative post in France. Exhausted, he decided to stay in France, and to rest at home in the Lot-et-Garonne.

After a year, Marie and the children went back to Indo-China, alone. She begged him to join them. In the end Henri gave in and set out for Saigon.

A few days after his return, their third child was conceived. Henri was present at the birth. Like her two brothers, Marguerite Germaine was born at home in Gia Dinh, on 4 April 1914, at four in the morning. When Marguerite was six months old, her mother became so ill that the military doctors in Saigon had her urgently rushed back to France. She was suffering from 'compound arthritis, malaria, heart problems and renal complications'. Once discharged from the military hospital in Toulouse, she returned to Saigon on 14 June 1915. Baby Marguerite had been separated from her mother for eight months and in the care of a Vietnamese boy.

The family had not long been reunited when it was the father's turn to be in such agony that he was forced to consult the military doctors, who diagnosed double pulmonary congestion, acute colitis and chronic dysentery. He was ordered by the governor general of Indo-China to go immediately to France. Marie, worried to death about her husband, news of whom rarely reached her, was left to bring up the three children on her own. Henri, admitted to hospital in Marseille, kept the truth from her: the doctors had found him to be in such poor health, his body so wasted, that they didn't know how best to cure him. Different treatments were tried, until at last one allowed him to consider returning to Indo-China.

Fate was conspiring against the couple. This time it wasn't illness that kept them apart, but the First World War. Henri had just bought his ticket to sail for Saigon when he was picked up in Marmande, enlisted as a private in the army, and assigned to the auxiliary service. Fortunately, Henri once again became ill. This was to save him, for the time being. He never made it to the front. Invalided out of the army in March 1916, and readmitted to hospital, first in Marmande, then in Reims, he became a special medical case, an object of study – racked with pain and tired to the point of exhaustion. The military doctors tried out new remedies to treat his 'dysentery and chronic malaria'. He was so well looked after that in September 1916 his administration considered he was fit for military duties. But claiming paternal rights, Henri was finally allowed to return to Indo-China in October.

'When we were little, mother would sometimes play at showing us the war. She'd fetch a stick that was the same length as a rifle, put it on her shoulder, and march up and down singing "Sambre et Meuse". Then she'd burst into tears. And we'd have to comfort her. Yes, my mother loved man's war.'[24]

Henri's eldest son, Jean, stayed in France, having decided to leave school and join up. For two years Henri had no news of his son. While the mother loved man's war, the father experienced it in his flesh.

The Donnadieu family lived in a typical turn-of-the-century civil servant's house, with a few meagre palm trees at the entrance that gave it an exotic feel. Every day the mother would take the tram to the Saigon girls' school. The servants were left to raise the children. In the few photographs that exist, the children are dressed like communicants, and look as good as gold. As for the parents, they already look old, spent, tired.

Marguerite used to say she'd have loved her memories of childhood to be filled with nostalgia and wonder. Unfortunately it was drab and unhappy. Whenever the family thought they were settled, they had to decamp and start all over again. Marguerite's early childhood could be summed up as a long and restless wander through Indo-China's main towns. No memorable house, no lasting friendships, no school either: the mother taught this hard-working child, whose particular loves were reading and writing, unlike the two brothers who were already rebelling against any attempt at education. By the time she was an old woman, her childhood had lost all traces of the child. 'There is nothing so clear, so lived, less dreamed than the whole of my childhood. Without imagination, with none of the myths and fairy tales that crown a childhood with dreams.'[25]

Marguerite was three when her parents left Saigon. Her father had been posted to Tonkin; in a move up the colonial promotion table, Henri had been appointed director of primary education in Hanoi.

Hanoi. Thirty years earlier the city had been a foul and disgusting sewer. By the time the Donnadieu family arrived, it had been transformed into a tropical Parisian miniparadise. In the main street, Paris hairdressers abutted elegant perfumeries and shops that stocked the latest fashions. Then there were all the cafés – Café du Commerce, Café de la Place, Café Albin and of course Café Beine, where Madame Beine, a former canteen manager, would emerge into the cool of the terrace in her wide-brimmed hat to serve absinthe to the officers of the garrison. Pagodas had just been demolished in the heart of the ancient city to make room for new administrative buildings: Navy, Treasury, Post Office and Headquarters. Paths had been created around the lake, similar to those in French parks; and on the lake itself, young soldiers in boats pulled on the oars to show off their muscles. When the sky was overcast just before the arrival of the monsoon, you could imagine yourself strolling in the Bois de Bou-logne on a Sunday in autumn, surrounded by well-dressed young men and young women in ankle boots, their faces protected by ornate sunshades.

> It's the courtyard of a house by the Small Lake in Hanoi. We're together, she and us, her children. I'm four years old. My mother's in the middle of the picture. I recognize the awkward way she holds herself, the way she doesn't smile, the way she waits for the photo to be over. By her drawn face, by a certain untidiness in her dress, by her drowsy expression, I can tell it's hot, that she's tired, that she's bored.[26]

Although Marguerite's father had been promoted, her mother was unable to find a position. Already conspicuously out of place in what was a quiet white community, she grew bored and would spend her time running around in circles. She was unusual and people would point her out in the street. While the father seems to have found it easy to uphold the standards of the French administration, the mother was loud, extravagant and impulsive. Looking after her three children wasn't enough, so she continued to search for work.

Henri was worried about his son Jean who, now demobilized, had written to the French Colonial Office asking to join his father in Indo-China. Henri supported the application by writing to the administrative authorities in August 1919. For three months the father waited for the grown-up son he hardly knew, and the son waited in Marseille for a boat to take him to Indo-China. Permission was eventually granted. But then, at the very moment when he could leave, Jean decided not to go. Why? We do not know the reasons behind this sudden change of heart. Father and son would always miss one another and Marguerite would never know the big brother that could have protected her.

As for Marie, having been unable to find an administrative post, she borrowed money to buy a house and turned it into a private school. She couldn't not work. She began taking in pupils from Hanoi and a handful of boarders, the children of wealthy families, with whom the little Marguerite was brought up during her early childhood.

In this house Marguerite had her first sexual encounter. One day a young Vietnamese boy invited her to go with him to his hiding place, a secret den he'd built with bits of wood down by the lake. She wasn't afraid. He got out his penis and she did as she was told. 'I remember it very well: I felt somewhat dishonoured for having been touched. I was four years old. He was eleven and a half and hadn't yet reached puberty.'[27]

Marguerite Duras waited seventy years before committing this incident to paper. Why? Was she ashamed? Had she forgotten it? Or was it a case of fabricating a 'true false memory' over the years? We know that traumatic false memories abound and that the memory can release in detail events that never took place.[28] She said she'd been traumatized by the event and that for a long time she'd thought of it as something terrible, 'the scene shifted from itself. In effect it grew with me, it never left me.'

The world had opened up for her too soon, the mother–daughter relationship was seriously damaged. For the child told her mother, and the mother expelled the boy from the boarding school, then told her daughter to forget it had ever happened. Marguerite felt guilty for having told and responsible for the boy's expulsion. 'I never mentioned it again to my mother. All her life she thought I'd forgotten.'[29]

From this genuinely experienced distress or from the memory screen came the model for the sexual blueprint used in several of her books: sexual pleasure for women through 'the gaze', solitary and transgressive pleasure for men. In a sexual relationship each remains separate from the other. Love is used to forget momentarily the cruel nature of solitary pleasure. In Marguerite Duras's eyes, children are not asexual: they understand, arouse and experience desire. At the age of four, Marguerite was soiled, touched, defiled. A doll sacrificed to lust. Guilty already? Unhappy to be always feeling it was her fault. Her body was an object of pleasure. She knew it was. And she knew this very early on. 'It wasn't until much later and then only to men in France that I told the story. But I know my mother never forgot these children's games.'[30]

On a trip to China at the age of five, Marguerite watched an adulteress being buried alive. The lover too was also sometimes buried alive – they would be placed facing each other in the coffin. The wronged husband was the only one with the right to intervene. So sometimes the man was pardoned, but the woman never. In *Green Eyes* Marguerite gave a brief description of this trip made with her parents, and other evidence can be found in her archives. There is even an undated and never published piece of writing in one of her notebooks, where she describes finding a dead man in a dustbin outside a house:

He was folded in half, bottom down. He was too big for the dustbin. His feet stuck out and his head hung down, mouth open. He was grey, crawling with lice and as old as an elephant. And yet it was a man. My brothers and I couldn't take our eyes off him. We walked around him. All our lives we would see that dead man in a dustbin.

The remedy was silence, the mother once more pretending that nothing had happened. The mother's hands over the daughter's eyes. But how can you forget that a man's body can be put in a dustbin? And how can you have a carefree childhood?

Moreover, Pierre was a bully who would delight in rehearsing his talent for spitefulness on his brother, only to perform it all the more effectively on his little sister. He made sure Marguerite knew from early childhood that he did not want her in the family; he pursued her with sneers and taunts, driving the terrified child to hide cringing under the stairs.

After Hanoi, Henri Donnadieu was posted to Phnom Penh, Cambodia. It would appear that the family were not sorry to leave Hanoi. Their only regret was the boarding-school house they'd just bought and been unable to sell.

Of Phnom Penh, all Marguerite's memories were of sorrow, antici-pation and despair. Yet it had started off so well. A sumptuous baroque house came with the father's new promotion. They moved in on 31 December 1920. Situated in the heart of the city and surrounded by an enormous garden, the magnificent residence delighted the family. During the day the servants had charge of the children. Still not at school, free and wild, they spent their days in the park, studying only when they felt like it. A good student, Marguerite learned everything her mother taught her. And luckily this time the mother had no difficulty finding a job in the public sector. On 19 January 1921, she was appointed headmistress of the Norodom school.

The father had little to do with his children, needing to preserve all his energy as he struggled against the permanent exhaustion, lethargy and drowsiness that had the doctors baffled. In February, drained of all his strength, he was forced to stop working. In March he became so seriously ill that he took to his bed. On 24 April he was rushed on board the *Chili* and repatriated on health grounds. Alone.

The colonial doctors at the city's military hospital took him in hand the moment he landed in Marseille on 23 May, but in vain. Henri Donnadieu was obviously a medical conundrum. In desperation the doctors sent him to Plombières, also to no avail. Henri was getting worse. He was officially informed by the colonial office that he couldn't return to Indo-China. In any case he didn't have the strength, but his wife was demanding his return. On 23 September, Dr Fraus-sard from Plombières diagnosed Henri Donnadieu as having 'an untreatable condition that has resulted in weight loss, weakness and generally poor health. He is at present unable to return to his post, being in need of a period of prolonged rest so that he can be properly looked after. Several months of complete mental and physical inactiv-ity is recommended.'

Why didn't Marie get the first ship back with the children? Why didn't she go and look after him? After all, the authorities would have given her leave of absence and paid their travelling expenses. Was she frightened of seeing her husband's family again? Had Henri said he never wanted to see his wife again?

Although the doctors talked of rest, Henri Donnadieu was in fact dying and he knew it. Suddenly and without warning he discharged himself from the clinic and holed up in a house he'd purchased during an earlier visit, the Le Platier property, in Pardaillan par Duras, Lot-et-Garonne. His son Jean moved in with him.

He took to his bed, where he waited for death. He would only see his two eldest sons, his brother Roger and his former mother-in-law. A month and a half later, on 4 December 1921, Henri was dead. As requested, he died alone. His brother found him in his bed, at peace, staring at the window.

In far-off Phnom Penh the mother awaited word of her husband.

All four of us sleep in the same bed. She says she's afraid of the dark. It's in this house she'll hear of my father's death. She'll know about it before the telegram comes, the night before, because of a sign only she saw and could understand, because of the bird that called in the middle of the night, frightened, lost in the office in the north front of the palace, my father's office.[31]

Had Marie really believed that her husband would pull through again? It would appear so. There had been so many health scares. But Marguerite didn't understand. Only later did she speculate about her mother's motives. 'My mother refused to join him in France, she stayed where she was. As though rooted.'

On 5 December a brief telegram from Jean, the eldest son, left Duras for Phnom Penh. Worried how Marie would react to the death of her husband, on 7 December, Jean Donnadieu wrote to the French Colonial Office asking them to look after Marie (whom he called 'my mother'), 'my little brothers and sister' and to 'take all necessary steps'.

The mother couldn't accept the news from France. She wanted to double-check the information in the telegram. Yes, it is your husband who's died, the colonial government officials confirmed. We too have just been informed.

Marguerite was seven, her brothers ten and eleven. She would later maintain she didn't remember being affected by her father's death. Her mother had already taken on the role of guardian and bread-winner. Some have come up with the somewhat far-fetched inter-pretation that Marguerite was saying her father was not her father, that her real father had been Chinese.[32] In adult life, Marguerite even bragged about her lack of feelings and the fact that there had been no great drama resulting from the news of his demise: 'I was very young when my father died. I obviously felt no emotion. No sadness, no tears, no questions. He was away on a trip when he died. A few years later I lost my dog. I was inconsolable. Never had I suffered so much.'[33] Time distorts. Three years before she died she admitted to having been extremely fond of her father. In her opinion he was better-looking than her mother, more charming, more courageous, more upright, less crazy.[34]

For a long time the authorities were ignorant of the circumstances of the father's death. Henri had refused medical treatment towards the end and no death certificate had been issued. His death appeared to them so suspect that five years later the government of Indo-China was still not sure whether Henri was dead or alive. No death certificate meant no pension for Madame Donnadieu. Marie would spend years trying to persuade the authorities that her husband was well and truly dead and that she was indeed the widow of Henri Donnadieu. She bombarded the military doctors of Agen, Marseille and Plombières with letters requesting his death certificate. The doctors eventually gave in and produced the papers, but the Indo-Chinese government was obdurate and continued to be so for a long time. 'It is the view of the Director of Health responsible for the troops of the Indo-China group to whom this file has been passed, that these certificates do no more than state that Henri Donnadieu was suffering from chronic dysentery contracted in Indo-China. The certificates do not allow us to conclude that the said condition was the cause of death,' said a note from the government of Indo-China dated 18 December 1926. It was six years before Marie received any of her widow's pension. Her dogged perseverance forced the authorities to capitulate although the file on Henri Donnadieu was never closed. And so in 1927 she was finally granted an annual pension of 3000 francs, a quarter of which was to go to Jacques, the younger of her husband's two sons from his first marriage. But neither Jacques nor Roger Donnadieu, his uncle and guardian, ever received a penny. Marguerite's mother was so determined to save her own children from destitution when she was widowed that she had a tendency to forget that she had a financial and moral obligation to her stepsons.

To Marguerite, the death of the father was more like a continued absence than a sudden tragedy. The mother was already alone, with her misery, her world-weariness and her endless problems. What was the point of struggling? Marguerite's mother loved misfortune, and misfortune smiled down on her like a beneficent and perverse lover.

When I was a child my mother's unhappiness took the place of dreams. My dreams were of my mother, never of Christmas trees, always just her, a mother either flayed by poverty or distraught and muttering in the wilderness, either searching for food or endlessly telling what's happened to her, Marie Legrand from Roubaix, telling of her innocence, her savings, her hope.[35]

Marie returned to France on leave in 1922; she spent a few months in the north and then moved into the Le Platier house, which in the eyes of the neighbours was now hers. But her in-laws refused to sign the property over to her. Today the house is a ruin, destroyed by a fire in 1953. Trees grow through the middle, the floorboards have disappeared and nature has taken over what was once a beautiful property with an orchard, a bread oven, tree-lined paths and arable land – eleven hectares in all, looked after by a tenant farmer. In 1962, Marguerite tried to buy back the house and one hectare. She even began to clear some of the land, but it came to nothing in the end. Two years before she died, she wanted to spend some time in quiet contemplation at her father's grave. She was on the phone for hours trying to find out where he'd been buried, but to no avail. It had been Henri's dying wish to be buried with his first wife. Family affairs were complicated, even in the hereafter.

In Duras they remember (and still talk about) the Donnadieu mother and her three children moving into the house. She was religious, extremely religious, and friends with Father Dufaux, the parish priest of Pardaillan, who would later become Pierre's private tutor. She was also a greedy, grasping woman who drove a hard bargain. She hadn't been there five minutes, and already she was trying to disinherit the youngest of her stepsons. The wealth of correspondence that passed between Henri's brother Roger and the governor general of Indo-China testifies to the intensity of the struggle. One letter from Roger Donnadieu, dated 22 April 1923, to the governor general of Indo-China stated:

She wants to get her hands on the house in Le Platier. She will no doubt succeed. She wants the pension that should be going to her stepson even though she is not the one bringing him up because her life as a widow being in sole charge of three children is hell. She will no doubt succeed. Madame Donnadieu who has no affection for her husband's children, is today challenging them in court with the obvious aim of deferring judgement on my brother's estate over which she in fact has control.

Marie did not get her hands on the house in Le Platier, but she did disinherit her husband's sons, and her attitude alienated her from her in-laws.

When Marguerite arrived in Le Platier, she was eight years old. It was her first encounter with France. The two years she spent there would be remembered as a time of great joy and of absolute oneness with nature, 'what with the purity of the landscape and aridity of the earth, a certain wildness in the landscape and the people'. Marguerite was a real country girl, who would stride with friends through field and forest in clogs. A wild child. Yvette, a grocer in Monteton until she retired, grew up in the area and vividly remembered her childhood playmate, known by everyone in the village as Néné:

> Every Thursday I'd spend the afternoon at the Donnadieus'. In the evening Marguerite, her brothers and mother would walk me home. As we didn't live far we'd go through the fields and across a stream called the Rieutord. Marguerite was a fairly solitary little girl with lots of personality. I remember how some Thursdays Madame Donnadieu would leave us with the parish priest of Pardaillan, and when it was time for afternoon tea, he'd get different jams out of the cupboard. She didn't like her house much and was happier when she was with the neighbours, the Bousquets, where she often stayed the night.[36]

Marguerite's homeland was Cochin China, it was where she'd been born, but by also secretly having Lot-et-Garonne as an adopted land, it became very much a part of her. 'To me France will always be Pardaillan, along with the smell of apples drying on wicker racks, the clear water of the Dropt and watercress beds,' she would write in 1992 to Patricia Gaudin, a native of Pardaillan. And when she decided to publish her first novel, she abandoned her father's name and called herself Duras, the name of the district the father's house was in, and for the setting of her first novel she chose the father's native land.

When she had come to the end of her statutory leave, Marguerite's mother applied to be allowed to remain in France on grounds of ill health. She informed the ministry that she had anaemia and chronic malaria. The military doctors in Agen did not agree. Having subjected her to a medical examination on 19 May 1924, they concluded, 'Madame Donnadieu is now fit to leave for the colony. She should therefore return to her post overseas.'

On 5 June 1924, accompanied by her three children, Marie set sail from Marseille. Her destination was Saigon, but she had no idea exactly where she would be posted. She secretly hoped it would be Saigon but openly dreamed of Hanoi. When they docked in Colombo, she was handed a cable informing her she was being posted to Phnom Penh.

This was a dreadful blow. She had no wish to return to Phnom Penh, the city where she'd learned of her husband's death. Moreover, she knew that the impression she'd made there hadn't been a good one. From Colombo she sent telegrams to the French Colonial Office in Paris as well as to the governor general in Saigon; she also got representatives to send telegrams on her behalf. The ship set sail again. Arriving in Saigon, she received final confirmation of her posting to Phnom Penh. Furious, she ranted and raged, then begged, then left under duress for Phnom Penh, from where she wrote this despairing letter to the governor general of Indo-China:

> Had I been alone I would have been delighted at the news that I had been appointed to Cambodia for, as headmistress of Norodom school from 1921 to '22, I was very happy in my post. But I have three children and the two boys are 14 and 13. They have completed their first year of secondary school and there is no educational establishment there that will allow them to continue with their studies.
>
> Moreover, the position of headmistress I used to have has been filled, which means that despite my qualifications and experience, I have to live at the hotel with my children while most of my salary is swallowed up by this inconvenient arrangement. And yet I own a house in Hanoi.
>
> Finally, sir, I should like to point out that my poor husband, who died in 1921, had children from a first marriage, and that one of them is still a minor. This situation has caused me a lot of problems.

I myself have been working in the colony for twenty years. I have always devoted myself to the education of the children entrusted me and it is intolerable, at a time when my own have need of support, that their future should be compromised.

This letter promoted the colonial authorities to investigate the matter. When questioned, Marie's colleagues went wild. Cambodia's director of primary education, in a cable to Saigon, stated that not only did Madame Donnadieu have 'a very bad reputation at the Norodom school but also with the examination board' and that her very presence 'was the cause of trouble and friction'.

Marie could sense that she'd been betrayed, and was permanently aware of an atmosphere of conspiracy. She tried to speak with her colleagues, demanded an explanation, but all were evasive. She couldn't understand and struggled on alone in this unlucky city. Was Madame Donnadieu paranoid? She was certainly extremely unhappy. In the face of her colleagues' stubborn silence she asked the education department to set up a committee of inquiry 'to ascertain the truth behind the criticisms'. But the very same people who were writing these accusatory letters acted surprised. She demanded a report and got one: 'Madame Donnadieu has never been the object of disciplinary action, the person concerned even appeared before the promotion board and was subsequently upgraded.' Her professional honour was safe and there was never an official reprimand, yet the gossip continued.

In the face of what was an increasingly hostile climate, Marie withdrew. She cabled her despair to the governor general of Indo-China. On 23 December 1924, her life took a turn for the better: she received news of a new posting. On 24 December, she was finally able to leave Phnom Penh and her birds of ill omen. Her destination was Vinh Long. Marguerite was ten and her true Indo-Chinese childhood was about to begin. She left the huge administrative buildings, homes-cum-schools, noisy colonial cities, the oppressive atmosphere of the white colony, to discover the river and the forest.

Marguerite was a child of Indo-China. She would describe its landscapes, lights and smells right up to the end of her life. What would she have been without Indo-China? Would she have become Duras? It was this native land, which she made the focus of her writing, and this sensory contrast, which she continued to cultivate, that always, to the day she died, recharged her batteries. As an olive-skinned young girl she even looked oriental, then later as a woman with high cheekbones and slightly almond-shaped eyes she could easily have been mistaken for a *congaï*.

Vinh Long was an outpost in up-country Cochin China. Vinh Long, plain of birds, the picture of paradise, a slow pace of life, time standing almost still; Vinh Long, the miniature dream world. As Marguerite would say, 'It came like a bolt of lightning, like faith. It came and it was for life. At seventy-two I can still see it as though it was yesterday, siesta time and the roads of the outpost, the white district, the empty flame-tree-lined avenues. The sleeping river.'[37]

CHAPTER 2

The Mother

There are no more tigers in Vinh Long. But the peasants still battle against the wild boar that appear at night to eat the tender shoots of the rice paddies. Large chattering monkeys called *co-rai* guard the entrance to the forest. Nothing much has changed there. The town looks sleepy and solemn in its dank indolence. Everywhere you go you feel the river, the heavy, eddying, muddy waters of the river. Smithies and jewellers hold their markets in its curve. You can still find traditional craftworkers in Vinh Long. Buddhist monasteries somehow survived under communism. And while Catholic missionaries were refused entry, a priest managed to get in and settle there.

In the twenties, the whites, dressed in white, kept mostly to themselves. The women wore wide-brimmed hats and lace dresses; young girls wore full-skirted dresses and patent leather shoes; and the men wore pith helmets, shorts and bow ties. Neat coconut-palm-lined streets, colonial roads cut at right angles, well-tended public gardens. A silent white town where a few gleaming Hotchkiss cars, their windows shut tight, could be seen cruising around. They were owned by powerful Chinese, wealthy whites or tiger hunters staying in the small town.

In Vinh Long they had built separate schools for girls and boys. Marie was headmistress of the girls' school. Hers was an administrative and not a teaching post. She had about one hundred girls in her care. They were mainly taught such practical subjects as sewing

34

and embroidery, but also basic French and arithmetic. Marie had Vietnamese teachers working for her, but she soon grew bored and did some teaching too. Proud to have a teaching qualification in sewing, she taught that as well as French. She loved her work and loved her pupils, her girls who in the Confucian system were not a priori excluded from school but were barred from the mandarinate, intelligent girls whose parents had taken them out of the fields so that they could be educated.[1]

The Donnadieu family shut itself up in a district that was also isolated, and observed the rituals of white Vinh Long. They were integrated, but only on the surface. The mother was respected but not liked. She was different, still pointed out in the streets, set apart. Probably because she was a widow, because she spoke her mind, because she made herself heard. Besides, she was a meddler, forever begging, complaining, judging, interfering and disapproving of all and sundry.

Marie Donnadieu had three children to bring up on her own. She was getting no help from her family, and her husband's family would have nothing to do with her. At the time she was earning 10,000 francs a month and teaching French in her spare time. Not a lot to live on. But it wasn't just a question of money. Marie wasn't interested in a life dependent on the teachers' promotion panel. Marie didn't want to be a civil servant for the rest of her life. She dreamed of adventure, of breaking from her daily routine and the bleak, dreary life of a petty little white.

The eldest son, Pierre, had left school; he was uncontrollable and made a nuisance of himself in the Chinese district. The mother just let him get on with it. The younger one, Paul, had also given up on school. And their mother was a teacher! They'd stay out all night and then sleep till five in the afternoon. All three children went around barefooted, spoke Vietnamese and lived with the servants. Gossip was on the increase among the whites. Had Pierre started to visit opium dens? Whatever the reasons, the mother needed more money. Marguerite didn't see herself as belonging to the world of the whites; she was no ordinary white girl, a child whose mother let her do anything. She was pretty much left to her own devices. At home there were tears, screams and shouts. Insults, blows and injustice frequently rained down on her. She'd hide under the stairs and wait for the storm to pass, as it invariably did. A bundle of fear, hate, desire and laughter. The only way of life she knew was that of the family. This family of extremes was both the tempest and the raft. The girl slept in her mother's bed, and so at night she was less frightened of God. Night falls quickly in the tropics, without any warning.

One evening in Vinh Long something happened in Marguerite's head and body. Something serious that would mark her, but also enrich her work. A childhood incident, repeated and distorted by recurring dreams, can never fully explain a fictional *oeuvre* but it can shed light on an imagination peopled with the same characters and tortured obsessions. 'My fear's so great I can't call out. I must be eight years old. I can hear her shrieks of laughter and cries of delight, she's certainly playing with me. My memory is of a central fear. To say it's beyond my understanding, beyond my strength, is inadequate.'[2]

Duras's universe from *The Sea Wall* via *India Song* to *The Lover* is permanently haunted by a madwoman, beggar, shrieker, siren who rises from the mud. In her unpublished notes, 'The flea-ridden beggarwoman is accompanied in the waters of the river near the banks where the carp sleep. She lies in wait for them and eats them raw.'[3] Half-man, half-woman, emerging from the frontiers of the night and running around in the Forbidden City of the whites, this beggar screamed words that heralded the apocalypse. As the day was drawing to a close, that was when the shrieking madwoman pursued Marguerite. For a few moments, that was all. But it was enough to have her shaking in terror. In the Vinh Long house, at the end of the street, past the gate, in the dark, little Marguerite ran, then, the moment she was through the door, dropped to the ground. Phew! Saved. The child was terrified of being touched. The madwoman was a smuggler and Marguerite could sense it. A smuggler of madness. All through her life Duras was afraid she might go mad, yet often she courted madness; she decided to befriend it rather than make of it an enemy to be defeated. 'To be one's own object of madness and not become mad, now that would be a most wonderful misfortune,' she wrote in *Green Eyes*. Very much later, when it was already too late, she realized her mother was mad. And as though to exorcize her own share of madness, she admitted it and wrote it.

The beggarwoman really did exist, as Marguerite described in an interview:

> She first came to us in Cochin China and has appeared in virtually all my books. She came with her little girl, a child of two although she looked as though she was six months old. She was riddled with worms. I adopted her. My mother let me keep her. She died. We couldn't have saved her. ... The beggarwoman ran away several times, she kept disappearing. She had a wound on her foot. We'd always catch up with her. And then one night she disappeared for good.[4]

Marguerite never had any photographs of Vinh Long, but the landscape was indelibly imprinted on her memory. When she was writing *The Lover*, she said in an interview:

> Vinh Long is a river of lagoons like the oxbows in Conflans. Endless sea deltas. Countless villages. Hundreds of sleepy creeks all around Vinh Long. It was so very beautiful. Gardens and parks that led down to the river, just like in *The Vice-Consul*. The teacher's house was on the fringes of the white town in the less fashionable area. Vinh Long is surrounded by alluvial plains and surgically unfinished areas.

On either side of the long streets, grass huts sit under the palms. Jewellers and grocers, their stalls stuck side by side. More Chinese shops than Annamese. A quiet, dreary life. Here you can taste time as you wait for dusk to turn the river pink.

It was in Vinh Long that everything began to fall apart for the Donnadieus. The mother started to have bouts of depression that frightened the children, the boys were labelled delinquents and the minor civil servants were beginning to ostracize her. They thought she talked too much, was too strict at school, and that she was sowing discord among her colleagues.

Pierre was becoming increasingly violent. Violent towards his younger brother, and very violent towards his sister. He'd hurl insults at her, beat her and generally mistreat her. He was always yelling at the servants, his brother, his sister, the world. He infuriated the neighbours. He'd buy a monkey and then spend hours on the terrace either delousing it or stroking its testicles quite openly. And all the while, amid the chaos, the shouting, the interminable fights and deadly silences, little Marguerite was working, surviving by working. She worked so hard that when she took her primary-school certificate, she came out top in the whole of Cochin China.

Pierre's violence would verge on insanity. Their mother said nothing. She never said anything. She knew she could do nothing to calm her son down and didn't want to. She seemed almost attracted to his evil side and, on occasion, quite shamelessly and even proudly endorsed it. But she had three children. There were times when she'd remember this. And although she might have said nothing, she wasn't blind. One day she took the plunge and decided to have him repatriated to France. In *The North China Lover*, Marguerite says it was after seeing Pierre take meat from the little brother's plate. 'And he ate it – the way a dog would. And he howled just like a dog, that's really what he was'.[5] Realizing it was a question of life and death, his mother reluctantly shipped him off to Marseille. From there, he returned to his father's region, to Pardaillan, where Father Dufaux, his guardian and tutor, took him in hand.

The troublesome son gone, the mother could breathe again. She started to plan for the future and to dream of making money. She was a woman obsessed with money. With money you can do anything. In Marie's mind – and it was something she believed all her life – only money could bring you respect and happiness. She was never to be satisfied with her lot. After years demanding her widow's pension, it arrived at long last. Around this time she also sold her little house in Hanoi. And so, with her meagre savings, she embarked on a huge project, one that she was sure would make them rich: to buy land, work it and end up queen of the rice paddies of the Pacific.

The plots were called concessions and consisted of a few acres of land stolen from the peasants and given by the authorities to whites interested in cultivating them. A decree had just been passed to encourage the small-scale colonist to own land made available in Cochin China, Cambodia and Annam. Thanks to this decree, Marie was entitled to a free 300-hectare concession. And so she applied. She was immediately offered 300 hectares of good land wherever she wanted. But 300 hectares wasn't enough; she wanted at least twice that much. Marie had ambitions. 'But it's not just the rich who have things: if we want it, we can be rich too.'[6] She began to dream. And the thieving authorities cleverly fuelled the dreams of little whites like Marie. She began to rave. She imagined herself a multimillionaire, a captain of industry, fabulously rich. So she said she'd wait.

Still, Marie wanted her concession on the Pacific. She pictured it in all its glory; she thought about it day and night. She pleaded with the authorities. Again they told her she could have 300 hectares straight away, but that if she wanted another 300, she would have to go through a complicated procedure: extra land could only be purchased by tender, and applicants had to be approved by the authorities. One of the officials showed her where the concessions available to colonist were.[7] Marie went through with everything: the paperwork, the endless formalities, the official inquiry, but there was still no news. She made great play of the fact she was a widow with three children, adding the names of her husband's two children to the application forms in a bid for sympathy. Two years she waited, and the anticipation was driving her crazy; two years of building her dreams of a new life out loud to the children, who were beginning to believe in them. She'd have liked her land to be nearby, but the plots in Cochin China had already been taken. It would have to be Cambodia.

She was in Sadec when she heard the news. It was in September 1928 and she'd just taken up her post as headmistress of a girls' school. Sadec (now Sa Dec) was considered the most beautiful city in Indo-China. At the end of the thirties, travellers would visit the sleepy little town that stretched along the curving banks of the Mekong, hidden by the tropical vegetation. Today in the Chinese quarters, overrun by cackling chickens, blacksmiths still work in an atmosphere heavy with the scent of mint. People visit the Ile des Blancs in the centre of the town, a relic of colonial times. To reach it, a boat pitches and tosses you through the muddy ferment of the Mekong. The stony promenade, edging the island, with its fringe of drooping tamarind trees and coconut palms, hasn't changed since Marguerite's time. The school is a typical colonial administrative building with an imposing façade and small, very basic classrooms inside. Wild mango trees now grow in the playground. Everything has survived, though it looks on the brink of collapse. There's a variety of tiger lily that grows so quickly that in a matter of days the front steps of the small bamboo houses are covered and you can't get in. In Sadec there's a tall, imposing

1910 house hidden from view by hedges of oleander. You clamber over the metal gates, cross the neglected garden, push open the front door careful not to break it down, and, accompanied by a gang of cheeky kids who appear from nowhere, move through the reception rooms into the huge ballroom, touching as you go the old, now torn prints, part the shutters and glide in a waltz over the tiled floor. Her novels, her films – it's all here. What if Marguerite Duras made nothing up? What if this house had haunted her so much that she was able to conjure it up later, elsewhere? But then with her, elsewhere was everywhere.

In Sadec, a smiling and courteous old man, Mr Dong, told me that yes, he remembered Marguerite well. He was four years younger than she was. He'd been her neighbour, and the one who, every evening, delivered the food his mother had cooked to the Donnadieu family. Especially sautéed pork. The mother never went to market and never cooked. Liked? Respected. The girls at the school were frightened of her. The locals called her Madame Dieu. It wasn't exactly a compliment, it was just that she often acted as though she were God. Strict with her students and not terribly pleasant to her colleagues. Evaluation reports invariably stressed her faults and her superiors never missed an opportunity to criticize her and give her a low rating. At the end of the 1929 academic year, for example, Monsieur Tondet, an ex-headmaster and head of Sadec's education committee, gave her a 'fair' for behaviour, appearance and academic abilities, whereas he spoke of her colleagues in glowing terms. The same Monsieur Tondet concluded, 'Madame Donnadieu has made little effort this year to improve teaching standards. As a headmistress she can be very disdainful. She finds it difficult to take orders and makes my task as Head of the Education Committee increasingly difficult.' Was this a kind of reprisal or something more personal? An investigation was called for. Her reputation had obviously followed her. Monsieur Taboulet, the local administrative head, was called in, and he confirmed, 'Temperamentally, this particular teacher is not easy. She certainly looks after her school but appears to be more concerned with increasing student numbers.[8]

Today Mr Dong can still clearly recall his days at school when he was a small boy. He can remember the timetable, the subjects and the names of his teachers. The lessons were in French. He learned to sing 'La Marseillaise' and knew the stories of Clovis and Napoleon off by heart. The speaking of Vietnamese within the school compound was strictly forbidden and punishable by expulsion, though the children spoke it quietly among themselves. School was compulsory until the first year of secondary school. Mr Dong says 'Madame Dieu' was quite right to be strict with her pupils. She wanted to do the right thing, to get them through their elementary-school-leaving certificate so that they could one day get a secretarial job with the Provincial Department.

Mr Dong remembered the shy little girl always clinging to her mother; the weary mother, perpetually tired, slumped in an armchair, lost in thought for hours on end, on the veranda where everyone could see her. And the eldest boy who one fine day arrived from France, and the violence and screams that started up again in the Donnadieu household.

The archives of the Colonial Department corroborate Mr Dong's recollections. A penniless Pierre did in fact suddenly, and without seeking his mother's permission, leave Pardaillan and rejoin the family via Marseille, Saigon, Sadec. His excuse was that he'd had a feeling his mother was seriously ill and that he needed to protect her.

Pressure was mounting: the adored son was ever more violent, the authorities were causing difficulties and Marie was having to borrow money to secure the concession at last. She felt alone against the world.

At the time there were five opium dens in Sadec. For one piastre you could smoke for two or three hours, depending on the dose. From the outside the dens looked like darkened shops, with a smell reminiscent of burned chocolate. Inside there wasn't a sound. There were three rows of beds in the largest one, just planks of wood with a mat on top, Mr Dong explained. You lay on your side and smoked from long wooden pipes. A dormitory of dreamers. A coolie kept watch at the door and counted the money. Mr Dong smiled. Rich or poor, everyone smoked, and the French encouraged it. 'It earned them money, a lot of money and it was supposed to have a numbing effect on us,' he told me.

It is certainly true that profits from the sale of opium poured into the coffers of the Treasury, hence its vindication in an official report issued by the government of Indo-China: 'as a commodity, opium is

of interest only in so far as it brings money into the tax department.'
State-produced opium alone represented over a quarter of the annual
revenue; in other words, over 7 million piastres went to the state
every year. In collaboration with the Institut Pasteur, pharmaceutical
companies set up opium factories in Saigon and Hanoi with the aim
of producing a drug that was not only less harmful to the consumer
but would also guarantee an increase in tax revenue. But it was
obviously not enough, for the authorities continued to complain
that they didn't have sufficient staff to cover opium distribution
throughout the area. France surpassed its wildest dreams. By the end
of the twenties, thousands of Vietnamese were addicted to opium.
Like sleepwalkers, addicts skulked around outside opium dens, as
emaciated as the victims of famine. Poor wretches, they'd do anything
for a smoke, just a smoke.

Pierre Donnadieu lived in an opium den by the river. He'd come
home only to squeeze money out of his mother. Desperate, she
confides in her daughter. Together they weep as they lie in the same
bed. The daughter yells at her mother, then asks for forgiveness. The
two of them there in the night, holding one another. 'Let me tell you
what he did, too, what it was like. Well – he stole from the houseboys
to go and smoke opium. He stole from our mother. He rummaged in
cupboards. He stole. He gambled.'⁹

Eventually Pierre left again. 'For several years he was no longer
part of the family. It was while he was away that my mother bought
the land, the concession. A terrible business, but for us, the children
who were left, not so terrible as the presence of the killer would have
been, the child-killer of the night, of the night of the hunter.'¹⁰

Christmas holidays, 1928. At the end of a long and tiring journey, the
Donnadieu family and two servants at last set foot on the plot of land
so long coveted by Marie. Marguerite discovers a Beauce-like region
of rice paddies, the water shrimp-coloured or sand-pink depending
on the time of day, and an oppressive sky. Marguerite had always lived
in small colonial towns designed to look like a French provincial town
or even a public garden. In the Cambodian region of Prey-Nop, at
the edge of the Pacific not far from the Elephant Mountains, she
found a landscape of rivers, lagoons, muddy earth and foaming seas,
surrounded by a forest that sheltered tigers. She would say that it was

here she discovered nature. The concentration of wild animals, the fish that inhabited the shallow basins beyond the trees, the rustling, terrifying tropical jungle: all that is true. Marguerite invented nothing.

The concession was situated eighty kilometres from Kampot, in southwestern Cambodia, on the vast crescent-shaped indentation then called the Gulf of Siam. Before the arrival of the Donnadieu family, the Gulf of Siam had been a haven for smugglers. Armed gangs of Chinese whose headquarters were on a nearby island had terrorized the whole area. The concession was three kilometres from the sea. Between sea and plain there lay a huge expanse of coconut and pepper plantations. *Filao* vegetation spread over the white sandy beaches. The hidden pagodas, paths through the jungle, deserted Buddhist temples in the middle of the forest, the sun-baked earth, chattering monkeys, clear rivers, pure air – all that would always fill Marguerite with wonder.

Prey-Nop seemed to be the end of the world. It took two days to get there from Saigon; from Sadec a night and a day. The journey was an escapade along rutted roads in an overloaded old banger. Every time they stopped, Paulo, as the younger brother was nick-named, would get out his rifle and sniff for wild animals. With a chauffeur and their faithful servant Do, the family crossed the vast plains and rice paddies broken up by coconut and areca palms to reach 'the kind of terrain where there are no more villages, no more houses; a country full of water and swamps. And there, at the edge of the ocean, were forests of mangroves, which was all that could be seen for miles around when it was high tide season.'[11]

All summer, Paulo and Marguerite were left to their own devices, there in the middle of the plain, to shoot at wading birds, to walk in the sun when they should have been taking a siesta, to climb up through icy waterfalls to get to the withered hectares of banana trees. Marguerite was fourteen, her brother seventeen. Together they killed monkeys and birds. 'It was terrible, we killed everything we came across.' There were alligators, panthers, snakes. They walked under a sky hidden by forests of lianas where chattering parrots frolicked, travelled the length and breadth of the salt marshes behind the sea wall and bathed in the stagnant water of the lagoon where carcasses of wading birds lay rotting. Brother initiated sister, teaching her to listen to animal sounds, to sniff their smells, not to disturb the big cats. Marguerite and Paulo lived like the Vietnamese, spoke Vietnamese, played with Vietnamese children. It was a happy period. The beauty of nature, the lights, smells and colours would remain forever engraved on her memory.

It would be some time before Marie Donnedieu realized that her dream of being rich had been foolish. Anyway, what did she know about rice paddies, about agriculture? Nothing.

> Yes, it was what you would call a concession. But they must have seen her coming, this woman alone, completely on her own, a widow with no one to defend her. The land they had given her was unworkable. She had no idea that to get a fertile concession you had to bribe the officials of the Land Commission. They gave her land, but it wasn't land, it was land that was covered with water for six months of the year. And it swallowed all the money she'd saved over twenty years.[12]

Even today in Ho Chi Minh City learned old Vietnamese men will speak to you of Marguerite's book *The Sea Wall* with their eyes full of tears. They're moved not so much by the mother's despair as by the passion with which Marguerite pays tribute to the men who died in the blistering heat, cutting and laying roads through the swamps for France. The men were chained together. Ordered to work them till they dropped, military leaders, veterans of the French colonial army, rounded up and oversaw political prisoners and poor peasants dying of starvation. Numerous testimonies speak of having seen groups of them dragging dead bodies around. This orally transmitted historical fact has never been properly recorded. Marguerite paid tribute to these unsung heroes who gave their lives for France. There are students in Vietnam today who still tremble with gratitude towards Marguerite Duras. She was the only one to speak of the children of the plain who the moment they were born were condemned to die of hunger, cholera or dysentery. 'The children simply went back to the land like wild mountain mangoes, like the little monkeys from the mouth of the lagoon.'[13]

Faced with the problem of the advancing sea, Marie Donnadieu attempted the impossible – to build a sea wall. She was challenging God. And she wasn't the only one, as can be seen from colonial documents found in Ho Chi Minh City. Dozens had been given land unfit for human habitation, and dozens battled, driven by despair, to build, with the help of the peasants, mud- and log-walls to hold back the Pacific.

Fortunately Marie had built their bungalow on solid ground, two rooms and a veranda with a view of the banana trees and tired cannas. This permanent structure, standing as it did on loose soil, would buy her time in her battle with the authorities. The little house next to the road that skirted the plantation cost her 5,000 piastres to build, an enormous sum at the time. Built on stilts because of the flood waters, and made of wood that had to be cut and sawn into planks on site, the house survived the humidity, the weather and the foam of the Pacific breakers.

However, Marie wanted more than a house, she wanted an estate. So she had some fifty workers brought from Sadec. She paid them a pittance and told them to build her a village in the middle of the swamp, two kilometres from the sea. She took rash decisions, rushed into things and then panicked. Soon she felt overwhelmed by the scale of the undertaking and felt she should stay on to supervise the work, so she obtained temporary leave of absence from the education authorities in Saigon.

In a first, unpublished version of *The Lover*, which contained passages that turned up in *The Sea Wall*, Marguerite describes this six-month period: 'While our house was under construction, we, that is my mother, younger brother and I, lived in a grass hut adjacent to the one belonging to the "upstairs" servants. The village was a four-hour boat ride from the road and therefore from our house. So our lives were in every way like those of the servants except that my mother and I slept on a mattress at night.'

Then her mother became ill. Bouts of despondency and depression would force her to lie down. The attacks could last for days. Marie told the children she was going to die. They were frightened. The nearest doctor was hours from the road and there were no telephones in that area of Cambodia. The mother would occasionally open a weary eye to tell her children not to worry. 'It'll pass,' she'd sigh and then slip back into a lethargic state, which would be followed by prolonged fits of weeping. Financial problems exacerbated her anguish and her physical deterioration.

45

These crises of my mother's appalled and alarmed the native servants who, each time, threatened to leave. They were worried they wouldn't be paid. They'd come over to the grass hut and sit in silence on the embankment that ran down the side until the attack was over. Inside, my mother just lay there, unconscious, quietly moaning to herself. Now and then my brother and I would go out to reassure the servants and tell them Mother wasn't dead. They found it hard to believe. My brother would tell them that if Mother died he would do everything to get them back to Cochin China and pay them himself.[14]

The mother felt her husband had forsaken her. She wanted to join him in the hereafter. Marguerite told me she was brought up with the 'conversations' her mother regularly engaged in with her late husband. She would talk to him out loud, rationally, ask him for advice and report back to him. Night was the only time she could talk to her favourite dead person. 'She wouldn't do anything without first consulting him; he would "deliver" his plans for the future to her. According to her, these "deliveries" always took place around one o'clock in the morning, thus justifying my mother's vigils and, in her opinion, giving her incredible prestige.'[15] She only spoke with the dead; to the living she ranted.

Forced to grow up too quickly, Paulo became a man, the boss of the concession, the guarantor of the lives of his mother and little sister. 'My brother . . . was the bravest person I've ever met. He found the strength to reassure me and urge me not to cry in front of the servants, that it was pointless, that mother would live. And indeed, the moment the sun left the valley and went down behind the Elephant Mountains, mother would regain consciousness.'[16]

An excellent hunter, Paulo had a Winchester 10.7-mm-calibre rifle and a .357 magnum. His life revolved around the hunt. He'd store rotting meat under the veranda, for use as bait in traps, and then go off into the lookout posts he'd built in the forest. When not out hunting, Paulo was dreaming of blondes with ruby lips, as he sat in the evening on the veranda listening to love songs on the worn-out gramophone. In *Eden Cinema* and *The Sea Wall*, Marguerite recollects the wild dreams and thwarted ambitions of the brother–sister duo. Both appear to be caught in an eternity of waiting, rooted in the stinking earth, consenting slaves to misfortune.

Every penny of their mother's savings had gone into the concession – twenty-four years in her job as a civil servant. Yet in one
night the waves of the Pacific swept through the plantations and razed
the harvest to the ground. The bungalow ended up marooned in the
middle of a vast swamp. Next day the mother, taking her two children
with her, spent eight hours in a boat inspecting the devastation,
unable to accept the extent of the disaster. She would take on the sea,
the land and the general government of Indo-China.

When her temporary leave of absence came to an end, she returned
to Sadec to oversee the start of the academic year. Worn down
by money worries, she tried to borrow from the chetties, Indian
moneylenders found all over the Far East. The atmosphere was
tense in Sadec too. The white community thought she was strange,
aggressive, eccentric, and was finding her increasingly difficult to live
with. The children stayed at home, shut off from the rest of the world.
The school was beginning to see the mother as a problem too. Once
again she was criticized for being too strict, too extreme, quick-
tempered. Of course the other whites were nothing like her, not in
the way they dressed, lived or spoke.

Every weekend Marie would take her children to inspect the concession. She had to keep an eye on the sea walls. The walls were one
of the brilliant ideas to come from the father in the middle of the
night. When you inhabit the hereafter, it's easy to imagine that the
sea can be tamed. In an unpublished piece, Marguerite Duras
describes her mother's first attempt at constructing the sea walls: 'We
brought in several hundred workers who built the walls in the dry
season supervised by my mother and brother. Then disaster struck.
The walls were worn away by hordes of crabs sucked into them when
the tide came in.'[17]

Next, the mother had the idea of using rocks, but it's not easy to
find rocks on land liable to flood. In the end she opted for mangrove
trees. The mangrove trees held fast and the rice was at last able to
grow. But her employees, upset by her authoritarian manner, har-
vested the early crop and sold it to a neighbouring planter. Once they
had pocketed the money they cleared off back to Cochin China, never
to return to the concession. The mother discovered the extent of the
disaster during the school holidays. Marguerite recalls her reaction:
'Again my mother came to terms with it. She tired of the sea walls

and chose to ignore the fact that those still standing would collapse the following year!"[18]

The mother kept the concession but decided as an experiment to farm only a part of it, the handful of slopes furthest away from the sea. Finally she abandoned the whole thing for good. She was ruined. Now and then she'd go there with the children, to dream. Paulo would polish his weapons; Marguerite would dream of writing. There their mother was at last able to rest. Together they'd gaze at the blue of the sky and breathe the scent of the velvet nights. The house in *The Sea Wall* became their holiday home.

Pierre would turn up in Sadec without warning. And with him, discord and violence returned to the Donnadieu household. Pierre wanted to kill Paul. Marguerite wanted to kill Pierre. Pierre stole from his mother, who was then forced to borrow money from the chetties. Pierre bought a new baboon and made him the sole object of his affection. He'd play the piano for him at night, and make him swallow coins. But with love came torture. He made the monkey swallow so many coins that he would walk around with his head permanently bowed. He bought the monkey a cockerel, which the monkey plucked. The cockerel screeched. The money carried on. The cockerel died. Pierre bought another cockerel. The monkey turned nasty. To the active encouragement and delight of his owner, he'd spend hours on the veranda masturbating for all the world to see.

CHAPTER 3

The Lover

~

When the mother finally understood that she was completely ruined, and that the concession would never make her a millionaire, she put all her energy and dreams for the future into her daughter's education. The year was 1929. Marguerite was fifteen and Marie Donnadieu was thinking of sending her to the lycée Chasseloup-Laubat in Saigon. Just as she had decided the concession would make her rich, so she decided her daughter would succeed.

Marguerite, a bright but disruptive pupil, was not popular; not with her teachers and not with her classmates. She'd just had a disastrous academic year and failed in every single subject. She'd been reprimanded for serious breaches of discipline, and been summoned to appear before the disciplinary committee for having thrown a satchel into her teacher's face at the end of a French lesson. But she was clever and had the ability to do well at school. Her mother was very aware of this, and hadn't forgotten the brilliant marks Marguerite used to get as a little girl.

The school didn't take in boarders, and so Marie Donnadieu moved heaven and earth to find somewhere not too expensive for her darling daughter to lodge in Saigon. Marguerite was never a boarder at the Lyautey School, immortalised in *The Lover*. In fact, the Lyautey Boarding School never existed. Marguerite ended up a lodger with Mademoiselle C. There were three other boarders in Mademoiselle C.'s small house: two teachers and Colette, two years younger than Marguerite and also a pupil at the lycée. Mademoiselle C. wanted

49

a quarter of Marie Donnadieu's salary for this so-called rounded education. 'Only Mlle C. knew my mother was a teacher, we were careful to hide it from the other boarders in case they took umbrage.'[1] In the short story 'Boa', Mademoiselle C. turns up as 'la Bardet', a coquettish old maid with a roving imagination and a body that trembled with unfulfilled yearnings. Marguerite became Mademoiselle C.'s sexual hostage. There's a very disturbing scene in 'Boa' that turns up almost verbatim in Marguerite's personal diary. It describes how every Sunday afternoon, after having been to the botanical gardens, and taken her afternoon tea of biscuits and bananas, la Bardet would wait for the young girl in her bedroom.

> Her own eyes lovingly lowered, she'd stand very straight so that I could admire her. Half-naked. Never had anyone ever seen her like this, only me. But it was too late. At over seventy-five no one would ever see her like this again, apart from me. I was the only one of our household she ever showed herself to, and always on a Sunday afternoon, after the zoo and when the other boarders were out. I had to look at her until she told me to stop. 'How I love this. I'd rather go hungry,' she used to say.[2]

Our little secret. Mademoiselle C. insisted on these weekly sessions. No, no touching, just looking. Looking, saying nothing. Conspirators. She'd position herself in front of the window – the half-naked, shrivelled body in the full light. Marguerite had never made love. Imagined it, of course; thought about it all the time. So, feigning desire, Marguerite looked at the old spinster enamoured of her body. The young girl was disgusted, upset, aroused. Having closed the door to Mademoiselle C.'s room, Marguerite would station herself on the balcony and sing to catch the eyes of passing colonial soldiers and wink at them languorously.

Marguerite claimed she'd been forced to agree to these sexual sessions and that they went on for two years. Fact or fantasy? Telling a friend about them years later, she referred to them as 'traumas'. She says Mademoiselle C. reeked of death. 'Mlle C. had a cancer under her left breast but she only ever showed it to me. She'd uncover her breast as she made her way to the window and would show it to me. I would tactfully gaze at the cancer for two or three long minutes. "You see," Mlle C. would say. And I would say, "Ah yes, I see."'[3]

Denise Augé, a year younger than Marguerite, and today a lively, cheerful, sweet lady with, funnily enough, that same oriental look as Marguerite – environmental influences, she explained, smiling – vividly recalled Mademoiselle Donnadieu arriving at the lycée Chasseloup-Laubat in 1929. A thin, pretty girl with long plaits. She was pleasant, sociable, very good at mathematics, so good in fact that she used to help all the boys in the school; she was fairly shy, not especially noisy, and always gave the impression she wasn't up to scratch. Particular about her appearance? Absolutely. Denise remembered an occasion when, invited to a game of tennis, Marguerite turned up in high-heeled shoes. All the girls laughed. Marguerite blushed and ran off without a word.

Classes at the lycée Chasseloup-Laubat began early in the morning, when the heat was still bearable and the scent of the tamarind trees less heady.

> This is the road to school. The time is seven-thirty, it's morning. In Saigon. There's the wonderful freshness of the streets after the municipal carts have passed, the time when the smell of jasmine inundates the city – so powerful some whites 'find it appalling' when they first arrive. And then miss it once they've left the colony.[4]

When it was siesta time Marguerite would go back to the boarding house and shut herself in her room. Like many adolescents, she spent hours examining herself in front of the mirror. 'I had neat, white breasts. They were the only things in my life in that house that were a pleasure to look at.'

Her fourth year at school was a disaster: she failed almost every one of her subjects. But the beginning of year five was a revelation: 'The whole school was reading my essays. They were so good the fifth-year teachers were refusing to mark them and yet I knew nothing about French literature,' she told Claude Berri. Denise confirmed this. Suddenly Marguerite was an exceptional pupil. From zero out of twenty she was getting nineteen out of twenty, without trying. As she said, 'It had made me less frightened.' By the time her mother came to collect her at the end of term, she was feeling more confident. She handed her mother her report book. Marguerite remembered that her mother burst into tears right there in the courtyard. For once she actually felt like hugging her.

At the Chasseloup-Laubat school Marguerite had to sit at the back of the class with the children of customs officials because of her social position. Her academic success did not allow her to forget her origins. The pupils came from all over Indo-China and the whites were in the minority. There were five, six white girls per class. The Vietnamese boys, at the time referred to as Annamese or natives, often fell in love with white girls in the higher classes. As Denise said, blushing despite her eighty-two years, 'One of the natives in my class was in love with me, he wrote me poems every day, it was very embarrassing. Love was out of the question. We weren't brought up to be racist but a relationship like that was, by definition, unnatural. My generation didn't despise the Annamese, but we would never have dreamed of socializing with them outside school.'[5] They were closely supervised, these young white ladies, and not allowed to roam the dangerous streets of Saigon. Every family had its chauffeur waiting at the school gates. Except for Marguerite's.

Denise had quite forgotten Marguerite when in Paris one day she came across the poster of Jean-Jacques Annaud's film *The Lover*. She rushed to see it and bought the book. But she was quite adamant:

> I just don't understand this story about a Chinese lover. It wasn't like today. There were no lovers, especially not Chinese lovers. There were two scandals at Chasseloup-Laubat school. One was a friend of Marguerite's who fell in love with a married man (white, of course). Her family soon had her packed off to a convent in Hong Kong. And then there was another who at fifteen and a quarter wanted to marry an old lawyer. She was divorced before the month was out.

Another classmate of Marguerite's, Marcelle, said that while Marguerite gave the impression of being timid, reserved and well behaved, she was very secretive. She never confided in any of her friends and no one knew anything about what she did once classes were over. Marcelle did recall that twice Marguerite boasted of leading a double life, although she never explained what she meant. She did, however, have a vivid recollection of a jubilant Marguerite turning up at school one morning, flashing a diamond ring on her finger to some of the girls, saying she knew a rich man.

Is the story of the Chinese lover true? All through her life Marguerite had a talent for confusing the issue, for having us believe lies she then ended up believing herself. There are so many different versions of the story that a biographer has to remain sceptical. Even so, a trip to Vietnam and the discovery of an unpublished notebook have shed new light on the affair.

The lover existed. I visited his grave, saw his house. Marguerite had a relationship with a Chinese man. His nephew told me about it when I met him at the pagoda the grandfather had built in Sadec. He invited me to his home in a suburb of the city, where he runs a small restaurant, and told me the story of Marguerite and his uncle. He showed me photographs of the lover's wife, who now lives in the USA with her children. He took me to the house outside Sadec formerly owned by the lover's father. We went on a strange tour of what had been the family estate: agricultural land where unfinished buildings lay like giant beetles among well-tended rice paddies surrounded by straw huts with rickety roofs. On our way back to the main road he turned on to a muddy track that came to an abrupt end in the middle of a field. Plunging through the wild grass, he led me to a kind of burial mound: on a large grey stone slab eroded by tropical rains, dirty and neglected, surrounded by the insistent buzzing of bluebottles, sat two identical tombs. One contained a coffin. The other was empty. Two dates had been engraved on the first, a date of birth only on the second. The lover's wife knows that one day she'll have to lie here next to her husband, despite his double life.

The lover's blue house that appears in the novel exists too. Several years ago it was converted into a police station and so the taking of photographs is banned. Across the potholed street is the river. In the courtyard three policemen and a group of small children kick a ball around. Despite the interpreter's warning I discreetly reach for my camera. She was right. The angry policemen rush over and want to confiscate it. But what secrets could this run-down house possibly hold today? We leave. The nephew takes me home, to the restaurant-cum-house he is so obviously proud of, despite its location in a poor suburb. Outside, there are four wooden tables. It's five in the afternoon, the light is beginning to change and night is fast approaching. The man tells me about the lover's life after Marguerite, the arranged marriage, the many children, his uncle's great love for his wife's sister, the double life, difficult to lead in a small town where everyone's watching everyone else. Night falls. Beers are downed. When the revolution came, he told me before he left, the guards came and arrested the family. The lover was the only one to escape, thanks to an old school friend. The others? They were taken to the heart of their own lands and forced to dig holes in the soft soil of the rice paddies. One hole for each man, who was then buried alive up to his neck in mud. Then they sent for the peasants who'd worked for them, handed them stones and stood them in front of the heads. The peasants were forced to throw stones until the sun rose and dispersed the night.

It took the lover three months to get back to Saigon, travelling by night, through the irrigation canals of the rice paddies. Before taking his leave, the nephew handed me the address of the friend in Saigon who'd saved the lover's life. Then he seemed to change his mind and, with a conspiratorial air, went off to fetch two documents, neatly tied with string, which he kept under his bed. I was expecting to see old photographs from the family album, love letters, unpublished material, things never before seen … But what he was proudly displaying was nothing more than a faded copy of an old French magazine. On the front page was a copy of the photo from his uncle's identity card. The story must be true if the lover's photo appeared in *Paris-Match*.

It was at the end of 1929 that they first met.

She hesitates. She says apologetically:
'I'm still small.'
'How many years?'
She answers the way a Chinese would:
'Sixteen years.'
'No,' he smiles, 'that isn't true.'
'Fifteen years, fifteen and a half – all right?'
He laughs.
'All right.'[6]

There are many men in Marguerite's work, including three versions of the lover. The one immortalized in *The Lover* is weaker, smaller, sicklier than the healthy, more confident 'north China lover'. Both these lovers are Chinese, from Manchuria or elsewhere; Chinese with pale, virtually white skins. Chinese, not Vietnamese. Chinese was more chic, gave you more status. The Chinese stood apart, were often shopkeepers, wealthy, extremely wealthy. But the first lover Marguerite describes – in *The Sea Wall* – is white. In his first appearance she dared not depict him as being Chinese. Skinny, drab, depraved, a voyeur. He is completely lacking in charm and yet loves seducing girls. That's all he thinks about. And he smells of game.

All three lovers are around twenty-five years old, own large black limousines and are badly proportioned. Their bodies are quite obviously deformed despite the way each wears elegant, well-tailored, loose-fitting tussore suits. The first lover allows the heroine's older brother to call him a monkey. Indeed 'it was a fact, he did not have a beautiful face. His shoulders were narrow, his arms short, he said he was of below average build.'[7] Fortunately there were his hands. Durassian lovers all have beautiful hands, and Marguerite describes them brilliantly and in great detail. The hands are erotic. The hands are a prelude to passion. Even the first lover, the puniest, the most grotesque, the most pathetic, had this redeeming feature: 'his hands were small, well-manicured, slim and rather beautiful.' And all her lovers' hands are adorned with diamond rings. The presence of the diamond gives them a princely quality.[8] Marguerite always loved diamond rings. She wore hers until the day she died; never taking them off, not even to wash rice. In Duras's universe the elements of the love ceremony are always the same. First the sight of the diamond excites desire, and then there's the smell of amber on the skin after lovemaking, and the touch of the lover's silk clothes and in their folds a whiff of opium.

Smooth, perfumed bodies, abandoned to love. The man is effeminate. The lovers are anti-macho, slaves to feminine desire. With Marguerite it's always the girl who calls the tune, who gets into the limousine, who takes the hand, who keeps him waiting, who leads him on with meaningful looks, her voice suddenly soft, her body seductive. It's always the girl who marks the stages, decides how events will unfold. But for all that she's not sure what she's doing or where she's got to. Having closed the door of the limousine, the young girl in *The Lover* feels weary, drained. Not because she's broken a sexual and social taboo but because, through this act that will commit her, she's excluded herself from the family for the first time in her life. A few years before she died, Marguerite Duras admitted that at the time she was still very much caught up, drowning almost, in her love for the mother.

The lover fails to separate mother and daughter, or to make the girl exist apart from her brothers. But he does offer her another life: that of writing. For the lover is the first to hear and believe that the child wants to become a writer. The affair with the lover disconnected Marguerite from the family group. While she was living the experience, she was thinking it, already selecting words so that she could write about it later. All her life, in one form or another, Marguerite never stopped telling the story of the lover.

It would be too easy to say that at the end of her life Marguerite's memory was beginning to fail her and that she thought what she'd written was more real than her own life. But the discovery of a document after her death does shed new light on the affair. It is an undated notebook which, according to handwriting experts, most likely dates from the war. In this piece Marguerite Donnadieu never intended should be published, she wrote:

It was on the Sadec–Saigon ferry that I first met Leo. I was on my way back to my lodgings and someone – I can't remember who – happened to be giving me a lift as well as Leo. Leo was a native but he dressed like a Frenchman and spoke perfect French, he was just back from Paris. I wasn't fifteen yet and I'd only ever been to France when I was very young. I thought Leo was very elegant. He was wearing an enormous diamond ring and a suit of oatmeal tussore silk. I'd never seen a diamond like it except on people who until then had never noticed me, as for my brothers, they wore white cotton ... Leo told me I was pretty.

'Do you know Paris?'

Blushing I told him I didn't. He knew Paris. He lived in Sadec. Someone living in Sadec knew Paris and this was the first I knew about it. Leo courted me. I was stunned. The doctor dropped me off at my lodgings and Leo found a way to convey that we'd meet again. I'd realized he was unbelievably rich and felt quite dazzled; I was so impressed, so uncertain I couldn't answer Leo.

Written in a clear and careful hand, with no crossings-out, the piece had been carefully placed in an envelope, sealed and never again opened. Is it a confession? Or is it the outline of a novel? Who knows? This story, recorded like a diary, certainly has a ring of truth about it. It was the first time Marguerite was telling the story of a love and betrayal that was to haunt her for the rest of her life:

> Next day, it was siesta time. I heard a car horn sound loudly. It was Leo ... Leo drove past thirty-five times in succession. As he went past the house he slowed down but didn't dare stop. I didn't go out on the balcony ... I dressed as best I could and at two o'clock set off to go to school. Leo was waiting for me on the route, leaning against the door of his car, again wearing an oatmeal tussore suit.

Something that never really comes out in any of the 'official' versions, but is quite blatant in this piece, is the fascination with money – money the driving force behind desire.

> I was absolutely fascinated by Leo's car. The moment I got in I had to know the make and how much it had cost. Leo told me it was a Leon Bollée and that it had cost 9000 piastres. I thought of our Citroën that had cost 4000, which mother had paid off in three instalments. Leo seemed delighted we'd had no problem striking up a conversation. He turned up in the evening and appeared again next day, and the days that followed. I was so proud of his car and was relying on its being seen. I'd stay in it on purpose to be sure my friends would spot me.
>
> That way I was hoping to end up friends with the daughters of the top civil servants in Indo-China. None of them had a limousine like it with liveried chauffeur, black limousine and jacket, specially ordered from Paris, of impressive size, and exquisite taste. Unfortunately, and despite his wonderful car, Leo was Annamese. But I was so dazzled by the car I chose to overlook this drawback.
>
> I continued to see Leo over the next few weeks. I always managed to manoeuvre the conversation so that he'd talk about his fortune. He had around fifty million buildings scattered around Indo-China; he was an only child and had access to vast amounts of money. The figures on which Leo's fortune was based staggered me; I'd dream about them at night and think about them all day.

At the time Marguerite's mother was earning 22,000 francs a month. A quarter of that went to the owner of the Saigon boarding house; another quarter to Pierre's tutor in France and a third went to the chetties to pay off loans made for the concession. She had nothing to live on. It was the bleakest period of her life. In Marguerite's grim words, 'We suffered so much from being poor but what was worse was having to hide it.' When the family was living on the plantation far from prying eyes, their poverty was bearable because it was inconspicuous. But not in Sadec where

> it was imperative we do everything to prevent the sixty French people on the post from knowing anything of our situation. And so my mother, on the last day of the month, would wait until nightfall and then go under cover of darkness to give the chetties a third of her salary. There were times when she couldn't go. I can't remember why now. The chetties would come round to the house, ensconce themselves in the sitting room and wait. On more than one occasion she broke down in front of them and wept, begging them to go away because the servants could see them. But the chetties wouldn't leave and my mother ended up chucking the money in their faces.[9]

The ferry's no different from in her writings and the banks of the Mekong haven't changed much if we're to believe the few photographs that exist. The old bus still makes the journey, somehow. Loaded inside and out, with passengers squeezed or perched or precariously balanced on steps, on roof; wobbling with caged animals, a menagerie of bikes and sacks of rice, it manoeuvres on to the ferry, amid a cacophony of shouts, led by the mob of itinerant vendors who besiege the passengers. At last, time to move off. Slowly the riverbank retreats. The ferry looks so old, its frame so rusty, its cable so worn that you begin to imagine an accident, a sinking, and to recall Marguerite's fears, 'In the terrible current I watch my last moments. The current's so strong it could carry everything away – rocks, a cathedral, a city. There's a storm blowing inside the water. A wind raging.'[10] Today it's diesel lorries, not a Leon Bollée, but the Sadec bus is still there, and the lucky, fat, hand-painted Buddha still sits next to the driver.

The crossing lasts barely fifteen minutes, but the ferry is the height of activity. Accompanying himself on a rattle, a blind musician sings; two small children at his side hold out the begging bowl. Steam comes out of an ingeniously modified bicycle to keep sticky white cakes warm. There are women loudly praising the virtues of quails' eggs. The wind is strong, you can feel the sea nearby, the water churning. On either side of the river, gangs of small girls sell nougat, rice- and corn-cakes sweetened with molasses and wrapped in a banana leaf. 'The Chinese treats her to one. She takes it. She devours it. She doesn't say thank you.'[11]

Between the My Tho ferry and Saigon the road is straight, flat and monotonous. Banana trees, water palms and coconut palms bend in the wind. The rice shoots quiver. In the fields grey and white tombstones sit in the green expanse, erected, since time immemorial, to face the setting sun. In the small town, at the side of the road, a little girl lying in a bamboo cot plays with a piece of wood. Behind her, a man is painting red characters on a wooden coffin. Life, death, the waiting, immortality.

Apart from the fact that I was ungainly and dressed in a way that was so ridiculous it defied description, I wasn't exactly conspicuous for my beauty. I was short and still underdeveloped, covered in freckles, weighed down by two auburn plaits that hung to midway down my thigh, and sunburned from living outdoors all the time at the plantation (in Saigon white skins were in fashion).

Some might have found my regular features attractive, but my sulky, sullen, stubborn expression so completely ruined them that no one ever noticed. My mother described my horrible countenance as poisonous. I've examined my features in vain hoping to find some sign of gentleness, of sweetness.

Sometimes, but not often enough and always in private, her mother tells her she's pretty. Yes, yes, you can look pretty, Marguerite. You'll get there one day. She tells her not to worry too much about it. Whenever Pierre beats her, he insults her, tells her she's a failure, a good-for-nothing, so ugly she puts men off, ugly, so ugly she'll have to get used to the idea of being an old maid.

It's true I had no dowry and the knowledge that one day she'd have to marry me off made my mother anxious. As soon as I turned fifteen the subject was already being discussed at home. 'However hard you try to find her a husband,' my older brother would say, 'you'll still be lumbered with her when she's thirty.' It was a sore point with my mother and she'd get angry, 'I could marry her tomorrow if I wanted to and what is more, to whomsoever I wished.'

The prospect of being an old maid made my blood run cold, death would have been the lesser of the two evils. I listened. I knew my mother was lying when she said she could marry me off to whoever she wanted, but even so I dreamed of finding a 'suitable match'.[12]

Marguerite was for sale. The brothers had no intention of working for a living and as far as the mother was concerned, it was normal for a daughter to leave home in return for a large cash payment. Even before the affair with Leo began they were on the lookout for a suitable match. 'Why did Leo notice me? He found me to his liking. I can only conclude that it was because Leo himself was so ugly. He'd been left badly scarred by smallpox. He was much uglier than your average Annamese but his taste in clothes was impeccable.'[13]

Never mind if he was ugly. A member of the opposite sex was at last looking at her, paying her attention, making her feel she existed. In fact, Marguerite had already attracted the attention of one of her classmates at the lycée Chasseloup-Laubat. He'd been making advances for months. But he was even uglier than Leo. Even more disgusting! And moreover, he wasn't rich ... 'He was one of the dunces in the class, a half-caste, his teeth were so rotten, I wouldn't let him touch me. Everyone treated him with contempt. His brother owned a shop in the Chinese district. He was over twenty and still in fourth grade because he'd had to repeat the year so often.' The poor man would beg Marguerite to sit next to him at the back of the class. Then he'd grovel for her to give him her hands, which he'd cover with kisses. 'I'd look at him, curious ... He was a tragic being: I couldn't stand him because he embodied the species I was wanting to escape. The poor and despised with whom I belonged.'[14]

Marguerite saw herself as a wild, wicked and solitary child. Apart from Colette, Mademoiselle C.'s other boarder, who may have been the original of the Hélène Lagonelle character in *The Lover*, she had no friends. The few girls who congregated around her were more an adoring group of admirers than a core of confidantes. Today, Denise feels bad she never invited her to the parties and tea dances organized by the worthy society of Saigon. Marguerite was trapped. She felt it was up to her to save the family from destitution. It was something that she alone could do. At first she said nothing to her mother. In the afternoons, car windows tightly shut, she and the lover cruised the streets of Saigon together. She enquired of Leo and the inhabitants of Sadec how much his family was worth. It was soon confirmed that he was extremely wealthy. On holiday in Sadec she introduced him to her family; then, egged on by her mother and elder brother, she gradually worked on a deal: a love affair in exchange for a lot of piastres.

> With Leo as a newcomer to the family there was a complete change of plan. The moment we knew the extent of his fortune, it was decided unanimously that Leo would pay the chetties, finance a number of ventures (a sawmill for my younger brother, a design studio for my older brother) the plans for which my mother had already carefully studied; and also, moreover, he would provide each member of the family with their own car. I was given the task of taking these proposals to Leo and of 'sounding' him out without offering anything in return.[15]

In this perverse game where Marguerite took the initiative, was she dupe, accomplice or victim? She was hooked on the game. The game of love she metamorphosed when she wrote her versions of the lover. The writer's revenge on reality! Expanded and romanticized, the story rang so true, was so moving and apparently authentic, that the episode with the lover became a part of her life that was never challenged. *The Lover* was her revenge. She eventually turned an abject story into an erotic tale and happily pocketed the money. Honour had been satisfied. But was what she told me true when she said the family had absolute control over her, that her hands had been tied? The girl wasn't giving in to the lover but to her mother. The daughter was a gift from the mother. He could have all of her except her sex. No marriage, no sex. But the mother wanted to avoid marriage – he was after all a native – while continuing for as long as possible to reap the financial benefits of the relationship.

The affair with the Chinese lasted for almost two years. During the first year Marguerite was still a boarder in Saigon. The young man would collect her from school in the chauffeur-driven car. Enclosed in the car, the height of luxury to the young girl, they talked and got to know each another. A few weeks into the relationship, the young man took her hand and said, 'I love you.' It was the words that quickened desire. The words that moved her so, words she'd read so many times in a book she ranked above all others, a book she knew by heart (boasting she had read it at least fifty times): *Magali* by Delly.[16] In *Magali*, the words 'I love you' are only ever spoken once. But they have the effect of sanctioning the indestructible bond between the lovers fashioned by months of waiting, a painful separation and the suffering they have both endured. In her diary she wrote, 'Not only was he saying it, but he would never say it again and it was to me that he was saying it. It could have been anyone saying it to me. Under the same conditions it would have had the same effect on me.'[17] But Leo was ugly. She didn't find him attractive. How could she overcome his lack of appeal? In her diary Marguerite gives a detailed description of the young man's repeated advances. Leo had a method: he'd begin with the hair, move down to the waist, round to the breasts attempting to caress them, and then in despair up to the mouth. The battle went on for months. The first kiss is described like a rape:

> He caught me off guard. I cannot describe how repulsive it was. I hit out at Leo, spat, wanted to get out of the car. Leo didn't know what to do. In the space of a second, I had become as rigid as a bow lost forever. I kept saying, It's over, it's over. I was the very personification of revulsion ... I had to keep spitting, spat all night, and again the next day whenever I thought about it.[18]

Leo was growing bolder. Leo wanted to touch. Leo introduced Marguerite to pleasures never before experienced. Leo became ferry-man of the night. He dragged her off to Cholon, she who knew only the torpor of native posts. Cholon is life itself, a constant crush, a riot of colours, sensations, smells, movement; a shifting, intense beauty.

A plain once separated Saigon and Cholon. When the early white colonizers arrived, they found it was a vast graveyard. Today tarmac covers the cemetery, and streets busy with rickshaws and mopeds lead to Cholon. Everything leads to Cholon. It has one of the biggest markets in Indo-China. No one sleeps in Cholon. Night and day outside tiny shops, old men stand in the mud and sell dried crab claws, guaranteed to prolong an erection, while just next door heavily made-up girls take the heads off huge, shiny carp. Cholon smells of mud and *nuoc-mam*, of spices and aromatic teas. People tear around and knock you flying; everyone's always in a hurry, except for the small children. In the midst of all this hurly-burly, in a neat hand they conscientiously copy into pretty exercise books the Chinese characters a grandmother has drawn for them. In Cholon, nothing has changed since the thirties. The rue de Paris is still decorated with multicoloured bunting and the restaurants with their mirrored staircases are still guarded by portly Buddhas. The opium dens are open. Outside, men wash and, laughing, splash themselves with mud. There are people playing dominoes, shouting out numbers, and a small girl lying in a canvas cot, left there in the street, is singing. Below, the labourers gather around sweet pepper soup. Above, the rice kings get drunk on champagne. The restaurants are just as they were described in *The Lover*, huge steamships overflowing with food, light and noise, waiters bellowing out the orders. The to-ing and fro-ing is enough to make you giddy. It's a city without inhibitions, a city of traffic, of scum, of prostitution. Everything is for sale. Nowhere compares with Cholon.

Leo's jealous. He spies on Marguerite, waits for hours outside the school, insists on knowing her timetable, follows her in the car from the lycée to Mademoiselle C.'s. The child lets him touch her, every day a little more. She doesn't want him to but doesn't know how to stop his advances. He says, 'If you're unfaithful, I'll kill you.' He takes her to see American gangster movies so he can grope her in the dark. Not daring to rebuff him, she lets him stroke her as she stares wide-eyed with wonder at the beautiful and brave heroines. In *The Sea Wall* Marguerite Duras gives a wonderful description of how Suzanne gradually allows her future fiancé to possess her through the gaze but not yet through touch. We find in Marguerite's diary an analysis of this skilful heightening of pleasure. 'I felt so guilty about Leo and it bothered me I couldn't do more.'

Then her mother was appointed headmistress of a girls' school in Saigon, and moved with her sons to a house not far from the lycée

Chasseloup-Laubat. The young girl returned to the bosom of her family, where there was laughter and good times, but also beatings. Anyway, that's what Marguerite says in her diary. At times it is heart-rending to read her account of the physical violence she claimed she was subjected to and so powerfully describes. Was Marguerite a child martyr? An object of lust, broken for an unnamed pleasure by the elder brother and his co-conspirator, the mother? Appearances were kept up, as was their seemingly petit-bourgeois family life. Not for one moment did Denise Augé, her classmate from the Chasseloup-Laubat school, suspect that Marguerite was being beaten. And Max Bergier, who at one time boarded with Marie Donnadieu in Saigon, thinks it was highly unlikely. Marguerite said on seueral occasions in later life that her brother was physically violent and that she was frightened of him, and told a friend that Marie had beaten her regularly but that the beatings had in no way diminished her love for her mother.

Mother would often beat me, especially when she went to pieces. She just couldn't help it. As I was the youngest and the most amenable of her children, I was the one she beat the most often. She'd send me spinning, she'd hit me with a stick. Anger would give her such a rush of blood to the head that she'd say she was having a stroke. My fear of losing her was stronger than my wish to rebel. But while I might have agreed with the reasons behind the beatings, I could never accept the means. I knew Leo wouldn't understand, that he could never go along with the way my mother treated me, and yet I agreed with her completely and could not have tolerated anyone criticizing her, not even Leo.[19]

Some of Duras's lovers used to boast to their friends that she enjoyed a beating. Later on in her life she came to blows with her son. They say, don't they, that children who suffer physical abuse in turn abuse their children? At school Marguerite had a malicious streak and enjoyed making pupils cry and then never speaking to them again. She became bolder still, targeting some of the teachers. She could make them ill just by staring at them. Some of the monitors suffered breathlessness and fainting spells and were forced to leave the school. She ended up fearing the fear she provoked, and therefore 'deserved' beatings that might quell what she claimed was a deep-seated evil. An unhealthy rivalry brought mother and son even closer together in violence.

They both wanted to beat me. If mother was beating me in a way that didn't suit him, he'd say 'wait' and take over. But she always regretted it because each time she thought he'd end up killing me. She'd let out these terrible screams, but even then he found it difficult to stop. One day, he changed tactics and sent me crashing into the piano; I caught my temple on the corner and it was some time before I could get up again. My mother's fear was so great that she was later haunted by these battles. This Herculean strength of my brother's, who to cap it all had overdeveloped biceps, so overawed my mother it made him want to beat me more.[20]

Her relationship with Leo inflamed Pierre, who then added insults to injury. After 'whore', 'swine' became the favourite, then 'bitch', 'little shit' and 'serpent venom'. In her diary, Marguerite wrote:

The difference between my mother's and my brother's beatings was that the latter's were much more painful and difficult to take. Every time he beat me, I'd reach the point where I'd think my brother was going to kill me, and where anger would give way to fear, fear that my head was about to be separated from my body and roll across the floor or fear that I'd end up going crazy.[21]

At night, Marguerite writes, Leo would take the whole family out. At the restaurants of Cholon, the brothers would select the most expensive items from the menu and never say thank you, before ending the evening in a fashionable nightclub, the Fountain.

The Fountain, mentioned in the diary and *The North China Lover*, really did exist. Older Saigon inhabitants recall the nocturnal outings of heavily made-up white women arriving in their big cars at the outskirts of town to rendezvous with already tipsy Frenchmen. Once known for its ostentatious luxury and its 'alcoves' for debauchery, scattered around the tropical gardens, the place has now been razed to the ground. Today the small river that used to feed the swimming pool flows through an ocean of refuse. Market stalls stand where the dance floors once were. A crowd of children follow me into the small house belonging to an old man who used to be a waiter at the

Fountain. He recalls with nostalgia that wonderful era when wealthy Chinese men went out with young white women, buying them drinks and dancing till dawn. No more foxtrot, no more charleston.

Leo was supporting the mother financially, and the brothers too. But it wasn't enough. Mother and elder brother were in need of ready cash. Without actually saying so, the mother made sure her daughter understood that she needed piastres, that she should hurry things up. The girl would obey, but in her own time. Leo was allowed to kiss her, to hold her hand. Then to tango. She did not consent to making love in the bedroom until a few days before they left for France, and, according to the diary, only once.

In the diary the young girl describes how bringing home the money made her feel she at last existed in the eyes of her family. So she asks for more. But Leo hesitates, he's seen through her game, finding it obscene, disgusting. The mother is waiting when the girl returns from seeing Leo. How much did he give you today? The girl doesn't answer, prolongs the suspense. The mother follows the girl around the house; the brother, half-naked, circles around them. At last the child has power over her mother. And the mother's pleased with her daughter. She worries less about her, thinking she might after all be able to stand on her own two feet. She might not get married but she'll know how to handle men. And that's what counts.

At school, Marguerite was gradually alienated from her friends. She met with disapproving looks. They called her a prostitute, the youngest slut in Saigon. She started skipping classes. There were threats from her friends, she said, and she couldn't ask the teacher in charge for help, because he'd once locked himself in his office with her and tried to kiss her.

It was at that time that she discovered literature. She abandoned Delly in favour of Shakespeare and Molière, whom she loved and never grew tired of. She also fell in love with Lewis Carroll, come across by chance during an English lesson. How she envied Alice the world she'd invented!

Leo talked about the future and the child resigned herself to spending the rest of her life with him. In any case, she had no expectations. She even felt she was falling in love with him, just a little. Life might be easier with Leo than with her mother. 'I accepted Leo's stupidity.

66

I accepted everything. My mother, my elder brother, the endless beatings. Everything. As I saw it, my only way out was to marry Leo because he had money, and because his money could get us back to France where life would be good. I couldn't imagine staying in Indo-China because to live alone with Leo was beyond me.'

But towards the end of their almost two-year-long relationship, Leo one day informed Marie Donnedieu that his father had forbidden him to marry Marguerite. Things moved quickly after that. Her mother wanted to return to France as soon as she could to make a new life for herself. But she didn't have a penny to her name. The mother saw herself as a victim. 'She used to say, "I'm fettered to adversity, worn out, it would be best if I died ..." She said it too often, we became immune to it.'²² The Chinese lover's father enquired how much it would cost to hasten the departure of the Donnadieu family. Marguerite's mother asked for two million piastres. In Duras's books, the lover's family give her a diamond, a huge diamond but, alas, a flawed diamond, as the mother discovers when she tries to sell it. I don't know whether the family ever really gave her a diamond, but cash they certainly did.

In the summer of 1931, Marie and her two children boarded the *Bernardin de Saint-Pierre*, destination Marseille. The mother did not pay for the voyage, to which as a civil servant she was entitled. The lover's father had finally given in. The family thought they were leaving for good, but Marguerite would return a year later with her mother.

Very little is known of their stay in France. Temporary addresses found in official files reveal that Marie and her children lived first with the mother's family in Doullens, in the Somme, then in Le Platier par Duras. There her mother resumed her vain attempts to gain possession of a house she knew she had no claim to. The reasons behind her relentless determination emerge from a careful reading of Marguerite's first book, *Les impudents*. It's the story of a vicious, good-for-nothing brother, a fiery but indecisive sister and their biased, violent mother, blinded by her love for her son, who live on a country estate. The mother wants her son to become attached to the soil in the hope he will turn into some kind of gentleman farmer.

She's wasting her time. He's only interested in easy money and city girls.

According to her childhood friend Yvette, it wasn't the same Marguerite who returned, the one who used to run laughing through the fields and who talked and ate like a peasant. Marguerite had become a secretive and solitary young woman, not interested in re-establishing her ties with the villagers. She shut herself away and would talk to no one. Her beauty was intriguing. The boys would watch her and whistle as she passed them on her way to the cinema with her brothers on a Sunday afternoon. There are a few photographs taken around this time, where the Donnadieu trio can be seen posing calmly for the camera, looking united. A skinny Marguerite, hair pulled back, is meticulously dressed, her expression sad.

Having spent the school holidays in Le Platier, Marie decided to move to Paris. In a piece entitled 'Le train de Bordeaux' in *La vie matérielle*, Marguerite Duras describes what happened or what she thought happened – since the account sounds like an instalment of a photo-novel – during the night journey. She was in a third-class compartment with her mother and brothers. Sitting in front of her, a man of around thirty was staring at her. 'I was still wearing the light colours of the colonies and sandals on my bare feet. I wasn't tired. The man asked me about my family. I told him we lived in the colonies, talked about the rains, the heat, the verandas, about how it was different from France, the forest walks and how I'd be taking my baccalaureate this year ...' Marguerite was speaking so quietly that everyone dozed off. And then it happened 'with just one glance'. She lay down. She fell asleep. She woke up. The man's soft warm hand was moving up her thighs. The night, the train, next to her the brothers fast asleep and the embrace. When she opened her eyes as they drew into Paris, the seat opposite was empty.

Once in the capital, Marie Donnadieu approached Paris city council to find her lodgings. Widow with three children, long-time civil servant. She was so persistent that they gave her a flat in Vanves, at 16 boulevard Victor-Hugo. In *Les impudents* Vanves has become Clamart, where the heroine, Maud, endlessly trails her melancholy through the icy streets of a dreary suburb. 'And as time went by, she felt more and more alone, always further away from the familiar shores of life.'

68

Daily life in Vanves for the Donnadieu family soon became a living hell. Pierre was gambling and every evening he'd blow the money he'd stolen from his mother, before disappearing into the night and coming home at dawn, haggard. The savings so carefully put aside by Marie were soon all gone. As a result there was no money for basic necessities. No money to buy Marguerite a winter coat and not enough for a hot meal every day. 'I was obliged to ... not exactly steal ... but, if you like, ask for money. I would ask people for money, people in my class. I knew they were rich ... and then the cops turned up ... no one said anything ... but they still found out it was me ... I never gave anything in return ... no, nothing.'[23] In her diary there's a brief mention of this period and of the financial situation: 'When we were living in France and I'd gone back to peddling my wares with the boys at school, my brother got into the habit of going through my pockets every night. Then he'd beat me, accusing me of living off immoral earnings. He said he'd teach me how to live, that it was for my own good.'

Marguerite talked to me a lot about money at the end of her life. She was a wealthy woman, yet always worried she might go short. Greedy Marguerite, never satisfied. In a conversation with Jacques Tronel, just before she started work on the screenplay of *The Lover*, she admitted to having felt ashamed when she first came to France and started asking for money. Then she got used to it, initially asking only the boys at school and then moving on to men. Years later, in an attempt to justify her actions, she added with childlike insistence, 'Not even once, cross my heart and hope to die, did I ever keep a penny for myself. Everything went to the mother or older brother ... Nothing. Not even a chocolate. So it proves I can't be stingy.'

For Duras, money and writing were inseparable. She took money to give it away while retaining the intensity of the injustice and her disenchantment so that the process of writing could begin. At seventeen she was already writing a lot: short stories and poems, most of which she burned. And during this chaotic period, she was conscientiously studying for her baccalaureate. I never found out which school she attended. All Marguerite ever said on the subject was that the results were displayed at the Sorbonne, and that her mother, beside herself with worry, camped out all night in the courtyard like one possessed, only to discover her daughter's name at the top of the list.

For a long time Marie Donnedieu couldn't decide whether to return to Indo-China. The knowledge that her husband's property would never be hers made her realize she would have to continue working beyond the statutory retirement age. The pension she was due to receive in four years' time would not be sufficient to meet the needs of the family, particularly those of her eldest son. At the beginning of an unpublished manuscript of *The Lover*, Marguerite wrote in the margin, 'When the mother decided to return to Saigon so that she could draw her pension, the girl chose to go with her.' Pierre stayed in France.

Indo-China was attracting a growing number of investors from France, and the number of companies being set up there was on the increase. For the white colony living in Saigon, the early thirties were a time of expansion and greater wealth. With the help of loans from the Bank of Indo-China and the freer movement of the piastre, the owners of rubber and rice plantations saw their fortunes swell. Racism and brutality towards the local people continued. The white society was hierarchically structured. Right at the top were a few immensely rich families who made the laws; and right at the bottom, the poor, destitute Vietnamese, exploited and humiliated by whites who didn't think twice about beating them, knowing they had nothing to fear from a corrupt legal system. The way of life was established with the arrival of the early settlers. In 1895 if an infantryman killed an Annamese it would cost him forty francs – deducted from his wage – to cover the cost of the burial. The army sacrificed hundreds of men – mostly political prisoners and criminals – to the building of the roads and railways. The government of Indo-China in 1926 announced that it was against the law for a white to strike an Annamese. Many of the settlers were outraged.

Marguerite's return to Indo-China coincided with the start of a relationship based on respect and friendship between a small group of French intellectuals and educated, keen young Annamese, who were demanding independence for their country and threatening revolution. These sons of wealthy Annamese families had been sent to universities in Paris. There they studied the French Revolution and law, and some associated with Marxists and anarchists. When they returned they were qualified lawyers, engineers and doctors. In the eyes of French law these Annamese were neither subjects nor dependants. In fact they had the same rights as French citizens. Naturally they were indignant at the treatment the settlers and the colonial government of Indo-China continued to dole out to their fellow countrymen.

Admittedly there were some extremely wealthy Annamese families. These had become Frenchified and, in the process, tame allies of the colonial authorities. They saw nothing unusual in their children, on being admitted into the lycée Chasseloup-Laubat, abandoning the black tunic in favour of European clothes. They put up with the fact that the colonial government would not allow their sons to apply to French universities without first obtaining permission from the governor general. Those who went to France discovered white people very different from those who were in the colonies. Some even found the inspiration and theoretical notions they needed to fight oppression and desire independence. These were called 'anti-French' and 'Bolsheviks'. Those Annamese and French who, through their thoughts, words or deeds, undermined the colonial government, were considered anti-French. The Vietnamese looked to the Chinese for inspiration. In 1927, the Viet Nam Quoc Dan Dong party was founded along the same lines as the Kuomintang. In February 1930, in Hong Kong, the Vietnamese Communist Party was formed, and in the autumn, it was renamed the Parti communist indochinois (the Indo-China Communist Party). In Indo-China, in the early thirties, hard-line nationalists were of Chinese origin, but they were few in number. They wanted to free their lands from the white man, who was basically nothing but a conqueror. The peasants, the masses, could and should rise up. Weapons were obtained. But to expect the embryonic nationalism one day to be transformed into an actual group feeling or a protest against oppression was still utopian.[24]

As a young woman Marguerite was not interested in politics. But she may well have been aware of the repression of the communists carried out at the end of 1931, a few months after her first departure from Indo-China, and familiar with the articles of Andrée Viollis, exposing conditions in Indo-China. In her book *Indo-China S.O.S.*, published in 1935 with a preface by André Malraux,[25] Viollis revealed that at the time there were 1500 political prisoners rotting in Saigon's main jail. Their captors were subjecting them to unimaginably cruel tortures, sometimes leading to death. Annam was devastated by a terrible famine. As part of the entourage of Paul Reynaud, the colonial minister, Andrée Viollis had been able to avoid the speeches and official functions to meet the editors of independent newspapers. She had gone into prisons and travelled the length and breadth of north Annam. She saw hundreds of destitute peasants starving to death in hospices set up by the French where they were given nothing to eat. She saw Saigon, sweet, perverse Saigon, still ruled by planters and colonists. She saw the opulence, the champagne, the gambling joints, the pianolas, the Paris clothes (the white suits of the men, the pale colours of the perfumed white women), the colourful crowds flocking to the smart shops in rue Catinat, the white dinner jackets of the jazz bands playing on the terrace of the Continental Hotel after dark. Nothing had apparently changed in this sleepy oriental Passy.

And it was here – where the streets are lined with tamarind trees, where the white houses have verandas and surrounding gardens and are enclosed by railings, and at street corners you may hear the odd note from a piano – that Marie Donnadieu, with her daughter and younger son, decided to settle.

The *Bernardin de Saint-Pierre* docked on 14 September 1932. Marie purchased 141 rue Testard, now Vo Van Tan. Max Bergier, Marie Donnadieu's first lodger at the end of 1932, remembers the house well. There were twelve rooms that opened on to verandas and a small garden at the front with an ornamental fountain. Every morning Madame Donnadieu and Max would go by rickshaw to the local school opposite the shipyards where she taught. Marguerite grew fond of the little boy, taught him to read, and took him to the zoo on a Thursday afternoon to see the elephants splash about and the boa swallow dead chickens. Max slept upstairs in Marguerite's room. She liked to have the shutters open all night. When it was too hot, she'd get the canvas beds out and they'd sleep on the terrace under the stars.

Life appeared to be highly regimented: school, siesta, school. Little Max felt he was part of the family and didn't seem to miss his father, a former baritone turned tax collector. Max's mother was a dressmaker and the representative in Indo-China of three major fashion houses.

They lived in a small, remote town over three hundred kilometres from Saigon. Apparently Max's parents never paid Marie any money but from time to time Max's mother would give her dresses. In the evening Marie would make him practise his reading and writing in the big dining room. Marguerite would work either in her room or with her mother. 'Some evenings we'd go into the drawing room. Néné [Marguerite] would read, Madame Donnadieu would play the piano. When my parents came to visit she'd play while my father sang light opera.'

Marguerite returned to the lycée Chasseloup-Laubat to take her second baccalaureate. The photographs Max's parents took show a very intense but pretty and well-groomed young lady with made-up eyes. At school, she was again alone and isolated, never going out, and rarely invited to the tennis-club parties or tea dances given by Saigon's young white community. But she was hard-working and often complimented.

Paulo worked. He was an odd-job man at the naval docks, and then a garage mechanic, before eventually finding an administrative job in Cholon. He had a passion for cars and was always changing them. He'd spend all day Sunday tinkering around with them outside the house. His favourite was a convertible Delage he did up himself. His mother then spent all her money buying him a Hotchkiss. Max remembered Paulo and Marguerite getting on really well, each showing great affection for the other. They'd eat together as a family. The mother never said much, opening her mouth only to give the orders. They had two servants to wait on them. Max never witnessed any verbal or physical outbursts, and mother and daughter appeared to have a fairly normal relationship.

It was the best year I ever had with her. We weren't living in fear any more. My mother got used to the girl she hadn't much liked; that year she probably grew to like her. Afterwards she'd forget me. The elder son would be her only child again. It was because she missed that child that she kept me close to her. But despite knowing her better than she knew herself, I still loved her.[26]

Marguerite thought a lot about God, read the Gospels, developed a taste for philosophy, became a disciple of Spinoza, devoted herself to her studies, examined herself less in the mirror. There was no sign of the lover. Leo had disappeared. (The mother saw him again, much later, after Marguerite had finally returned to France for good.) She passed her baccalaureate with distinction. Mother and daughter were both happy. 'My mother packed me off on the ship. She wanted me to continue my studies in Paris ... To have a child with a degree, it was as simple as that. And that's what I did. I got my degree. She got everything she wanted, but I didn't love her any more. Like a lover I fell out of love with her.'[27] Mother, brother and Max accompanied Marguerite to the docks of the Messageries Maritimes. Max recalled how happy she looked that day.

On the passenger list at the Marseille colonial office, it said that Mademoiselle Donnadieu, Marguerite, nineteen and a half years old, daughter of Madame Donnadieu, former teacher, had disembarked from the *Porthos* in Marseille. Nature of leave: anticipation! The date was 28 October 1933. Max Bergier's paternal uncle was on the quay waiting to take her to Saint-Charles station. Destination: Paris.

CHAPTER 4

Rue Saint-Benoît

~

When Max's uncle put Marguerite on the Paris train, her brother Pierre was waiting for her at the other end. Pierre would continue to use and abuse her. He was in a dreadful state. A petty criminal in Indo-China, in Paris he'd become a small-time dealer and pimp, quite happy to put his girlfriend on the streets of Montparnasse outside La Coupole. He introduced her to Marguerite and they became firm friends. When the young woman fell ill with tuberculosis and couldn't work, Pierre abandoned her, and it was Marguerite who got her admitted to hospital and who nursed her until she died.[1] Marguerite later told a friend that Pierre sold opium in Montparnasse and that he was sometimes a 'voyeur' at middle-class parties, where he would charge a lot of money for the depraved serenity in his eyes and his services as a professional lover.

Whatever the truth of the situation, Marguerite refused to live with her brother and, wanting to have nothing to do with him, moved into a rather prim and proper boarding house for fairly well-off students, just behind the Bon Marché. She had the little money her mother had given her before she left Indo-China, which allowed her to live reasonably well; in fact, she was able to buy an expensive car at the end of 1935.

She enrolled as a student at the faculty of law in rue Saint-Jacques. Out of what she claimed was love for her father, she also signed up for further maths. She later confessed that her life at the time was somewhat 'hectic', that she was having one affair after another. Not necessarily for payment, though some men gave her money, but particularly because – and she never hesitated to admit it – she had until late in life a real passion for physical love. She wanted and needed to make love. She said this and wrote it, and several men who lived with her confirmed as much. At the time it wasn't so common. Men loved it, a beautiful, emancipated girl who said she loved love. Love for love's sake. Not the forever-after kind of love, more the ensnaring kind of love. 'What saved me was that I was cheating on the men I was living with: I would walk out on them. That saved me. I was unfaithful. Not always but most of the time. But that's what I wanted. I loved love and that's what I wanted.'[2]

Little D. was what the men called her, because she was small and because she'd told them she hated her given name. Gold-flecked green eyes, hair tied back, well turned-out, impeccably dressed, with an aura about her that was both dreamy and amused, an oriental icon. You could fall in love with her at the drop of a hat. And that was what she wanted, it was in her eyes, in the way she gave herself to you when she looked at you, said Georges Beauchamp, a fellow law student who, with a twinkle in his eye, admitted to me that he was fortunate to escape Marguerite's extraordinary powers of seduction. Those who weren't so lucky came out badly, he added, laughing.

She wrote to reassure her mother, telling her that she was studying hard and that she was still planning to become a teacher. In Saigon, Marie bought a house in rue Catinat and converted it into a boarding school rather than a boarding house to accommodate a handful of friends' children. She was undecided what to do with the rest of her life and didn't know whether to stay in Indo-China once she had retired or join her daughter in Paris. There was growing unrest throughout Indo-China.

Marguerite was not yet politically committed, although she was outraged by the events and actions carried out by fascist groups in the Latin Quarter.[3] 'We were still young, still innocent, politically apathetic,' said Marguerite's university friend France Brunel.[4] Marguerite soon began to feel isolated and so restless that she suddenly and without warning dropped out of university and joined the Salvation Army for six months. 'Why? I don't know. It was so depressing.'[5] Six months living with the destitute, helping them, keeping them warm, cooking for them. Six months of charity work, of being involved in people's day-to-day misery. Six months she rarely talked about, but which contributed to her becoming politicized.

Marguerite had left the university but not her lodgings. One night at the end of 1935, fire broke out on the roof and began to sweep through the boarding house. In the middle of the pandemonium, there in front of the firefighters, Marguerite met her neighbour from the room next door, one Jean Lagrolet. A fiery meeting in every way.

This handsome, elegant, aristocratic-looking and highly cultured young man, born in Bayonne in 1918, fell madly in love with Marguerite. They discovered they were fellow students, and both wanted to become writers. Jean Lagrolet introduced Marguerite to foreign literature, especially to American authors. She read Faulkner's *Light in August*, discovered the poetry of T. S. Eliot and the works of Joseph Conrad. She loved Conrad and would read him over and over again, all through her life.

Jean Lagrolet was handsome, like the Hollywood star Tyrone Power but much more charming, France Brunel told me in a voice trembling with emotion. He slept little and spent his nights playing chess or cutting newspapers up into thin strips. Marguerite would sleep cocooned in tiny pieces of crumpled paper. He chain-smoked and was subject to bouts of depression. He'd scream out in the night, frightening Marguerite, who didn't know how to heal his wounded soul. He talked to her about his unhappy childhood – his mother had died in childbirth, and his father blamed the boy.

Marguerite and Jean were in their third year at university. At that time the ratio was one female to ten male students. Marguerite worked hard and, with her desire to charm, would always go and see her lecturer at the end of a class, France added, laughing. She loved political economics and while she continued with her maths course she was also enrolled at the Ecole des sciences politiques. Her results were brilliant and she had a reputation for being lively and intelligent. Her friends were amazed at her capacity for work. France remembered that she did a lot of walking, and that when the two of them went away for the weekend, they would go for long walks, their law lecture notes and a pad of paper in a pocket. Law was all very well but Marguerite had no intention of making it her career. She told France she wanted to become a writer. They were both crazy about the cinema and together they'd go to see the latest releases.

It was also thanks to Lagrolet that Marguerite discovered the theatre. The screen was replaced by the stage as her passion. Thereafter she went to the theatre at least twice a week, hanging on to every word that came from the Comédie-Francaise's classical repertoire, particularly when it was a play by Racine. She discovered the director Antonin Artaud in *The Cenci*, and saw Jean-Louis Barrault making his debut with *Autour d'une mère* at the théâtre de l'Atelier, five years before the Comédie-Française took him on to direct a deeply moving *El Cid*. He and Marguerite developed a lasting friendship which would later be translated into a fruitful partnership. But her passion for the stage peaked when she discovered Ludmilla and Georges Pitoëff – he was a director and stage designer. Thanks to the special student rates at the théâtre des Mathurins, she was able to see *Romeo and Juliet* over and over again, and plays by Claudel, Ibsen and Pirandello. She used to describe how night after night she'd go to this particular theatre and wait for the auditorium to empty before she could leave her seat and stagger out, so haunted was she by the words. The desire to hear words she had written, spoken on stage, dates from that period.

One of Georges Pitoëff's secrets was that he could poeticize everything he touched and make the most basic of sets and crummiest of costumes look spectacular. Cocteau said he brought something fiery to the theatre, something wild and terrible like the beat of a heart. A few cubes, two grey curtains and three projectors were enough to stir the emotions. The Pitoëffs were the first to get rid of stage curtains and prompt. They focused on text, no special effects, nothing but the text sublimated by the voices. To direct, you have to return to the author's original idea, to enter his universe, Pitoëff used to say. Once the source has been discovered, the director can take possession of the whole, in a natural way. Marguerite would remember the lesson. To purge the text of dross, to reach its very essence so as to go straight to the spectator's body, that was what she always aimed to do on the stages of Europe.

Political events were making the atmosphere tense in the law faculty. The majority of students were right-wing, some extremely so. France and Marguerite would perch on café tables in the boulevard Saint-Michel as they sought refuge from the orderly battles between left- and right-wing students. Heart and soul, they were leftists. Republican, antifascist certainly, but more on the level of emotions than politics. Marguerite was never part of any group action; crowds frightened her. When in the general election the Popular Front won the second ballot, at midnight on 3 May 1936, she didn't go out into the streets, as did a good many intellectuals, singing 'The Internationale' and chanting, 'Down with Fascism.' Marguerite was leading a very bourgeois life. She wanted to do well and get as much out of life as possible.

However, her relationship with Jean Lagrolet had become complicated. Jean would occasionally sink into a terrible depression. There was nothing Marguerite could do to bring him out of it. She needed to get away, to distance herself. And so she had moved into an apartment at 28 rue Paul-Barreul. One day in January 1936, Jean introduced Marguerite to two friends from Bayonne: Georges Beauchamp and Robert Antelme. The trio had been inseparable since they first sat together at school. Having come to Paris to study law, they were all three cultured, attractive, middle-class charmers. Marguerite was soon integrated into the group. Together they went for walks. Marguerite was their queen. Together they went to the races at Vincennes, Longchamp, Auteuil. Marguerite was a wild gambler. She always had some system she had to try out, given her by a waiter in boulevard Raspail. They went to Trouville and the south of France in a Ford cabriolet – at that time a luxury car. Marguerite was in the driving seat in every sense of the word. Georges Beauchamp recalled their wild escapades – the nonchalance, the fun, the friendship, the laughter. They would stay devoted friends through thick and thin.

What can one say about Robert Antelme? Everyone I met told me in a voice choked with emotion that he was an extraordinary human being. He was charismatic, extremely wise and tremendously generous. A secular saint, many agreed, and an exceptionally astute intellectual. A great bearlike metaphysician, a poet of everyday life. He wore a permanent grin; in his presence, people felt safe. His father had been subprefect in Bayonne and then a tax inspector in Paris. Robert had two sisters, Marie-Louise, nicknamed Minette, and Alice. Photographs taken in the mid-thirties show him to be a jovial fellow with a mischievous smile, sensuous lips and penetrating eyes. He was studying law because that was what the sons of the middle classes did and he had to do something. His interests, however, were literature, the theatre and ancient history.

'Of all the men I've ever known, he was the one who had the greatest influence on those around him. The most important man to me personally and to others,' Marguerite explained. 'I can't put my finger on what it was. He didn't speak and he did speak. He never gave advice, yet we did nothing without his advice. He was intelligence personified but hated intelligent talk.'[6] 'He was the most exceptional man I ever met,' added Georges Beauchamp. 'And I'm eighty and knew François Mitterrand.'[7] 'He reminded me of the hero of Dostoyevski's *The Idiot*,' another said. 'He was a very good man, an extremely compassionate man. In reality, of course, he was more complex. People admired him. He always gave the impression he was listening.'[8]

Robert and Marguerite fell passionately in love. This led to a crisis of friendship. Georges Beauchamp takes up the story: 'Things were not so good between Jean Lagrolet and Marguerite Donnadieu. She was growing tired of the tormented boy. She'd introduced him to opium and his intellectual ramblings were beginning to get on her nerves. But Robert was always there at Jean's side, available, obliging. He wasn't as good-looking but he was always cheerful. Jean Lagrolet was a Dorian Gray. She wanted peace and quiet. She left him for Robert.' Georges took the revolver from Robert's hands, the revolver stolen from his father's desk, when Robert wanted to kill himself because he'd betrayed his best friend. And while this was going on, Jean was overdosing on laudanum. Marguerite locked herself away in her flat and wept.

It was Georges who sorted things out. Leaving the two lovebirds Marguerite and Robert to get on with their lives in Paris, he took a doped-up Jean Lagrolet, against his will, on a long trip around central Europe. Georges was bewitched by the area, but not Jean, he was too broken-hearted. Jean Lagrolet never touched a woman again, and faced up to the reality that he was a homosexual.

Robert still lived with his parents in rue Dupin, Marguerite in rue Paul-Barruel. France Brunel was the go-between. In the eyes of the world – no doubt in order not to upset Jean Lagrolet – theirs was an intellectual and not a physical relationship. Marguerite had enormous respect for Robert. She who, throughout her life, so rarely listened to anyone, actually listened to him. She admired him for his intelligence, his generosity and his sense of the absurd. With him she felt safe.

Students and intellectuals in the prewar Latin Quarter of Paris often ended up sharing their affairs with friends in the back rooms of cafés in Montparnasse, where endless discussions went on through the night on the consequences of Hitlerism, the future of the Popular Front and the most effective way of helping Spanish republican fighters. It was a time when Jean-Paul Sartre and Simone de Beauvoir could be seen in cafés, a famous couple who led separate lives. For modern, financially independent female students, the lover-friend did not necessarily become a husband. Marriage was an ideal only in the eyes of the parents of these emancipated young women who lived love a day at a time.

Marguerite was considered to be emancipated and independent. Her friends said she had money, quite a bit of money. It came at regular intervals from her mother, who had decided to keep open her school in the rue Catinat, Saigon, during the school holidays. The number of boarders had grown so much that she had taken on the wives of officers and noncommissioned officers to supervise and teach them. She ran her establishment with a rod of iron. 'To her, children were cattle that brought in money,' said one of her former students. He had been at the school in 1938 and remembered the iron discipline and Spartan way of life endured by the pupils: lessons, rest, afternoon nap, all in the same classroom, at the same desk. He went on to say:

The contrast was striking between this forbidding woman always dressed in black, the look of a widow about her, and the son with whom she lived, ostentatiously dressed in tussore suits and shiny shoes. He regularly bought luxury cars with white tyres that he'd bring to a screeching halt in front of the children. The mother was killing herself working to pay for the son's expensive tastes, pandering to his every whim and sending substantial sums of money to the daughter, who did well in all her examinations.[9]

As their faith in the Popular Front was slowly eroded, Robert, Georges and Jean turned to pacifism. They knew that change was essential, that the corrupt old order couldn't deal with the economic problems facing France.[10] They rejected communist and fascist dogma in favour of those philosophies that encouraged individual spiritual growth. At a political meeting they first met their fellow law student François Mitterand,[11] although it would be another six years before they really got to know him properly, when they joined the Resistance. At the time François Mitterrand was working for *L'Echo de Paris*, a newspaper that supported Mussolini and fascism. Jacques Benet, who would be called up in 1938 with Robert Antelme, was a school friend of François Mitterrand. They had got to know one another when they were both living at the same boarding house. He said that at the time Mitterrand was 'a bit bewildered'. 'We were a couple of innocents just arrived from the country.'[12] François Mitterrand was a Catholic socialist, a diligent student, though keener on literature than civil law.

At the time Claude Roy was hanging around the students of Action française and writing for magazines. François Mitterrand and Claude Roy spent endless nights discussing literature. 'Our sole passion at the time,' Mitterrand told me, 'was the search for our truth.'[13] 'At that time there was a certain glamour to be had from claiming to be a monarchist, a sort of antiquated dandyism,' Claude Roy admitted in *Moi je*. Called up in 1939 and captured in Lorraine, he escaped in October 1940 to free France, where he worked for the Vichy press and radio.[14] Claude Roy eventually joined the Resistance.

Some of the young people from that period, disciples of Nietzsche and yearning for a revolution they couldn't name, met up again after the war at Marguerite Duras's, united by their shared passion for communism. But meanwhile the time for defeats had come and rearranged the pieces on the chessboard of passions. These young students were plunged into events that were to mould them. Enlisting at the end of summer 1938, Robert Antelme was to be profoundly affected by the experience. Before taking the giant leap, he sent his friend France a letter full of nostalgia. 'Yes, I'm getting ready "to set off" in I don't know which direction and in a suit I am alas more than familiar with. What will happen to the gradual evolving of my energy reserves and poetry?'[15] This is how François Mitterrand, who joined up at the same time and the same rank, cynically described the experience of military service: 'To us, called up to be soldiers in 1938, it was a lesson in how an honest citizen in all this mediocrity could so quickly get used to filth, sloth, drink, brothels and sleep.'[16]

And so the moment Robert was granted leave he returned to Paris. On several occasions, having turned up without warning, he waited all night for Marguerite asleep on the doormat.[17] Robert discussed his despair in conversations with Jacques Benet. Europe was dying, democracy was capitulating, what hope was there? A letter written to France Brunel on 17 September 1938 anticipates the Munich agreement of the following week:

How can we not be utterly sickened as we gaze upon this new face of France? Is this the face we were taught to love in those early history books? Pale and cringing and practically perfidious ready to hide at the hint of a drumbeat. A small country relies on us alone and we give in. We are the lowest, the poorest. You will instantly say 'I want war' or rather that you dread it but is it really to love peace to permit an action that will instigate and endorse an era of barbarity? If the rule of law, if justice is no longer applicable, then has the spirit itself lost its last chance and shall we be compelled to await the advent of a German revolution for there to be an end to this? ... All we hear is talk of Wagner and *Lohengrin*, where intrinsic legend is confused with bloody epic, and harmony confused with standardization.

And it is the blundering French, the 'discerning' French who so admire the dynamism of the Third Reich, the spirit of the Third Reich.

In Munich, the British prime minister Chamberlain and his French counterpart Edouard Daladier accepted Hitler's demands on Czecho-slovakia. When Daladier returned to Paris and saw the crowds waiting at the airport, he expected to be booed. Instead they cheered him for a long time. His only comment was 'Bloody idiots.' Truth was, the French had no wish to go to war. In her journal Simone de Beauvoir wrote that nothing, not even the cruellest of injustices, was worth going to war over. Sartre's response was, 'We cannot give in to Hitler indefinitely.'[18]

Marguerite had graduated in political sciences and started looking for a job. 'It wasn't difficult,' France exclaimed. 'I immediately found a job with the Ministry of Defence and Marguerite with the Colonial

Office. At the end of the day I'd collect her from her office.' Marguerite joined the Colonial Office on 9 June 1938 as an 'assistant' and was earning 1500 francs a month. She was assigned to the intercolonial department of information and documentation situated at 11 rue Tronchet. Had she chosen this ministry because of her family background? It would appear so. Her mother had fought to be allowed to continue to work beyond retirement age, as can be seen from the mountain of correspondence that passed between the office of the governor general of Indo-China and the head of the department of statistics at the ministry. The mother's requests were forwarded to the Paris office via her daughter, who tried in vain to intercede with the minister for colonies. Was this when she first met him?

According to France, Marguerite found her work fascinating. She was quick to memorize information on such diverse topics as the quality of the tea from the mountain plateaux, the courses of rivers in west Africa and how vanilla is processed. Then she had to write technical reports for internal consumption on a variety of subjects. Her brilliance didn't go unnoticed and her name was put forward for the job as the minister's political speechwriter. Her rank, importance and duties were in fact about to change, thanks to the influence of a powerful cabinet colleague, Philippe Roques, who singled her out for greater responsibilities. Engaged by the minister himself in June 1938, Philippe Roques at the age of twenty-eight was posted to the department that had just recruited Marguerite: the intercolonial department of information.

Previously with the post and telecommunications ministry, Mandel had reluctantly agreed to take on the colonies portfolio. It was a small ministry with no money, no structures and no resources. It was a strange irony that Mandel, a former disciple of Clemenceau who was so against the colonies, should end up in the rue Oudinot. But the man had a will of iron and was renowned for his pigheadedness. He set out to revolutionize the sleepy ministry with the help of a team made up of such faithful colleagues as Philippe Roques and Pierre Lafue, who would soon become good friends with Marguerite Donnadieu. Philippe Roques was put in charge of press relations and Pierre Lafue became assistant ministerial speechwriter. Mandel completely restructured the ministry, made new appointments and sacked anyone regarded as incompetent, those he referred to as 'colonials in colonies'. He did not stop with ensuring the efficient functioning of the ministry.[19] Convinced the next conflict would not be limited to Europe, it was his intention to turn the colonies into an additional military and strategic force ready to go on the offensive in the event of war. He set up a general staff for the colonies, responsible for the organization and mobilization of troops, and appointed General Bührer to head it. 'There can be no delay. We have a war on our doorstep and we are not prepared,' Mandel admitted. With a view to weakening the threat of fascism, the strength of the colonial army had to be increased and its complete autonomy guaranteed. 'From now on, we, the colonies, are going to wage a subversive war from our frontiers against the *Boche* and fascists,' he never tired of telling a political class that found him somewhat egocentric, extreme and pessimistic. On a strategic and military level, Mandel was in fact highly efficient. In June 1939 he would inform the government that he was in a position to deal with any eventuality and that he had 600,000 men ready to fight on any terrain.

On 16 September 1938 came Marguerite's first promotion: assistant to the committee responsible for publicizing French bananas, formed in June 1938. She left bananas to work with tea before returning to the intercolonial department of information on 1 March 1939. Her task was clearly defined. In collaboration with her superior Philippe Roques and helped by a close aide of the minister, Pierre Lafue, a historian and writer (who the following year published a novel entitled *La plongée* with Gallimard), she had to produce a book outlining the virtues and greatness of the colonial empire. It was a commission. The minister explained there was no time to lose, the book had to appear as soon as possible. Marguerite – as we have seen – had already been noticed for her ability to synthesize, her capacity for work, her aptitude for writing and her knowledge of the history of Indo-China. She got on with the job and scribbled away night and day, producing pages and pages of writing that Roques revised and corrected.

Robert Antelme was bored stiff in his Rouen barracks. One day, he received a telegram: 'WANT TO MARRY YOU STOP RETURN TO PARIS STOP MARGUERITE.' Jacques Benet remembers Robert's joy. Robert took three days' leave and caught the first train to Paris.

On 23 September 1939 at 11.15, he married Marguerite at the town hall in the fifteenth *arrondissement*. Marguerite had taken care of the formalities. The wedding was a private affair. They said 'I do' in front of two witnesses. Marguerite's witness was Joseph Andler, an English journalist who soon disappeared from their lives. One evening thirty years later Robert would tell his second wife that years later he learned that Marguerite's witness had been her lover at the time. Robert's witness was Fernande Figli. Marguerite had picked her. None of Robert's or Marguerite's friends had ever heard of her and they never met her.

When France Brunel returned from her native southwest the next day, Marguerite just dropped it into the conversation that she'd married Robert the day before.

Why did they get married? Some of their close friends said that it was because war had broken out. Dionys Mascolo, who became Marguerite's partner later on in the war, still maintains today that – given the gravity of the situation – they wanted the strong bond of friendship they'd had for some years legally sanctioned. 'She married Robert because they got on extremely well and because Robert had been called up.'[20] Monique Antelme fiercely disputes this unromantic version. Robert had told her that he was madly in love with Marguerite and overjoyed that she wanted to marry him. For it was Marguerite who proposed to Robert. Was it an experiment for Marguerite but love for Robert? We mustn't forget that it was a tense period and a marriage certificate provided a degree of help and security. Besides, the climate at the time was such that young people exchanged wedding rings so that separation could be all the more dramatic later.

On her wedding night, having seen Robert off at the station, Marguerite went quietly home. He returned to Rouen to be a soldier. The following month Robert wrote to France:

> We don't yet know when we shall be leaving this place. I can't tell you how deadly it is here. What is there to lead us to believe we are still men? Yes, we are in for a long sleep and each of its respites will be painful.
>
> We, we join in, we join in the chaos. At the centre of this foulness we are committed body and soul to the struggle. The forthcoming battles

will in a way echo the skirmishes you and maybe I have had against the consequences of man's barbarity. Let us suppose it is a relief we are about to perform, the relief of forces exhausted by an era of folly and nothingness...

I am sitting on straw as I write and a huge cloud is darkening my words, in the dark, in the midst of the howls of those who are now my neighbours.[21]

And François Mitterrand wrote:

'If men fight, so be it; let them learn to live; let them track their stupidity back to its lair; let them beat their breasts at the sight of their barbarity; there are those who, for fun or through ambition, are about to lose their liberty, their sensitivity, their tranquillity. What would distress me so would be to die for values in which I do not believe. There are things I have to sort out with myself.[22]

As for Sartre the soldier, he described himself as 'a civil meteorologist', 'a company penpusher'. He reread Stendhal, finished writing *The Age of Reason*, annotated Jules Renard's *Journal*, was bored stiff, played chess, wrote numerous letters to Simone de Beauvoir making only rare and brief references to the political situation. Sartre, like so many others, suffered the war without rebelling. 'I think that it's having totally forgotten peace that helps us put up with the war. Bombs could be dropping all around me, I'd be terrified of course but no more than before a natural cataclysm,' he wrote on 12 May 1940. He went on to say, 'We have grown used to the idea that blood is made to flow. It is no longer the sacrilege it was at the beginning.'[23]

In Paris Marguerite Donnadieu was working flat out on the book commissioned by the minister. Mandel was determined to leave his mark on the ministry in rue Oudinot and to drive through his ideas. No means of communication was overlooked. His speeches were broadcast on the radio, there were promotional inserts on the wealth and advantages of the colonies, and propaganda committees set up by Philippe Roques, who regularly released information on the important role of the ministry and, of course, on the heroic deeds of the minister. And then there were the enthusiastic reports and comments from those newspapers that supported him. Some journalists mocked Mandel and his desire for recognition: 'Radio Toulouse, at the request of Mr Mandel, congratulated Mr Mandel on Mr Mandel's fortuitous initiative. The same Mr Mandel, more Mandel than ever, asked Radio Toulouse to devote a programme to the colonies.[24]

Later, in the draft of a novel, Marguerite drew a vitriolic portrait of him:

> He had nothing but contempt for us. A great politician had once treated him with contempt when he was young. And because of this he thought he held the key to authority. The key was the contempt he'd endured and that he now inflicted on his colleagues. He never shook hands with anyone. Whenever he returned a file he'd fling it on the floor saying, 'Pick it up.' You'd have thought he had a million things to do. Everyone trembled before this larger-than-life character. Except for me. Me, the son of a top civil servant, reared on Nestlé milk, aluminized water, chlorinated salad and who secretly masturbates every day. They say masturbation makes morons of children. It wasn't the case with me. On the contrary, it brought me reason, revolt and joy.[25]

On 18 March 1940, François de Roux, a member of the cabinet, sent the finished manuscript, entitled *L'Empire français*, to Gallimard, rue Sébastien-Bottin. François de Roux was a friend of Gaston Gallimard, founder of the publishing firm, who at the end of August 1939 had taken refuge in the town of Mirande in the Pyrenees. In Paris the publishing house continued to function under Brice Parain, the company secretary who had been appointed chief administrator in Gaston's absence.[26] A few days later, Louis-Daniel Hirsch, the commercial director, gave the go-ahead for *L'Empire français* to be published. The contract allowed the ministry to purchase 3000 copies. It was essential that the book be ready by 1 May when the exhibition France Overseas was due to open. In the correspondence Roques was described as a close colleague of the minister. The name of his co-author Marguerite Donnadieu was never mentioned.

L'Empire français came out on 25 April 1940, with an initial print run of 6300 copies. The 240-page book, written in an academic and technical style, had but one aim, which was quite clearly set out in the first few lines: to inform the French that they had extensive territories overseas, an empire that every Frenchman and every

Frenchwoman should know about. The book did not attempt to hide the fact that its aim was militant. France had to know about its 'colonizing abilities' so that it could be proud of them. 'And that is the task of this book. The understanding the reader will gain from this book is: the Empire is made. The war helped complete it.'

The book lists the colonies and records the history of French colonialism in a paternalistic tone. *L'Empire français* is a work of pure propaganda that endorses France's dominion over the colonies. The very principle of colonialism was acknowledged as a universal truth[27] even though the colonies were becoming a greater economic and financial burden. In a survey of 1939, 'Would you rather fight than forgo a fraction of our colonial possessions?' 44 per cent of French people answered no, 40 per cent answered yes. There was a feeling of 'social humanism' predominant in France at the time which gave rise to the idea of a brotherhood of man. Those familiar with the pro-independence theories of communist intellectuals were few and far between. Those who subscribed to them were even rarer. To the majority of the French, the colonies stood for exoticism, a change of scene. They represented an elsewhere with hazy geographical boundaries and virtually unfamiliar cultures. The book's vocabulary reveals the authors' mindset: people born in the colonies are 'natives' who love their homeland, who have 'a child-like faith' in 'sweet France'. To the two authors the white race was by nature the con-quering race, and although the book pays homage to the courage and pride of the 'native', it is teeming with clichés that point to a human hierarchy. At the top of the ladder of the inhabitants of the colonies we find the Annamese – was this Marguerite favouring her native land? – and at the bottom the black African: 'The Negro is the victim of the forces of nature. Undeveloped, sickly and suspicious, he hides in the shadows of the forest and is incapable of dispelling the mysteries that surround him. The Negro penetrates deeper into the forest as the European moves in and makes way for more robust indigenous races.' But as the forest thins out and the white occupation advances, it is the view of Marguerite Donnadieu and Philippe Roques that 'the type of native changes'. Indeed 'the Negro from the steppe is braver and bolder.'[28]

Natives are not altogether the same as other people. In other words, they are different from us Westerners. And that is why, the authors explain with many arguments to support their view, we must continue to fashion them in our image by passing on to them the benefits of Western civilization – education and medicine having been found to be the most effective weapons. But how can the point of view of indigenous elites who want to be acknowledged rather than dominated be taken account of? Marguerite Donnadieu and Philippe Roques envisaged the gradual evolution of a policy: in exchange for what some 'natives' gave France, certain local councils, especially in Indo-China, would be granted additional powers. Particularly brilliant subjects would be allowed to study in some of France's great institutions of learning, such as Saint-Cyr and the Polytechnique, or to become high-ranking army officers. But a distinction would have to be made between those races that were not equal: 'It would be insane to impose on a young Annamese, whose country had achieved historical and intellectual greatness, the same working conditions as a young black child, whose evolution has been held in check for thousands of years.'

L'Empire français upheld the status quo and hoped colonialism would survive the upheavals of the forthcoming war. While it was possible for some colonies to envisage the gradual implementation of a policy diplomatically described as 'of association, indeed of collaboration', it was considered essential to remain circumspect. The extending of citizenship was not an option. Although there were reformers suggesting that the empire should have its own parliament made up of representatives from the colonies, in the eyes of Marguerite Donnadieu and Philippe Roques that idea was too innovative and too dangerous because 'the black race was still in its infancy'. 'It is through a process of trial and error that the black native will gain an understanding of the administrative, political and commercial structure of the area to which his village belongs. Were he given the vote, he would be confused, unable to use it or swayed by witchdoctors or marabouts.' So the betterment of 'our natives' would be a gradual affair. The important thing was to have them ready to provide cannon fodder against Germany in the forthcoming conflict. And, as these zealous authors remind us, Monsieur Mandel had 'with extraordinary foresight' fortunately already made all the necessary provisions.

The tone of *L'Empire français* is quite startling. To understand where the authors were coming from it is essential to see the book in its historical context. Marguerite Donnadieu was acting like an average Frenchwoman rather than a nasty antiquated colonial. It was only the far left that was opposed to France's colonizing efforts. Mandel openly supported the giving of aid to the Spanish republicans, and was therefore considered a worthy opponent by totalitarian states. Destiny robbed us of the chance to judge the effectiveness of his plans for a colonial army; in the words of one of his biographers, the tool was disregarded or misused.[29] But in 1944 the colonial troops played a vital part in helping the forces of the Free French fight in France and Italy.

As a propaganda book relevant to that time, it had very little impact. Gallimard sold 3700 copies, in other words 700, since 3000 had already been purchased by the Colonial Office. Marguerite had to 'forget' the book and had it deliberately dropped from all her biographies. She did not, and I can vouch for that, like to be reminded of it. She would have liked to obliterate it, to pretend it had never existed. But facts are difficult to get rid of. And so, since she couldn't disown it, she spoke of it as an oversight, a youthful error of judgement. And although she didn't find an audience, the book did launch Marguerite into the world of publishing. It was a useful experience, and her status as a co-author for the Gallimard publishing house would stand her in good stead a year later when she was looking for a publisher for her first novel.

On 18 May 1940 Mandel was appointed minister of the interior. He took his friend and colleague Philippe Roques with him and gave him an important position in his cabinet. Officially Marguerite stayed with the Colonial Office, but she continued to see and to work in secret with her friends Lafue and Roques.

On 6 June 1940, the Germans broke through the Somme front and on 10 June they crossed the Seine. On 19 June, General Weygand declared Paris an open city. That same evening, the Council of Ministers moved the government out of Paris. And so the exodus began. Seven million men, women and children took to the roads of France and made their way south. The members of the government stopped in Tours. Mandel was the last to leave Paris. He was still minister of the interior but he no longer had any power. During the night of 10–11 June, he left for Tours with a much reduced team and converted the prefecture of

Indre-et-Loire into a Ministry of the Interior. With him were Philippe Roques, Pierre Lafue and Marguerite.

Ministers were found accommodation in the surrounding area, in remote castles in the middle of the countryside with no means of communication. France Brunel, as a civil servant with the Ministry of Defence, had been part of the delegation that left Paris on foot, then by cart, in the mass exodus. On the afternoon of 12 June she saw Marguerite arrive in the grounds of the Château de Cangey, the official residence of the president of the Republic, Albert Lebrun. Looking fresh and nicely turned out, Marguerite was stepping out of a plush car that belonged to the prefecture, still in the company of Roques and Lafue. That evening an unforgettably sad meeting of the Council of Ministers was held. Mandel and Reynaud were wondering whether they should leave Tours and go to Bordeaux. At the end of the meeting, Weygand spoke the word 'armistice'. Everyone was shocked. 'Fight, fight to the death,' Mandel pleaded. 'Let's go and fight.'

On 13 June, Mandel, in the presence of Reynaud, received the new British prime minister Winston Churchill at the prefecture of Tours. At 18.00 hours, Mandel attended another meeting of the Council at the Château de Cangey. He could see that an armistice would gain them some ground. At 20.00 hours he sent a telegram to all prefects ordering them to hang on. During the night he had a long conversation with the undersecretary of state for war, General de Gaulle, on the need to fight.

Marguerite was an unwitting participant in the events of those hapless days as the fate of France wavered. Yet curiously enough, she never recalled the deadly climate of the dying Republic, not in any of her interviews, nor in her novels. On 14 June, Mandel left Tours for Bordeaux. Their destinies led them off in different directions, and Marguerite never saw him again. She followed Pierre Lafue to Brive, where he went to his cousin Madeleine's house. She was to become a writer under the name Madeleine Alleins, and one of Marguerite's most loyal friends.

France Brunel also eventually turned up in Brive. She found that not only had Marguerite settled in there, but as a civil servant on secondment from the Colonial Office she had even found herself a job as a writer at the prefecture. Happy and busy, she stayed on until the end of the summer (according to some of her friends, she was playing happy families with Lafue).

In September 1940, Robert Antelme returned to Paris. So did Marguerite; and on 1 November she handed in her notice at the Colonial Office.

At the end of September Robert got a job at police headquarters in Paris, probably thanks to his father, who worked there as an assistant writer. He stayed until May 1941. By becoming a humble civil servant he was soon able to involve himself in the activities of the Resistance. Robert was lucky enough to be assigned to work for Jacqueline Lafleur. She'd been working as a writer at police headquarters since March 1938, and had, from the moment the Occupation began, been working for the Resistance on a daily basis. She helped out foreigners in difficulties, stole compromising files and systematically destroyed the denunciations sent her by the first bureau of the cabinet. She'd try to find out who was sending them in so that she could pass the names on to her group of 'patriots' and, whenever possible, warn those who were under investigation. She sent military plans to England, supplied London with headed notepaper from police headquarters and housed English airmen and gave them French lessons in her office at the prefecture. Jacqueline and Robert would be lifelong friends. Robert was an efficient work colleague, took risks, aided and abetted his boss, and helped wanted men to escape by plane. After the Liberation, Jacqueline Lafleur received the Resistance medal and the Franco-Britannic Distinguished Service award for acts of resistance carried out between August 1940 and August 1944.

In February 1941, Robert bumped into his old barracks roommate Jacques Benet in Saint-Germain-des-Prés. 'I was an escapee,' he explained.

I was looking for lodgings. I didn't even have to ask. Robert just came out with it. And so I stayed with Robert and Marguerite in rue Saint-Benoît. I got myself a little job so that I had something to live on. But every evening I'd go back to their place. In 1941, I suppose their life was fairly typical of any married couple. She was a pretty young woman, very warm, with a touch of exoticism. She spent a long time telling me the story of her family in the Dordogne and talked a lot about her mother who lived in Indo-China.[30]

As for Georges Beauchamp, he met up with Robert again at the end of 1940. 'Through the Museum of Man network, I was helping pick up English and Canadian parachutists and Robert was helping me,' Georges Beauchamp explained.[31] The couple had just moved into rue Saint-Benoît, and night after night, Jacques Benet, Robert Antelme and Marguerite discussed the situation, looking for ways to oppose the occupying forces. Friends would drop in and they'd drink as they put the world to rights. Lafue, for example, was a regular visitor, as were France Brunel and old friends from the faculty of law. Number 5 rue Saint-Benoît became a place to meet, to talk; where they could discuss Stendhal, Nietzsche or Saint-Just. Marguerite had turned the apartment into a permanent forum, a raft of freedom and friendship. During the war it was a bolthole, a place to hide members of the Resistance. After the war it became home to a group of minds that attracted a fair number of French intellectuals. Rue Saint-Benoît was the home Marguerite shared with Robert, but she had her own room and would take her men there. Some stayed long after the affair was over. Rue Saint-Benoît was a space shared, the home of the group, a place for exchanges – culinary, ideological and literary.

Marguerite had come across the apartment by accident. It was a neighbour in a bistro who one day told her an apartment was about to be vacated in her block. The neighbour was Betty Fernandez, second wife of Ramon Fernandez, a writer and one of Gallimard's readers since 1927, a friend of Jacques Rivière and Marcel Proust, and at that time a collaborator. The apartment in question was below theirs. Lower-middle-class apartments, fairly spacious, not too expensive and most important of all, ideally situated at the heart of Saint-Germain-des-Prés. 'We talked. Betty Fernandez's intelligence was irresistible. And so we met again.'[32] The formalities for the apartment were soon concluded. Robert Antelme signed the lease and moved in. From being neighbours, the Fernandezes soon became friends. 'I never met people more charming than those two beings, the Fernandezes. An essential charm. They were intelligence and goodness personified,' said Marguerite, who always defended the memory of

Ramon.[33] Marguerite and Robert were aware of his political leanings. In the intellectual and literary circles in which they moved, it was impossible not to know. In his flat you were likely to meet Gerhardt Heller, an officer from the *Propagandastaffel* and German delegate on the Board of Censors; Karl Epting, the director of the German Institute; and the writers Chardonne, Céline and Pierre Drieu la Rochelle. Before joining such French writers as Chardonne, Drieu and Brasillach on their sorry journey to the Weimar in the autumn of 1941, he worked at the *NRF*, previously headed by Drieu, and was a member of the political bureau of Dorriot's PPF. Yet between the two floors in the rue Saint-Benoît there was neither disapproval nor fear. Quite the contrary. Secretly working on her first novel, on a Sunday Marguerite would go upstairs to talk. She said she never met any Germans there. Ramon Fernandez was highly cultured and sometimes brave. He was the only collaborator to praise Bergson when the Jewish philosopher died in January 1941, which earned Ramon an insulting letter from Céline. Marguerite was very sensitive to this charming man, a racing-car enthusiast and tango dancer, already suffering the effects of age and alcohol. She would listen captivated as he talked of the authors he'd written about: Balzac, Molière, Gide and soon Proust.[34] Marguerite went to his weekly salons, but she never invited him to her place. With Betty, whom she adored, she'd go to the café to talk.

Their friendship lasted for almost two years, but when Robert and Marguerite joined a Resistance cell in 1943, Marguerite ended their relationship. 'Ramon was coming down the stairs. I went up to him. "Ramon," I said, "we've just joined the Resistance. We have to stop speaking to one another in public. Stop seeing one another. Stop telephoning one another." ' Marguerite never forgot Betty or Ramon. Betty, she told me, was at the source of *The Lover*[35] – her personality, her charm, her unpredictability, the life she led. The very first version of *The Lover* begins with her. 'Betty Fernandez. As soon as I say her name there she is, walking along the Paris streets, she's short-sighted. She's a plant whose long, thin stem bends with the wind. She's beautiful, strikingly beautiful. In a poetic analysis of life, she was nearly always an attentive friend, extremely loyal and extremely loving.'[36]

*

The biographer of Gaston Gallimard says that 'to be a French writer in 1941, to send a manuscript to Gallimard, meant that you accepted being read and judged by a committee [that included] R. Fernandez.'[37] Marguerite of course sent the manuscript of her first novel, *La famille Taneran*, to Gallimard, but under the name of Donnadieu, giving as her address that of her husband's family and without mentioning the then influential name of Fernandez. In the accompanying letter she wrote:

Dear Sir,

My name is perhaps not completely unfamiliar to you as I co-authored the book on the French Empire you brought out last year. But the enclosed manuscript, *La famille Taneran*, is in no way related to the first book, which for me was nothing more than an occasional book. I now wish to embark on a career as a writer.

Henri Clouard, André Thérive and Pierre Lafue have read the enclosed manuscript. They liked it very much and urged me to get it published. I value their opinions and hope it will meet with your approval.

Marguerite Donnadieu
c/o Antelme
2 rue Dupin – Paris 6

She heard nothing from Gallimard. Time dragged for the impatient Marguerite. Pierre Lafue reassured her, telling her it was quite normal. He was still madly in love with her. As for Robert, although he had encouraged her to find a publisher for her first novel, he had been quick to point out its weaknesses, the stylistic irregularities, the sloppily developed plot. Robert's opinion was more important to her than Lafue's. She begged him to go to Gallimard. According to Gallimard's archives, it was Marcel Arland who had been given the task of reading the manuscript, and his reaction was negative. The verdict had been given but the rejection slip not sent out. The day Robert visited Gallimard, he bumped into the writer and editor Raymond Queneau in a corridor. Robert's enthusiasm was such that Queneau decided to salvage the manuscript, and he read *La famille Taneran* on 6 March 1941. He did not like it either, although he recognized its underlying qualities. He considered the story muddled, lacking in control, and overinfluenced by American literature in general and Faulkner in particular. But there was still no official response from Gallimard. Finally Marguerite, who for some reason didn't want to appeal directly to Fernandez, asked Pierre Lafue to have a word with the publishing house. Her former lover, companion in flight and colleague from the Colonial Office was also, as it happened, a friend of Ramon Fernandez. On 8 May 1941, he sent this letter to Gaston Gallimard:

> My Dear Sir,
> Ramon Fernandez informs me you are going to come a decision regarding *La famille Taneran*.
> The book of course is not without flaws, but it has an atmosphere reminiscent of Emily Brontë.

His intervention paid off. On 16 May, Marguerite received a letter from Gallimard signed by Raymond Queneau:

> Dear Madam,
> We read your manuscript with great interest. We are at present unable to undertake its publication. However, should you one day be passing the rue Sébastien-Bottin I should be happy to discuss the matter with you.

Queneau was then thirty-seven, and had published seven novels. The meeting was crucial to Marguerite. Queneau suggested she abandon her American models, simplify her style and get straight to the point. He was gentle and kind and persuasive, and Marguerite listened to what he had to say. He helped her see her qualities, the intensity she put into depicting certain traits in her characters and the style she used to describe particular landscapes. He gave her the courage to go on. She would recount how during this first and incredibly decisive meeting, Queneau gave her just one piece of advice – to write and to do nothing but that. Being a writer is a profession. You have to stick at it. She never forgot the lesson.

A lively and fruitful friendship soon developed between him and Marguerite. Queneau also became a friend of Robert Antelme and the mentor of Marguerite's future partner Dionys Mascolo, with whom he would work in rue Sébastien-Bottin. Queneau would be one of the regulars at the postwar dinner parties held in rue Saint-Benoît. He'd run circles round the men and have women falling at his feet with his wild humour and wonderful sarcasm.

Queneau was not one to impose his tastes. At Gallimard he was there to listen, not to influence. Marguerite appreciated this attitude and the way he treated people as equals. He helped her get over Gallimard's rejection so that she could approach other publishers. Through thick and thin Queneau was always there for her, offering help and support.

Marguerite took her manuscript to several editors, all of whom turned it down. In her memoirs, Dominique Arban remembers that Robert Antelme turned up at her house at eight one morning in the summer of 1941 with Marguerite's manuscript under his arm. Arban was then working for Plon as a reader. Mutual friends had introduced her to Marguerite and Robert, and she had liked them. However, she was taken aback by the early morning call and the urgency in Robert's voice: 'I should warn you, if you don't tell her she's a writer, she'll kill herself.' She tried to explain she would not be blackmailed into reading it, but Robert disappeared, leaving the manuscript behind. Arban picked it up. According to her it bore the title *Les complices*. The influence of Hemingway and Faulkner was strong, but there was nothing unusual in that. 'First I read without displeasure. And then with pleasure. She was undoubtedly a writer. I carried on, turning the pages over, one after another. No, I wasn't wrong.'[38]

Dominique Arban went to see the owner and managing director of Plon, Bourdel, and at last Marguerite had an agreement in principle. But she would have to wait two years for her first novel, by then entitled *Les impudents*, to be published.

At the end of autumn 1941, Marguerite discovered she was pregnant. She had confided on more than one occasion to Georges Beauchamp and Jacques Benet just how much she wanted a child. After much persuasion, Robert finally agreed. She had a difficult pregnancy. Entries in her journals speak of physical fatigue, growing anxiety, palpitations, her changing body and her inability to comprehend the changes. Marguerite grew so fearful that Robert found her difficult to live with. She couldn't bear to be separated from him and would follow him down the street shouting. Did Marguerite intuit that he was having an affair? She always claimed there was a touch of the witch in her, that she had presentiments and premonitions. Although he still loved Marguerite, Robert was falling in love with a young woman called Anne-Marie. But he did not leave Marguerite, and their life together went on as before, with no apparent rifts.

Their friends knew nothing of Robert's liaison with Anne-Marie. France Brunel, who saw a lot of Marguerite, said she was very agitated, and admired Robert for his saintlike patience. France was also pregnant; they were due the same month. She remembers how difficult it was to follow a healthy, well-balanced diet in occupied Paris and how they would waddle, two conspirators, through the streets of the Latin Quarter.

Marguerite went into labour before France. The baby was badly positioned, and the couple panicked. Robert drove Marguerite to the maternity hospital she'd chosen for the delivery and where she'd been for regular check-ups. It was a maternity home run by nuns, and ill-equipped to deal with emergencies. Her labour was long and painful, lasting twenty hours. The nuns weren't used to it, and Marguerite suffered terribly.

The child was born in the middle of the night. He didn't cry. He had died coming into the world. Marguerite was appalled. Her world was plunged into darkness. She was filled with the most terrible feelings of guilt. Guilt at not having known how, at not having been able to bring a child into the world. Inside her he'd been alive, but she'd killed him as he left her. And she, was she still alive?

Marguerite was in hospital for a few days. She found some of the nuns particularly nasty. Instead of comforting her, they were punishing her. But why had Marguerite chosen a hospital run by nuns? Some of her friends reproached her and she regretted it. She was spared none of the clichés. Little children go to heaven. Stillborn babies become angels. As far as Marguerite was concerned, the nuns had stolen her child in the name of God. She wasn't allowed to see the child and spent nights trying to picture him. Robert was lucky, he'd seen him; they'd even let him hold him. Marguerite kept asking: 'What was his mouth like? His hair?' 'He looked like you, Marguerite, yes, just like you,' came Robert's gentle reply.

The little boy's death haunted her for the rest of her life and sometimes surfaced in her books. What is a woman if she's not a mother? Nothing, unless she's a depressive nursing her gloom as she waits for death. Duras admired young girls in the first flush of womanhood and had great respect for women who were mothers. To be fulfilled, a woman had to experience motherhood. Marguerite adored babies. In her opinion childless women were not real women. For months, Marguerite couldn't sleep. For a long time she blamed herself. Later, much later, when she tried to rationalize what had happened, she blamed the war, the way things were during the war, the nuns, medicine.

According to Georges Beauchamp, things were never the same between Robert and Marguerite after the baby's death. Emotionally they may have been closer, but physically something had gone. After the baby's death Robert was wonderfully attentive, extremely kind and considerate. Marguerite shut herself off from the world: 'I said to R, "I don't want to see anyone, just you." '[39]

To Marguerite a child was an inventor of worlds, a DIY enthusiast of the universe, a being equal to God, a philosopher who asked real questions, an innocent close to the truth who challenged the games played by adults. Marguerite Duras's work is teeming with children. Eternal vagabonds, they always personify truth and freedom. Instead of always telling them to be quiet, we should listen to what they have to say. In Duras it is the child who is right.[40] In her literary world, children and women are the mad ones, the prophets of truth.

CHAPTER 5

From Collaboration to Resistance

∼

In May 1941, Robert Antelme left the Préfecture. He had been taken on by the cabinet of the minister for industry to work as an attaché in the department of information and documentation. The minister was Pierre Pucheu, a company director and graduate from the École normale supérieure. Robert was soon a close colleague of Pucheu, and as one of his most trustworthy advisers he was given the sensitive role of private secretary. When Pucheu was moved to the Ministry of the Interior, Robert went with him as a contractual attaché, then became a writer at the Ministry of Information, where he stayed until the end of 1943.

In July 1942, Marguerite was taken on to the payroll of the Book Organization Office. She was appointed secretary to the agency in charge of allocating paper to publishers. Was it thanks to Ramon Fernandez that Marguerite got this job? Highly likely but impossible to verify. Fernandez, like Brice Parain, was one of the forty or so official readers to belong to the Paper Allocation Agency. Created by Marshal Pétain on 1 April 1942, the agency was in charge of over-seeing the use publishers made of the paper allocated to them. Marguerite was responsible for the readers' reports. The majority of publishers decided to continue in business, even at the expense of having to sign an agreement with the Germans. Three months after the armistice, and under the auspices of the president of the asso-ciation of French publishers, they signed a censorship agreement with the occupying forces. Publishers agreed to print nothing that was anti-German or proscribed in Germany. If a publisher was in any doubt, the association was responsible for preliminary censorship. It would then submit the manuscript to the Germans pointing out any 'controversial passages'. The notorious Otto list was drawn up of books to be withdrawn from circulation – a strange homage to the German ambassador Otto Abetz. The works of Freud, Malraux, Aragon, Koestler and many others were banned as a result. The books were piled up in a huge garage in the avenue de la Grande-Armée and subsequently destroyed. It was impossible not to be reminded of the book burnings that took place in Berlin as early as 1933.

Marguerite could not have been unaware of the extent of collaboration of an organization under the constant surveillance of the Bureau of Propaganda. The Paper Allocation Agency sieved manuscripts to see whether they were worth publishing. Depending on the quantity of paper available, it then drew up a list which was submitted to Propaganda for approval. The system lasted until the Occupation ended. It suited both the French and the German authorities since 'Propaganda can adjust paper allocation as it sees fit and censor books it does not wish to see published'. Marguerite as secretary of the agency made the decisions and had the power of arbitration. But 'the Germans had absolute control', said Georges Duhamel, who as permanent secretary of the Académie française was a member of the Agency, 'approving those books that promoted their policies, passing those that were no threat and silencing any authors they regarded as adversaries.'[1]

Claude Roy first met Marguerite Duras in her office. 'I wanted to publish a book of poems with Julliard. They'd said, "As paper's in short supply, be a good chap and run along and see the lady at the Cercle de la Librairie." I thought the lady was divine. "What are your poems about?" she asked. "Love," said I, all shy. She burst out laughing and said, "You'll get your paper." '[2]

Marguerite no doubt did what she could to frustrate the censorship machine and to facilitate the maximum number of publications. But she had to associate with the Germans during management meetings and was obliged to follow their instructions. She had limited room for manoeuvre even though, in her purely literary domain, she gave the impression she was in charge of the decision-making process. Later, whenever questions were raised about this period of her life, she would brush them aside with an irritated wave of the hand.

The paper shortage was giving cause for concern; reprints had come to a virtual standstill and readers' reports on new books were becoming less detailed. Marguerite needed new readers. The authorities must have trusted her for they let her hire them herself. That was how, on first meeting Dionys Mascolo – when he came to plead the cause of a book for Gallimard in November 1942 – she suggested taking him on. The readers' payment was calculated on the thickness of the manuscript, the average price being 150 francs for a 200-page novel. 'I was poor and out of work,' he told me in 1996.

I'd studied philosophy for a year but never taken the examination. I was a messenger, a telephonist, but I wanted to be an intellectual. I was in a state of general revolt. My hero was Saint-Just, and at the time I was living with my mother, who would go to the soup kitchen with milk jugs to get food to feed her family. Thanks to a college friend, Michel Gallimard, I went to work for Gallimard, doing odd-jobs. When Marguerite offered me a job with the agency, I accepted what was a clerical literary job.

He added, 'It was a board of censors, we couldn't publish what we wanted. We knew that.'

Marguerite never hid the fact that for her it was love at first sight. Dionys was 'handsome, extremely handsome', 'like a god,' she said, to the day she died. She used all her charms to seduce him. Dionys found her charming and beautiful but demanding. 'She was always wanting me to tell her I loved her, and they were words I just never said.'[3] It was a period of discovery, of wonder, of afternoons in hotel rooms. 'She really enjoyed making love and would tell me so. Our passion was mutual.' They discussed literature a lot. Dionys was finding Stendhal 'exhilarating' and made her read him. She was working her way through Balzac. Although she hadn't yet found an editor for the first novel, she was planning the second. They often went to the cinema and protested loudly whenever Marshal Pétain appeared on screen during the news. 'Small gestures, tiny gestures. The serious stuff came later,' Dionys told me. It wasn't until they'd been going out for a fortnight that she told him about Robert. She'd say, 'If you knew Robert you'd know I demand a lot from men.' She described their independent lives, Robert's relationship with Anne-Marie, her relationship with her lovers, her collection of lovers, especially the latest, whom she referred to as 'the Neuilly lover'. But with Marguerite and Dionys it wasn't the same thing. From the outset, they both wanted their love to last. With the others, Marguerite hadn't felt she was cheating on Robert or betraying his trust. With Dionys, she did. 'It was adultery,' he said. Dionys took her to meet his mother. Their relationship started looking more official. Marguerite broke off with the others, although Dionys hadn't asked her to. She broke up with the Neuilly lover. He was keen on the Bible and all holy texts, and would chant them in the back rooms of cafés in Saint-Germain.

> He was thin, slightly stooped, with dark, wavy hair and very beautiful blue eyes framed with thick dark lashes, a pale complexion, an extremely expressive mouth that rippled over teeth set just behind his lips, high cheekbones. He was not particularly clean, his shirt collars left a lot to be desired, as did his nails ... he had a concave chest. He had spent his childhood reading the holy Scriptures.[4]

Insane, rich, locked away in mystical isolation, the Neuilly lover would remain imprinted in Marguerite's memory. She was eternally grateful to him for having introduced her to the Bible, which (along with the seventeenth-century novel *La princesse de Clèves* by Madame de La Fayette), was the book she turned to whenever her batteries needed recharging.

Marguerite often talked to Dionys about Indo-China. She described the smell of the earth after rain, the colour of the sky after the monsoon, the swamp that stretched from her mother's house to the Pacific, where she loved to walk wallowing in the blue of the sky, the purity of the night; and expeditions into the mountains, swimming in lagoons with her brother Paul. To her Indo-China was still the motherland from which she was cut off. Returning like leitmotifs were the mother's nastiness and the elder brother's perversity. The admonitions that followed the beatings still rang in her ears. 'I had the impression she'd been seriously abused by two people dear to her,

her mother and elder brother.' She was still obsessed with her mother, who, though never able to love her, kept her fed by sending money orders, sacks of rice too that Marguerite would open jumping for joy. And then one day in December 1942, a telegram arrived from her mother in Indo-China. 'PAUL DCD' (Paul *décédé* – deceased). Dionys never forgot the shock it gave Marguerite. She couldn't move, couldn't breathe! She spent months doubled up, broken. Her little brother, dead!

Marguerite never understood how it could have happened. The circumstances surrounding Paul's death were strange. He hadn't been ill. He had a modest administrative position in Cholon, tinkered around with cars, raced his horses. He was in love with a young woman who had been working as his mother's secretary for over a year. On the eve of a holiday weekend, Paul complained to her and his mother that he was having difficulty breathing. The mother wanted to wait for her doctor to return from his weekend away in Saigon. The fiancée complied. By the time the doctor returned, Paul was already in hospital. The fiancée said, 'He went very quickly. He was still conscious when he died. I held his hand until his eyes shut forever. His mother was at his bedside.' Paul's funeral was held a week later in Saigon cathedral. She often talked to me of the brother she called her little brother, of his goodness, his beauty, his gentleness. The softness of his skin washed in rainwater – that was him, not the lover. The languid siestas in the sweltering heat, body to body, stretched out, still, listening to the other's heartbeat – that was him, not the north China lover. The brother she initiated sexually,[5] the brother to whom she gave her mouth, mouth not sex, her mouth for his sex. 'Look at those deep eyes,' Marguerite would say to me, showing me the photograph pinned to the frame of the mirror in the hall of rue Saint-Benoît. 'Never, do you hear, never did he ever hurt me.'

Marguerite spent her life searching for that lost brotherhood. It haunts a whole area of her work. Her lovers, the real ones, were brothers. Brothers in arms too. Unto death! Robert became a true brother after Paul's death. Dionys was the lover-brother, the one of perpetual rows and constantly renewed desire.

Philippe Roques, Marguerite's co-author of *L'Empire français*, had abandoned words early on in the war in order to join the Resistance.

He was one of the freedom fighters who, through their courage, determination and political awareness, helped form the early pockets of resistance. He remained loyal to Mandel and visited him in the prison du Portalet, and in 1941–42 he carried out a secret mission to contact and liaise with the members of the French government. Even before he joined the Free French, he maintained that 'every day there are Frenchmen who risk their lives or freedom for General de Gaulle. No one else would make such sacrifices except the communists who also know how to die gloriously for their convictions.' He sent a list to London of all the members of the government who were in the Resistance and able to form a clandestine executive committee. Then Roques was arrested by the Germans in February 1943 and gunned down trying to escape.

Jean Lagrolet was taken to Germany as a prisoner of war. He escaped and returned to Paris, where he contacted Georges Beauchamp, who put him up until the end of the war. The latter was part of the Poldery network, helping British pilots and carrying out contact missions. Robert Antelme was of course aware of his activities.

Six months into their relationship, Marguerite introduced Dionys to Robert. 'It was love at first sight for both of us,' said Dionys. Just like every one else who ever had anything to do with him, Dionys instantly fell under the spell of Robert's charm. Robert continued to see Anne-Marie and Dionys started to visit Marguerite and Robert. He became a regular visitor so quickly that he was soon being invited to Sunday tea at Betty and Ramon Fernandez's flat. Queneau, on learning of Dionys's frequent visits to his collaborating colleague's apartment, advised him to distance himself from them. 'The longer the Occupation went on, the more politicized we became,' Dionys explained.[6] Despite not wanting to join a group, he still claimed he was an anarchist. 'Marguerite was one too,' he declared.[7] 'I bought a revolver with the help of some friends and told Marguerite I'd hidden it up the chimney at my place in case I ever needed it.'

Marguerite spent all her free time writing and amending the manuscript she was desperately trying to find a publisher for. She worked on it every night, revising chapter after chapter. She'd pass each reworked section to Robert, who always said it was wonderful, and then to Dionys, who was more critical. 'It struck me as facile. She wasn't complacent and took my comments on board. I'd just moved to literary management at Gallimard and was getting to know the work of young authors.' Marguerite introduced him to the writer Jacques Audiberti, who became a social and literary friend. But Queneau was without a doubt her real guide when it came to literature. Dionys confirmed this: 'Queneau was a determining factor. He helped Marguerite when self-doubt crept in. He'd rejected her first manuscript but encouraged her to carry on.'[8]

Much later Marguerite published an interview where she asked him, 'How do you decide a manuscript is publishable?' Queneau replied, 'Is this a future writer, or someone who will never make it? It's not really a question of deciding whether a manuscript is good or bad, that's very subjective. But you can see if the author belongs to the category of writer, future writer or whether he is simply an amateur.'[9] Queneau made Marguerite understand she was a future writer. Marguerite believed him. Thereafter she would only be a writer.

Her first novel was published by Plon under the name of Duras and entitled *Les impudents*. The moment the book was published Marguerite was not sure about it. She later disowned it, blocking it from her mind until 1992, when she agreed to have it brought back into circulation. Was she right to disown the book for so long? The style is clumsy and the word 'disgust' is repeated ad nauseam. In fact the word aptly sums up the atmosphere the fictional family inhabits: the gambling, thieving brother brings financial ruin to his mother and constantly betrays his nearest and dearest, and the rebellious daughter is unable to tear herself away from the oppressive family. The Durassian framework is already in place. We have the mother besotted by the perverse brother, money as the root of all their problems, the little brother tormented by the big brother, the mother who, out of sheer exhaustion, allows the brother's iniquities to rule the family and the terrified child. This strange family's cloying and yet protective bubble of love and hate forms the subject of the book. Writing it helped Marguerite exorcise some of her end-of-adolescence fears.

The setting of the book is not Lot-et-Garonne, but only because of a slight geographical shift made by an inexperienced novelist who did not – then! – want to be accused of confusing her life with the subject of her novel. The estate is very much like her father's house and some of the events are obviously taken from the time when Marguerite's mother was thinking of settling in France. The heroine becomes pregnant, and her mother encourages her to leave so that she can get on with her shameless love for her son. And so she dispatches her daughter like a parcel to the man who has shamed her. 'There are loves, even between mother and child, that are inescapable, loves to be lived to the exclusion of all else.'

Marguerite already knew how to convey a young woman's desperate lucidity on discovering the world of men: the impudence of love, guilt at having felt hate, 'the constant fear, the filthy bartering, the impurity of the world – everything is already there. The wish to speak, to spit out the disgust in order to bring about desire.' But the style is convoluted, the writing too precious. 'How stupid can you get?' Marguerite said later. 'When you start out as a writer you should always put your first novel away in a drawer. I was twenty-four and extremely stupid.' It wasn't a bestseller but it was well reviewed in a couple of places. Anyway, she had achieved her goal – publication; and on the way she had found a godfather in the person of Queneau, and a name: Duras.

The coast of Duras, near Pardaillan, in Lot-et-Garonne, is a white-wine-producing area, a region of vines, tobacco and plums. Our real name is the one we give ourselves, not the one we are given. By changing her name, Marguerite was separating herself from the Donnadieu family. 'She told me she'd taken a pen name because she wasn't proud of her brother, she wanted to distance herself from her non-literary identity,' Dionys explained. 'She said it would spare her from being accountable to those who'd known her as Donnadieu. I took Gratien as a pseudonym at the same time because I was born in Saint-Gratien.'[10] She took Dionys to Duras and they spent two summers there in a house belonging to an uncle.

Her brother Pierre, prowling the streets of Montparnasse, would often turn up unannounced in rue Saint-Benoît, demanding money or helping himself from cupboards. He was still involved in shady deals and kept bad company, boasting that he was once more living off girls on the streets around La Coupole. He was living with a young woman who didn't care where the money came from, and who went on the game herself when the need arose. Marguerite was moved by her, and she tried to protect and look after her.

Although Marguerite was ashamed of her brother, she couldn't get away from him. He depended on her and that was enough to satisfy her.

François Mitterrand, together with some of his colleagues on the executive committee for prisoners of war for southern France in Vichy, gave in his notice in January 1943, when Pinot was dismissed. Back in Paris he looked up his old school friend Jacques Benet and set about organizing a Resistance movement while continuing to play on his former Vichy connections. It enabled him to meet members of the internal Resistance and patriotic organizations. Through Jacques Benet and thanks to him, Marguerite Duras also joined the Resistance – she and her husband and her lover.

After escaping from Germany, Jacques Benet saw a lot of Mitterrand. The two men liked, valued and trusted one another implicitly. Benet, who was having to keep out of sight in Paris, had been sent by Mitterrand to recruit in Lyon. Returning to Paris in June 1943, he went to see his friend Robert Antelme, with whom he had kept in regular touch since his escape. 'I asked Robert and Marguerite if they could put me up. The response was an instant yes. But in exchange I had to get them into the Resistance.'[11] Jacques Benet moved into rue Saint-Benoît. 'They told me, "We want a one-hundred-per-cent commitment." We were very good friends. The atmosphere at the time was one of defeat.' Night after night Jacques Benet, Robert and Marguerite discussed politics.

Robert was still seeing his old school friend Georges Beauchamp, who was having problems. Involved in more covert operations, he had the job of picking up English parachutists, hiding them, then helping them get out. He was looking for contacts. Robert told him about Benet and arranged a meeting. Benet told Beauchamp about François Mitterrand. A meeting was set up in a café opposite the Convention metro station. Although they had been contemporaries at the law faculty, Georges Beauchamp and François Mitterrand had never met before. From now on they were to become inseparable.

Marguerite insisted that she could do more. Putting Benet up wasn't enough. 'We want to work with you,' she told him. 'Our movement still didn't have a name,' Benet explained. 'It was very early days. We were fighting for the honour of the prisoners of war.

I asked Robert to pass us any information he could glean from the ministry where he worked and whether he knew people in other ministries.'[12] Robert Antelme arranged for Jacques Benet to meet David Rousset, who published a small newsletter. Robert was taking more risks and introduced several people to the group. 'We met in cafés. We took precautions. We had to watch out for informers,' Beauchamp recalled. Marguerite started putting up Resistance fighters and acting as a go-between. The risks were enormous. She had just handed in her notice at the Book Organization Office. The action of a new Resistance fighter? It would appear so. She suggested that a neighbour replace her, the woman who lived downstairs, Madame Courant, whose daughter Nicole, despite being only seventeen, was already in the Resistance.

Jacques Benet remembers bumping into Ramon Fernandez on the stairs of rue Saint-Benoît house on more than one occasion. Ramon would drag him off to Lipp's to drink white wine and discuss literature. Benet desisted from judging him and thought that his wife Betty did not hold the same views but said nothing out of love for him. This little world got together, chatted in bistros, put the world to rights.

Georges Beauchamp was sent to the struggle against the STO (Service du travail obligatoire/Forced Labour Service). He managed to get himself taken on as a runner in the department of labour, which gave him access to files on young conscripts. He would tell them not to go. Marguerite, who was there too, delivered letters and met members of the network. 'She made herself useful and always showed willing,' Jacques Benet added. 'She was also a liaison officer. She did as she was bid. The moment she took me in, she took every risk there was to take.' Marguerite delivered and helped Robert with recruitment. 'They wore out their shoes in the streets of Paris enlisting people,' Benet and Beauchamp stated.

In July, François Mitterrand committed his first act of public resistance. On 10 July 1943, the national day for the prisoners' movement, he disrupted the session in Salle Wagram and protested against the government of Occupation. He was challenged by the police but to their bewilderment walked out of the meeting with some friends. Mitterrand was always changing identity, profession and hiding place. He was involved in a frenzy of activity in Vichy and Paris, and kept in with people close to Pétain as well as with all branches of the Resistance, in Algiers as much as in London. In the words of General de Gaulle, 'he ran with the hare and hunted with the hounds.'[13] During the summer of 1943, he gained stature and gradually established himself as a leader – if not *the* leader – of former POWs. 'I can be a leader only by resorting to cunning or terror or through the merciless networks of inhumanity,'[14] he wrote to a close friend in July 1943.

In 1986 Marguerite Duras and François Mitterrand described their first meeting for a magazine. Marguerite, who sometimes claimed to have forgotten everything about it, said she remembered the event quite clearly. 'It was late one evening. There were two of you. You were in the drawing room, sitting in front of the fireplace, on either side of the stove, the kind made out of old drums in which we burned newspapers pressed into balls. I can't remember if I gave you anything to eat. Mascolo was there. You talked together, the three of you, but not a lot. And then suddenly you lit up and the whole room was filled with the smell of English cigarettes.' In fact he would not go to England until the following year. 'I never knew where the English cigarettes came from. But that evening I understood we'd joined the Resistance, that it was done.'[15]

And that's how she took a few elements from a real event to produce a better story and endeavour to create a myth. That is pure Duras, to enhance reality, to make it more attractive, even if it means reinventing it, in order to escape banality. In the novel Marguerite was then writing, which would become *La vie tranquille*, the heroine says, 'If I'd known that one day I'd have a history, I'd have chosen it; I'd have been more careful how I lived it, so that it would be beautiful and true with a view to pleasing myself.'

Mascolo too remembers that first meeting with Mitterrand, who took him on to work in the propaganda section of the embryonic Resistance organization and put him in charge of editing an underground newsletter. Mascolo got hold of paper and machines.

Mitterrand's recollection of Duras was of a lively, enthusiastic and determined young woman, who was always offering to undertake the most delicate of missions.[16] He moved into the back bedroom at rue Saint-Benoît.

That summer was a passionate time for Dionys and Marguerite. She sent him heart-rending letters every day. 'Tell me you love me.'

'Happiness is unbearable.' 'She wanted more lovemaking,' Dionys told me. 'Mutual desire drew us together. She was in love with me but me, not yet. It was never enough.' They would meet in cafés, then go and make love in a hotel bedroom. Marguerite would beg him to tell her he loved her. Dionys wouldn't. 'It drove her crazy,' he said. Dionys was actually having a fling with an attractive, sweet young woman and he felt torn between the two. He desired Marguerite but not enough to give up the other woman. Marguerite kept plaguing him. She wanted him, smothered him, was all around him. And he didn't know what he wanted.

And then of course there was Robert. Robert loved Marguerite but pursued his relationship with Anne-Marie. Anne-Marie visited rue Saint-Benoît but never stayed the night. Mascolo also visited rue Saint-Benoît every day but never stayed the night. He and Robert were so close that Marguerite felt excluded, jealous. It made Dionys laugh. 'Robert was wonderfully unpretentious. I never met anyone as genuine as Robert. He was more than a brother. The moment I met Robert, I loved him better than I loved my three brothers.' The two men would talk for nights on end. They had a high regard for one another and before long a great affection developed between them. But Marguerite hadn't told Robert the nature of her relationship with Dionys, as letters from her to her lover, written in the summer of 1943, testify: 'I have just got in. He suspects something. He telephoned the *NRF* and asked if I was with you. If you see him, you have been warned. Speaking is not enough. I am without you. Write to me poste restante.'[17]

Robert decided to take her to Doubs, near the Swiss border, for a few days' holiday. She went along but was miserable at being separated from Dionys, to whom she wrote: 'I am very much alone. The kind of aloneness you feel after you have been writing and feel the need to tell someone but the world is asleep. I feel trapped, drowning in solitude. I have put my watch next to me to hear it tick. You can always be more and more alone. It is fathomless.'[18]

Marguerite and Robert went on long afternoon walks together. She dared not leave and return to Paris. So she threw herself into her writing and sent secret messages to Dionys without arousing her husband's suspicions.

To love you is even better than writing. I know that absolutely. Of course there are nights where we listen to the nothing, deep in our bodies, without desire. We are separated. Every day I wonder what I am going to do without you. One day tell me, send me a telegram, say I love you, I desire you, I don't know what to do with these naked words. I am going to sleep in you. Here, I am sending you a page I wrote tonight. Is that how I should write? Don't lose it, I would never find it again. It's the girl arriving at the seaside.

Marguerite was working on her next novel, *La vie tranquille*. A young man one day walks into the dull universe of a young woman forced to live a monotonous life in the country. His name is Tiène. Marguerite Duras likens him to an angel, an apparition. Tiène is based on Dionys. All the young woman can think about is Tiène, Tiène's naked body, an inexhaustible source of pleasure. Until he came along, there had been a hollow, something amorphous inside her body. 'There came from inside it an empty cry that was calling no one. Since then a force has been growing I am powerless to resist, a thought has taken root there, in me, against me . . .'

Still Marguerite said nothing to Robert. At the time, writing was an attempt to understand herself, a search for the truth. How could she continue to write if she herself was living a lie? She could imagine Dionys flirting, showing off in the corridors of Gallimard. Robert couldn't understand why his wife was suffering from mood swings, charming one moment and the next spiteful. He went for long walks on his own, while Marguerite tortured herself, unsure how Dionys felt about her. She wanted proof, made some complicated calculations: if I left Robert, would Dionys want to live with me?

One stormy night Marguerite had a lucky escape when lightning struck the field she'd just crossed. She was plagued by morbid imaginings, tormented by the thought of her dead child. She approached Dionys. 'She told me she wanted a child. It was her way of saying she loved me,' he recalled. Dionys was taken aback. He couldn't see himself as a father just yet and had no real desire to see his life turned upside down. He had plans for a book, his new job was taking up a lot of his time and he was still seeing his girlfriend regularly. But Marguerite wasn't one to give up:

If ever you were keeping me on hold . . . me the greatest coward of all at the thought of bothering you for a child. We don't carry a child without love. We are attached to the man who's done that for us. The only choice left me is to attach myself to Robert. In the ashes of the future, my only hope is the hope of betraying you.

Marguerite and Robert returned to Paris. Anne-Marie was waiting for Robert. Marguerite went in search of Dionys.

A lot of people dropped into rue Saint-Benoît, they'd go and have a drink, a chat. A community spirit was forming. (In 1943, Marguerite Duras, like so many other young left-bank intellectuals, was of course passionately existentialist. However, she never acknowledged this and even denied it vigorously. Neither on a philosophical nor a friendship plane did she ever have any affection for or complicity with Jean-Paul Sartre or Simone de Beauvoir.) Jacques Benet stayed the night a few times and moved into the back bedroom with François Mitterrand. 'We had a single bed between us.' At the end of August, Robert and Marguerite asked Benet and Mitterrand to change hideout and to go and stay at Robert's mother's flat in rue Dupin. No reason was ever given by either of them. With hindsight, Benet thought they were probably going through a bad patch, although there was no evidence of this.

Robert was becoming more involved. He recruited from administrations and passed on documents that turned up at the ministry. Dionys did some breaking and entering so that he could get a Roneo stencil machine to print his newsletters. He was also helping out with the magazine *Combat* and, thanks to Camus, ended up editor. Mascolo suggested Camus join his group of irregulars, but Camus, after hesitating, at first refused. Mascolo was busy carrying weapons around, passing on military secrets, walking around with his revolver, taking risks. 'I kept my revolver in the saddlebag of my bike. At home I hid it up the chimney in my mother's sitting room.'[19] Camus was producing pamphlets and writing articles. His and Mascolo's offices were used as postboxes. 'I joined the irregulars because I wanted some action,' Dionys explained. Even the drafting of a pamphlet could lead to arrest and deportation. 'I didn't know that François Mitterrand had been in Vichy, and frankly I couldn't care less, not even now. We were rising up and we were fighting. The National Movement for Prisoners of War and Deportees was not offering its activists any chance of military action. Its men were in the underground.'[20]

Georges Beauchamp was still a runner in the department of labour, which controlled the collaborationist militia – the Milice française, formed in January 1943, made up of volunteers and headed by Pétain's deputy Pierre Laval. To steal the call-up papers for the STO, he and an actress friend used to put on small shows in the building. He'd disappear during rehearsals. One day Georges told Edgar Morin, a spy for the Communist Party and a member of the Resistance propaganda team, 'Just you wait and see, I've got you a great present today.' They went to the avenue Trudaine. The present was Dionys Mascolo. 'I took to him straight away,' said Morin.[21] 'He was calling himself Masse. He hadn't tried too hard with his false name.' Beauchamp, Morin, Mascolo, Benet, Mitterrand and Munier, head of the irregular force, often met in the Antelme family apartment in rue Dupin where Robert's sister Marie-Louise, known as Minette, lived. Marguerite rarely attended the meetings, to which she had in fact not been invited. She carried on with her work as a liaison officer and was soon working on the underground newsletter. She wasn't afraid and never thought of her actions as particularly remarkable.

Robert was still working for Pucheu's cabinet as an editor. He took advantage of his position to compile lists of people sought by the authorities, many of whom were communists, and helped them escape. In October 1943, Mitterrand suggested to his comrades in the Resistance that they start an underground paper and call it *L'Homme libre*. The meetings at Minette's in rue Dupin, where Benet and Mitterrand were living, became more frequent. Mitterrand remembered the warmth of his friendship with the group. He liked Marie-Louise enormously, and found them all to be generous, enthusiastic and above all cultured. In rue Dupin they were as likely to be discussing Stendhal and Faulkner as military advances and the latest from the Russian front.

On All Saints' Day Mitterrand made it clear to those closest to him that he was about to leave for London:

I have my eye on the future and I am preparing myself body and soul to be part of the century. There are those who believe in me and I fear for them. I believe in no one and that makes me fear for myself. But the road ahead is exciting, the stakes are high, and behind this personal quest, there is what we call tactical politics and strategy, the games men play and the understanding of things, which I find absorbing and intriguing.[22]

He left for London during the night of 15–16 November. Four days earlier he had narrowly escaped being arrested by the Gestapo, who had paid his lodgings in Vichy a visit. From London he went to Algiers, where General de Gaulle received him. Mitterrand asked de Gaulle to let him head the Charrette network. De Gaulle refused and suggested he either serve with the expeditionary forces in Italy or as a parachutist. 'He turned down both propositions. I dismissed him. We had no more to say to one another.'[23]

Marguerite was having problems with the end of her manuscript. She saw Lafue, who made encouraging noises, echoed by the poet Robert Desnos and Queneau. Robert and Dionys read it. Again the latter was scathing about the stiffness of her style and the obtrusive influence of American literature. 'She listened to me. My comments had to do with technique, nothing else,' he said. As for Robert, he protected Marguerite and helped her find the strength to continue. He felt that Marguerite had talent and that she should not debase it by producing literature that was overtly feminine, in other words in the style of popular romances. Robert wanted stringency, purity and strength. He believed in Marguerite and thought she could become a great writer as long as she didn't give in to the demons of seduction and to an already evident narcissism. Dionys, on the other hand, was bolder, more sarcastic. He was impressed by her persistence but could still not see a style, a vocation as a writer.

Emotionally Dionys and Marguerite were playing a game of cat and mouse. He was the curled-up cat needing no one, not even Marguerite, getting out his claws if the need arose. She was tormented by the situation. It was war, with the war 'outside' as their accompaniment. Behind closed doors it was love to the death. 'I took her as though to kill her, as though I was going to axe her to death,' Dionys wrote in his diary.[24] 'Marguerite taught me that physical love was an art,' Dionys told me, 'that no other school was as intensely serious or tragic.' Marguerite won. Dionys eventually became her one and only lover. 'After that we stopped being frivolous. At the time we couldn't have coped with the other having an affair.' Marguerite and Robert continued to live their love-friendship, and Marguerite chose not to tell Robert what was going on nor to leave him.

The moment François Mitterrand returned from Algeria via London, at the end of February 1944, he contacted Jacques Benet and Robert Antelme. He moved back into rue Dupin; he went underground and used various false names. On 12 March representatives from the three main organizations for prisoners from the French Resistance met and decided to merge into one organization, to be called Mouvement National des Prisonniers de Guerre et Déportés (National Movement for Prisoners of War and Deportees). Mitterrand became the leader of this officially recognized movement. But soon pressure began to mount at the heart of it. Denunciations, betrayals? Members of the militia and the Gestapo were after them and appeared to have gleaned detailed information on their hiding and meeting places. 'There was treason in the air,' Marguerite told me in 1995. 'I had my suspicions but what could I do? I had no proof. I felt I couldn't trust anyone, not even the members of the group.'

The first of June was a black day. An important meeting of the movement was supposed to be taking place that morning in avenue Charles-Floquet. There was a ring at the door of the apartment. Mitterrand opened the door. A stranger asked to speak to Berard – Jean Bertin's name in the Resistance. Having no reason to suspect him, Mitterrand went to fetch Bertin, who went to the door. The man drew a gun on him and ordered him out. From the window, his helpless friends saw him leave the building, ashen, escorted by the man who'd asked to talk to him. Initially held in the prison of Fresnes, where he was tortured, Bertin was deported to Germany in August. Mitterrand and the others escaped.

There was supposed to be another meeting that same day at 18.00 hours in rue Dupin. Robert, his sister Marie-Louise, Paul Philippe and his wife, and Jean Munier, alias Rodin, head of the irregular forces, were already in the apartment waiting for their friends. Georges Beauchamp was to meet Mitterrand outside Lipp's and they were to make their way to rue Dupin together on foot. Mitterrand, who had not yet acquired a reputation for always being late, didn't come. Beauchamp was growing impatient, pacing, hopping up and down. A few hundred metres away Marguerite was at home. She hadn't been invited to the meeting. Dionys Mascolo left his mother's house in avenue du Maine and made his way on foot to join his friends. Jean Munier wasn't feeling well. In the apartment he was walking around in circles. 'I had a premonition,' he told me in 1996. A breathless Mitterrand arrived outside the Café Flore and whispered to Beauchamp, 'Don't go. I just called. A woman answered, very formal, "Monsieur, you are mistaken." It was Marie-Louise. Wait for me. I'm going to phone again.'

In the Antelme apartment it was as silent as the grave when the telephone rang again. A few minutes earlier Munier had looked out of the window and seen, on the pavement opposite, a tall man in civilian clothes with two policemen. He sensed danger and ran downstairs. At the entrance to the building the police stopped him, demanding to see his papers. He responded with his fist, sped off and didn't stop until he was out of breath. Then he stationed himself at the corner of the street to warn his friends of the trap. Moments later two Gestapo cars turned up. Robert Antelme and Paul Philippe came out, flanked by police. Madame Philippe was confined to the apartment along with Marie-Louise.

Mitterrand called again from a public phonebox in boulevard Saint-German. Beauchamp was lookout. This time Marie-Louise's voice was curt. 'Monsieur, I have already told you, you are mistaken.' Then Mitterrand understood. Later they learned that the man from the Gestapo had been telling Marie-Louise to get her interlocutor to join them right away. Munier saved several of his friends from being caught in the trap. Mascolo was warned outside the Bon Marché. He ran round to rue Saint-Benoît to fetch the lists of names and plans hidden in the chimney. On the way he collected his revolver from under an armchair and threw it into a sewer. That morning Georges Beauchamp had passed Robert Antelme the plans of a German munitions factory. Robert swallowed them before his interrogation.

Paul Philippe and Marie-Louise were deported; Philippe's wife was imprisoned, then released a few months later. She wasn't a Jew. Philippe survived deportation, but Marie-Louise never returned. An inmate of Ravensbrück, she died of exhaustion after the camp was liberated. She didn't have the strength to return to France.

On the evening of that 1 June, Mitterrand called Marguerite at rue Saint-Benoît. He told her there was a fire, the fire was spreading fast and she had ten minutes to get out. She went down and found him waiting in rue de l'Abbaye. 'I looked at you and took rue de l'Université. Only today,' Duras told Mitterrand forty years later, 'do I understand that you were showing me where to go and where not to go. You were barring the way to the rue Saint-Benoît. Only today, forty years on, can I see clearly what your body there in the middle of the road was telling me. Oblivious, I obeyed.'[25] Later on that evening, Mitterrand tracked down Rodin, who gave him a blow-by-blow account of the events in rue Dupin. Mitterrand came to the conclusion that the man who had rung at the door in avenue Charles-Floquet that morning, and the one who had made the arrests in rue Dupin, were one and the same. The man had obviously been given inside information by someone at the heart of the group. Now he knew about the network and was therefore able to continue to go after its members.

Wanting to know where her husband was being held, Marguerite went to the offices of the German police. When she arrived in rue des Saussaies, there were at least a hundred women there who had already been waiting for hours. In the queue, there was a heavily pregnant young woman dressed in black. The Germans had written to inform her that her husband had been shot and she should collect his belongings. The woman had been queuing for twenty hours.

Marguerite waited a day and a night outside the offices of the Gestapo, but in vain. They told her to come back. And so she scoured the railway stations to see if her husband was in any of the convoys of deportees. There were rumours. She thought he might be in Fresnes, and at dawn on 6 June she made her way to that prison with her parcels. She was one of a dozen or so people in the waiting room. She waited patiently. A few hours later the Germans shut the doors. There was the sound of planes over Paris, and the air-raid warning sounded. 'They landed this morning at six o'clock,' a young man whispered. Marguerite didn't believe him. 'It's not true – don't spread false news!'[26] The Germans threw them all out. There would be no parcels that day.

Marguerite returned to rue Saint-Benoît, where Dionys Mascolo joined her. Nicole from downstairs – the seventeen-year-old acting as go-between for their Resistance group – saw them leave on their bikes. They tore back to Fresnes, but food parcels had been suspended. Marguerite went to Fresnes several more times, but in vain. She approached a friend of hers, a secretary at the Ministry of Information and former colleague of Robert Antelme, to get a parcel permit. Her friend told her to go back to rue des Saussaies. She waited three or four days before being admitted to the offices of the German police. At last she reached the office of the man who could perhaps help her, only to be told he was absent. His secretary gave her a note allowing her to return the next morning. He was still not in and her pass expired at midday.

> I go up to a tall man in the corridor and ask him to be good enough to extend my pass till the evening. He asks to see my card. I give it to him. He says, 'But this is the business of the rue Dupin.'
>
> He mentions my husband's name. He tells me it was he who arrested him. And he who was the first to question him. This is Monsieur X., here called Pierre Rabier, an agent of the Gestapo.
>
> 'Are you a relation?'
>
> 'I'm his wife.'
>
> 'Oh! ... It's a bothersome business, this...'[27]

What happened next is described in *La Douleur* in the story entitled 'Monsieur X. Here Called Pierre Rabier'. The man's name was really Charles Delval. As Duras describes it, he talks about Resistance organizations, plans found on the table in the apartment, and asks her if she knows her husband's friends. 'I say I didn't know most of them very well and didn't know others at all, that I wrote books and wasn't interested in anything else.'[28] Delval says he knows; he likes to think he is cultured, chats to her conspiratorially. He feels honoured to have found an interlocutor from the intellectual milieu to which he dreams of belonging. Marguerite hopes that through Delval she'll be able to find her husband, protect him, even get him released.

Marguerite was very depressed at the time, jumpy and extremely anxious. Mitterrand felt responsible for Antelme's arrest, and so did Jacques Benet, who had recruited him into the organization. Dionys Mascolo, who was living with his mother and visiting Marguerite every day, observed the trancelike state she was in. She wasn't eating or sleeping properly. Every night they paced up and down station platforms waiting for the convoys. For reasons of security, Mitterrand asked her to leave the organization. Her only contact was Dionys, who, when not with her, telephoned her regularly. Three weeks went by. The Gestapo hadn't been to search the apartment, so she contacted Mitterrand and asked if she might go back to work for them. He said yes and suggested she work as a liaison agent.

Her first task was to establish contact between two members of the MNPGD – Godard and Duponceau – opposite the Chamber of Deputies. As she was waiting, she ran into Delval-Rabier again. 'I smile at Rabier, I say, "I'm very glad I've run into you – I've tried several times to see you, coming out of the rue des Saussaies. I haven't had any news of my husband." ' Marguerite gave three versions of this meeting.[29] Her overriding feeling was one of fear. Did Delval know of her activities in the Resistance? Was the Gestapo waiting to arrest the three of them? Marguerite was just going up to Godard when Delval appeared, but he didn't notice. Later Marguerite claimed that Mitterrand insisted she should see Delval regularly, but he told me she was the one who asked him and that he had agreed. 'It was only natural, she was desperate to use Delval to get news of her husband.'

What was going on between Marguerite and Delval? An affair? Questioned today, some of her Resistance friends seem to think so. Mitterrand thought it was quite likely, but anyway, what really counted was that 'Marguerite was a loyal friend'. Georges Beauchamp, Mitterrand's comrade in arms, thought Marguerite was playing with fire and enjoying it. Jean Munier thought Marguerite was courting disaster.

According to more recent witness accounts, it would appear that Marguerite was the one who initiated the relationship with Delval. In *La Douleur* she wrote, 'I play along with him, as I often did later, and insist on seeing him again, on making an appointment.' Delval gave her important information: Robert was in Fresnes but likely to be deported to Germany. Marguerite went to Fresnes, hoping to catch a glimpse of her husband; she tried to bribe Delval into taking him a parcel. She wanted to believe Delval had some kind of control over the situation.

She went back to the Resistance group, where the matter was discussed and it was decided that Marguerite could continue to see Delval, but armed protection should be provided by the organization. Georges Beauchamp challenged this:

> François Mitterrand never ordered Marguerite Duras to see Delval on a regular basis. In fact the whole business bothered François. Munier and his boys were sent to protect her. If they'd fired into the crowd Munier could have done nothing to prevent it. But Mitterrand went along with it; what mattered were the lives of Marie-Louise and Robert Antelme. Delval never saw Marguerite as a member of our movement. He saw her as a pretty young woman with whom to have trysts.[30]

Who tried to seduce whom? There was more than an unhealthy attraction between Marguerite Duras and Charles Delval. There were a lot of meetings, one or two a week. Delval would call around midday, to arrange to meet later that day. Delval let drop bits of information, perhaps without realizing it; for example that some of the prisoners were about to be transferred from Fresnes to Drancy.

One evening she telephoned Dionys from Fresnes to tell him to hurry to the Gare de l'Est with cigarettes and sugar. She had just learned from some of the prisoners' wives that Robert could be in the convoy. Dionys called Nicole and they pedalled like mad to the station, but they didn't see Robert.

In the morning of 17 or 18 August Marguerite caught sight of Robert being taken out of Fresnes under armed guard. He was standing on the platform of a bus. With the other prisoners' wives, Marguerite ran after the bus, waving. 'I run after the bus and ask where they're going. Robert L. shouts something. I think I hear him say "Compiègne".'[31]

In the end Delval muttered the name of a secretary working for the prison administration at Compiègne who was open to bribes. Next day Marguerite gave Delval a gold topaz ring. She never met the woman and never saw the ring again. Robert never received her parcels, not at Fresnes, nor at Compiègne.

To Jean Munier, who kept a watchful eye on Delval so that he could protect Marguerite when they were together, it was glaringly obvious: 'Delval was in love with her. In the restaurants where they lunched and drank freely, they gave the impression of being a couple that got on very well. Elegant, conservative, well dressed, with round gold-rimmed glasses, he was the very epitome of the well-to-do bourgeois.' Munier wondered which of the two was going to eat the other. With the benefit of hindsight, he thinks they were both hooked. 'Mitterrand had said to me, "I trust her but keep an eye on her." One day at the end of a meeting, a haggard Marguerite made her way towards me and whispered, "I almost crossed the Rubicon. I won't be going back." '[32] But the affair continued.

Still Delval told her nothing – not what had happened to Robert or Marie-Louise or any of the other friends he had arrested in rue Dupin. Did he actually know anything? Beauchamp continued to disapprove of the meetings and said as much to Mitterrand. Benet agreed with Beauchamp, and thought that the Delval affair was taking too many men away from the organization and that if Delval really was an important man in rue des Saussaies, then Marguerite was neither confident, discreet nor level-headed enough to lead a double life.

Around this time the Resistance was dealt a major blow. Many of the networks were crushed, and the members were running out of steam. To each meeting Mitterrand first sent a liaison officer in his place who automatically changed the time and the venue. Sometimes he sent a second agent who would again change the meeting that had already been shifted. Mitterrand knew there was a mole in the organization and suspected a member of the group. Some of the meetings he attended were followed by arrests. But still he went free. Just how far did the corruption go? Mitterrand didn't know. He was obliged to move around more and therefore to take more risks. The Delval–Marguerite affair weighed heavily on him.

According to Marguerite, her relationship with Delval-Rabier fell into two distinct phases. The first started with Robert's arrest and ended with the meeting where the group asked her to write a letter to François Mitterrand promising 'on my honour to do all I can to help the movement kill Rabier before the police get hold of him, just as soon as I know my husband and sister-in-law are out of his reach'. It was a time of fear – dreadful, overwhelming fear. The second phase, after Dionys had delivered the letter to Mitterrand, continued until Delval's arrest after the Liberation.

At their meetings, Delval is always there ahead of her, waiting, across the street or round the corner from the designated venue. She never finds him waiting for her inside. One day he arranges to meet her at the Café de Flore. She's had time to give a warning, and so two members of the group keep watch. There in front of everyone he takes a revolver and handcuffs out of his briefcase, lays them on the table, opens the briefcase again and gets a bundle of photographs out. He selects one and puts it down in front of Marguerite. ' "Look at this photo," he says. I look. It's Morland [Mitterrand]. The photo's very large, almost life-size. François Morland looks back at me, straight in the eye, smiling. I say, "I don't recognize him. Who is it?" I didn't expect it at all. Beside the photo, Rabier's hands. Shaking. Rabier is trembling with hope because he thinks I'm going to recognize François Morland.' Delval offers her a deal: Robert Antelme will be set free in the night if she tells him where he can find Morland-Mitterrand. 'I say, "Even if I knew him, it would be disgusting of me to tell you what you ask. I don't know how you dare to ask me." '33

Marguerite warns Dionys, who warns Mitterrand, who warns Beauchamp, Munier and the others. During one of the meetings they again discuss the possibility of killing Delval. Mitterrand asks Marguerite to describe the photographs. He comes to the conclusion they must have been stolen during the rue Dupin arrests. Some were portraits taken at the Harcourt studio, others a set taken when a friend got married in Toulouse. But the photos were not only of Mitterrand. They were also of Danièle Gouze, his future wife, and several friends, most of whom were members of the underground. Delval had passed them on to the Gestapo.

Delval has to go. Several ideas are under consideration. Marguerite doesn't know them all. Dionys volunteers. With some of the members of the network, he hatches a scheme that will allow him to kill Delval with complete impunity. He needs an open space, a spot where he can make a quick getaway. No luck; Delval arranges to meet Marguerite on street corners, not in open places. And so Dionys decides to kill Delval in the apartment at rue Saint-Benoît. Marguerite invites him up on several occasions, but Delval doesn't fall for it.

The net is tightening around the MNPGD. In Vichy, on 20 June, a member of the network, Pierre Coursal, is arrested and beaten.

Mitterrand asks Danièle to leave Paris and to go and hide in Cluny. The photographs in Delval's possession have put her in danger. Since the Normandy landings, the Germans have been growing frightened and the members of the Resistance worry about the fate of prisoners. Will they speed up the deportation to Germany or shoot them? Marguerite writes in her diary, 'I can't hold my head up any more ... If he comes back we'll go down to the sea, he'd like that best. Except that I think I'm going to die. And if he comes back I'll die.'[34] Now that Marguerite knows her husband's been moved from Fresnes to Compiègne, the marshalling yard from which trains go to the camps, she loses any qualms she might have about Delval. 'Suddenly there isn't much time. I'm afraid of dying. Everyone's afraid of dying.'[35] She tells Dionys that Delval must be handed over to the movement so that they can kill him before he has time to escape. But Mitterrand has more urgent matters to see to. 'Most of the Resistance movements were falling apart, leaders being arrested; the organizations were decimated,' he explained.[36]

On 7 July Henri Guérin, a close friend of Mitterrand, is arrested and taken to the fourth floor in rue des Saussaies for interrogation. The Gestapo show him the photos of Mitterrand, the ones stolen when the rue Dupin arrests were made. The Gestapo torture Guérin, beat him and plunge him into an excrement-filled bath. All the questions are about Mitterrand and his network. Marguerite keeps her appointments with Delval in the black-market restaurants. Less frightened of him, she tries to get him to talk. 'He's less important already. He's nothing. He's nobody, just an agent of the German police.' However, she's growing impatient with the group for not having executed him yet. Dionys tells her they'll try to kill him in the next few days. 'We'd even chosen the place – in the boulevard Saint-Germain, I can't remember exactly where.'[37]

Dionys Mascolo didn't kill Delval. Had he ever actually intended to? He didn't bow to Marguerite's wishes, and when Delval was arrested and tried, he sought not to condemn him too much. There were several attempts by the military wing of the MNPGD to gun him down but they ended in failure. One was outside Les Deux Magots, another in a nearby street. 'We weren't killers,' Mitterrand later told Marguerite.[38] He had entrusted the task to three men. 'But the situation was very serious. Delval knew a great deal about our ring, he'd already arrested fourteen of our friends. So we decided to kill him.' A specialist in this kind of 'job' who insisted on remaining anonymous told Mitterrand, 'Delval is easy to kill but we'd have to take the little lady as well.' Marguerite had a lucky escape.

Marguerite claimed her relationship with Delval lasted three months. One of their last meetings was on 16 August in a black-market restaurant at the intersection of rue Saint-Georges and rue Notre-Dame-de-Lorette. She describes it in *La Douleur*, the lunch-time crush, the benches covered in artificial leather, the clients, all agents of the Gestapo. Delval-Rabier's a regular. He knows everyone, he's on familiar territory, among collaborators. Marguerite is ashamed and frightened. 'I'm ashamed of sitting here beside Pierre Rabier of the Gestapo, but I'm also ashamed of having to lie to this member of the Gestapo, this hunter of Jews. The shame extends even to the shame of perhaps having to die at his hands.' Marguerite and Dionys have laid a trap. Marguerite has informed her lover where they're to meet. He's come with a friend to identify Rabier. In *La Douleur*, she writes, 'I see them parking their bikes out in the street. It's D. For the second person they've chosen a girl. I look down. Rabier looks at them and then looks away again, he hasn't noticed anything. She must be about eighteen. She's a friend. I could watch them go through a furnace more easily than this.'

The friend was Nicole, the daughter of Suzanne Courant from downstairs. More than fifty years later, she remembered the day vividly. Dionys came to see her and asked if she could go with him to protect Marguerite. They cycled across Paris. There was nothing unusual in this. Nicole had been in the Resistance since the outbreak of war. It was a beautiful day. But Nicole had a problem: she didn't have a lot of time. At three that afternoon she was due to be a witness at a friend's wedding on the other side of Paris. For some reason Dionys was in a hurry too and in a great state of agitation. 'Everything happened very quickly. He told me Marguerite was in such-and-such a restaurant. We had to go and identify some bloke so that we could kill him.' And so Marguerite sees Dionys sit down at a table opposite, with Nicole at his side. 'I was reckless in those days,' Nicole said. 'I told Dionys we had to go and sit near them. We sat down against the light on two benches.'[39]

In *La Douleur* Marguerite describes how Dionys asks the restaurant violinist to play a tune she loves. Marguerite is laughing; she looks at Dionys and he looks back at her, her with Delval. She thinks the Delval affair makes Dionys want her more. She loves the idea that Dionys might execute Delval. Marguerite leaves the restaurant with Delval, watched by Dionys and Nicole. She's had too much to drink. 'It wouldn't take much to make me tell him he's going to be killed.' In a few minutes maybe. They get on their bikes. Delval's in front. She laughs. 'I raise my right hand for a moment and pretend to aim at him – bang! He pedals on into eternity. He doesn't turn around. I laugh. I aim at the back of his neck. We're going very fast. His back stretches out, very big, ten feet away from me.' Before leaving her he suggests they go up to a friend's studio. She says no. He doesn't insist and gives up.

She never saw him again except at his trial.

CHAPTER 6

The Road to Liberation

~

On 17 August 1944, Dionys found himself caught up in violence at the intersection of boulevard Saint-Michel and boulevard Saint-Germain. The irregular forces of the movement also stormed the town halls of Colombes, Bois-Colombes and Asnières. Armed, and with Patrick Pelat and Jean Munier in charge, they took over strategic points in Paris. They had just joined forces with the FFI (Forces françaises de l'intérieur, the French Resistance forces). Munier moved into a building in the Chaussée-d'Antin and occupied the basement of the offices of the *Petit Journal* in rue de Richelieu. The following day, Pelat requisitioned the whole building as well as the printers in rue du Croissant. He gave Dionys Mascolo the job of editing the movement's newspaper *Libres*. The first four issues were sold underground. François Mitterrand signed his name to the first editorials.[1]

> For three days Paris has been fighting. For three days an army raised in each district, in each street has been chasing out the invader and winning us back our right to live ... Now that we can at last shout our joy and hope in public, we should not forget the many dark battles, the many friendships woven and tragically unwoven, the many human exchanges inexorably linked to the most painful of memories.[2]

During this period Marguerite was with Dionys, Georges Beauchamp and Edgar Morin. With Dionys she was part of the campaign that took over the former *Petit Journal* in rue de Richelieu. She started

128

working for *Libres* immediately, first anonymously, then after a few months she wrote her editorials under the name of Marguerite Duras. She accompanied Edgar Morin and his partner Violette when they drove off to occupy the Ministry of Prisoners, in place de Clichy, taken over by the Paris branch of the movement. She then went to 100 rue de Richelieu where a company of some hundred and twenty young men had just moved into the premises. Beauchamp asked her to oversee the arrival of supplies and the cooking. She became a cook and the manager of the canteen to feed the euphoric but famished young men. She and Lisette cooked day and night for the FFI, newly allied to the MNPGD. One day, between meals, she goes out into the streets of Paris to join her friends working on the underground *Lettres françaises* in the offices of *Paris-Soir* guarded by armed members of the FFI. The French flag is flying over the Sorbonne. Two lovers embrace. 'The most beautiful day of our lives,' declares Claude Roy, war correspondent for the newspaper *Front national*. Marguerite has her FFI pass and isn't worried about stray bullets. She walks for hours through a Paris busy liberating itself.

At the junction of rue Jacob and rue Bonaparte, she's caught up in crossfire. 'We'd met up with Claude Roy and were on our way to the Seine. You can't imagine how straight the rue Bonaparte is. German or French, we had no idea, but the firing in this corridor-street was coming from the direction of the river. We went from doorway to doorway. We must have been mad, we should have waited.' The crowds are shouting, throwing flowers. Parades alternate with violent clashes. In rue des Écoles Claude Roy sees pools of blood. Marguerite helps distribute tobacco and bread taken from German lorries.

Over the next few days and nights, the FFI went round picking up collaborators. There were those who wanted to beat them, to interrogate them; they wanted blood, revenge. This was particularly true of a Spanish group. Ignoring her friends' warnings, between meals Marguerite wandered around the building in rue de Richelieu, seeing the arrested collaborators, talking to the FFI, meddling in everything. Dionys was not happy, and nor was Beauchamp. But Dionys and Beauchamp went out into the streets of Paris on military expeditions. 'We carried out difficult military operations,' Beauchamp confirmed, 'we blockaded German convoys and took prisoners. We'd take them to the town hall in the ninth arrondissement or to rue de

Richelieu. We executed no one.' Their fear and risk-taking bolstered their euphoria. 'We did some reckless things during the insurrection. No one except Dionys and I would go out when there were snipers on the roofs,' Beauchamp said. 'Dionys found the whole thing very romantic. These days I realize how lucky we were, given the unnecessary risks we took at times.'³

The movement requisitioned another building in which to assemble and interrogate prisoners, a seedy hotel in rue Beaubourg. But Dionys Mascolo, Georges Beauchamp, Edgar Morin and François Mitterrand were later adamant: each solemnly swore they committed no acts of violence, not even minor ones, against prisoners; instead they hurried to deliver them to police headquarters so that they would be protected from overzealous colleagues who resorted to torture, claiming it would make them talk. According to the historian Pierre Péan, the MNPGD in Paris could be held responsible for only one summary execution. Dionys, Beauchamp and Morin did not allow beatings. But at the heart of the MNPGD there was a yearning for vengeance. Marguerite was sympathetic to the young men who were eager for revenge. In a notebook discovered after her death, dated 24 August 1944, she noted: 'Men shout. They smack their blood-smeared lips. It's sweet. It's milk. This night, 23 August, men forage in the night like newborn babies. Search for the breast. Blood. It's good ...' Further on, in the same unpublished piece, she goes a bit further: 'Festival of blood. Flowers offered. Opened. Instantly. The condemned filled with blood not yet spilt. But already the adorable lips part as they pass. Lips in love ... Disorder. Bliss of bliss.'⁴

As well as performing her duties as canteen manager, Marguerite worked alongside Captain Champion. 'He was a pigheaded, violent bloke,' Beauchamp said. 'They'd go to hotels together to carry out interrogations. There are friends who still think Marguerite Duras's attitude at the time was very hard.' Another fellow Resistance fighter confirmed her violence and her wish to fight the enemy who, in her words, 'had to suffer'.⁵

The Paris insurrection put a stop to the plan to kill Delval. Dionys, on Marguerite's insistence, went to his house in rue des Renaudes to arrest him, but Delval had vanished. A neighbour had denounced him for being pro-German. He'd been arrested and sent to Drancy, but the MNPDG were unaware of this and it was quite by chance that they discovered his whereabouts. Delval had told the police he'd lost his papers. He was on the point of being freed, as the police, after a hasty inquiry, had nothing to charge him with. A member of the MNPDG informed Mascolo of Delval's imminent release. He got there just as Delval was being let go, and arrested him. It was 1 September 1944.

Dionys took Delval to the hotel in rue Beaubourg. The interrogation, led by Mascolo and Mitterrand, could begin. (Morin confirmed that they all had their own prisoners. 'He was our prisoner. We had him put in our prison. From time to time, we had to go to that hotel to collect information, Dionys too. We didn't enjoy it one bit. We saw men in chains, badly beaten, faces covered in blood. There were a lot of North Africans among the prisoners. We were told they were neo-fascist. There was no proof of this. It made us sick.'[6]) Neither of them resorted to violence. Mitterrand wanted to know who had betrayed them and knew Delval was the only one who could tell him. 'We had an intense and fairly frank discussion,' he said.[7]

While Mitterrand continued to try and get proof of guilt out of Delval, Mascolo went to rue des Renaudes to search for incriminating evidence. Delval's wife was there. Paulette Delval described what happened next.

> He was extremely polite. He asked me to accompany him. My mother and little boy were with me. He allowed them to leave. I'd been permitted to see my husband a few days earlier in the prison visitors' room. I learned thanks to Mascolo that he was in the rue Beaubourg. He took me to the rue de Richelieu. When I arrived, a woman – next day I found out it was Marguerite Duras – said, 'As for you, you have no right to a bed, you can sleep on the floor.' In the early hours of the morning, they took me to see my husband in the hotel where he was being held. They had no evidence against him.[8]

All night Mitterrand interrogated Delval in the room in rue Beaubourg, but he didn't get the information he was after – neither the names of the informers in the group, nor any proof of guilt. In 1995 he was still not sure how important Delval had been and wondered whether he hadn't lied about his role in the Gestapo.[9] The day after the interrogation, Mitterrand said that in his opinion, Delval was a poor sod who'd betrayed out of wickedness.[10] Paulette maintained that Marguerite had participated in her husband's interrogations. She claimed she saw Marguerite go into Delval's cell-room in rue Beaubourg. 'The night before, when I arrived at rue de Richelieu, a woman said to Mascolo, "She looks nice but you're going to have to get nasty with her. She's pretty. Pity, we're going to have to damage that one." ' Paulette said she knew what Marguerite had in mind, but Mascolo stood up to Marguerite in front of their comrades in arms. In a fit of pique, she went to join the Spanish in the streets. Next day, Mascolo interrogated Paulette about her husband. 'He was very kind,' she stated solemnly. Then it was Mitterrand's turn. 'He too was very considerate, very polite.'[11]

The two men saw no point in continuing. 'At the time she struck me as naïve and innocent,' François Mitterrand said, 'beautiful and generous, madly in love with her husband,'[12] whom she'd married in 1939. She had obviously told them everything she knew. Delval was working for a petroleum company but had recently become an expert in art objects.

When the interrogation was over, Paulette, in the presence of her husband, was locked up in a room at the rue Beaubourg hotel. One morning Marguerite fetched her and took her to rue de Richelieu. There she blindfolded her and interrogated her for some time, according to Paulette. In a story in La Douleur entitled 'Albert of the Capitals', Marguerite describes a woman, Thérèse, who takes great pleasure in torturing. Who is Thérèse? 'Thérèse is me,' she says in the foreword. 'The person who tortures the informer is me,' she writes. In 'Albert of the Capitals', there is also a D. – Dionys. D. leaves the room to go and eat. Thérèse is alone with two men thirsting for revenge. They shut the door and train the light on the informer's eyes. Thérèse is lonely without D. and among her comrades, for she's the only one to think prisoners should be ill-treated. Her comrades don't have a high opinion of Thérèse, they think she's hard, she shouts too much and too often. No one likes her, except D.; while he doesn't agree with her, he doesn't criticize her either.

Paulette still loved her husband in 1996. 'The man had a heart of gold. He was handsome, tall and blonde with blue eyes. He was always lending people money. Yes, he was pro-German. Before the war he had a German friend, they spent too much time together. And then of course his family was from Alsace.' As far as Paulette was concerned, Delval was a collaborator but not a Gestapo agent. She always denied her husband had had an office in the rue des Saussaies. For a long time afterwards people pointed her out in the street of the suburb where she lived. Her son couldn't go to holiday camps because his father had been a collaborator. When he died, the town hall even refused her permission to bury him.

'Albert of the Capitals' makes grim reading. A man suspected of being an informer is told to undress and is then humiliated by men who want him to confess. Thérèse is in charge of the interrogation. Duras describes the pleasure to be had from torturing. She hides nothing. She exorcises through her writing a moment of perverse pleasure. The reader is spared nothing. The informer's body is described as fat and pink, not made for love, with old shrivelled testicles, the smell of unwashed flesh. Thérèse is slightly embarrassed. But she believes she has a mission: to save the honour of the Resistance, to avenge the dead. For her, the war is not finished. She and D. are not of the same opinion – prisoners are soldiers who have been captured in battle. Thérèse wants to kill them all, but D. hands them over to the police.

It was a time of great confusion for Marguerite. She had no idea how Dionys felt about her and she had no idea what had happened to her husband. Since Robert's arrest nothing had gone on between her and Dionys, though he remained a loyal and thoughtful companion. Marguerite had become Robert's wife again and Dionys was about to have affair with another woman. He thought about it, he set it up. The woman was there, locked up not far from where they were. Her name was Paulette Delval. Did Marguerite intuit this?

Thérèse doesn't hit the victim. She orders her men to hit him. Marguerite never hit anyone. Words can be more painful than blows. 'Go ahead,' says Thérèse. She encourages them to hit harder, faster. 'The more they hit and the more he bleeds, the more it's clear that hitting is necessary, right, just.' During the interrogation the door opens and the others come in. They don't all approve of what's going on. D. has still not returned. 'Go to it,' Thérèse tells the men she's supervising. 'It's not enough yet.' The informer lies on the ground, naked, badly beaten. The men carry on, their fists bloodied. Thérèse is flushed with pleasure. The words must be read over and over again.

'Thérèse jumps up and says, "Don't stop any more. Then he'll tell."
An avalanche of blows. It's the end.'
D. stops the massacre, and tells Thérèse to go and get some sleep.
'Thérèse picks up a glass of wine and drinks. She can feel D. looking
at her. The wine is bitter. She sets the glass down.' You have to strike.
'There will never be any justice in the world unless you yourself
are justice now.' And Marguerite believed that all her life. When I
broached the subject in 1994, she gave a wave of the hand to indicate
she didn't want to discuss it. But when *La Douleur* was published in
July 1985, she was interviewed for *Les Cahiers du cinéma*, and admitted
that she'd tortured a man and that she had no regrets. In 1991, she
explained.

> It can happen just like that – you torture someone, you become a cop.
> It couldn't be helped. I'm not saying I regret it. And I'm not saying I'm
> happy or unhappy I did it. All I'm saying is it can happen ... It was
> horrible. Horrible. The man was bleeding, he'd been beaten, he was fat
> ... Well, torturing the guy couldn't be avoided, and that's all there is to
> it, it just couldn't. It was something I had to do. I think my hate was so
> great it was killing me. I didn't want to kill him. He didn't die. But not
> to have tortured him. No. And that's all there is to it.[13]

I came across the shorthand notes of this interview in Marguerite's
cardboard boxes after she died. It was filed away with the *La Douleur*
notebooks. In the margin she'd written, 'It must never happen to me
again, never.' In blue ink, in capital letters, she had added, 'These are
stories that happened.'

On 14 September 1944, Charles Delval was handed over to the
French criminal police. That same day Mascolo freed Paulette Delval.
'They took me to my mother's house. Next day I went home; everything had been stolen.'[14]
A court of investigation was set up. Charles Delval stated he was
an agent working for the German authorities in rue des Saussaies, his
profession: art expert. He admitted to having a great admiration for
the German people: 'I admire that disciplined nation, its institutions,
its faith and courage.' His first contact with them had been when he
was arrested by their department in rue de la Pompe on suspicion of

Gaullism. Having convinced them of his good faith, he was subsequently released. A few days later he got himself taken on in rue de Saussaies. He 'accompanied the Germans and was put in charge of searches and checking papers found in suspects' homes'. He confessed to having participated in the arrests of Resistance members. Delval disclosed he had also saved, through the intermediary of the Germans in rue des Saussaies and in return for a substantial sum (300,000 to 400,000 francs), Jews interned at Drancy and Compiègne.[15]

Paulette Delval wasn't allowed to see her husband and could only communicate with him through his lawyer, Maitre Floriot, who had defended him before the war in a business matter. One afternoon there was a ring at the door in rue des Renaudes. Paulette answered. It was Dionys Mascolo. 'I hear you were burgled while you were being questioned. I've come to apologize and return your belongings. I found some photographs. I've brought them back.' Paulette thanked him. As she was closing the door, Dionys insisted on seeing her again. Paulette agreed to meet Mascolo for dinner in a restaurant in two days' time.[16]

Meanwhile, the investigations continued. The second time Delval was examined, he insisted that he had never denounced anyone to the German authorities, and that the only arrests he had ever made were of members of the MNPDG. There was a Delval–Marguerite confrontation. Marguerite gave evidence against him. Delval alleged that he had saved Marguerite Antelme from being charged when her husband and friends were arrested in rue Dupin, where he had found the plans of German installations on the table. Marguerite told the police she had doubts over his true identity and that she suspected him of being on a secret mission for the Germans. Delval vehemently denied the accusation levelled against him that he was a spy. 'As to being involved in any kind of mission in France once the Germans had left, that's pure fantasy. I might have said as much to Madame Antelme to impress her.'

Between the end of the investigations and the beginning of the trial, Dionys paid court to Paulette. 'He wasn't bad-looking. We saw a lot of one another because of the business with my husband. Mascolo promised he would do everything he could to save him,' she told me.[17] Later, Dionys and Paulette would have a child. Dionys always maintained Marguerite never knew about his affair with Paulette, let alone about the child. Paulette never saw Marguerite again.

Delval's trial opened on 4 December 1944. For reasons still unclear today, he was put on trial with Bony and Lafont, two sinister *Gestapists*, although he was never mixed up in the gang's activities. On 7 December, 'Delval confessed to almost everything. Tall, blond, wearing horn-rimmed glasses, his voice composed, conspicuous for his cynicism and self-control,' the journalist André Marianne observed. He said there were two traitors in the MNPDG. Mascolo took the witness stand to confirm this. Three days later the judge cross-examined Marguerite Antelme. The MNPDG newspaper *Libres* reported: 'Quietly, confidently, our friend gave her account of those fatal days in June and July 1944 as the net closed around our movement. She told of her enforced relationship with Delval, the lengths he went to to get her to identify Morland, the prisoners he boasted having deported to Germany.' Her deposition was heard in deadly silence. Marguerite said she had nothing but hate and contempt for Delval and described her shame. The jury was greatly affected by her statement. No one was in any doubt. Not Delval's lawyer, not the courtroom, not André Marianne, who wrote, 'Thanks to Madame A., Delval's fate was sealed today.'

Throughout the proceedings, Mascolo had kept reassuring Paulette Delval, who did not attend the trial, that her husband would be all right and that there was no way he could be linked to the gang of assassins. But when Floriot told her of Marguerite's deposition, she lost all hope and begged Mascolo to find a way to save him. Paulette Delval claims Mascolo made Marguerite go to Floriot's house the night of 11–12 December 1944. Marguerite offered to retract her earlier statement. Floriot wasn't sure, he thought the jury might be suspicious, but since everything looked so bleak, he accepted Marguerite's offer.

Floriot was right. No one could understand what she was trying to do. The second time she gave evidence, there was uproar in the courtroom. Marguerite appeared to hesitate, she was awkward, contradicting her previous statement. She said, 'Delval always behaved very correctly towards me and always refused the money I offered him to save my husband. He did, however, say he had intervened on his behalf.' She added:

One day he told me he had to arrest a Jew. The Jew was not in. He and the other policemen had to break down the door. The people really were out, they were not hiding, there was nobody in the apartment. On the table there was a child's drawing, and under the drawing, it said 'To my darling daddy' or something like that. Delval said, 'I left. I didn't have the heart to arrest the father.'

THE JUDGE: Unfortunately he arrested many others!

MARGUERITE ANTELME: Maybe ... but, anyway, your honour, I'm here to clear my conscience, not Delval's. My husband's in Germany, I don't even know if he's still alive. Yet despite all that, I wanted to tell the truth.

THE JUDGE: Your honesty does you credit.

But at the end of the trial, a woman came forward and said Delval had asked her for 400,000 francs to get her husband out of a camp in Alsace. He got the money, her husband was released. Did this witness statement sway the jury? When the verdict came all the accused were sentenced to death. One of them had a heart condition and died before sentence was pronounced. Delval showed no emotion. His wife said he waited quietly for death, reading and writing in his cell.

Charles Delval was shot at the beginning of 1945. His lawyer was present, and Delval gave him a letter for Paulette in which he assured her of his love. Paulette and Dionys's son was born six months later.

Two weeks after the trial ended, on 28 December 1944, Marguerite Duras's second novel, *La vie tranquille*, was published at last.[18] The Gallimard reader Marcel Arland had again strongly opposed the publication of Marguerite's novel, and Raymond Queneau's report had been quite critical: muddled narrative, lack of control and too marked an American influence – chiefly Faulkner. Yet he stressed that despite its faults the book was publishable, and he edited it himself. Queneau still had the office next to Dionys Mascolo. At the time Marguerite was a regular visitor to Gallimard. She even did the odd job for them from time to time, which was how she came to be paid by Gallimard in November 1944 for correcting the proofs of *Patrice ou l'été du siècle* written by her old comrade in arms, Pierre Lafue. It was Raymond Queneau who commissioned her to do it. She was still seeing André Thérive regularly. He was the Gallimard author she'd used to get *Les impudents* published. His name appeared along with those of Céline, Drieu La Rochelle, Charles Maurras and Henry de Montherlant on a recently drawn-up list of writers banned by the French society of authors.

She was also very busy writing political editorials for the newspaper *Libres*. She supported purges and the imposition of heavy sanctions on collaborators. Her condemnation of Delval in her first statement to the court proved just how determined she could be. Some of her friends in the Resistance were critical of her intransigence. They were appalled that Delval had been sentenced to death and would have preferred him to be imprisoned so that they could find out who the informer in the group had been. And yet Marguerite had no qualms about her novel being published by Gallimard, even though there was a demand that sanctions be imposed on Gaston Gallimard by the committee responsible for purges.[19] Marguerite complained that the book's launch did not get a high enough profile from Gallimard, but in fact it attracted a great deal of attention for a second novel and by the summer of 1945 the initial print run of 5500 copies had sold out.[20]

La vie tranquille is a short novel divided into three parts. The action takes place on the parental farm, set, like *Les impudents*, in Duras country. The subject is also similar, a sombre family drama with – once again – the predominant perverse relationship between a brother and a sister. For the most part the book was written in 1943 during the holiday she had spent in Doubs with Robert. Every day Marguerite had gone for long walks in search of adventure, allowing herself to be overcome by the fear nature can bring. Every night she wrote. As she went along, Marguerite had sent Dionys the pages Robert had corrected. The husband had encouraged, the lover criticized.

The heroine is twenty-six. Her name is Françoise and she's lived on a farm since she was a child. Françoise likes to swim and to feel the cool running water ripple over her body. And when she's out riding the mare, she likes to feel the animal's panting through her body and to lift her skirts so that she can feel the powerful sweaty flanks in contact with her naked thighs. Only one boy has ever got close to her, the handsome Tiène, the Dionys character. He's her brother's friend and one day he moves into the farmhouse. Sometimes Tiène goes up to Françoise's room at night. When he vanishes, in much the same way as he arrives unannounced, she thinks she's going to die.

Three deaths occur and Françoise is directly or indirectly responsible for them all. Death doesn't frighten Françoise. She is there when they close the coffins, watches fearlessly over the dying and looks on unmoved as a man drowns. Françoise is death's young fiancée. Françoise drives her brother to murdering his uncle before committing suicide. It was while writing the novel that Marguerite had learned of her brother Paul's death. The pain she felt is translated in the book. Her brother, her love, her protector is gone and the physical, sensual, spiritual love she had for him is fully described in *La vie tranquille*. Françoise goes to the cemetery to find him: 'I'd like to kiss the empty sockets of his eyes. To breathe these blinded eyes to know my brother's smell.' Marguerite never visited her brother's grave in Saigon, but for at least a month, she wailed night and day and literally banged her head against the wall. Marguerite said the book came pouring out of her. She soon forgot it, however, and when she reread it in 1993, she was struck by its depth. 'It was a book that came out in one breath, in the banal and very dark logic of a murder. It's possible to see beyond the book itself, beyond the murder in the book.'[21]

Marguerite was still waiting in anguish for Robert. She was going around collecting 'information on the movement of prisoners and transfers from one camp to another', which she then published in *Libres* in September 1944. She was also seeing a lot of Suzie Rousset, who was still without news of her deported husband David. Together they preserved meat, helped returning prisoners of war and tried to find out where their husbands were. They also discussed politics. Marguerite claimed she was passionately communist. She criticized the silent majority of the French who had just accepted Pétain's paternalism, who were frightened of the Russians and were never openly committed during the Occupation. Those who today make up modern-day France, she wrote in 1945, 'do not know and will never know that one can suffer from honour'.[22]

Marguerite was bearing up but she couldn't eat, couldn't sleep, she cried and was slowly sinking deeper into depression, as we see in this extract from a notebook written at the time:

Two plates on the kitchen table. D. and her. Even the bread looks dead. They're dead, their stomachs empty. Every day they die for want of bread. And the calculation begins again: a finger for a piece of bread. Lying on the ground, corpses in place of wheat, corpses but no bread.

How can a being, a hungry being, preserve his self-respect, continue to grow in harmony with himself, think of his soul, pray to God. How can he continue to be a part of the human race, which involves living life to the full.

In Buchenwald, a Belgian teacher died. Nine of his students witnessed his death and when it was over, they took his bread. They broke it into nine parts.[23]

Several people testified to how thin and lethargic she was.[24] Day and night Dionys watched over her. He told her she was mad. 'Yes, I am mad, it's written on my forehead,' she declared.[25] Marguerite 'sensed' Robert's death, she was certain of it. In her diary she wrote: 'He's been dead for a fortnight. Fourteen days, fourteen nights, abandoned in a ditch. The soles of his feet exposed. With the rain, the sun, the dust of the victorious armies all falling on him. His hands are open.' She decided that on being officially informed of her husband's death, she'd commit suicide: 'alive I shall die for him.'

As a journalist with *Libres*, Marguerite received military information as it came in. Whenever the liberation of a camp was announced, it gave her more anguish than joy. She wrote: 'I can't take any more. I keep thinking something's going to happen. It's not possible. I should describe this waiting in the third person. Compared to this waiting I no longer exist.'[26]

Then on 23 April 1945:

Silence. Silence. Silence. No change. And yet change. I stood and I went to the middle of the room. It happened in the space of a second. What's happening to me? The dark night is at the window watching me, I draw the curtains. Still it watches me. What's happening to me? ... Robert Antelme, who's he? You're waiting for a dead man, okay let's go see a dead man then, yes, right, let's go then.

No more pain, I'm on the point of realising there's no longer anything in common between this man and you. Who is this R.A.? Has he ever existed? What is it that makes him Robert and not someone else? What have you been playing at for the last couple of weeks working yourself up? Who are you? What's going on in that room. Who am I? D. knows who I am. Where is D.?

The following day, 24 April, Marguerite learned that Robert was still alive, or at least he had been alive two days before. Witnesses saw him in a column during the evacuation of Buchenwald. Mitterrand and his friends redoubled their efforts and inquiries.

On his return, Robert would tell Marguerite and Dionys that he had walked for ten days before his column was broken up at Bitterfeld. The survivors were put on a train to Dachau. When they arrived they were in a state of unimaginable exhaustion. After that, accounts of Robert Antelme's return differ. Those of Mitterrand and Marguerite are the same.

Summoned by de Gaulle, Mitterrand flew to Dachau on 1 May 1945 as a member of an American-led military mission. Crossing an enclave of corpses, he heard someone murmur his name. He went over to the man, who was barely breathing, and cradled him in his arms, unable to identify him. Robert had recognized his voice. He asked Mitterrand to take him with him, but the Americans refused to let him.

Mitterrand called Marguerite from Germany, saying, 'Listen carefully. Robert's alive. Now keep calm. He's in Dachau. Listen very, very carefully. Robert is very weak, so weak you can't imagine. I have to tell you – it's a question of hours. He may live for another three days like that, but no more. D. and Beauchamp must start out today, this morning, for Dachau.'[27]

The story became a legend. Robert got out alive, and it would appear that Mitterrand saved his life. But the sequence of events was not quite as described by Marguerite and Mitterrand in their respective accounts.

Following a request from General Lewis of the US forces, a delegation of members from the Provisional Consultative Assembly was set up on 30 April to record the liberation of certain camps in Germany. Dachau had been liberated the day before. Mitterrand was on the delegation as president of the MNPGD. Their first stop was Landsberg, a so-called convalescence camp, where the ditches were filled with snow-covered corpses. Not a single survivor. Those who saw it never forgot.[28] At midday the delegation made its way to Dachau. Mitterrand was in the American general-staff hut when Bugeaud, another MNPGD member, who'd gone off to look around, came tearing back shouting, 'I've found Leroy [Robert Antelme's Resistance name].'

'We ran over to the sanitary block and found Robert in the shower,' Jacques Benet said. 'He was shivering and weak. He spoke in a dying voice.' To this day Jacques Benet can't forgive himself for not insisting that the Americans allow them to take Robert with them. Mitterrand begged, but orders were orders. They talked of the risk of typhus and of sanitation quotas. So, the men returned to Paris without him. Before they left, Robert wrote Marguerite a deeply moving letter, 'My darling, a stolen letter. Stolen from time, from the misery of the world, from suffering. A love letter.' He'll be home soon. He knows he has the will to live. He's thinking of her. 'Goodbye, Marguerite, you can't imagine how painful your name is to me.'

The moment he touched down in Paris, Mitterrand arranged to meet Georges Beauchamp. Mitterrand told him that the camp was under quarantine and that huge numbers of inmates were continuing to die. 'Find someone to go with you,' he said. 'You'll need passports, petrol coupons, staff permits.'

Beauchamp went to Mitterrand's house and borrowed his colonel's uniform. Then he thought of Dionys, his assistant during the Liberation, and borrowed a lieutenant's uniform as well. Next morning Mitterrand provided them with mission orders issued by the DGER. They set off at once in George's recently repaired old car, driving nonstop. 'Fighting was still going on around Dachau,' Beauchamp remembered.

The camp guards were wearing gas masks. They wouldn't let us in unless we agreed to take the masks. In the camp the Americans were executing members of the SS. We spent hours looking for Robert. We searched in huts and between the huts. Living and dead had been thrown together. We found him, one of a group of people standing around. It was a beautiful day. It was he who called to us. He was standing in an alley, between the blocks. He weighed thirty-five kilos. We hadn't recognized him.[29]

With the help of a communist detainee, they took over a sentry

without dying. But he couldn't go on not eating without dying. That was the problem.'[33] His body wouldn't even take a drip. Dr Deuil watched over him night and day. He saved Robert, and Marguerite saved him too. Her devotion, self-sacrifice and selflessness were amazing. Anne-Marie visited Robert regularly in the rue Saint-Benoît, but it was Marguerite who looked after him. Between Marguerite and Robert it was for life.

Marguerite told me she couldn't remember the early days of his return. Her memory was a complete blur. As Georges Beauchamp saw it, 'Robert was returning to Marguerite. While he'd been in the camp he thought about her all the time, forgetting he'd ever left her.' Her generosity and courage were such that Georges forgave Marguerite everything, her infidelities, disloyalties, exaggerations, even her narcissism.

Dr Deuil waited four weeks before telling Marguerite that Robert would live. During the whole of this period Beauchamp and Mitterrand were regular visitors, and Dionys was there virtually all the time. Robert confided in him a lot. When his strength returned, he went out for walks with David Rousset, who weighed thirty-eight kilos when he returned from the camp. Suzie and Marguerite would join them on these slow walks.

In mid-June, at Benet's suggestion, Robert and Marguerite went to a convalescent home for returning deportees, which the MNPGD had just opened near Verrières-le-Buisson.

Like so many deportees, Robert would experience terrible feelings of guilt: Why me and not the others? On 21 June 1945, he sent Dionys his first letter as a 'solidified living being', which is how he referred to himself. 'It is to you that I write first for I want you to nurture, for a little longer at least, the wonderful feeling of having saved a man.' In this long letter, written on Paper Allocation Agency letterhead, Robert Antelme first set down in black and white his thoughts on the effects of his return and the changes in his self. He asked to be forgiven, for 'in hell you say everything'. Having fought to return to the human race, to be a man who could hold himself upright, who could eat, talk, even sleep a little, Robert didn't know how to be morally reborn into the world. His mind was unbalanced and he knew it. Like a phenomenologist, he observed himself striving for self-knowledge. He drew strength from his understanding of philosophy – his compass as he embarked on a thrilling yet morbid journey to reconquer himself. He studied the slowly emerging new being like an entomologist studying a chloroformed insect – with interest and rigour. 'It will not all have been pointless and I progress painfully in a good solitude,' he told Dionys. 'Sometimes my sense of honour is still too strong, but that too will no doubt soon be ironed out, neutralized. And then perhaps I shall accept the likeness to myself because I shall know it is not: I shall accept the portrait: there will be no more portrait.'

Meanwhile Marguerite kept a watchful eye on the progress of her book. Witness the irate letter she sent her editor Gaston Gallimard from the rest home the day Robert was communicating his existential turmoil to Dionys:

> For reasons with which you are familiar, I have until now been psychologically incapable of looking after my book *La vie tranquille*. Since its publication, in other words since January 1945, I have had neither the time nor the inclination to see to my interests. Today however I feel able to do something, particularly since no one – and I say this without acrimony – no one has been dealing with it in my absence and my book has been left high and dry.

Having established that her book had sold out, Marguerite raised the alarm over the situation of young writers at the end of the war. In the dramatic way she draws attention to herself, which she would use time and again, we detect her determination to be an author in her own right, her fear of remaining for ever unknown:

> Michel Gallimard whom I saw for five minutes some three months ago informed me that for the time being there are no plans to reprint my book and that authors like Aragon and Eluard were in the same situation. *I cannot agree.*[34] Aragon and Eluard can *wait*. Firstly they have money. Secondly they are not likely to be forgotten. *I need money and I am likely to be forgotten.* ... Sir, will you reprint my book? You could not have treated my book with more contempt had it been a flop. What am I to do in the face of such indifference? I never go to see you, know no one and belong to no literary circles. Is that why?
> This really is most tiresome! Tell me what the young should do if

after four years there is still no one willing to help them, and if they are still being treated like the pains in the arse of the era?

Marguerite was right to fight. On 11 July, Gaston Gallimard sent her a three-page letter justifying his decisions. He set out the problems with paper suppliers, the rising costs of production, the rapid depreciation of novels by young authors. Being polite and wise, he assured her of her talent: 'I liked your book very much. I know the place you should have and will no doubt have.' A clever, pragmatic man, he came up with a proposal regarding the reprint: 'Many are the authors at the *NRF* who, conscious of the state of things, provide the paper needed to produce their book. Is there no way you could help out in this way? It would greatly facilitate matters.'

In August the book was reprinted, with a run of 6500 copies. Marguerite had contacted the neighbour from downstairs, who had replaced her at the Paper Agency. Madame Courant arranged for 800 kilos of paper to be delivered to Gallimard.

Marguerite was living with Robert again. Anne-Marie, whom she had contacted when Robert was deported, was a frequent visitor to the rest home. Dionys's friendship with Robert was so very intense that it monopolized him completely. Marguerite didn't know where her heart belonged. She loved Dionys, with whom she had resumed sexual relations, but what she was experiencing with Robert was binding them together. And Dionys was beginning to avoid her. For the present the love was between the two men and Marguerite was an outsider. She could feel it, could intuit it. From the rest home she wrote to Dionys:

> I'm coming to Paris on Tuesday. Robert is asleep. He loves you very much. He told me he thought he was wearying you.
> We shall probably never be together again.
> Everything's a mess! I'll never have your child . . .
> We don't want to live with anyone. We won't have that child.
> I wait to grow old and good. To die. Who will save us from this affliction of the heart?[35]

At the end of June Dr Deuil told Robert he could go somewhere for a rest but under medical supervision. Marguerite and Robert went to Saint-Jorioz and stayed in a hotel on Lake Annecy. Robert learned to walk properly again, to eat, to breathe. He hadn't said much since they told him of his sister Marie-Louise's death. 'It was at night. His youngest sister and I were there. We said, "There's something we've been keeping from you." He said, "Marie-Louise is dead." We stayed together in the room till daylight, without speaking about her, without speaking. I vomited. I think we all did. He kept saying, "Twenty-four years old." Sitting on the bed, his hands on his stick, not weeping.'[36] Marguerite respected his silence.

From post-Liberation Paris, Mitterrand wrote to Marguerite and Robert:

Everyone's out dancing all of the time. The nation-king laughs and feasts. Anniversary after anniversary. Liberation after Liberation. People are decorated mechanically. The fireworks splutter. The cops are being honoured. Every honest man knows they were heroes.

All that is not very serious. Pleasure is at last running out of steam. However much Thorez [leader of the French Communist Party] goes on about production, it is through singing that the Revolution will come and not through work.

Robert was gloomy. In the hotel a convalescing young deportee with a shaved head played the harmonica. Marguerite wandered the forest, leaving Robert to his thoughts. For hours he stared at the ripples the breeze made on the lake. Can the surface of things be punctured? he asked Marguerite. In the field next to the hotel, where the washing was spread out to dry, a former German soldier scythed the grass. Robert was waiting for Marguerite to talk but Marguerite initially said nothing. Was he hoping their life together would revert to what it was before? He had thought about her constantly during his ordeal in the camp. She was a beacon, his motherland, his anchor in reality.

Anne-Marie came to see Robert and stayed for a few days at the hotel. Dionys eventually made the journey too. He arrived just after the dropping of the atomic bomb on Hiroshima. In *La Douleur*, Marguerite writes, 'It's as if he [Robert] would like to lash out, as if he's blinded by a rage through which he has to pass before he can live again. After Hiroshima I think he talks to D. D. is his best friend,

Hiroshima is perhaps the first thing outside his own life that he sees or reads about.'

Marguerite was there, by Robert's side, like a caring mother, a loving friend, attentive, compassionate. But she was going to leave without him. 'I told him we had to get a divorce, that I wanted a child by D., that it was because of the name the child would bear. He asked if one day we might get together again. I said no.'[37]

CHAPTER 7

The Party

~

'We in the underground, ghosts come back to life, we did not know then that many of us would abandon reality and slowly become ghosts once more.' In *Autocritique*, Edgar Morin captured the pervading climate of troubled exhilaration in which their small group of liberated liberators floundered. The future no longer belonged to them, and disenchantment was setting in as they viewed tomorrow being planned without them. Political life again centred on the National Assembly and the government. The revolution had not come. Mitterand had joined the tiny party born of the Resistance – the UDSR (Union démocratique et socialiste de la Résistance/the Democratic and Socialist Union of the Resistance) – but the Resistance itself appeared to have been forgotten.

Marguerite blamed the Catholic Church. She wrote in her diary:

> Right now, the hunger of those who do not share our hate makes us want to vomit. The Church is quaking in its cassock because it's scared of the ravages it will cause, this hunger of the people's bestial reaction … The Church will have them once again swallow the Nazi crime, the black host of the Nazi crime. The Church makes no distinction between Nazi crime and God's blows. Hitler is His dearest lost sheep. Filth, filth.[1]

She and her friends had known revolutionary fervour during the days of the Liberation, then euphoria as Robert returned to life. It was impossible to imagine life ever being the same again, to imagine themselves thrown back into humdrum monotony. The fall would be hard. In a country weak and shivering, the time was not right for avant-gardists and utopians to dream of creating a new world order.

As the summer of 1945 drew to a close, Marguerite and Robert returned to the flat in rue Saint-Benoît and learned what had happened to Betty Fernandez. After her husband had died of an embolism a few months after the Liberation, Betty went to ground in her apartment. She thought Ramon's death meant she would be forever exempt from the judgement of men. But mid-summer came and Betty Fernandez-Van Bowens, of Hungarian origin, was arrested, shorn and paraded through the streets of the Latin Quarter. Duras would make her live again in *Hiroshima mon amour*; the twenty-year-old woman, head shaved, paraded through the streets of Nevers as the Marseillaise booms out, is also her. 'I can remember her grace,' Duras wrote in *The Lover*, 'it's too late now for me to forget, nothing mars its perfection still, nothing ever will, not the circumstances, nor the time, nor the cold or the hunger or the defeat of Germany, nor the coming to light of the crime.'

For a long time Marguerite was torn between her desire for vengeance so violently expressed in the early days of the Liberation and her longing for a peaceful future, represented at the time by the banner of a communism that promised to free the world. She wasn't the only one to be tormented by the poisonous past that some would have liked to see erased. Intellectuals were divided over the purgings. Should we forget? Can a nation be reconciled only by agreeing to forget the horror? François Mitterand criticized Albert Camus for his contempt for charity. Camus challenged both hatred and forgiveness. So did Marguerite.

In November 1945 Robert made his position on the subject of revenge quite clear in the magazine *Vivants*. There were still German POWs on French soil and there were those who objected to their being well treated. But the death of one former enemy can never erase millions of deaths. 'Only the victory of the ideas and way of life they died defending can have any sense of vengeance,' Antelme said. Neither hatred nor forgiveness could eradicate what the victims should never have seen, what they should never have had to experience. 'Only respect for man will allow us to live together once more.

To preserve that hatred, to play at being barbarians will keep us locked up in the prison of war. And what is more, to the folly of vengeance, to secret abstentions, to the cowardly acts of those unharmed, we say: no.'

Marguerite had been a communist since 1944. She hadn't consulted anyone about joining, not even Dionys. She said she was euphoric when she joined the clandestine PCF (Parti communiste français/French Communist Party), based at the time in the Catacombs.[2] On her return to Paris she became an activist. She belonged to cell 722. Like any self-respecting militant, she used party jargon and therefore believed she was fighting for a world where equality and justice would prevail. Several witnesses, notably Jacques-Francis Rolland, Edgar Morin, Claude Roy and Dionys Mascolo, recalled the passion with which – whatever the weather – she used to sell the party's newspaper *L'Humanité* in her area on a Sunday morning. She very conscientiously recorded in a notebook the number of copies sold each week (usually around forty to fifty) and how regularly she attended cell meetings. She was proud to belong to a party that presented itself as the 'party of the shot', to don her resistant patriotism and enjoy the same kind of prestige as the Red Army.[3] Marguerite was a communist because it was the party of the working classes, because it defended the poor and the pure. But she was a particular kind of communist, a euphoric, utopian, idealistic communist. In the same way that she had suddenly and briefly dropped out of her comfortable student life to work night and day for the Salvation Army, so Marguerite gave herself body and soul to the Party. Night after night, she left Robert and Dionys discussing the future of the world while she went off to carry out with dogged devotion her work as a militant. She couldn't tolerate anyone challenging the Party. Dionys wrote in his diary, 'Marguerite, her genuineness, her distress, her inability to lie, and her terrible insincerity.' She'd put on her so-called communist uniform – army jacket and fur-lined boots – to go and ring at doors, stride around the streets and go into cafés where she'd collar people and spread the good news. There is a very stern photograph of her on an official campaign. The writer Jacques Audiberti, who loved her dearly and who called her 'my little sister', would tease her fondly whenever he saw her at the Café Flore or Les Deux Magots: 'And how's my darling little Chekist?' he'd ask.

From time to time she took her concierge, Madame Fossez, along on her trips and eventually persuaded her to join up. To Marguerite, Madame Fossez was 'the' proletarian. There were in fact not many of these glorious representatives of the Latin Quarter proletariat to join the Party. They were fought over. So Marguerite wooed Madame Fossez and took her along when she did her rounds.

Robert and Dionys preferred books to following orders. Marguerite and Dionys listened for nights on end to Robert. They were forever transformed by what he told them; it was a kind of revelation. Crushed to the core of their beings by the Nazi denial that Jews belonged to the human race, they became Judaized – Jewish, had it been possible. Edgar Morin recalled his special status within the rue Saint-Benoît group because he was a Jew, 'a real one,' Morin said laughing. 'I had something extra. In their eyes, I was endowed with an existential and philosophical aura that gave my opinions added depth.'[4] This Judaization of their being never deserted them and it left its mark on many of Marguerite's books. Many of her fictional characters are Jewish, have Jewish names or are taken for Jewish. Even when it is not explicitly there, it can be the clue to understanding certain obscure recurring themes. As though she is constantly asking forgiveness, as though plagued, tormented by guilt.

At the time the 'Jewish question' – and its aftermath – was not exactly on the public agenda. Jews were embarrassing. The general reaction to the few camp survivors who dared speak out was in effect indifference. Very few postwar intellectuals and politicians denounced the anti-Semitism of Vichy or concerned themselves with the moral and intellectual consequences of the Holocaust. The newspapers at the time made references to the 'persecution of non-Aryans'. Not once during Marshal Pétain's interminable trial was the term 'anti-Semitism' ever used. And Mitterand never referred to it in his newspaper *Libres*. It was Albert Camus in 1948 who first broached the subject in his preface to Jacques Mery's book *Laissez passer mon peuple*.

Even before Robert returned from the camp, Marguerite had had first-hand experience of the authorities' problems in dealing with the deportation. In the autumn of 1944, Edgar Morin, prominent in the MNPGD, had suggested Marguerite and Dionys might mount an exhibition on Hitlerian crimes. The Ministry of Justice appointed some of their own to help out, who lost no time in creating an atmosphere in which it was impossible to work. A disgusted Marguerite was the first to leave, but the documents on concentration camps lent her by the Americans while she was preparing the exhibition remained forever imprinted on her memory.

All three of them, Robert, Dionys and Marguerite, wanted to be as though in exile. Avid readers of Marx and Hölderlin, they felt their only homeland was this land of friendship. 'The life of the mind between friends, thought formed in the written or verbal exchange of words are indispensable to those who search. Otherwise we are ourselves without thought,' wrote Hölderlin. They sought to put his philosophy into practice and debated heavy moral issues. Together, they strove to understand and analyse the extent of the Jewish genocide. In response to the enormity of the Holocaust, Marguerite Duras created the fictive character Aurélia Steiner, born in Auschwitz. The Americans had told Marguerite that some fifty children had been born and grown up in Auschwitz. Some had survived. None said 'I'. All they knew were their numbers. For a long time Marguerite dreamed of the extermination of Germany: 'I was punishing the Germans and Germany for having killed the Jews. It was an extremely violent, terrifying and exhilarating dream.'[5]

'Pity I'm not Jewish,' Duras said. 'Even writing won't make me Jewish.' In February 1996, Dionys Mascolo explained to me that not being Jewish meant there were more opportunities to languish in stupidity. It also meant questioning Western culture, rejecting Catholicism once and for all, trying to understand the Jewish faith, denying the notion of personal salvation, finding a new conscience and hoping for a hybrid culture.

At the end of 1945, Marguerite and Robert became publishers. Robert needed a job; Monsieur Benoit, a printer, agreed to help them; and Robert Marin put up the money to found Cité universelle, based in the Antelme family home in rue Dupin. 'The small publishing house,' Dionys added, 'was our dream for independent come true.' They produced three political books with distinctive red and white jackets before being forced, within two years, to give up for financial reasons.

Marguerite was experimenting with a new style of writing based on the gaze. In the short story entitled 'Eda ou les feuilles', the hero witnesses the death of the woman he loves. Today the long philosophical meditation reads like an amateurish and repetitious stylistic exercise. Marguerite Duras's inspiration came from her obser-vations of an apparently banal reality, which she then slowly distorted. 'Each morning the leaves were that bit more distinct. Soon they would be open, thought Jean, flat and straight at the ends of their stalks. For the moment, they still clung to the tree. They were reminiscent of things, painful things. Their flesh was so alive.' This short story, rejected several times, was reworked by Robert, Dionys and Marguerite. At the time Marguerite accepted corrections, lot of corrections. As always, the moment she finished a manuscript, she would submit it first to Robert, who would say 'It's fine', and then pass it apprehensively to Dionys. 'Yes, I was critical of her writing,' Dionys recalled. 'And at the time, she was grateful.' Marguerite was going through a period of self-doubt. She'd start writing and then give up. She'd write the beginnings of short stories on the backs of communist pamphlets. Marguerite never threw anything away. In much the same way that she'd make excellent stews with yesterday's leftovers, she'd keep these bits of paper and recycle them in other writings later.

Robert and Marguerite were still living together in rue Saint-Benoît, though they had separate rooms. Dionys, though still living with his mother, was a frequent visitor. He never slept in the rue Saint-Benoît apartment, although he'd sometimes crash on the sofa in the hall. To those who were not close friends, Robert and Mar-guerite were a couple and Dionys the couple's friend. As Mascolo said laughing, 'We went to a hotel to make love. No one made love in the rue Saint-Benoît.' Like a mother, Marguerite protected, provided for and comforted Robert, and saw to it that Dionys was happy. The door was permanently open and Marguerite's reputation as a cook was spreading fast among the intellectuals of the Latin Quarter. She loved entertaining. Queneau, Merleau-Ponty and Audiberti dropped in from time to time. Edgar Morin was always there. The meals were informal. They drank a lot and occasionally danced. They all said the same thing: Marguerite was cheerful, pleasant, extremely funny, charming and exciting. She loved having people around her, loved feeling desirable. She'd sit on men's laps just to see if she aroused them.[6] The men enjoyed these slightly perverse games of hers that never came to anything. 'You were always left with that feeling that it could be possible, that you could leave with her and start an affair,' confided someone who preferred to remain anonymous. Rue Saint-Benoît was a place where you could relive your adolescence. People could come and stay whenever the mood or love took them. With the key always under the mat, the spare beds made up and sleeping bags available, Marguerite was as welcoming and hospitable as the Corsican villages of old.

Those who knew of the relationship between Dionys and Marguerite worried about the pretence she kept up to maintain in public her image as Robert's wife. In the street, Marguerite held Robert's arm and Dionys walked by her side. Robert observed these rites while continuing his affair with Anne-Marie, who was expecting a child he didn't want. Before long he was having an affair with an ex-lover of Dionys's.

At the beginning of summer 1946, Marguerite went to the Dordogne on her own. She wanted to rest and to think; she was finding it impossible to continue to live torn between the two men. But how could she choose? She wrote to Dionys, 'This mutual adoration we three have for one another is both extraordinary and monstrous. Christ Almighty, will I never get any peace? Not to have to worry about you any more … All I am is the love I have for you. I always seem to be in the tow of suffering. There is no solution. This situation is so wearing.'[7] Marguerite was reluctant to destroy her life with Robert and hoped Dionys would suggest she go and live with him. But Dionys said nothing and stayed with his mother. He was seeing a lot of Paulette Delval, although Marguerite knew nothing of his double life. According to Paulette, who was expecting his child, he wanted to leave Marguerite and set up home with her. But it was all talk and no action. It took him thirty years to admit he was the child's father. He said nothing to Robert, but Robert felt in the way, so he started looking for another apartment. Marguerite persuaded him not to leave.

One inauspicious spring day in March 1946, Dionys and Robert had joined the Communist Party. 'Having decided to delay no longer and in full knowledge of the misery awaiting us, Robert and I, in one of those sombre moods so well suited to weddings and funerals, made our way to the place Saint-Sulpice and – in that mutually supportive way, the strength of the one bolstering the weakness of the other – arm in arm we crossed the threshold.'⁸ And so it was without enthusiasm that Dionys and Robert joined Marguerite at the Latin Quarter meetings of cell 722, where she had already been an ardent activist for two years. In his diary Dionys described the absolute belief she had at the time in libertarian communism as the only thing capable of effecting a break from the world of the past. The cell was short of rank-and-file members from the working classes. The rue Saint-Benoît printers sent along a few workers, and there was of course Madame Fossez, the concierge from 5 rue Saint-Benoît. Meetings always began with fifteen minutes of politics; then there followed the distribution of tasks. Marguerite loved sticking bills, handing out leaflets and visiting the poor. Regarding herself as one of the privileged, she was the first to ask to be given menial chores. She'd take on anything. In one of her notebooks I came across a pamphlet from that period. On the reverse she'd written:

- Politics: calm – we are going to fight for better rates of pay and working conditions. Points to remember: no radical action. To move towards a free market for some commodities.
- Constitution: we shall not disarm. Union with the socialists is the key to the success of our politics. Electoral law to be obtained. Full proportional representation.
- Local: satisfactory results of new methods. Effectiveness of pamphlets. Must not force public opinion. As far as possible to deliver our literature to private homes – make contact with sympathizers. Work base.

She had proved to be such a good communist that she was soon secretary of the cell, a position she held for a year. She was nominated for the position of delegate to the Federal Conference of the Seine, but turned it down because she wanted to stay with the rank and file. She openly challenged the notion of promotion within the Party. The cell was a bit like an early Christian community. They'd help one another out and look for old people with problems. Dionys wrote, 'For months on end, in silent carefree generosity, more relaxed doing unrewarding jobs on her own, she was experiencing such perfect self-effacement that she hadn't a care in the world except when she wasn't sufficiently absorbed in work that demanded dogged devotion.'⁹

Dionys was averse to party affiliations; it bothered him to be a card-carrying member of the Communist Party and he detested the idea that anyone should curtail his freedom. 'It was the same with marriage. We were never married. We were against such rituals.'¹⁰ Robert was a communist before he joined. To him communism was the only alternative, the only possible theoretical structure to help him survive the death of the human race. Robert would always be a communist, even after his distressing expulsion in March 1950. And Marguerite too – all her life she claimed she was a communist. In rue Saint-Benoît, by the third whisky, however, Robert was confessing he preferred Michelet to Marx. The philosopher Maurice Merleau-Ponty was analysing the Party's fallacious interpretations of Marx; Morin was holding forth on the future of proletarian rule. But they were all blind, or rather choosing not to see.

Marguerite got hold of the shorthand transcripts of the Moscow trials and circulated the retranscribed text around the comrades. Moscow was a long way away but her faith in the Party began to waver. She attended fewer meetings. She laughed at the recommendations being distributed to Party members, entitled 'All you need to know to be a good Stalinist'. However, to all intents and purposes Marguerite was still a perfect communist. She organized local fund-raising events for the cell and commandeered the apartment before and after. Cans of beer were stacked high before the event and afterwards it was bundles of unsold copies of *L'Humanité*. People came and went, stayed for an hour, a night. 'We believed in the future,' said Jacques-Francis Rolland, 'we wanted to live with the people, to let them have a voice.'¹¹

It was when Robert and Dionys officially joined the Party that doubts crept in, and she began to distance herself. She reported her doubts to the Party. She went to see her superiors and protested at the Stalinization of minds, threatened to stop selling *L'Humanité*. They calmed her down, allayed her fears – for the time being. One evening the following month, in that hive of activity that was the rue Saint-Benoît Claude Roy turned up with an Italian friend, Elio Vittorini. This was a momentous meeting for Marguerite not only because of the intense friendship that was to develop from that first encounter, but also for the literary influence he would have on her work and political vision.

The writer Elio Vittorini was a handsome, private and charming man. He radiated an ironically cheerful sensuality. In Italy Vittorini was regarded as an important political thinker, and since the end of 1943, European intellectuals and writers had been claiming him as one of their own. Vittorini became an emblematic figure. He was a poet, Resistance fighter, modern philosopher and a committed actor. His 1942 book *Conversation en Sicile*, banned in Italy by the Mussolini regime, had circulated illicitly in France during the Occupation.

Marguerite saw Elio Vittorini as not only a great writer but also a real Resistance fighter, one who, having joined the Communist Party in 1943, believed in a moral and liberating communism. Like Antelme, he wanted to wash away the 'trespass against the world', committed by Fascism and Nazism. Artist, philosopher, aesthete, cook, walker, swimmer, great company during evenings full of fun and booze, Elio Vittorini became a lifelong member of Marguerite's circle of friends. When Marguerite loved, she loved to distraction and wanted it all, there and then. Two months after they met, she suggested to Dionys and Robert that they spend the summer in Italy with Vittorini and his wife Ginetta. The heat, the sea, Robert's body confronting the sea, confronting the world, alive, definitely alive. She and Ginetta lying in the sun, naked behind a clump of reeds, drinking in the heat. And finally Dionys still as beautiful, his body sleeker from swimming; Dionys with whom she loved so much to make love. Marguerite said it was the happiest summer she ever experienced.

She was much inspired by Vittorini, who got her to abandon classical aesthetics in favour of a new kind of writing. From then on she makes the same use of the words in a novel as a musician of the words of a libretto. She adds poetic weight to the mechanical and external weight of the language. As in the work of Vittorini, over and above the reality of actions and objects there is a mythical reality that can only be achieved through writing.[12] Duras's art owes much to the Vittorinian technique of repetition, the incantatory return of words, a position in the sentence that compresses their usual meaning and a certain indistinct aura, distinctly resistant to analysis.

The meeting with Vittorini was to have quite an impact on the political thinking of the rue Saint-Benoît group. He offered these ideologically bewildered French intellectuals a way out. In place of the constraints of French Stalinism, he offered them a theoretical reformulation of a liberating Marxism. Invited to France by the Comité national des écrivains (National Association of Writers), Vittorini attacked the Stalinism of French communist intellectuals and their slavish mentality. 'We were amazed,' Dionys recalled. 'There was an instant spark. Unto death. And the wish never to be separated.'[13] A well-connected man, Vittorini had worked for the underground press of the Italian Resistance. With the Liberation he became chief editor of *L'Unita*, the Italian Communist Party's daily newspaper. But more importantly, he had his own magazine, *Il Politecnico*, in which he published writers he liked, whether they were communists or not.

Marguerite was finding it increasingly difficult to accept the dogmatic party line. Outraged at the blind obedience of Stalinists, she'd write rude letters to the intellectual executives of the Party. She suspected them of treachery and lies. Vittorini provided her with confirmation of her worst fears. Having been officially invited by a delegation of the PCF, he was able to ascertain the state of mind of those whose mission it was to embody the future of the Revolution. He was alarmed to discover that intellectual Stalinism in France was more like a military psychosis and that ideological and cultural questions were approached in the line of duty rather than truth. Marguerite listened to Vittorini and knew he was telling the truth. But she was torn. Where should she stand? Which camp should she join? Where were the real enemies? How was she to fight? And with whom?

All her life Marguerite had nothing but contempt for Jean-Paul Sartre and she detested Simone de Beauvoir; she hated her work and said as much. She poked fun at the writer Louis Aragon and despised Camus. At the time, Sartre, fascinated by Stalinism though challenging its ambiguities, was postulating the notion of commitment. Marguerite never subscribed to this notion. She chose to follow the model purported by Vittorini: the free, communist though not necessarily Marxist intellectual, the affective, protesting communist. Any transformation of the world produces a moral philosophy. Morality can only truly begin to exist through revolutionary action. By claiming to create a new type of intellectual, the CPF was running the risk of producing a new kind of bloody idiot, Vittorini told a delighted Marguerite before returning to Italy.

Yet Marguerite, Edgar Morin, Dionys Mascolo and Robert Antelme continued to believe they could impose a new understanding of morality, politics and love on the Party. With this in mind they founded the Groupe d'études marxistes (Marxist Study Group), meeting in rue Saint-Benoît. The group, which also included Maurice Merleau-Ponty and David Rousset, appeared flexible, ironic, distant and mistrustful. They wanted to remain in the Party and yet be in a position to criticize some of its activities. And they wanted a return to the philosophy of Marx and Engels. Looking back, Dionys Mascolo believed there was genuine theoretical and political dissent within the group. Morin was more sceptical; he remembered a lot of idle chatter and endless discussions on the Party's praxis and endeavours to recapture these impossible-to-discipline bohemian intellectuals. In any case, to be of any use to the working class, the group decided it was necessary to classify the information in *L'Humanité*. And so some buried themselves in newspaper cuttings and the ideologically incorrect group died a quiet death.

Like everyone else, Marguerite was indifferent to what was going on in the country she'd grown up in. The French fleet had bombed Haiphong and when war broke out Marguerite had no idea her brothers were battling in an Indo-China in flames. She was more interested in events in Czechoslovakia and Poland. 'Our anti-colonialism spoke for itself,' Morin stated in *Autocritique*. 'We weren't drawn to Stalin but what was so absolutely crucial to us was commitment,' Dionys explained. For Marguerite this persistent and agonizing desire to perpetuate communist commitment was like a search for an absolute. She stayed in the Party so that she could continue her spiritual search. How can man be redefined? How can the human condition be changed? What was culture doing to alleviate the suffering of man? Thanks to Elio Vittorini, she read philosophers and economists, wrote on such issues as exploitation, slavery, poverty. While she continued to revere the proletariat, she was more openly contemptuous of the Stalinist machine. The French and Italian Communist Parties were growing apart. In France, for example, Henry Miller was being accused of pornography and Sartre of being a smarmy rat. In Italy, on the other hand, one of the Communist Party's greatest intellectuals was quietly writing about Camus's moralism, existentialist doctrine and the power of desire in the new American novel. In the opinion of Marguerite, Dionys and Robert, who followed the Italian model, to be a Marxist did not mean you had to be narrow-minded. In the eyes of the group, who saw themselves as revolutionary intellectuals, Italy, whose Communist Party was at the time the most important in Europe, was the Promised Land. Communism in Italy was drawing on genuine spiritual strength, even though hope was supplied by a predominantly Catholic culture. Communists in Italy took communion on Sunday. 'I had stopped believing in the divinity of Christ,' said Vittorini, 'in order to believe in his humanity more.' This Christo-communism suited Marguerite.

The cell Marguerite belonged to at the end of 1946 had six to twelve participants, depending on the sessions. Marguerite always arrived early, arm in arm with Robert. Dionys was always late, reluctant to forsake his piano for a lesson on Marxist dialectic. Dionys projected the detachment of the aesthete and dandy familiar with the real pleasures of life – music, love and literature – as well as the conviction that he understood real Marxism, the one re-examined in the light of the Greek philosophers and Saint-Just. There were frequent altercations at the end of the meetings. Marguerite always supported Dionys. These tiffs over the revolution didn't stop them from all going first to the bistro and then on to finish the evening in rue Saint-Benoît.

In the rue Saint-Benoît, Robert was working on his book about his wartime experiences, *The Human Race*, and Edgar Morin, returned from a stay in Germany, had moved in with his wife Violette. The days were spent in discussion, the nights drinking cheap booze and singing. Edith Piaf was their favourite; Marguerite knew all her songs by heart. She and Dionys would sing duets together. 'And an ebullient, anxious Marguerite,' said the Jansenist and fanciful Claude Roy, 'was queen of the happy hive of activity. She had the unpredictability of a goat, innocence of a flower, gentleness of a cat. Baroque preciosity and the simplicity of a peasant.'[14]

Dionys's mother was ill and moved into rue Saint-Benoît for a few months. Marguerite liked her very much. She was a kind, sensitive and very affectionate woman. So there are mothers like that! Marguerite enjoyed her company and told everyone that she was the very opposite of her own mother.

As everyone knows, activists have large holes in their pockets. And so when the sacks of rice arrived from her mother in Indo-China, Marguerite would invite them round for a meal. On high days and holidays she'd serve grilled rabbit to go with the rice. She cooked for her buddies – Raymond Queneau, the anthropologist Michel Leiris, the philosopher Georges Sichères, who had a soft spot for Marguerite and used to say, 'That woman is the epitome of the magic of words, the very epitome'.[15] The novelist Georges Bataille, Ponge the poet, Atlan, Clara Malraux, Jean Duvignaud, and the novelist Romain Gary turned up one evening; the psychoanalyst Jacques Lacan on several occasions; Dominique and Jean Toussaint Desanti, known as Touki, were regulars until they fell out for good. In 1949, on the instructions of the Party, Dominique wrote a Stalinist booklet, thus betraying her friendship with Marguerite, whom she had christened 'Marmonne' (Mumbler), and the rue Saint-Benoît friends. 'That is how Stalinism came about. We were undoubtedly but uninspiringly vile,' she said. Later, as she explained in her autobiography, she regretted it. For Dominique Desanti, the rue Saint-Benoît had been a tonic, an antidote. But Marguerite refused to forgive or see her again. She was never under Party orders, never a Party soldier, but she did admit she had been naively uncritical of a party that eventually came to embody weakness and lies.

The friends were otherwise inseparable and life was like one long uninterrupted conversation. They drank a lot, laughed a great deal, especially Marguerite, who laughed uncontrollably. She was the life-blood of the group. Most of the men admitted in old age to having been in love with her: Jacques-Francis Rolland, Claude Roy, Edgar Morin. 'I was under her spell,' Edgar admitted, 'she was a prick-teaser.' And she knew it, and used it to make Dionys jealous. 'She was the spark, she liked taking, she was a real collector,' Claude Roy confirmed. With Marguerite in charge, political attachments, emotional attachments, sexual attachments, all became jumbled up. There weren't many women in this world. One was Clara Malraux, whom Marguerite admired and would allow to talk. Violette Morin she could just about tolerate; however she might only watch but not speak. In fact the women chose to keep their mouths shut rather than challenge the jealous authority of the mistress of the house who couldn't bear another woman to be in the limelight and risk eclipsing, albeit for a few seconds, the brilliance of her presence. She was therefore the only one to state her opinions. Robert, eternally patient, stayed in the background; Edgar would expound amusingly; and Dionys would charm with his ideological intransigence and theoretical passion. Edgar Morin was astounded by the intellectual virtuosity of the debates.[16] The warmth of the understanding they shared was infectious.

Rue Saint-Benoît – where the paths of communists, crypto-communists and future ex-communists crossed – was a place for banter and confrontation. Freedom of speech was still on the agenda, but yet a climate of suspicion and accusation hung over the apartment. Some of the comrades' opinions were seen as suspect. There were those who kept quiet for fear of being denounced. And others were fearful they'd be accused of subversive activities and left the rue Saint-Benoît, never to return.

When Marguerite found out she was pregnant, Dionys's first child, with Paulette Delval, had just been born. Until the day she died Marguerite never knew her son had a half-brother. Her belly huge, Marguerite was rattling away on the typewriter in rue Saint-Benoît as she kept an eye on the cooking. She radiated happiness and felt fulfilled at last because a child was growing inside her. She would help him into the world and bring him up to be as free as possible. This had always been more important to her than belonging to a literary circle. And so she waited impatiently for the baby, observing the changes in her body and recording her feelings:

> He started to move around just above my pubis, so I placed my hands flat on that part of my abdomen so that I could feel him. He raised my hands and fidgeted around so mischievously I had to smile. I wondered whether he was sleeping. With my hands I tried to feel his shape but all I could make out was his outline, especially at the top! He was deep within me almost touching my back and in the warm pool he stretched and made himself comfortable, living inside me without shame, playing happily, bigger and stronger with each day that passed, sucking a little of my blood, each day stronger until the day when, fait accompli, he'd

stop and with great solemnity, take the path out through my flesh that separates him from the world.[17]

When Marguerite first announced she was pregnant, Robert said he wanted to move out of the way, but Marguerite and Dionys wouldn't hear of it. Marguerite was in seventh heaven. She loved being between these two men. To be carrying a child made her feel incredibly strong. It made her feel superior to the men and she had no hesitation in telling them so. They were willing to accept the superiority of feminine splendour. Closely and affectionately watched over by Marguerite, they entered 'in feminy'.

Everyone in the area, even Madame Fossez, thought Marguerite was expecting Robert's child. Marguerite said nothing. But while among the friends and neighbours, she nurtured the ambiguity of the situation, she wanted her relationship with Robert to be set straight legally. Although Dionys mocked the divorce Marguerite wanted, calling it a ludicrous and disagreeable formality where one of the parties had to admit to impropriety, on 24 April 1947 and on Marguerite's initiative, the couple's marriage was dissolved in the civil court of the Seine.

CHAPTER 8

Motherhood

~

On 30 June, 1947, a boy, Jean, was born. At a cell meeting, after the baby's birth, Robert's latest girlfriend whispered to the woman who two years later would become the second Madame Antelme, 'Whatever you do, don't congratulate Robert. Dionys is the father'.[1] But the birth further strengthened the friendship between the two men. Dionys was Robert's saviour. Robert was Dionys's mentor. It was never a very manful, demonstrative and noisy friendship. It was reflective, intellectual, poetic, sensual too. Robert had been the father the first time Marguerite became pregnant. In the future he and his wife Monique would make sure they were always there for Jean.

Physically and intellectually Marguerite found the birth a deeply moving experience. She had at last brought a child into the world. She had shown what she was capable of. She had created a life and nurtured it inside her. She was back living in the world. The fact that her first child had been stillborn had made her fearful that she would not carry her second child to full term. She found the experience of the child physically separating from her womb and continuing to live exhilarating:

> I rubbed against him. In my flesh, bathed his nascent but distinct flesh. His independence deep within me was so striking and stark that I responded as though torn apart by truth, a Woman glistening with truth ... Now as I read these lines, he is there, out of me, sleeping a few feet

away. His freedom is no less complete than mine. My life is linked to his, dependent on it down to the smallest detail.[2]

At the beginning of August Marguerite, Dionys and the baby left Paris for Château-Chinon. Their friend Mitterrand had loaned them a cottage set in the middle of the fields. Comfort was minimal but the river not far away. Unfortunately Mitterrand had forgotten to warn them that the idyllic spot was infested with insects. The harvest mites feasted on the baby's tender flesh: hence he was given the nickname Outa (Mite), which has stayed with him to this day. Marguerite was an overpowering, possessive, anxious mother, but she was also cheerful, mischievous, easygoing and particularly respectful of her child's liberty. She treated Outa as an equal. She felt indebted to a child who had brought her so much. And she was in love, madly in love with him. Together they invented codes, rituals, secrets, languages. She and he, hand in hand. Together they created a protective bubble, an invisible fortress into which none could penetrate. Her son meant more to her than her career as a writer. In *Outside* there's a description of the two of them out in the street when he was little. People, street, noise:

He laughed and out came the sound of his laugh. It was windy and a tiny fraction of the sound of this laugh reached me. And so I half-raised the hood of his pram, gave him back his giraffe so that he'd laugh again and stuffed my head under the hood so that I could catch the whole of the laugh. My child's laugh. I put my ear to the shell and heard the sound of the sea.

The child's birth didn't have much impact on life in rue Saint-Benoît and didn't affect Marguerite's political activities. As she was giving him the bottle, she'd be busy with her work as an activist, as well as doing the cooking and writing.

In the autumn of 1947, she gave up – apparently for good – on a novel that turned up in one of her manuscript notebooks, the grey notebook, entitled *Théodora*. In all there are some forty pages in the archives of IMEC. When Marguerite came across them by chance in a cupboard, she had an extract published in *Les Nouvelles littéraires*, in 1979. It begins as follows: 'Cinzano's in short supply, it's in shorter supply than anything else at the moment. Soon there'll be more, then later even more. I don't know if Pascal will give me some. There's no knowing how he decides to give his clients Cinzano. Discreet, he serves, wipes his tables, says a couple of words . . .' Marguerite was seeking to write about insignificance, banality. She wasn't sure about the title, abandoned *Théodora* for a time in favour of *Le cachet d'aspirine*. 'In all modesty,' she wrote, 'it's a fantastic title. Its insignificance fills me with the kind of vertigo you get when confronted with insignificance.' It is set in a hotel, and boredom slowly becomes the main theme. 'And then one night a vague glimmer of hope stirs in the hotel – a mother is worried. Her young son is ill. Very ill.' But the story wasn't going well. She noted the problems. 'I keep asking myself the question, What happens next? I'd like each of the characters to feel the frightful problem as deeply as I do and regret as much as I do that the little boy couldn't have been as ill as we'd have liked him to have been!'

At the time, Marguerite was terrified of losing Outa. Day and night she had to reassure herself he was still breathing. Her writing was an unsuccessful attempt to exorcise her morbid obsessions. So she started talking to herself, invented an imaginary interlocutor to whom she confided her fears.

Robert Antelme's book *The Human Race* was brought out a month before Outa was born, by the publishing house Marguerite, Dionys and Robert had founded, Cité universelle. In the preface, Antelme explains he wanted to go back over the life of a commando (Gandersheim) from a German concentration camp (Buchenwald). The book is a contemplative, philosophical and materialist journey through a still undefined universe. It is not so much a return to the camps as a return to that indestructible essence that is the self. Robert Antelme became a writer in the space of a book. In *The Human Race* he went to the very limits of literature, breaking down the door Marguerite talked about all her life. Marguerite was in fact extremely indebted to him. Taking over from Robert, she drew on his language and rid herself once and for all of linguistic affectations, grammatical conceits, games of hide and seek with reality. Had *The Human Race* never been published, *The Sea Wall* would not have been written. The revolution that took place in Marguerite's writing – her way of seeing literature as a stripping bare of the self – dates from that period.

Robert Antelme demonstrated just how far language shapes us as human beings in the world. In both his mind and body he felt the sudden surge of new words. The tremor of language, the vertigo of meaning, the poetics of being, the living human being seen as resistance fighter – all are conveyed in his unique book. Before his camp experiences, Robert had written poetry. In 1948, in a work published by *Le Patriote résistant*, he returned to the importance of poetry to describe the tireless resistance of the conscience, 'It is the essence of poetry to express what was threatened by the camps – experience as a continually lived reality. The testimony of prophetic witnesses, the poetry of the camps is the closest to being the poetry of truth.'[3] To name the real is to be able to envisage a tomorrow.

With the publication of the book came some extremely complimentary reviews, but despite this it was met with total indifference. It was squeezed out by others' accounts. Some were promoting David Rousset's book and others Geneviève de Gaulle's, and there were those Fascists who were already claiming the concentration camps had never existed. This came as no surprise to Robert Antelme who could see the curtain of the Phariseeism of forgetfulness and silence was about to fall. Come on, you must forget, forget all about it, the deportees kept being told. OK so they were allowed to talk, allowed to get on with it, but people really wanted them to shut up, so very much wanted them to move on. Society assimilated, digested everything. In 1948, on the subject of the camps Antelme wrote, 'Witness testimonies, no use any more, not even as alibis; they despise them, deny them. Digestion is done.'[4]

The Human Race is also a combative book, a committed book, a book that asks the proletariat – whether Jewish, black, yellow, Christian or communist – to be aware. In 1948 Antelme wrote, 'We found or realized that the nature of the "normal" regime, which exploited man, was no different from that of the camps. That the camp was simply the clear image of the virtually veiled hell in which so many nations still live.'[5]

Elio Vittorini, who was in Paris for the launch of *The Human Race*, appreciated the political and philosophical implications of the book. He was quick to buy the rights for the prestigious Einaudi imprint he edited. An interview with him by Dionys Mascolo and Edgar Morin, published on the front page of *Lettres françaises* on 27 June 1947, led to his break with the Party. Vittorini stated that, essentially, a communist was nonviolent, that the very notion of revolutionary crime was scandalous and that the ends never justified the means. 'We are drawn to communism out of love for man's absolute freedom.' By way of a reprisal, his magazine *Politecnico* disappeared six months later. Financed by the Italian Communist Party, he had published Sartre, Camus, Faulkner, Hemingway, Pasternak, but never any official Soviet writers. The Italian communist leader Togliatti reproached Vittorini for informing rather than 'forming' his readers. Soviet realism was gaining ground and corrupting all the European communist parties. The Italian comrades accused Vittorini of being a lyrical deviationist. In France, the article upset the Party's cultural masters. Abuse was hurled at Vittorini. Marguerite joined the fray and passionately defended her friend Elio.

But at the end of the summer Marguerite returned to Paris to learn that Elio, in a long open letter to the secretary of the PCI, published in one of the last issues of his magazine, had broken away from the Party in the name of cultural freedom. To be a communist, he wrote, means you are searching for truth and not the possessor of this truth. Culture should never be the vassal of politics. Anyway, what is a political man? 'He is a man of culture who abandons the search in favour of action.' In this well-argued, enlightened and courageous text, Vittorini accused the Communist Party of using the political lie as a murder weapon. 'It is impossible to understand how Italian communists can condemn Kafka and Hemingway, the Soviets, Dostoievski and the French, Proust. The sin of lying holds up to public opprobrium a category of minor intellectuals who, incapable of making a living, turn aggressive watchdogs.'

Although they never stopped criticizing it, Marguerite, Robert and Dionys remained in the Party for another two years. But by this time it had become dangerous to discuss misgivings with your comrades, and a surveillance system based on denunciations was set up. No more carrying a card and saying what you think, except in rue Saint-Benoît, where the illusion that you could change the Party from within had not been shattered. So as to neutralize the most recalcitrant, the Party functionery Laurent Casanova had just set up a

committee of intellectuals. 'It was a question of encircling the dissidents in order to disarm them, not to expel them,' explained a
participant recalling the attempts to regain control. 'It was a question
of appearing to allow them to express themselves without the other
comrades actually being able to hear them.'⁶ Mascolo, Morin, Duras
and Antelme fell for it and signed up at once. Yet the circle of writers
was directly linked to the Central Committee.

Among friends you can say anything, but outside, no. At least that's
what Casanova kept repeating whenever the opportunity arose to the
few comrades who still believed him. 'As it happened the retreat
had sounded and we wanted to preserve the ties we had with the
Communist Party, which were in fact what set us apart from real
Stalinism,' said Morin. During one of the meetings Robert and
Dionys criticized Jean Kanapa, another apparatchik. Party reaction
was instantaneous, and an explanation was demanded. At a meeting
in the spring of 1948 they had to defend their views. Robert, in the
name of truth and honour, first defended Malraux and Faulkner, two
of the writers the Party had insulted. 'On an intellectual level the
accusations are extremely damaging and make us look ridiculous,' he
declared to a packed hall where the whole of the Communist Party
old guard sat. The battle was lost in advance. Marguerite, Robert and
Dionys were the only ones who thought his words could prevail upon
the consciences of these hand-picked activists. But Antelme's tone
was so sincere, his arguments so well presented, his passion so strong
that some of them gave him a standing ovation at the end.

But Kanapa was still out to get Marguerite, Robert and Dionys,
who were regarded as miscreant and lawless. The Party slowly but
surely ostracized them. The Cercle de la commission des intellectuels
disappeared and a new literary group was supposedly created. The
dissidents had in effect been banned, but not yet expelled. They had
absolutely no intention of resigning. Today it's difficult to understand
why, being anti-authoritarian, they were so keen to remain in the
Party. But Party membership was a way of life, a way of hope, of
building a future – whether glorious or not – and of being part of a
'family'. Party membership meant you were never alone.

In the summer of 1948 Marguerite set off with the baby to Quiberon,
Brittany. It was too hot in Bocca de Magra, she told Ginetta and Elio

Vittorini, who had invited her to stay. To Dionys, who had stayed in Paris to work for Gallimard, she wrote, 'Actually I've always found forests (bloody) boring. Here there's nothing but sea, sky, heavy dew, more sea and rocks. I think it's what I've always loved.' She was a devoted mother, taking Outa for endless walks, watching him learn to walk and wanting to soak up everything about him. Being alone with her child delighted and disconcerted her.

'Tell me you love me,' Marguerite demanded from Dionys as usual. Dionys didn't go to Brittany, but Robert and his new girlfriend Monique went to stay with her. He had met Monique at a meeting of the Saint-Germain-des-Prés cell but their relationship was not yet official. They celebrated Outa's first birthday together. Marguerite was wondering whether or not to return to Paris. She wrote and told Dionys she hated her life in rue Saint-Benoît and 'you're so obviously bored with me, with your endless piano playing that has me on the verge of a nervous breakdown and I know you despise me ... You want to put me down, to bring me down to your level ... I'm waiting for you, wait only for you. We could get on together and not love one another. We could love one another and never get on. However, we only ever get on when we're fighting.'⁷

A war-weary Dionys fetched Marguerite from Quiberon. And in rue Saint-Benoît life was back to normal: boozy evenings, impromptu parties, literary discussions, friends unto death. Mascolo invited round foreign authors who were passing through: Marguerite fed Italo Calvino and John Dos Passos. Financially, Marguerite and Robert were living from hand to mouth, but Marguerite always managed to keep open house. She had contacts, knew a wheeze or two and could come up with cheap dishes. There were evenings when the discussions were heated. Cracks began to appear even in the inner circle of friends.

On the ideological front, the battle raged. They were surprised but not shocked when Marshal Tito was expelled, unlike their friend Clara Malraux who supported the Yugoslavians. In February 1948, Marguerite, Robert and Dionys accepted the underhand way the communists seized control of the Czech government. But they were torn. Dionys said it was a time of inner resignation. Meanwhile Marguerite was closing the door of rue Saint-Benoît to the friends who, through Stalinist subservience, screamed that Sartre was a hyena typist and Picasso a bourgeois formalist.

Morin lost his job as chief editor of *Patriote résistant*, the newspaper of the National Federation of Deportees, because of a disagreement over the Party's cultural policy. Robert, with the help of Monique, continued to send in articles and to run the deportees' cell. 'To him the Party was the friends,' Monique summed up. Strong ties of friendship, deep-rooted solidarity, a loving environment. He had been to Czechoslovakia and some of the communist writers had told him of their worries. But the writers were part of the intelligentsia, he told Marguerite and Dionys. What mattered were the people and the future of the people.

In April 1949, leaving Outa behind, Marguerite went to stay with Elio and Ginetta in Milan. They travelled to Piedmont, then stayed in Varese. 'Stunningly beautiful. Great spirituality. Enough to drive you crazy,' Marguerite noted. 'A Pascalian nature.'

Back in Paris, Marguerite again became caught up in cell 722's politico-ideological arguments. Friends and about-to-be ex-friends confronted each other in the bistros of Saint-Germain-des-Prés. To be a communist, Marguerite later explained, meant being on the side of life, it did not mean breaking with impunity from what kept you alive and gave you hope.[8] But to the apparatchiks, the intellectual was, by definition, suspect because he was a product of the middle classes. He spread rumours of defeat instead of uniting body and soul with the proletariat. Marguerite, Robert and Dionys didn't know it but the drama had already been played out. The Party had decided to sever its links with them but had not yet informed them of the decision. They had been accused of cynicism and inappropriate behaviour towards certain Party members. Today, looking at the official notification filed away in the archives of the PCF, we would probably find the reasons for their expulsion farcical, but Robert Antelme was devastated and Marguerite humiliated as a woman, an activist and a writer. Marguerite's letters and those of Dionys Mascolo, Robert Antelme and Monique Régnier, and the Party's responses, are also on file.

The whole affair began one evening at the Bonaparte Café in May 1949 following a boring cell meeting. Marguerite, Eugène Mannoni, Robert, Dionys, Monique Régnier and her partner Bernard Guillochon and Jorge Semprun were propping up the bar. They were drinking, joking; howling with laughter at everything and nothing.

They were enjoying themselves. According to several witnesses, Mannoni was supposed to have said, putting on a Corsican accent, that Comrade Casanova was a pimp – 'Casa's a big ponce' – and that in Corsica it was a well known fact. Guffaws of laughter from all those present. But in the file in Party archives, there's no mention of Casanova's name, only Aragon's. 'Everyone participated in the conversation. There was a lot of criticism of Comrade Aragon.' A few days later Bernard Guillochon heard that one of the comrades had reported the conversation to Party officials. Robert Antelme and Bernard Guillochon suspected Semprun and decided to confront him. Bernard Guillochon recalled that 'He began by denying it and then agreed to come along to a meeting of the friends in rue Saint-Benoît. Marguerite, Robert, Jacques-Francis Rolland, Monique, we were all there.'[9] 'The mood of the meeting was extremely heated, aggressive,' states the file in the PCF archives.

Today Jorge Semprun denies the facts and insists he had nothing to do with the denunciations:

> I do not accept I had a hand in their expulsion. It's mostly myth, a kind of family fiction. It's as though they needed to hound me, metaphorically, because I was closer to them than the others. I discussed it with Robert Antelme at the time ... In fact, when the wheels were set in motion to expel them from the Party, I had already moved out of the area to Montmartre, because I didn't want to get involved. And I took advantage of the situation not to renew my membership. I belonged to the Spanish party, and that was enough![10]

Summer postponed the polemic. Robert, Monique, Marguerite and Dionys rented a big house outside Paris. Marguerite wanted to start afresh and live in the country not too far from Paris. She wrote to her mother and asked her for money, but never got a reply. That summer, Marguerite read Diderot but found him longwinded and boring, blissfully immersed herself in Racine, knitted, pottered about and marvelled at her son who was starting to talk. 'He calls me Mummy and I call him rascal,' she wrote to Dionys. 'He is so bright. I really love this little chap. This morning as a funeral cortege was going past the church and the priest was chanting, the child danced so much and so well we had to calm him down. How worthy of your son.'

On 27 September 1949, Marguerite informed the cell secretary
that she would not be renewing her Party membership, and at the
end of December she handed in her card. But you don't leave the
Communist Party: the Party leaves you and demands explanations.
Marguerite refused to give any until on 16 January 1950 she sent a
letter to the members of the cell, saying

> I have found it impossible to overcome my sense of disgust and, I
> have to say, absurdity, at having once again to confront the sordid and
> ridiculous machinations of pathetic little fanatics from what might well
> be called the 'Martinet faction', since the word faction is being misused.
>
> My reasons for leaving the Party are not the same as Dionys Mascolo's.
> I am under the influence of no one. I took the decision alone and long
> before Mascolo. Viscerally I shall always remain a communist. I have
> been a signed-up member for six years and know I could never be
> anything but a communist. I would have been more than willing to give
> you my reasons for leaving the Party myself, had it not been for the fact
> that I know certain comrades are bent on distorting the most elementary
> of truths. But, rest assured, since I am unable to give you these reasons
> in person I shall not be giving them to anyone else in the world.
>
> My confidence in the Party remains intact. And I am sure that in time
> the Party will rid itself of the Martinets of the world who, in the name of
> vigilance (or should we say viciousness), have but one thought in mind
> and that is to feed and satisfy their own petty grievances. The Martinets
> missed their vocation. It's not the Communist Party they should have
> joined but the fire brigade (where in addition to the prestigious uniform,
> they would have received a few salutary showers) or the priesthood where
> they could have revelled in the joys of the confessional. But I am convinced
> the Party will one day set them on the right road.

More indignant correspondence followed. On 8 March 1950, the
following letter was sent to Marguerite by the branch of the 6th
arrondissement:

> The Saint-Germain-des-Prés cell wishes to inform you:
>
> 1) that after carefully examining your general political attitude, which
>   reveals an enormous divergence from the Party political line in
>   relation to literature and the arts in particular;

2) that after lengthy discussions within the cell during the Wednesday and Monday meetings, you refused to come and explain yourself;

3) that after reading and discussing at length your insolent and politically unsubstantiated letter regarding the Party and its democratically elected leaders.

The majority of members present voted (19 to 11) to expel you forthwith from the ranks of the Party. Before pronouncing judgement there are seven comrades who, whilst condemning your letter outright, wish to hear what you have to say despite your repeated refusals to do so.

Reasons

1) Attempts to sabotage the Party by disrupting the cell, with constant attacks against the branch committee through insulting and slanderous behaviour, and resorting to subterfuge to conceal divergence from the Party political line.

2) Frequenting Trotskyites, such as David Rousset, and other enemies of the working class and the Soviet Union (in particular a former attaché at the Yugoslav embassy at present chief editor of *Borba*).

3) Frequenting nightclubs in the Saint-Germain-des-Prés district where political, intellectual and moral corruption prevails, an activity vigorously and justifiably condemned by the working population and honest intellectuals of the arrondissement.

The motion to expel was passed unanimously by the branch committee on 16 February 1950. Marguerite was not one to sit back and argue. When she heard her name was being dragged through the mud by some of the comrades, that she was virtually being accused of being a whore, feeling that she was on trial, she decided to make a written statement in order to re-establish the truth.

I have been a member of the Party since 1944. Throughout 1946 and 47, I was an active campaigner, until such time as the difficulty of being pregnant prevented me from doing so (I should however like to add that I was still selling *L'Humanité* a month before I went into labour). I was cell secretary for a year and represented the branch on various committees (social, Paris VI, festivals, etc.). In 1949 I was delegate at the Federal Conference of the Seine … I was lucky enough to be secretary for 724, Visconti-Beaux-Arts, where there were workers, and it was there that I was my most active. You see, my distrust of intellectuals was such that it was only at the end of two years, maybe longer, that I admitted to a comrade that I was an author with Gallimard. The fact became known in the cell and I was subsequently criticized because I could probably have 'done something different from what I was doing.' At that particular time however, the criticisms levelled against me were very different from present ones. 'You're doing too much, you're going to make yourself ill,' people kept telling me. Now, those same comrades, whom I have not seen since I transferred to 722, send reports into the branch where they accuse of being a 'whore'. Perhaps they accuse me of being a whore because they can find no other insult. It's easy to accuse a woman of being a whore, it's vague and facile. Is it because I'm divorced? Because I live with a man I'm not married to? I find that difficult to believe since my accusers, Semprun and Martinet, are themselves divorced and the majority of comrades from the cell cohabit like us.

... Nightclubs? In two years I have been to Club Saint-Germain twice. It is precisely because I don't want to bump into communists or other intellectuals (an idiosyncrasy of mine) that I avoid going to them. I very much regret that there is no comrade from the Federation living in the area who could look through the windows of the cafés in Saint-Germain to see which of us were most active among the Sartrian youth. 'I suffer from insomnia, I can't bear staying in bed ...' one of the most regular told me to explain his nightly visits to local clubs. I refer to the first comrade to suggest we should be expelled. As for us, we sleep well and have no need of such pretexts.

One final point. I am accused of not agreeing with Party policy concerning politics and the arts. Very well, I admit that but let's set the record straight. The Party said we had to knock on doors. I knocked on doors. The Party said we had to raise funds. I raised funds on café terraces and elsewhere. The Party asked us – as this was crucial – to take in the children of strikers. For two months I took in the daughter of a miner. I signed up housewives in the markets, I sold *L'Humanité*, I stuck posters, I contributed by getting Antelme, Mascolo and many more to become members, etc. Everything I could do, I did. What I can't do is change some of my tastes in for example literature, which are what they are, and which would be physically impossible for me to give up. But since I have never shouted them from the rooftops, why are they suddenly being dug up at the last minute to be turned into my principal crime? During the six years I've been in the Party, not once, never once in the cell, did I ever discuss or express any reservations I might have had. I once confided in a comrade from the cell for the simple reason that he had encouraged me to do so, being of the same opinion as myself … I would like to repeat what I said in my letter of resignation, that viscerally I shall always remain a communist, I do not see how I could ever be otherwise. Given the circumstances, I should like to say that I shall never involve myself in anything that could damage the Party and that I shall continue to do everything within my means to be of assistance.

Robert was also expelled. That was the end of the friendship between Jorge Semprun and Robert Antelme.[11] That sarcastic comments and bar talk could forever damage and besmear so deep a trust today sends shivers down your back. However, everyone who lived through this black period of Stalinist activism confirms that this was the case – toeing the line could entail betraying your best friend. Pierre Daix confirmed Robert's depressed mental and emotional state following the expulsion. 'I shall never forget the devastation on Antelme's face the day he came and told me he'd been expelled. He just couldn't understand. He came to find me in my office at *Lettres françaises*. I reached out my hand to show him that nothing had changed between us. He hesitated before taking it. "What's the point, it's over," he said with tears in his eyes. In his eyes it was a rash sentence, an injustice, fate dealing him a terrible blow. He was ashen when he arrived, trembling. They had certainly broken something in him.' Pierre Daix said that after Robert's expulsion he went in and saw the person 'right at the top' of the Federation of the Seine to request his reinstatement. There was nothing doing; his appeal was refused due to 'Marguerite's sleeping around and her immorality'.[12]

From one day to the next friends can turn into traitors. But how do you survive expulsion from the Party? To be outside the Party was to be outside the world, Edgar Morin explained. 'It was so warm in people's homes, at meetings. I was like a ghost alone while all over the world workers were on the march. I had lost the communion, the fraternity, for ever. Excluded from everything, from life, from warmth, from the Party. I wept.'[13] It was the same for Marguerite. In her diary, she described the feelings that dogged her after her expulsion. She felt guilty, orphaned, spoke of 'trauma', of 'distressing situations'. It made her ill to see people turn and cross the street. She thought she'd never get over it psychologically.[14]

Some of their comrades tore up their Party cards as a mark of friendship, like Monique Régnier and Bernard Guillochon; others stayed in the Party but didn't abandon their friends. Embarrassed they continued to go to the rue Saint-Benoît to listen to Marguerite, Edgar and Robert analyse the shifts of Stalinist totalitarianism with the feeling they were committing a mortal sin. Jacques-Francis Rolland and Claude Roy saw their comrades expelled and were then expelled themselves. Then it was the turn of Jorge Semprun. And little by little all those who dared to continue to think were in their turn expelled: the philosophers, the poets, the scholars.

After her expulsion, Marguerite continued to call herself a communist, free to define herself in the morning and to redefine herself at night. At the end of her life, she confessed she was still a communist. 'The communist hope never left me. Hope was my sickness, hope in the proletariat.'[15] It was 1993. 'I should like to rejoin the Communist Party, and one day I shall,' she declared in 1994,[16] but she never did.

Just before Christmas 1949 Marguerite gave the manuscript of *The Sea Wall* to Raymond Queneau. On 15 January 1950 a contract was signed with Gaston Gallimard. The name Madame Antelme had been deleted and replaced by Donnadieu. They agreed on a royalty of 10 per cent on the first 1000 copies sold, 12 per cent on 1000–2000 and 15 per cent on further sales.

Constructed along the lines of a classical drama, stripped of any psychologizing that might hinder the plot, but modern in its style and development, *The Sea Wall* is one of the greatest twentieth-century books to have been written on motherhood, on a particularly anguished, violent and pernicious motherhood. As the story unfolds, the main character – an ageing woman – loses the vital energy needed to face the world. The tragic heroine sacrificed on the altar of colonial vampirism, this woman battles on behalf of her children against officialdom, against corruption, against destiny, and even against the waves of the Pacific. Her land – a miserable bungalow in the middle of salt marshes bought for a premium from colonial land agents for the cultivation of rice – crumbles, washed away by the tides. But she fights on so that the children of the plain won't die like mangoes falling before the rainy season, so that the peasants can at last eat their fill, so that ex-convicts enslaved by a century of colonialism will no longer be humiliated.

To convey the sound of the soul – that is how Marguerite defined her task as a writer. To give voice to the cry from the depths of time, the cry of injustice mingled with revolt. The cry of anger too, that sudden flash of dignity that each and every human being possesses when confronted with catastrophe. Human, too human, the mother in *The Sea Wall*, the egocentric, hypochondriac, moaning, over-possessive mother inhabits a no-man's-land where reality is but a tracery of illusions, and time an ever-erratic rudder. From the kingdom of the dead, her late husband sends her an occasional sign. The book opens with the death of a horse and ends with the death of the mother. Marguerite Duras never denied just how auto-biographical the novel was. Yet the book is not simply the story of Madame Donnadieu, it is universal.

Marguerite owed its success to her style. To describe childhood and adolescence she descended, without making awkward fictional detours, into her own memories. She put aside the fondness for American fiction that was holding her back and captured her feelings by refining her sentences, going straight to the point. The reader is transported to the places she describes. The humidity of the atmosphere, the dust raised by the vehicles as they take the only road across the arid plains, the bad smell of the wading-bird stews the mother dishes out to her children at every meal, the loose boards of the veranda that overlooks the quivering jungle – through the precise words she chooses, the rhythm she uses, the succinctness of the sentences and her art of ellipsis, Marguerite Duras makes us experience this world. In this intensely visual novel, the writer with her camera-pen scans the lands through which she travelled and knew so well. Marguerite invented nothing but allowed herself to be guided by her sensory memory.

The Sea Wall is also a novel about dream-life. The characters, like hallucinating ghosts, spend their waking hours dreaming of another life. Between dream and magic, the cinema is the ultimate retreat, where it's possible to enjoy the world as a spectacle and not be hit by it. 'Only there in front of the screen did life become straightforward. To find yourself with a stranger in front of the same image made you desire the stranger. The impossible was within reach, life's problems were resolved and became imaginary.'

Almost six years had elapsed between the submitting of *La vie tranquille* and *The Sea Wall*. A wonderful reward for our patience, commented Queneau. Marguerite Duras was now considered to be 'one of the best novelists of her generation'.[17] When it appeared, the book attracted the attention of a small circle but it did not receive wide critical acclaim. Writing in *Combat* on 22 June 1950, Maurice Nadeau drew his readers' attention to what he deemed to be a revelation. 'We believe this book will bring the author fame and fortune,' Nadeau announced, 'and put Marguerite Duras where she belongs – among the very best of our young writers.' He called it a cinematic novel. 'The narrative, flawless and never slack, is carried forward from beginning to end with inspired eloquence and brings together a succession of perfectly constructed tragic and comic scenes.' Nadeau and other reviewers pointed out the obvious influence of Erskine Caldwell.

Claude Roy, who proved to be a true friend, loyal through thick and thin and a fervent and sincere admirer of Duras as a writer, published an ecstatic review in *Les Lettres françaises* on 29 June 1950. When you're a member of the Party and addressing your comrade readers you don't say what you like in a communist newspaper. It was therefore the politically committed aspects of the novel that Claude Roy focused on, for example the description of the 'huge concentration camp that Indo-China with its viscous, humid and atrocious scenery had been turned into by colonialism'. Duras was describing an 'Indo-China that was calling for, justifying and needing an uprising'. Claude Roy 'preferred Marguerite Duras's troubled lyricism, the great burst of indignation that she wrenches from her heroes, broadening their dismal horizons, showing them at last within the immense framework of the immense injustice with which the White Man devastated the lands he governed ... A novel imbued with a dreadful beauty, with the pure white of goodness and a profound pity for man; a novel of stubborn hope,' he concluded and hailed the 'sea wall that at last stemmed tide, war and death'.

The Sea Wall was short-listed for the Goncourt literary prize that autumn.[18] Despite the support of Gallimard and some journalists, Marguerite received only one vote. She was not a good loser and was convinced the judges had gone against her because she was a revolutionary communist.

The moment the book came out, Marguerite went on holiday with Outa. On her way to Cap Ferret on the Bay of Biscay where she'd rented a house, she stopped off to see her mother. The latter had returned from Indo-China six months earlier and bought a property in Onzain, Loir-et-Cher, a kind of mock Louis XV castle. In Marguerite's bag was the book. Much later Marguerite described her anxious wait.[19] The mother, upstairs in her bedroom, spent all night reading *The Sea Wall*, the daughter, downstairs, awaited the verdict. It was negative. Marguerite was accused of having lied, of having betrayed and, the ultimate obscenity, of having used – to satisfy the world's baser instincts – fragments of her mother's life. 'I told myself one always wrote on the dead body of the world and similarly on the body of love.'[20] The daughter thought she had written a book about the mother's anger, the mother's dignity. She saw her book as a ringing tribute to her mother. All the mother saw was the condemnation of her malevolence and an attack on her as a mother. The hearing was brief. The mother returned the book to the daughter. 'She thought I was accusing her in the book of defeat. That I was condemning her! One of the great sorrows of my life is that she never understood,' Marguerite once said.[21] When Sartre's mother read *The Words*, her comment was: 'Poulou understood nothing about his childhood.' Can a mother understand what her child has written? Should a mother who thinks she owns her child's childhood not be automatically barred from reading what her child has written on the subject? Anyway it was too late. To the day she died, Madame Donnadieu would never be anything other than the widow of her husband and the mother of her oldest son. There could never be anything between mother and daughter.

The mother was a rich woman when she returned to France. Rich from being the owner of an upper-crust Saigon boarding school; rich from the houses – five – she had purchased, which had risen in value; rich from the trafficking in piastres that all whites in the colony went in for. She initially moved into a hotel in Paris and never spent a single night in rue Saint-Benoît.

Marguerite hatched a plot with 'her men' to get some answers from her mother. She wanted things clarified and to get an apology from her mother for all the harm done her when she was a child and an adolescent. And so one evening Marguerite had her mother to dinner in rue Saint-Benoît. Dionys, Robert and Edgar Morin were there. Edgar described Marguerite's mother as being extremely reserved, dignified and a bit on the cold side.[22] After dinner, Marguerite left the room. Dionys began by asking her about the violence inflicted on her daughter and demanding explanations. The conversation became more like an interrogation and lasted well into the night. The mother appeared not to understand any of it. The daughter did not reappear until the mother was leaving.

Marguerite spent the whole of July 1950 at Cap Ferret with Outa. She had established a loving relationship with him. She watched everything he did, wanted to remember everything about him, the way a shell remembers the sound of the sea. In her diary, she wrote:

> I'm not a crazed mother ... No. I know what a child is worth. It's because I lost one and because I know it could die that I'm like that. I've weighed up the cost of the whole horror of the possibility of such a love. Motherhood makes you good they say. Bollocks. Ever since I've had him, I've become spiteful. Anyway I'm sure about the horror.

Outa was a wonderful child. Lissome and funny, he delighted the adults with whom he spent all his time. He didn't have his own separate life. Some, like Queneau, were astonished, others complained – his father Dionys for one. Fortunately Monique's son was around; they were the same age and with him Outa was able to have a child's life. During the day Marguerite saw to her son, worked, did the cooking, made and fixed things. The nights were for drinking and talking. Her life as a writer she incorporated into her daily life. She was good with her hands and writing was one of her many activities. She never discussed it but never treated it as something apart.

CHAPTER 9

How Can Anyone Not Write?

~

Marguerite's relationship with Dionys was as turbulent as ever. He would always leave her gasping in admiration, 'I love you. Tell me you love me.' According to Marguerite, Dionys objected to 'the tenderness of love' and wanted only 'to live love like a bullfight'. That autumn, they continued to tear each other apart. Marguerite suspected Dionys of being unfaithful, and maybe she was right. Raymond Queneau often refers in his diary to Dionys having trysts with the pretty women working at Gallimard or spending a few hours with women writers after work. So Marguerite tried to make him jealous by seducing the regular visitors to rue Saint-Benoît. Marguerite was playing with fire and Dionys didn't fall for it.

On New Year's Eve 1951, everyone was drunk and the games of love and chance took an interesting turn. Marguerite had a long and passionate embrace with a new guest – the writer and journalist Jacques-Laurent Bost, a friend of Simone de Beauvoir, companion of Sartre, Queneau and Merleau-Ponty. Congratulating himself, he fell straight into the trap. Simone de Beauvoir in her *Lettres à Nelson Algren* gives a most amusing account of the beginning of this brief but turbulent affair. How could she sleep with a bloke who's never been a Party member? her ex-husband and present partner asks. 'She says nothing, pretending to listen, to knit, determined to sleep with Bost even though he's never been a communist.' A couple of days later 'Meg' (Marguerite) meets Bost in a café and says, in a most businesslike way, 'OK, let's go to the hotel for a fuck, I've got exactly

an hour.' Bost didn't want to, the discussion dragged on and they ran
out of time. They eventually did the business, but later and in secret.[1]
Marguerite's affair with Jacques-Laurent Bost lasted several months.
It was a relationship she valued but it ended badly. Dionys insisted
she end the affair, and Robert intervened too. Simone de Beauvoir
describes how 'Meg' tells Bost, 'It's actually my ex-husband who'd
like to kill you, not my partner.' In March Elio and Ginetta Vittorini
arrived from Italy and organized a family meeting. They all insisted
Marguerite finish the affair. In an attempt at reconciliation, Marguerite, exhausted and under duress, agreed to go to Venice with
Dionys.

Her next novel, *The Sailor from Gibraltar*, published in 1952, contains traces of these recent heartbreaks although Marguerite took the
precaution of reversing the sexes – it is the man who wants to leave
the woman. Judging by the state of the manuscript, the author had
problems getting the novel to hang together. For a long time *The
Sailor from Gibraltar* was going to be called *The Musketeer*. It was set
on land until the day Marguerite went to the cinema to see *The Lady
from Shanghai* and fell madly in love with the film and Rita Hayworth,
a sublime woman. Marguerite set to work transforming Orson
Welles's story and got rid of the temptress's taste for money so as to
be able to lock her into the passion and depravity of love. The setting
is the Riviera.

From a literary point of view, the book is bizarre, unbalanced and
unfinished. The first part is a muddled description of an insignificant,
spineless and impotent character – a man who can't stand his wife or
for that matter himself any more – and the reader is caught up in
repetitive prose, punctuated by rather vacuous dialogues too overtly
influenced by Faulkner and Sartre. And then he suddenly sees the
light. Quite literally. The vision – a white yacht – appears and everything changes; the light is blinding, love obvious and the story veers
off elsewhere. The woman from the white yacht appears on the beach
where the abandoned body of the man is lying. She wants to seduce
him, of course, to ensnare him, to make him her hostage, her sexual
slave, but the man has forgotten how to want, he's nothing but a dead
weight. So why does he agree to go on board? Probably because he
has nothing to lose and because he wants to learn to live with himself.
How do you make the best of yourself? That is the question that nags

at the heart of *The Sailor from Gibraltar*. For a long time the woman had done nothing with herself, it was time to face facts: 'You can't not. You must always eventually do something with yourself.' And so she searches the seas for her lover.

Duras was very much inspired by Maurice Blanchot, a writer who had also been active in the Resistance. She was a great admirer of his work and spent a lot of time with him. He advocated a literature that sought out the inherent power of words, a literature that existed only through and in literature, where the very act of writing risked impenetrability. 'We know that we only write when the leap is accomplished, but in order to accomplish the leap we must first write, write endlessly, write from infinity.'[2] *The Sailor from Gibraltar* is a novel about an unfulfilled search, about waiting that is by definition always thwarted, a great metaphysical novel. An angel goes by; visiting a museum, the narrator meets him and recognizes him. It's the angel that watched over his childhood, a picture of him hung over his bed. There are many angels in *The Sailor from Gibraltar*. In the ports, the prostitutes wait. In Duras's eyes prostitutes are heroines, the true muses of love. Paid by everyone, perfect performers of the repetitive mechanics of love, they give themselves to everyone while they wait to give themselves to just one.

On signature of the contract Marguerite received 120,000 francs, equivalent to royalties for 2000 copies. As soon as the book was published, she asked for an advance of 80,000 francs. In 1952, *The Sea Wall* sold 3200 copies and Marguerite had received a total of 175,000 francs in advances. At the time of signing for *The Sailor from Gibraltar*, she owed Gallimard a balance of 97,000 francs. Bear in mind that at the time Marguerite was living frugally, that she had decided being her profession was a writer and that she was not yet supplementing her income by working as a journalist. The only money she had coming in was from the publishing house. When the book came out, the reviews were restrained. By the end of 1952, 2800 copies of *The Sailor from Gibraltar* had been sold. On 15 September 1953, Marguerite asked for a further advance of 250,000 francs. She had just delivered her new novel *The Little Horses of Tarquinia* – 'two novels in two years, not bad, eh?' she said towards the end of her life, her voice brimming with pride.[3] She would publish a book almost every year.

Marguerite had no strategy, no blueprint. 'When I write a book I go off in search of adventure. But afterwards everything comes together to form a whole. The purpose, the subject is usually tiny at the start.'[4] Marguerite Duras knew nothing about the rules of plausibility. In fact, she couldn't have cared less about them. She liked making use of situation comedy and facetious remarks. Her books are always connected by visible or invisible themes, whatever the subject and despite time and distance. In *The Little Horses of Tarquinia* the link with the preceding novel is quite blatant: we are back in Italy, in the summer heat, with the ever-present sea. But for all that *The Little Horses of Tarquinia* is not a sequel to *The Sailor from Gibraltar*. The mood Duras was so good at creating is slowly established – psychological confusion, physical lethargy exacerbated by the sweltering heat, questioning the futility of life and the latent man-woman you-love-me-therefore-I-don't-desire-you conflict. The heroine's name is Sara and she's the mother of a young child (the same age as Outa), whose life with her partner Jacques is mad and miserable. Like Dionys he is handsome, an excellent swimmer, philosopher, ideologue, sardonic and scathing. The threat of imminent separation hangs over Jacques and Sara. Marguerite was about to turn forty, as was Sara. 'If you only want to make love with one man, it's because you don't like making love,' Sara tells her friend Gina, who is obviously based on Ginetta Vittorini. 'I feel I could make love to fifty men.' Sara would like to live in the hotel, far from Jacques. ' "You're fed up with me." He started to laugh. They both laughed. "As I am with you," he added. "We can't help it." ' Duras describes wonderfully well the automatic mellowing of love over time, the tedium and gloom of married life. Holidays – family – sun. In order to forget, they drink Campari, lie in the sea, dance under the stars in small restaurants. Sara can down ten Camparis in a row! I've known readers get hooked on that cheery, treacherous drink after reading *The Little Horses of Tarquinia*.

A strange man appears, well built and muscular, though his conversational skills are not brilliant. Sara falls into his arms after an evening of drinking and makes love on the flagstones of the veranda to the sound of 'Blue Moon'. 'She marvelled at being the object of his desire. In fact she had always marvelled at being desired by men.' Sara doesn't believe in herself. Sara can't find the words to express her thoughts. She needs her husband to sort out her ideas and to know what she should do. At the back of the *La Douleur* notebooks, there is in fact the story of an encounter Marguerite had while she and Dionys were on holiday with Elio and Ginetta Vittorini. And she probably danced under the stars to the husky voice of an Italian singer on a worn-out gramophone.

The Little Horses of Tarquinia is the existential acknowledgement of the failure of the couple as an institution. Marguerite and Dionys were weary of each other, and contempt would soon follow. A fatuous conventional life no longer appealed to her. 'Robert is the only one of us who still lives in the most infernal poetic chaos,' she wrote in one of her notebooks.[5] Robert whom she called her gentle rhinoceros, towards whom she'd been spiteful and who had – she knew – escaped her for ever. She missed Robert.

As usual Marguerite got Dionys and Robert to read the manuscript before she handed it in to the editor. They both said the book was unpublishable, too realistic and highly insulting to the Vittorinis, as it showed them in a very bad light indeed. Marguerite stood her ground and refused to change a single line. There was a meeting in Robert's house, attended by – among others – Jacques-Francis Rolland, Edgar Morin, Monique (the future Mrs Antelme) and of course Dionys and Marguerite. They had a very heated discussion, with the most biting and bitter criticism coming from Dionys. someone suggested the manuscript should be thrown in the Seine so that they'd never have to discuss it again. Marguerite fought tooth and nail to protect her manuscript, and even hid it under the sofa she was sitting on. Then, once tempers had cooled, after a few whiskies had been downed, she left with it tucked under her arm.

The book appeared as it had been written in December 1953. Marguerite had found a parry: it was dedicated to Ginetta and Elio! Confronted by this demonstration of friendship, what could they do but adopt a sardonic attitude as they read Marguerite's dramatic version of their conjugal wrangles? Anyway, Marguerite couldn't have cared less what Elio thought about it. They were drifting apart. Elio was too demonstrative, too opinionated. *The Little Horses of Tarquinia* is not only an excellent novel on the acrimony of love, it is also a wonderful treatise on failing friendships.

The critics were merciless. There were rumours before the book came out that Marguerite Duras was in line for a prize. Alas, 'Nothing happens in this novel to disturb the reader,' wrote Jean Blanzat in *Le Figaro littéraire*, even though he had been one of her first and most ardent defenders. 'People surrender to their fate, powerless to change it.' Marguerite Duras was repetitive without being innovative. 'This novel,' Blanzat added, 'is just like all the others, wholly inspired by American stylistic devices.'[6] Another critic agreed: 'After four novels, we have to accept that Marguerite Duras only wants to write in American French.'[7] Not wanting to be outdone, the satirical magazine *Le Canard enchaîné* pulled both author and book apart:

This lady, Marguerite Duras, plays the fool and displays a most concise vocabulary ... Example – we're all bloody idiots. Fuck me, now that's what I call virile. But it's all show, for when she chats Marguerite Duras gets her femininity back. It babbles. It waffles! Holds forth! Drones on! And on and on! People often talk about an author's tongue – well, Marguerite Duras never stops wagging hers.

For the rest of her life as a writer Duras had the reputation of violating the rules of grammar, of being the expert on nothingness and the Paris intelligentsia's mistress of navel-gazing. But she was not discouraged. She continued to write to exorcise her childhood and bewildering adolescence, and constantly returned to territory scorched by the absence of love.

In *Whole Days in the Trees*, a collection of short stories that takes its title from the main story, Duras once again portrays her mother. But this time she isn't a defeated, desperate mother with drooping breasts and worn-out cotton shifts struggling for her children's future survival at the edge of the Pacific. She an ostentatiously wealthy woman, but alone. And she wants to see her beloved son one last time before she dies. For the first time, Marguerite Duras sides with the detested brother, puts herself in his shoes. How is the brother going to get through the mother's visit? How long will it be before he has the courage to ask her for money or steal it from her? 'Outside there was a huge bright blue spring sun and light cool gusts of wind swept the streets. Walking along the pavements were free men whose mothers were far away or dead.'

Marguerite always said she was an early riser, that she loved the dawn and that it made her want to go for a walk, to write, to breathe. During her childhood and adolescence she was forbidden by her mother to make a noise in the morning in order not to wake the elder brother who had staggered home at dawn after a night in opium dens. All her life Marguerite was frightened of the night, which fell very quickly in Indo-China. It was nightfall in Vinh Long when the screaming beggar woman chased her, breathing down her back. It was in the middle of the night in 1940 that, returning from having had sex with another man, she found her husband waiting at the door, having come home unexpectedly. And we shouldn't forget all the long, anguished nights that followed, the nights of waiting, hoping for news of him when he was deported; then, after the Liberation, the drunken nights of rows when things were said that should have remained unsaid, and the dark nights of insomnia right up to her death. It's no accident that in 'Whole Days in the Trees' the son robs the mother in the middle of the night. The stolen money disappears instantly in a gambling joint. 'He came home at dawn, light and free, stark naked, an adult, at last – that night – exhausted like a man.' The mother goes home having noticed nothing, proud of her son who was already spending whole days in the trees when he was a little boy.

While Marguerite Duras was writing her book, Madame Donnadieu was living in her property on the banks of the Loire, with the chickens and sheep that kept her warm during the cold winters. With her lived Do, her faithful servant from Saigon, the one the elder brother raped, the modest, wonderful Do who could do everything – housework, cooking, sewing, reading. When she first moved in, Madame Donnadieu had thought she'd be able to carry on teaching, so she turned the property into a small private school and took in a few boarders, the children of wealthy Chinese and Vietnamese families living in exile. But it proved too much – Madame Donnadieu was too old, Do too tired. The venture came to an abrupt end. At that point she decided she would try her hand at rearing chickens. Equipped with a sophisticated and extremely expensive heating system, sold her by a canny shopkeeper, Madame Donnadieu branched into intensive battery farming. Less practical than Marguerite, she found the electric system difficult to master. It was a massacre. The chickens that survived had crooked beaks and a limp. Then she invested in sheep, thinking – but it never got past the thinking stage – she would have wool.

There was gossip among the neighbours. The son was useless, he was having problems again. And yet he only lived a few kilometres away, pretending to look after the mushroom bed his mother had also bought. He'd drop in on her every day and then disappear without warning into the trees on the Île de la Loire or into the gambling dens of the capital.

Marguerite visited her mother too, more often than she let on to her friends. She asked her mother for nothing – not money, not feelings. She wanted her company, waited for some kind of gesture. She used to make the trip from Paris to Onzain and back in a day so that she could cook her mother a steak because her mother had said she was the only one who could cook a steak properly. Sometimes she'd take her son, her friend Monique Antelme and her children down there for a few days. 'It was awful!' Monique recalled. 'She'd serve chicken for every meal and check we hadn't left any on our plates.' Authoritarian, terse, she was intentionally distant from her children. 'She never said much. She was more a woman of action. She'd follow us around, Marguerite and me. She was always so peremptory. She was quite modest to look at, with her tight bun and black dress. Penny-pinching. One knob of butter went into the soup and if we went to a café she used to take the sugar. It was quite obvious Marguerite was still afraid of her.'

It was only after her mother's death that Marguerite would say: 'These days, I don't love my mother any more.'[8] While the distancing had begun with the birth of Outa, *Whole Days in the Trees* marked an important stage in the continuing process. The mother had become literary material. Later, in *The Lover*, she would become 'standard writing', to quote an expression Duras used at every possible opportunity.

The mother is not the only heroine in *Whole Days in the Trees*. Madame Fossez is there, alias Madame Dodin, concierge by trade. Madame Dodin packs a hell of a punch, has one tooth, a great gift of the gab and moans all the time – the bins are too heavy, the tenants filthy, the stairs too steep. The story 'Madame Dodin' is a masterpiece of humour, a short treatise on the banalities of daily life. To Duras, who was speaking was less important than how they were speaking.

She didn't discriminate between a minister and a concierge. In fact, her friend Mitterrand was a minister at the time of writing. 'Madame Fossez is a better speaker than Mitterrand,' said Marguerite, who knew when to keep her mouth shut so that she could listen to others and then write down what she heard. She listened enthralled to the great diversity of the language, but she wanted to be a messenger, not a judge or censor. She let herself be impregnated by all the words, then put them into the mouths of her characters. To her literature was also a wish to show the unaffected, undisguised, unrefined aspects of language. She was often criticized for this.

It was probably in the last of the short stories from *Whole Days in the Trees*, the one entitled 'Les chantiers', that she took the most risks. Venturing into the land of nascent and indescribable loves, she invented a style of writing that challenged itself on the level of its function and future. In 1966 Duras would return to this short story to deconstruct and then reconstruct it to produce the film *Destroy, She Said.*

Following the relative failure of *The Little Horses of Tarquinia*, Gallimard decided on an initial print run of 3000 copies of *Whole Days in the Trees*. The reaction of the critics, while subdued, was more positive than for the preceding two books. *La Gazette de Lausanne* set the tone: 'It is difficult to believe that a woman could have thought up and put together in a form so abrupt, so intensely cynical and peremptory the short stories that make up this collection.' Marguerite would ask herself later how she so meekly and for so long put up with all the male advice, criticism and opinions. In a notebook dating from 1955, we find traces of these indignities and of what it did to her self-esteem:

I'd show Dionys something I'd written and he'd say, 'You've been reading Hemingway again, haven't you?' And I'd be left in a state of utter despair. I'd say, 'All right, so I've been reading *The Green Hills of Africa*, but what I've written there I could quite easily have written without ever having read it ...' Anyway, the story of Madame Dodin's bin, if you can call it a story, is mine. It's a slow, static story that brings me a joy and a sadness that has nothing to do with Hemingway's blazing stories.

The day will come when I give Dionys a definitive response. I've searched for it for four years but still haven't found it. He's always the one to come up with a definitive pronouncement about me. It's something we need to dwell on and explain that while I believe in Dionys's definitive statements and only in Dionys's, Dionys does not believe in mine.

In fact her reading of Hemingway's *Green Hills of Africa* in the mid-fifties had an enormous influence on her. Her friend Madeleine Alleins said Marguerite knew passages off by heart. If Marguerite never gave up writing, it was because she believed that, beyond the words she used, she could arrive at another indescribable reality. This was something she had in common with Nathalie Sarraute, who was one of the rare living writers whose talent she openly and frequently praised. She called this notion of writing the approach of the inner shadow, there where the archives of the self are to be found. Each one of us has an inner shadow. Therefore each one of us could write. The question for Duras was – how can anyone not write? Perhaps we don't necessarily want to risk venturing into those secret territories. Duras never tried to hide the fact that she thought she'd thrown away her life, riveted to a table writing to free herself, empty herself of everything mixed up inside her. She often felt she had missed out on 'real life', normal life, simple happiness, the lightness of being. Even when she could no longer write physically, she dictated or spoke phrases and sentences that could be turned into a book.

The apartment at 5 rue Saint-Benoît was Marguerite's universe, filled with her family photos, her bunches of dried flowers, her beautiful shining furniture, her broken stove, her shawls draped over the backs of shabby armchairs, loose parquet, the smell of rose petals. She was a talented DIY enthusiast and she entertained several times a week. Marguerite was considered an intellectual and charming hostess. Men would turn up alone just to flirt with her. She was careful to kindle their admiration and passion. The small world in which they lived encompassed a tiny area of Paris. A few hundred metres separated rue Saint-Benoît from the offices of Gallimard and the bistro Espérance, where Robert and Dionys often stopped for a drink after work. Head of rights and reproduction for Gallimard, Dionys was one of the six section leaders. Robert Antelme worked for another publishing firm, la Pléaide.

While continuing to attend her parties, professionally Queneau

had started to distance himself from Marguerite. Much to her annoyance, he had expressed reservations regarding *Whole Days in the Trees*.
She demanded that Gaston give her a new editor, and he gave her
Robert Gallimard. Robert was delighted to be editing a writer he
admired and a woman who over the years had become a friend. Even
so, she was not an easy author when it came to discussions. Only for
Whole Days in the Trees did she accept any of his comments. She would
brook no criticism when it came to her following book, *The Square*.
'She was all sweetness and light until it came to discussing her work
and then you weren't allowed to entertain the slightest doubt. I
remember one day I'd just begun to point out a nagging doubt when
she jumped in and said, "You're not up to the mark." ' From that
point on, editing Marguerite meant dropping everything to read
the latest manuscript, which she insisted Gallimard must send a
messenger to collect, even though the offices were a five-minute walk
away from where she lived. Then you had to call her within two hours
and tell her how brilliant it was. Dionys was no longer allowed to
read the books before publication. At the time it was Louis-René des
Forêts, a writer, editor and friend, who had the privilege of reading
her work and expressing his opinions. But the slightest comment
could throw her into an indescribable rage.[9] The only opinion she
still feared was Robert's.

Marguerite already considered herself to be a great writer and said
she wanted to be financially independent from Dionys. But her books
weren't bringing in enough money. And so she started to demand
larger instalments from her publishers and to listen to the calls of the
big newspapers, who were inviting her to write lucrative articles on
minor news items, fashion and cinema. 'That would be tantamount
to prostituting yourself,' said Robert. So Marguerite turned them
down, for the time being. She followed the rules of the pack over
which she reigned at rue Saint-Benoît – Blanchot, des Forêts, from
time to time Bataille, Queneau, Lacan, Barthes. The old guard of
Morin, Antelme, Rolland and Dionys met every evening. 'Those men
were all hers,' said Robert Gallimard. 'I wasn't hers. I had another
life, other people in my life. She didn't like that.' Marguerite was
authoritarian and opinionated – whether it was the colour of a new
jacket or the latest declaration from the Communist Party. She knew
where you could get the best and cheapest pigs' tails in Paris. She made

wonderful cold meat vol-au-vents and perfect spicy, moist Vietnamese rice. She was unflaggingly cheerful, playful, funny and lively. A touching, poignant, wayward, intolerable and extraordinary child. She knew the songs of Tino Rossi off by heart and loved to dance alone in the middle of the sitting room, going round and round for ages, drunk on music. Tantalizing, irresistible Marguerite! She was jealous of everything and nothing, but especially of her friends' wives, over whom she liked to wield a sophisticated kind of perverse authority. You had to be able to stand up to her. Only Monique Antelme had the charm and temperament to do that. Her children and Marguerite's son being around the same age, she was like a second mother to Outa and the only real friend Marguerite had at the time. Violette Naville, Edgar Morin's partner at this time, remembered that the day she decided to leave the rue Saint-Benoît group, her friend Roland Barthes pointed out she hadn't said a word for years. Violette hadn't even noticed ... Did Marguerite shut the other women up? She was only interested in the men, in their opinions, in being noticed by them. It wasn't until the militant feminism of the seventies that she had female friends and discovered 'sisterhood'.

Simone de Beauvoir was not a member of the clan and had no wish to join. During the fifties Marguerite approached Sartre a couple of times to see if he'd be interested in publishing some of her short stories in *Les Temps modernes*. Sartre met her and explained bluntly, 'I can't publish you. You're a bad writer. But I'm not the one who said it. If you don't improve, you won't get published in *Les Temps modernes*.' To the end of her days Marguerite Duras was sure it was Simone de Beauvoir who'd had the audacity to say she was a bad writer. She never forgot the slur. The animosity between them was also due to jealousy over the fact that they had both been in love with Jacques-Laurent Bost. But the root of the problem was that their approach to writing was radically different. Marguerite Duras used to reproach Robert Gallimard for on the one hand publishing Beauvoir while on the other claiming to like her books. He had Marguerite imploring in one ear, 'Tell me Beauvoir's a nothing,' and Simone in other confessing, 'I just don't understand Duras, explain her to me.' Marguerite did not like other women writers. There was the risk – and she openly admitted it – that they might overshadow her. She never made a secret of her contempt for Marguerite Yourcenar, with whom she unfortunately shared a first name. Again, the only woman writer she had any time for was Nathalie Sarraute. For forty years she admired her style, her determination to pave a way for herself and her legendary discretion.

Marguerite wrote nonstop and the moment a manuscript was finished she'd get it published. In 1955 *The Square* came out. It was somewhere between a short story and a philosophical tale. Deliberately prosaic, the book does, however, contain poetic illuminations, hallucinations and premonitory dreams. The two protagonists – a chubby commercial traveller and a fresh-faced young maid – swap opinions on the world one beautiful spring afternoon in a square. They talk all afternoon, and each thereby acknowledges the other's existence. They have moved into another dimension, another perception of the world. Talking, therefore existing. 'It certainly does you good, oh yes, but afterwards, when you stop talking, that's when it gets boring. Time begins to drag. Maybe you should never talk.' The square's about to close. They go back to their dreams. There's no message, no hope at the end of *The Square*. The characters are returned to their private solitude, to the futility of their existence.

In Marguerite's view *The Square* was a text that should be spoken, proclaimed, and it would soon be adapted for the stage. *The Square* had a print run of 2,200 copies – for three consecutive years the print run for each new book had gone down. The reviews were decidedly cool, and her friends were of the same opinion. During the time she was writing the book, Marguerite was having financial problems that obliged her to demand money from Robert Gallimard. 'To date, your account is in debt to the tune of 150,000 francs,' he replied. 'However, since your appeal has touched hearts notoriously sympathetic, I shall not be inflexible. I am enclosing a cheque for 50,000 francs, thus increasing your debt by as much...'

Another French colony was next to engage Marguerite Duras's attention. Algeria had first been occupied by French troops in the 1830s, and had repeatedly rebelled against French rule. In 1954, the war of independence broke out, setting the Arab Berber population against the French settlers and army. From the outset Marguerite was a fierce opponent of the repression of the Algerians. Dionys set up the Committee of Intellectuals Against the Pursuit of the War in Algeria, which brought together people from the left and right of the political spectrum. In October 1955, Marguerite was one of the first to sign a petition against the continuation of the war in North Africa, along with over three hundred other artists and writers. The petition described the war as a crime against humanity and a threat to the French Republic.

The poet and founding surrealist André Breton was at the committee's first meeting, as were the distinguished novelists François Mauriac and Roger Martin du Gard. Edgar Morin, Claude Roy, Robert Antelme and Louis-René des Forêts formed the main group. At the meeting held on 5 November, Marguerite made two proposals. One was to make a film on North Africans living in France, to show just how badly they were treated and to raise awareness. She had a director, Claude Jeager, and offered herself to write the scenario in collaboration with Marc Pierret. Her second idea was to attract to the committee as many artists as possible. She took personal charge of this and contacted, among others, Pablo Picasso and Jean Dubuffet. Everyone who had signed up contributed a small amount towards the financing of the film, but it never saw the light of day. The committee met regularly, produced a newsletter and elected an executive committee.

The petition provoked the wrath of Jacques Soustelle, the governor general of Algeria, who published in *Combat* on 26 November an article in which he rejected the notion that there was a war in Algeria, claiming that the word was being used by a group of agitated intellectuals to arouse feelings of guilt. According to him the Algerians – or rebels, as he called them – had neither aspirations nor principles. They were nothing more than racist, totalitarian obscurantists, torturers and arsonists. In response to Soustelle's arguments, a long political text analysing the situation in Algeria, entitled 'Reply to the Governor General of Algeria' was published on 3 December under the aegis of the committee. Having received no response, the committee two weeks later repeated its demand for the rapid setting-up of an inquiry. On 23 December, Soustelle responded by accusing those who dared harry the authorities and presume to tell them what to do, of bad faith and of being misinformed.

On 10 January 1956 Marguerite Duras was given the responsibility of replying on behalf of the whole group. In a letter that went on for

several pages, she made reference to camps in Algeria, to police use of torture, and accused civilians and servicemen of being guilty of the collective murder of the civilian population of Algeria. 'We have words to describe a man who puts all his energy into denouncing the atrocities of others while never mentioning those being carried out under his authority. It has to stop. Even the Statesman who appointed you governor general of Algeria now sees you as a has-been. He recently declared, "Economic and social feudalism are the law-makers in Algeria." As a man of action among men of action you have failed." '
The letter was sent to Jacques Soustelle on behalf of the committee. How could he have known who had written it? An informant? A police investigation? No one knows. However, the fact remains that he replied direct to Marguerite Duras, in much the same tone she had used to him: 'I would make so bold as to point out that you are mistaken in claiming that a thousand French intellectuals subscribe without a murmur to all that it pleases you and a few others to write.' He did not address the real issues.

At the next public meeting, on 27 January 1956, Jean-Paul Sartre and others formally denounced colonialism and colonialism by any other name, and demanded that an end be put to the myth that the Algerian assembly was going to be dissolved, negotiations sought with the leaders of the Algerian Resistance movement and Algeria made a French department. Sartre demanded that Algeria be made independent forthwith. 'I am very proud to have been there', Marguerite said later. 'We wanted to meet so that they [Algerians] could emerge from their fear, from their terror.' The committee produced a leaflet and lobbied the authorities. A telegram was sent to François Mitterrand, then French minister of justice, asking for a stay of execution for the Algerian Resistance fighters. As a result, for the first time in a long time Mitterrand and Marguerite talked together. It was a chilly meeting. Marguerite was disappointed in Mitterrand. After that she kept her distance, barely able to disguise her contempt for him. It wasn't until the 1981 presidential elections that they would make up.

In 1957, just as André Breton and other surrealists were joining the Committee of Intellectuals, it was dissolved and replaced by the Committee of Revolutionary Intellectuals.

French intellectual opinion was not unanimous over the Algerian question. Marguerite Duras belonged to what Albert Camus called the 'female left', which idly conjured an 'occupied Algerian nation struggling to free itself of the occupier'. Camus, himself born and educated in Algeria, regarded the Algerian nation as made up of two peoples, each of whom had as much right as the other to justice and to retain their homeland. There were disagreements in rue Saint-Benoît as well. Edgar Morin, and then Claude Roy, disclaimed some of the activities of the Algerian National Liberation Front (FLN) and refused to be associated with people who shot at the French. 'We knew very little about Algeria when we came out in support of it,' he later confessed.[10] The activities of the FLN in France reminded him of some of the Stalinist attitudes he had found so shocking. In rue Saint-Benoît, the arguments were often heated and lasted well into the night. Robert Gallimard left quietly. In late 1956, the failed Anglo-French occupation of the newly nationalized Suez Canal, and the Soviet invasion of Hungary, hastened the split between the communists and the rest. Deeply affected by the Hungarian issue, Marguerite subscribed wholeheartedly to the ideas of David Rousset, someone she had until then been quite wary of. The group disbanded. There were fewer meetings. But the old guard remained.

Marguerite divided her life between her three men. First there was her son Outa. Whenever she gave a newspaper interview she had to talk about him, saying he was the most important person in her life. 'Ever since he was born I have been living in madness,' she said.[11] And then of course there came Dionys and Robert, whose *The Human Race* was to be republished by Gallimard in 1957 and who was at last getting the recognition he deserved as a philosopher, writer and historian.

   Like all women, Marguerite knew the man she was living with was being unfaithful. Like all women, she knew even though she didn't want to know. Like a lot of men, Dionys denied it. This fuelled Marguerite's self-doubts and remorse, she was ashamed of her negative thoughts. All her friends, everyone knew Dionys was having affairs. Except for her. And although his friends didn't know about his double life with Paulette Delval, they knew Dionys was a womanizer. Marguerite was a woman who'd been wronged. Maybe she was excessively demanding of the man she was living with. Maybe she was overbearing, possessive, jealous, spiteful. And so the time came when he would go elsewhere, not far, just far enough away to be able to breathe. But she was never one for half measures, relationships dead but propped up for the sake of petty bourgeois conventions. In *The Little Horses of Tarquinia* Sara says of the man she lives with, 'He'd been unfaithful to me often enough, but me, I'd never yet been unfaithful to him.'

Marguerite and Dionys were finally drifting apart for good. The summer of 1956 was a difficult one. Marguerite went to Trouville, a resort on the English Channel, with her son. She waited for Dionys but he didn't come, and so she drove down to the south of France. Marguerite always enjoyed driving. Throughout her life she had a fanatical, wild and enduring love of cars, all cars, especially the biggest and the fastest.

Having arrived, exhausted by the journey, she wrote Dionys an umpteenth letter. In clarifying her position, she was in effect breaking up with him:

You never talk to me ... what do I owe you? I'm forty-two and I'm not prepared to go on like this any longer. I'm tired and I'm sorry. I think in my life I've been a person of enormous good faith and that I've been cheated. I'm probably wrong. My childhood was unspeakable, I was deprived and when you insult me I feel you must be right. I wish you all the best. But the kind of best you want from me is not what I want.

The decision was finally taken when she returned from holiday. They split but didn't separate, and Dionys continued to live in rue Saint-Benoît until 1967. Just as he'd found it difficult to move out of his mother's house and in with Marguerite, so Dionys couldn't cut himself off from her. He continued to live with her and together they saw to Outa's education. Marguerite at last felt free of Dionys's critical gaze. Above all released from having to wait up for him when she was sure he was being unfaithful to her. She could at last go to sleep without having to ask him – a need and a reassurance – to make love to her when he came home after an evening he didn't want to talk about. 'The pain, the agony of those brief flings, the constant watching, the silent screaming pain, and why? Why?' she wrote in 'I Wonder How', a piece recalling that period published in *Green Eyes*.

I

2

1. Marguerite Duras in Saigon with Max Bergier, one of her mother's pupils, 25 April 1933.

2. The Donnadieu family in 1920, posing for the photographer. 'From time to time my mother would announce: "tomorrow we're going to the photographer's". She'd complain at the cost but still spent money on family photos.'

3. Madame Donnadieu and her son Paul, Marguerite's beloved brother, 1st January 1964.

4. Madame Donnadieu and Paul on the road to Prey-Nop, Cambodia, to the concession immortalised in *The Sea Wall*.

5. The river crossing, where the first meeting with 'The Lover' took place: 'And the river, always that enchantment, whether by day or by night, empty or swarming with junks, calls, laughter, songs, birds.'

3

4

5

6

6. Jean Lagrolet around the time he met Marguerite Duras.

7. Duras and Jean Lagrolet in the early thirties, during their bohemian student life in the Latin Quarter.

8. In the rue Saint-Benoît. With Raymond Queneau's support Marguerite decides to take up writing. 'What is this constant, parallel to life, constant need to write?'

9

1◄

9. Robert Antelme around the time he first met Marguerite Duras.

10. Duras in militant gear ready to go and sell *l'Humanité-Dimanche*.

11. Duras, in the rue Saint-Benoît, 1955.

12. Marguerite and her son Jean, nicknamed Outa. In Marguerite's view, for a woman to be fulfilled, she had to be a mother. 'Woman gives her body to her child, to her children. They are on her as on a hill, as in a garden; they eat her, they hit her and she lets herself be devoured.'

13. Duras in Trouville, 1963. 'The more you refuse, the more anti you are, the more you live.'

14. Film shoot for *India Song* in the Trianon Palace, Versailles. Marguerite Duras with Bruno Nuytten, to whom she dedicated *The Lover*.

15. Elio Vittorini and Ginetta Vittorini, the couple immortalised in *Ten-Thirty on a Summer Night*, together with Albert Steiner and Duras.

16. Rehearsing *Shaga* with Marie-Ange Duteil and Claire de Luca, who along with Loleh Bellon and Jeanne Moreau was one of her favourite actresses.

17. Duras and Jules Dassin working on the screen adaptation of *Ten-Thirty on a Summer Night*, 1967.

UN FILM DE MARGUERITE DURAS

18

18 & 20. Duras and *India Song* at the Cannes Film Festival, 1974.

19. Typed manuscript of the beginning of chapter 3 of *Ten-Thirty on a Summer Night* (1967) with handwritten corrections. 'There are days you're frightened of dying before the page is finished . . . It's because of the nature of the activity that thoughts of death are with you every day.'

rive enfin.

_ Ne comptez pas que l'électr

dit la patronne, c'est l'habit

L'électricité n'était pas

dans la nuit. Le balcon où se

ses toits. Très bas, au dessu

Maria ~~avait~~ quitté la s

~~pour coucher la petite fille~~

Le couloir, par terre, é

couvertures. Parmis eux se t

maintenan

a lng

dix 1

revie

ag ie

ue. I

M

eux c

mange

tot

ein d

cette

co

utonne iti

peut voir que la femme de   ite

21

21 & 22. Duras at Les Roches Noires, Trouville, 1990. 'When I write about the sea, the storm, the sun, the rain, about fine weather, I am completely in love.'

22

2

23. Duras and Yann Andréa in Neauphle, in the early nineties.

24. Neauphle: the refuge, the writing-house, the house of contrasts, with its gardens, its roses, its cats.

25. 'Why do people write about writers? Surely their books should suffice.'

26. 'My head is full of vertigo and shrieks. Full of wind. And so sometimes I write. Pages, you see.'

27. 'We writers have very poor lives. I am talking of people who really write . . . I know of no one who has less of a personal life than me.'

Thereafter her relationship with Dionys was based on companionship, deep affection and mutual respect. They did not separate physically or geographically, only sexually and emotionally. To her dying day, Marguerite said she had rarely loved a man as much or had a lover as good. Whenever she was looking through an album that contained photographs of Dionys, she always admired his beauty and elegance.

René Clément had just bought the film rights to *The Sea Wall* and was deciding on the actresses. Marguerite wasn't consulted and expressed her disappointment at not having been invited to write the script. 'I shan't be the one working on it and that makes me very sad. They're keeping the title and my name will appear in the credits.'[12] She felt that people were taking liberties with her creative imagination and, even though the rights were important, she appeared quite shocked and disconcerted by this. However, she congratulated herself that the film project was coming off since the stage version, discussed two years earlier, had had to be abandoned through lack of funding.[13] At the time Duras had higher expectations of the stage than the cinema. She felt the latter had become an entertainment medium rather than an art form, a manufacturing process and no longer an invention. The theatre was unsullied by financial issues and was still a risky area. Duras believed in the sacrificial aspect of theatre, in the space come down from antiquity where the actors put their lives at risk with the words uttered on stage.

Marguerite Duras's first play, *The Square*, was performed on 17 September 1956 at the Studio des Champs-Elysées, directed by Claude Martin and performed by Ketty Albertini and R. J. Chauffard. Marguerite had simplified her novel, in which she claimed unintentionally to have written a play. 'Of course, not having done it on purpose, I don't know if I could do it again,' she explained modestly.[14] The director consulted her over the script and suggested she attend the rehearsals. She was soon completely hooked and had nothing but admiration for the two actors. 'They were instantly how I imagined them to be. There was nothing I could tell them.'

The play had a short run and attracted very little attention. Marguerite tried and failed to get it performed elsewhere, so the Studio des Champs-Elysées agreed to put it on again the following season, on condition they were paid. Marguerite obtained the money from Gaston Gallimard, and the play was revived on 1 May 1957. The reviews were on the cool side. 'A festival of platitudes, banalities and deficiencies formulated in a misleadingly simple language saturated with ellipses and punctuated with long thoughtful silences.'[15] Marguerite appeared to be unaffected by this lack of appreciation. She had just embarked on a new love affair.

CHAPTER 10

The Journalist

~

Today her friends say Marguerite was madly in love with Gérard Jarlot, a broodingly handsome, charming, funny, cultured man – a journalist, and a writer in his spare time. When Marguerite met him he was thirty-four and married with three children. He was to play a major role in her life, although she tried to dismiss him and made disparaging remarks about him once time had dulled the intensity of love. She attempted on two occasions to write about him, but in vain. The man defied words. She called him '*l'homme menti*' (the lied man). And yet she shared everything with him – her friends, engagements, houses, landscapes, paintings. She travelled with him, especially in Italy; drank with him, fucked with him. He was a great fuck, she used to say. He was the one who consoled her, who took her in his arms when she was in an alcoholic stupor. He calmed her when she tearfully mourned the absence of her son. Ignoring her opinion, Dionys had put Outa in a boarding school, so fiery had her relationship with him become. Thanks to this man, she would change her writing style, and write a wonderful novel. It was a literary as well as a physical love.

The circumstances of their meeting were extremely romantic. Some say they met playing poker one night, others say he bet his friends he could 'score' and get her into bed by the next day. Marguerite said they met at a Christmas Day party. They talked a lot and he offered to take her home. She refused. He got her address from a friend – Jacques-Francis Rolland – and left her a letter. The message was: I'm waiting for you in such and such a café. Eights days he waited, for five or six hours a day. Duras picked up the story: 'I resisted, went out every day, but not in that area of Paris. But I so desperately wanted to be in love again. On the eighth day I walked into the café like one going to the scaffold.' He was waiting for her and told her he would have waited through all eternity for her. She pretended to believe him.

With him she could laugh, say anything, not discuss politics, spend her evenings in bars, walk the streets until dawn and make love in the afternoon in his room across from the Jardin des Tuileries. It was in cafés that they continued to love each other. From café to café and in each, from table to table, as someone said. They would go home dead drunk and sleep until midday. There are very few photographs of Gérard Jarlot. A holiday film shows him swimming in the sea with Marguerite, athletic and smiling. The women who met him all agreed he was a handsome, dark-haired man. Not the typical Left Bank, boulevard Saint-Germain intellectual. More the daring-reporter-in-a-tired-raincoat-and-with-an-interesting-mouth type. He was very masculine, his friend Michel Mitrani explained, always bragging; he could be frivolous and serious. He had an 'English' complexion, a Saint-Etienne accent and spent his life drinking and picking up girls. At the time Marguerite called him a prince. Fickle, charming, frivolous, spending his days writing newspaper articles, film scripts, finished and unfinished novels. He was well educated, a darling son of the stout provincial middle classes; his roots were in Autun, a town he described in his second novel, *Un mauvais lieu*. Not keen on the life of a lawyer or solicitor offered him by his parents, he went to Paris, his dream being to mix with artists and to live among the Saint-Germain-des-Prés group. It wasn't difficult, given his natural charm, sensitivity and genuine kindness. He befriended the writer Boris Vian and was friends with Louis Aragon, with whom he worked until 1953. Great fans of jazz and contemporary art, he and his wife Eva opened the small Galerie du Luxembourg, run by his wife, which launched the abstract expressionist movement with the German-born Wols and the Canadian Jean-Paul Riopelle.

When Marguerite met Gérard he was a rewriter on *France-Dimanche*. Every weekend he wrote whole pages of the newspaper around subjects he'd been given. He wrote quickly and never had any qualms about scribbling page after page on these assigned themes.

His articles might just as easily be on some clandestine provincial love affair, a story of cruelty or a sensational trial as on a secret formula guaranteed to keep your husband's love alive. In other words, he was an expert hack. Claude Lanzmann, his boss at the time, knew it wasn't easy to find a style, write an intriguing story and deliver on time. Jarlot could have done it in his sleep. But he told Lanzmann he was only doing it for the money.

He modelled himself on Joyce, Swift and Proust, on whom he could talk for hours. He fancied himself as a writer, Claude Lanzmann recalled, and his two novels gave him a certain status in the world of journalism. Maurice Nadeau remembered him as a pushy kind of bloke who associated with real writers. 'I am weak, shy and not what you'd call brilliant. In a word, I am not a leading player and my desire for power can only take root in literature,' he used to say. 'The man was an incredibly gifted writer. He was very subtle, very witty, very charming. He was an exceptionally good talker too,' Duras said of him.[1] Maybe a writer, definitely a great lover and even a bit of a voyeur; according to Claude Lanzmann, Jarlot boasted to his colleagues on the newspaper that he'd had his bed raised so that he could install a mirror and watch himself and Marguerite make love. Anyone interested could go along to see his bit of erotic DIY. Our Jarlot was a braggart and a big-mouth, but a gentleman? Not always. With him, Marguerite explored forbidden caresses, reinvented pleasure, became addicted to it. It's like a delicious fall, she told a friend. 'Well, it wasn't a story ... I mean a love story but it was a story – how can I put it – I thought I'd never pull through. It was very strange.'[2] There had been times in the past when Duras thought her life was in danger – as an adolescent with the Chinese lover, before and after her marriage to Antelme when she was sleeping around with strangers, at the end of the war with Delval. For once she wasn't in control of what was happening to her. There was life before Jarlot and life after Jarlot.

She said as much herself. 'For a long time, I was part of society, I went to people's houses for dinner. All that was part of the whole. I went to cocktail parties, met people ... and I wrote those books ... That was it. Then one day I had a love affair and I think that's when it all started.' Her writing and her perception of writing changed. She discovered her true self through her burgeoning sex life and this gave her the will and the courage to cast off a few masters – Hemingway,

Vittorini and Beckett. Thereafter the strength to write came from within. Before, she was a woman who believed older and better-educated people could help her to learn. After – and at times to the point of caricature – she only believed in herself. She made what she termed her shift towards sincerity.

A few months into the affair, during which time she was unable to write, so obsessed was she with Jarlot, Marguerite received the news of her mother's death. The telegram reached her in a house near Saint-Tropez where she and Jarlot were spending a holiday. She decided they should set off immediately if they were to make it to the funeral next morning. They drove at breakneck speed through the night, taking it in turns behind the wheel. At dawn, exhausted, they stopped at a hotel. They set off again. They were drunk. It was light. Jarlot was shaking. He was at the wheel. Near the mother's house they stopped at a hotel. 'We made love again. We couldn't speak to each other any more. We were drinking. In cold blood he hit me. In the face. Certain parts of my body. We were shaking. Too scared to go near one another.'

She went to the mother's house. Jarlot stayed in the hotel. The undertakers were waiting for her. They were three around the coffin: Marguerite, her brother Pierre and the servant Do. Marguerite kissed the icy forehead and the lid was screwed down. Her brother wept. She watched him weep. She didn't feel like weeping. She was unmoved. She was thinking about the man she loved, the man who loved her and who was waiting for her. After the funeral she went to find Jarlot. They stayed in the hotel room – fighting, making love – crying, running about in the night, drinking and collapsing until the following morning.

The violence, alcohol and eroticism went on for six months. Marguerite said the madness lasted through the winter. 'After that, it became less serious, a love story.' And after a while she was able to write *Moderato Cantabile*.

The novel is permeated by this love story. It is in fact dedicated to Gérard Jarlot. Writers normally limit themselves to describing the outward manifestations of love. In *Moderato Cantabile*, Marguerite wanted to describe the indescribable. The principal heroine is a young middle-class woman who is bored with life. Her name is Anne

Desbaredes. She is the downhearted mother of an unruly young boy who completely overwhelms her and to whom she replies without ever really listening to what he says. Anne is an alcoholic socialite who slums it by going to taverns in the port; she sleepwalks through life and is a friend to the birds. Her idiosyncrasy is that she hates camellias. This woman, whose hand starts to shake after her third glass of wine, is of course Marguerite, and very similar to her later heroines.

The book opens on a piano lesson. It's impossible not to see Outa in the gifted but sullen and wilful child. Marguerite confirmed this during a radio interview in 1975: 'I went through a terrific upheaval when my son, a gifted musician, was learning to play the piano. I wrote nothing for a year, all I did was take him to his lessons and make him practise.'³

As they leave the piano lesson, mother and son come face to face with a crime. In the café downstairs, a woman has just died, murdered by the man holding her in his arms, murmuring, 'My love, my love.' Anne Desbaredes wants to know all there is to know about the dead woman. Soon Anne lives only through and for her. She feasts on the story and thinks she is satisfying her hunger for the absolute. For Anne the crime is a lesson in life. Can love change a life, become a destiny? With Duras it is always too late. Women never know how to seize the opportunity, to wake up in time. Anne Desbaredes is as good as dead, dead to herself, dead to desire and she knows it. Anne Desbaredes is a devourer, waiting for her prey. She plays on the fact that she looks so serene and gentle – all the better to terrify and ensnare people.

Published by Editions de Minuit, *Moderato Cantabile* came out in 1958. The book was unquestionably a turning point in Marguerite Duras's literary career. Marguerite knew her writing style had changed, so she was making a statement. In the eyes of an informed public, leaving Gallimard to sign up with Minuit placed her in a movement with which, despite her denials, she was so often linked: that of the *nouveau roman*, a concept introduced by Alain Robbe-Grillet in the mid-fifties. Why did Marguerite decide to leave what she referred to as 'her family'? Dionys and Robert worked for Gallimard, Gaston was an old friend, and Queneau, who still ruled over the reading committee, regularly spent an evening in rue Saint-

Benoît. She who had a reputation for refusing to talk with editors, and for never accepting the slightest criticism, nonetheless saw Queneau as a master in whom she had absolute confidence. Yet Duras told a friend that it was because at Gallimard they never read her books.[4] She had the impression she wasn't wanted any more. On the other hand, Jérôme Lindon at Minuit wanted her and never stopped telling her so. She preferred the enthusiasm and energy of a man who loved books to the daily round of a sacrosanct institution, even though, as Robert Gallimard reminded her, she published whatever and whenever she wanted. When pressing Gallimard for money, she had previously threatened to break off their relationship. 'We're ready to help you out as we have done in the past,' Claude Gallimard had written, 'but we can't just dish out money like that. Put yourself in our position.'

Never did Marguerite ever put herself in the position of any of her editors! As far as she was concerned, an editor was first and foremost a banker she suspected capable of robbing her. Of course, writing was her profession, her only profession and at the time her only means of making a living. Her need for money haunted her to her dying day. She never had enough money. Anyway, when you're a writer, how can you possibly be paid what you're worth? And then there was her insatiable desire for recognition. Odette Laigle, who played a crucial role over the years and, as time went by, became one of Marguerite's contacts at Gallimard, recollected that Marguerite would drag her into the Café de l'Espérance and anxiously enquire whether she'd read her manuscript. All in all, Marguerite didn't feel she was much liked by the publishing house, only ever visiting when a book was about to come out. The staff frequently found her cold and aloof. And so she was on the lookout for an editor who would believe in her, who would be more understanding. She was also trying to get some short stories published in magazines. But in vain.

It was Alain Robbe-Grillet, at the time an active editor with Minuit, who managed to persuade her. They had become friends on a lecture tour of England and Belgium two years earlier. Then he had read her books and liked them, and had therefore begun to woo her as an author.

As she had already done for *Whole Days in the Trees* and *The Little Horses of Tarquinia*, Marguerite had published in Maurice Nadeau's magazine *Les Lettres nouvelles* the very beginning of *Moderato Cantabile* in the form of a short story. Struck by its intensity, Alain Robbe-Grillet saw in these few pages 'a wonderful subversive strength at the very heart of the narrative'.[5] He encouraged her to take her work in a different, 'less traditional' direction, suggesting she do away with certain naiveties that were 'in the style of romantic magazines'. It was still possible at that time to make such remarks; she was still 'carefree, funny, friendly and open-minded'.[6] Marguerite took Robbe-Grillet's advice and at the end of three months she had finished the book he had asked her for. On 16 October 1957, she wrote to Gaston Gallimard:

> Let me publish my next book with another editor. You haven't made much money from my books (except *The Sea Wall*) and I haven't made much from you either. So let us divorce for the space of a book, Gaston. I would very much like, really very much like to try my luck elsewhere, just once.
>
> Why shouldn't the same rules apply to publishing as to life? Why should publishing be alone in demanding an individual's unconditional loyalty whereas in other human, economic and emotional activities it is otherwise? You can change your job, your life, your behaviour. Surely you can change your editor just once.

Gaston initially refused but eventually gave in: 'I want there to be neither acrimony nor bitterness between us. So give the others the book. But on the sole understanding that subsequent manuscripts will be brought to me. See this concession I am reluctantly making as proof of my continued interest in your work and of my friendship for you.'
Marguerite kept her promise and the following year Gallimard brought out *The Viaducts of Seine-et-Oise*. Ten books were to follow before, eleven years later, Marguerite went back to Jérôme Lindon at Minuit to have *Destroy, She Said* published, subsequently again returning to Gallimard. This shuffling back and forth between publishers sprang from her need for reassurance. Jérôme Lindon was not only an enthusiastic editor but he also understood how sensitive she was. The very same night after she had delivered a manuscript, he would read it so that he could discuss it with her the next morning.

Moderato Cantabile did not pass unnoticed, but the reviews gave a distorted image of the author by wrongly classifying her under the *nouveau roman*. 'Robbe-Grillet, Sarraute, Duras, all pioneers in the same struggle', was the headline in a particular literary journal delighted to at last be able to group together works that were, however, very different in nature. Marguerite Duras said nothing, happy and proud to be compared to writers she admired and with whom she felt a connection. In fact her book won the Prix de Mai awarded by the bookshop La Hune. Among the judges were Roland Barthes, Georges Bataille, Maurice Nadeau, Louis-René des Forêts, Nathalie Sarraute and Alain Robbe-Grillet.

Thirty years later, Duras publicly denounced the *nouveau roman* and fiercely denied ever having been one of its authors. She went so far as to insist proudly that she'd never understood any of it. Marguerite belonged to no one and compared herself to no one. It should be pointed out, however, that in the meantime she'd fallen out with Robbe-Grillet.

Jérôme Lindon remembered that after the praise, there came some bad reviews including one by the popular novelist Françoise Sagan in a major newspaper. The novel is open to any interpretation. In this way Duras is able to introduce the reader as a character in his own right, to irritate and unsettle him by repeatedly disrupting the logic of the plot. She always considered reading as a creative act. To read is in a way also to write. So many readers, so many creations. A text belongs only to the reader who gets hold of it. And with this appropriation the author disappears. It was the first time Duras was using a technique she would subsequently use a great deal and at times be excessively reliant on – leaving the work to the reader. She provides the pieces of the jigsaw but never puts it together. When you've read the story, you have to start it all over again to look for the clues. But there are always bits of the jigsaw missing. Literature-essay, novel-exercise, experimental, some said when it was published. The novel was caught in the crossfire between the old school and the moderns. Today it reads like a cross between a photo-novel, a treatise on style and a romantic tale. It hasn't aged at all and is a delight to devour.

Marguerite was not all that pleased with the finished product. She made numerous changes to the first edition, which were never included in subsequent ones. However, she never disowned the novel as she did so many others. She knew she had found a new way of writing but in future would have to guard against lapsing into self-quotation. She didn't like the film later made of it by Peter Brook and in 1974 said she wanted to make her own low-budget version.[7]

Life in rue Saint-Benoît went on much as before. When she wanted to spend time with her lover, Marguerite went to his room in rue de Rivoli where she sometimes slept over if they'd been out drinking all night. Dionys didn't like Jarlot, and Jarlot rarely went to rue Saint-Benoît, where the usual chaos reigned. Friends from all political persuasions returned after 13 May 1958 to help Dionys finalize his plans for a magazine, in which Marguerite would of course take an active part.

Le 14 Juillet was the magazine of absolute dissent, the magazine opposed to Gaullist power, founded by Dionys Mascolo and Jean Schuster. The first issue was distributed through newspaper kiosks on 14 July 1958, Bastille Day. The epigraph was a quotation from Pascal, 'We only spoke when it would have been a crime to remain silent,' and the opening article was on the political gravity of the situation and the role intellectuals should play. 'Allowing the bearers of *yes* to fall over each other at the palace gates and the shameful little Royalists to hug the walls as they make their way to the spies' entrances . . . it mattered to hurl that *no* as resolutely as possible.' The editors of *Le 14 Juillet* thought and printed that de Gaulle was a tyrant who had to be brought down, a hypnotist holding France in a trance. It was the responsibility of *Le 14 Juillet* to 'awaken public opinion and to protect the citizens from being robbed of their Republic'. 'The magazine was a great political achievement of which I am extremely proud,' said Dionys in 1997.[8] 'It was a basic reaction to the decline de Gaulle's personal power represented.' At the time Dionys and his friends were worried there could be a French-style Francoism and perceived Gaullism as a quasi-religious power likely to prevent the citizen from thinking clearly.

'We are in a state of historic disgrace, in a situation of historic shame. We are in a moment of political, intellectual and moral decadence. We are in an insanely vain political world, under the rule of a self-assured intellect, which cannot even be called stupid but instead appallingly narrow-minded, and the herald of all tyranny,' declared the editorial in the first issue. The collaborators on the magazine were André Breton, Benjamin Péret, Jean Dubignaud, Claude Lefort, and also the 'elders' of rue Saint-Benoît: Louis-René des Forêts, Robert Antelme, Elio Vittorini, Edgar Morin, Jacques-Francis Rolland, Claude Roy, Maurice Nadeau and Maurice Blanchot, who, when the call came, broke his self-imposed silence.[9] At this time Blanchot was a very regular visitor to rue Saint-Benoît. He got the poet René Char involved in the magazine and wrote (for the second issue) a long political tract entitled 'The Refusal'. One of the consequences of the magazine was to bring Dionys and Maurice Blanchot closer together: 'There was from then on a feeling of "togetherness" between us.'[10] To them, communism, true communism was 'the belief in the equality of man, the harmonization of consciences [sic], the right to the truth, more opportunities for the individual'. Far from Stalinist diktats, the magazine was a call for inner resistance, for the mind to enter a new era. Not all the contributors were as intransigent as Dionys but all were committed to what Blanchot termed the fellowship of NO: no to the Algerian war, no to the seizure of rights, no to authoritarianism.

Some of those on the intellectual left were disconcerted by this viewing of politics from a philosophical angle and could see no justification for the new magazine. 'It expresses neither a particular trend nor new ideas but is solely centred around the friendship and comradeship of authors who write or who could easily write elsewhere,' observed *France-Observateur*.[11] But to Marguerite it wasn't just another magazine, it was an organ of resistance. So much the better if it embarrassed some on the left. After the third issue it disappeared, but today it is regarded as having been of prime importance.

Only two women were ever featured: Colette Garrigues and Marguerite Duras. The former allowed *Le 14 Juillet* to use her private address as their headquarters, and the latter typed up articles and saw to practical matters. Marguerite contacted people willing to make a financial contribution, mainly artists whom she asked to donate paintings for a fund-raising sale. The list of those who accepted was long. The surrealist Matta and the sculptor Giacometti were the most generous. Marguerite was an active participant at meetings, often gave her opinion, witnesses say, and wrote two texts; one, 'The Assassins of Budapest', was on the sentencing of Imre Nagy, who was executed after Hungary's failed rebellion against Stalinism. As for Colette Garrigues, none of her texts were published in the magazine. 'All those intellectuals were male chauvinists,' she declared, 'and maybe we were too timid, not confident enough. They were the thinkers, the writers. We were the gofers.'[12] In a land of intellectuals who knew how to say no, male–female relations had not evolved much.

In 1957 Marguerite embraced journalism with enthusiasm. By this point newspaper editors were fighting over her. She chose two: France-Observateur for love, and Constellation for money. Marguerite invented a new kind of journalism as most of her articles were about stories experienced – they were moving rather than informative or thought-provoking. Marguerite saw herself as the great reporter of souls in torment. Looking to the margins of society, she despised centres of power, official assemblies, spokespersons, representatives of any kind. All you have to do to understand the world, she proclaimed, is open your eyes, go downstairs and out into the street, and know how to look and listen. Marguerite was returning to the tradition of the great nineteenth-century writer-reporters, but unlike them she never travelled further than the end of the street. 'The Algerian's Flowers', her first piece for a newspaper, published in France-Observateur in 1957, is a model of conciseness and emotion. It isn't political, but even today it has the ring of the committed article about it. The story is set in the Saint-Germain-des-Prés district. A young Algerian is out in the street getting his barrow ready to sell flowers illegally. Two policemen turn up. Papers? He has none. Then in front of all the people quietly shopping in the market, one of the policemen tips over the cart. To the annoyance of the police, one by one the flowers are picked up from the road by passers-by, who pay the young Algerian. 'Ten minutes later there wasn't a flower left on the ground. After which these gentlemen had plenty of time to take the young Algerian down to the police station.'

In her articles Marguerite often described the psychological repercussions of a war that masqueraded as something else – people arrested because someone didn't like their faces, a French woman insulted by the police for daring to be seen in public with an Algerian.

Through her portrayal of individuals, she raised public awareness. She also touched her readers. Her ability to listen to people not normally given the right to speak combined with her talent for transcription as she listened to children, to workers and to 'nobodies'. Marguerite carried out investigations in schools, wrote a wonderful piece on la Villette, went to Deauville in the summer and described women in the casino their hands trembling, children clutching bags of chips sitting yawning in cafés sheltered from the wind. Duras worked quickly in a telegraphic style, roughly sketching situations, depicting characters. Journalism to her was the art of the ephemeral, yet her stimulating, lively articles have not become dated and are still a pleasure to read today. She spent hours in cafés eavesdropping on conversations. Her approach to writing dialogue, perfected in her novels, allowed her to invent a kind of half-spoken, half-written language that was like the refrain in a popular song. Marguerite never picked over words but wrote for everyone. She never read through what she'd written. 'The thought of writing being careless doesn't displease me,' she said.[13]

Marguerite had no plans for a book; journalism enabled her to carry on writing. It was like being in training. She never did both at the same time. When she was tied up in a book, she stopped going out, lost interest in everything and had no time for the papers. Journalism filled the gaps, the empty moment. 'Writing articles took me outside, they were my first films.'[14]

Of the fourteen articles she wrote in 1957, only three had to do with literature. In one, the commissioning editor of a large publishing house (anonymous, but easily identified as Raymond Queneau) explains how he selects books for publication. Two are devoted to Georges Bataille, who was then her friend and model. 'Georges Bataille doesn't write at all since he writes against language. He invents how it's possible not to write while at same time writing. He unlearns us about literature.' And that's what Marguerite would attempt to do when she returned to the novel. Bataille and Blanchot were now her masters. Their influence on her oeuvre, though never acknowledged by her, was considerable.

All through 1958 Marguerite Duras wrote a weekly piece for *France-Observateur*, in their book section or in the 'news in brief' or 'everyday life' columns. She covered a wide range of subjects – the life of Confucius, the peregrinations of a yachtsman, the growing number of cars on the streets of Paris, major art exhibitions, Paris in August; book reviews, including a rave review of Sartre's 'Tintoret', profiles of celebrities from Brigitte Bardot to Peter Townsend.[15] She also contributed reports from the law courts.[16] In one particular article – ' "Poubelle" and "La Planche" are going to die' – which attracted great attention, and which she insisted should be republished twenty years later, she protested against a law by which two twenty-year-old murderers were sentenced to death. Legal rituals and the practice of extracting confessions outraged her. She described what she saw: a corrupt system of justice where the accused were denied the right to speak. The whole of their life was defined in terms of the wickedness of their act.

The criminal world always fascinated Marguerite. Having grown up with her younger brother's perfect immorality and her elder brother's constant thieving, she had a fondness for rogues and outlaws and openly admitted it. She always identified with those who had nothing – a throwback to her deprived childhood – even when she became wealthy later in life. Hypersensitive and permanently damaged by life's hardships and the injustice she had seen her mother suffer, she proclaimed loudly and sometimes exaggeratedly her admiration for those who dared put themselves on the fringes of society: robbers, tenants of night's shadows, prostitutes. She became so fascinated with them that she imagined herself a criminal. She sometimes emptied herself of a story that obsessed her by writing it down.

And so the following year she published *The Viaducts of Seine-et-Oise*, a book she subsequently disowned, and then rewrote ten years later with the new title of *L'amante anglaise*. It was based on a case she heard about from Gérard Jarlot. An ordinary couple live quietly in a village respected by all. One day they murder the deaf and dumb cousin with whom they have been living happily for some thirty years. The woman carries out the crime, cuts up her cousin's body and disposes of the pieces by dropping them on to trains passing under the nearby railway bridge. Why did she kill her? Neither can explain. Because she's crazy? the policeman asks the husband. Because she never really adapted to life, is his reply. They were both guilty of the crime – had both killed the cousin – he in a dream, she in reality. Criminals or fools? Both, Marguerite concluded. These individuals are close to us, she said. They are ghosts in a world that looks ordinary enough but where the murder of someone you love does not upset the inner order of things. We all have our dark side and every crime has its logic. We are all potential criminals. Perversion, pleasure and murder are all linked. Marguerite shocked; she loved shocking.

At the time *Constellation* was run by Madame Lecoutre, a mistress of Stalin's who liked to make Paris intellectuals work. Marguerite Duras's freelance work for *Constellation* was written under a pseudonym – she was using her mother's maiden name of Marie-Josephe Legrand to sign slushy articles on love and foolproof recipes. The titles of the articles set the tone: 'Telling lies kills love', 'Why did he leave his wife?', 'Advice for women on how to cope with the school holidays'.

In 1958 it was the turn of the world of cinema to court Duras. She had just been approached by Alain Resnais to work on a film script, and René Clément's film version of *The Sea Wall – Barrage contre le Pacifique* – was due to be released at the beginning of spring. 'It was an Italian-American co-production by Dino de Laurentiis and Columbia, in Technicolor and CinemaScope, starring Silvana Mangano and Anthony Perkins. Irwin Shaw and René Clément had worked together on the film script. The filming in Thailand had been a nightmare: mud, heat and discomfort. Duras and Shaw saw very little of one another and Clément was quick to inform Marguerite that he wanted no interference from her. She did manage to prevent the brother's role from being reduced to that of a pimp and demanded further changes. He had to be handsome, charming and driven by violent sexual impulses. James Dean was originally going to take the role of the brother, but Anthony Perkins was an inspired substitute. Realizing he was fighting a losing battle, Clément agreed to the changes and then took off to shoot his film. The maker of such films as *Knave of Hearts* (made in Britain) and *Jeux interdits* had not wanted to tackle the colonial issues but to portray a family's psychological problems. Made for international consumption, the film had a trial run in Hollywood and Italy. When it was released, René Clément was careful to distance himself from the book. Dreading the critics who would accuse him of betraying it, he made it quite clear the film was an adaptation and not a transposition. The exact term, he said, was 'inspired by ...' But 'I know I haven't betrayed the spirit of the book by shifting the film's prime focus. Marguerite Duras was deeply moved by the first screening. In the bungalow of the film, she recognized her childhood bungalow.'[17] Despite their friendship, however, Duras never liked Clément's film. She was to say later that he had understood nothing of the book's brutality. He had 'salvaged' her life and her mother's life by eliminating the violence. He created a happy ending by leading the spectators to believe that the son, once the mother was dead, would accept white society by building a sea wall himself. Duras felt betrayed and humiliated. She never again sold the cinema rights to her books but filmed them herself.

In the meantime she promoted the film, telling interviewers it was very beautiful. It was an opportunity to increase sales of the book. A month before the first screening in Paris at the Moulin-Rouge, she wrote to Gaston Gallimard, 'Are you planning to reprint the novel?' Gaston replied by return of post that there were 1200 copies in stock and that he was going to have these covered with a dust jacket based on the film poster. Marguerite also promoted the novel in her column in *France-Observateur*, and the book was given a new lease of life. Interviewed in the press, Marguerite again talked of her mother, of the issues in *The Sea Wall*. 'Some people will find the book embarrassing. That doesn't bother me. I have nothing left to lose. Not even my sense of decency. In writing the book I ran the risk of indecency.' She felt she had won a battle. The mother was dead, but the film's release rekindled her memory. 'For me the problem had been to make her disappear behind herself, to have her surpass her singularity, to assassinate her and have her rise from her own ashes. There were no two ways but only one to prevent her life from having been pointless: and that was to forget her. When I saw Clément's film, I knew she was dead.'[18]

The critics raved. 'The film is an outright success, a flawless masterpiece, genius replaces talent, the anecdotal rises to match the tone of the times,' wrote Robert Chazal in *France-Soir*. Henry Magnan, of *Combat*, left the screening so moved he felt he'd been rocked by 'an inner typhoon'. The dissenters were few and far between. Eric Rohmer in *Arts* voiced a few criticisms: too expensive, too 'blockbustery', too gimmicky, the *mise-en-scène* lacked grace, the shots of nature lacked breath. However, 'despite the few clichés collected along the way, it is a pleasure to hear Clément's moralizing voice once more'.[19] Another critic conceded that the film looked good despite the cold academicism that came 'from a rather dull, fairly boring book, where the characters solemnly talk a lot of twaddle'.[20] Today the film, regularly shown on television in France, looks like a Hollywood-inspired classic, with glimpses of Elia Kazan's universe. The brilliantly directed Mangano–Perkins brother–sister dyad still arouses sexual emotion. The incest is subtly sketched. Even today the film exudes a delicious violence mingled with a languid exoticism.

Duras promptly distanced herself from it. Two weeks after its release, having declared to *L'Express* that, although the film was good, 'readers of the novel might be disappointed', she was already toying with the idea of writing for the cinema.

> If I had to transpose another of my novels to the screen, I think I'd make a good job of it, I could take liberties with my book that an adaptor wouldn't dare take. In the final analysis I think adaptors are too faithful to the original. I could rewrite any scene for the screen, in the same spirit, without it having anything to do with the book. If one wants to remain faithful it is essential to preserve the tone.[21]

For her next film, the tone was something she found immediately – the tone for *Hiroshima mon amour*. She said there were times in life when to create was to be in non-work. For *Hiroshima* this was instantaneous.

The story behind the film was a series of coincidences. Anatole Dauman, founder and director of Argos Films, had just produced the documentary *Nuit et brouillard* (*Night and Fog*) about the Holocaust. Its director, Alain Resnais, wanted to break into feature films. Dauman, then involved in talks with a big Japanese company, told him about an idea for a documentary on Hiroshima. They had a title, 'Picadou', from the Japanese nickname for the atomic bomb. Alain Resnais wasn't exactly turned on by the idea but nonetheless asked the documentary filmmaker Chris Marker to work on the project with him.[22] Resnais viewed dozens of films on the subject, spent six months thinking about it and said to Dauman, 'If you want to make a film on Hiroshima, buy the rights from the Japanese; neither Marker nor I could do better. What we need,' he went on, 'is fiction. We don't need any more documentaries on the subject.' Dauman started to look for a scriptwriter. Two days later, he asked Resnais point-blank, 'How d'you feel about going to Japan with Sagan?' Resnais's reply was 'OK, I don't know her but she seems pleasant enough.' Dauman had wondered whether Simone de Beauvoir might be interested but opted for Françoise Sagan. He'd already met her and arranged to see her at the Pont Royal bar so that he could introduce her to Resnais. They waited for hours. Sagan had forgotten all about their appointment.

'That was when I brought up the name of Marguerite Duras,' Resnais explained. 'I'd just read *Moderato* and fallen in love with it and I'd really liked *The Little Horses of Tarquinia*. I'd just seen *The Square*, and found the musicality of the language so moving ...' Resnais saw Duras as an author who had 'tone'. He'd even thought of shooting *Moderato Cantabile* without telling her, and then showing her afterwards. 'It was my intention to get in touch with her anyway.'

Approached, Marguerite invited him round for tea. 'It wasn't tea, it was beer,' Resnais said, 'and it lasted for five hours. We had great fun.' They both agreed that it wouldn't be a documentary and the nuclear apocalypse would not be the primary theme. Their departure point was: Have our lives been changed by the horror of the dropping of the bomb? Three days after their long conversation, Marguerite phoned Resnais. 'I've written a piece of dialogue, do you want to read it?'

'It was a romantic conversation between a young French woman and a Japanese man; I was very taken by it. I contacted the producer.' The agreement was very quickly finalized, said Anatole Dauman.

Without going to Japan, without researching the subject, without preparation Marguerite worked flat out, day and night. She started to work within the framework Resnais had given her. 'I'd told her I wanted two different plots set at two different periods of time. One had to be in Lyon during the Occupation. But everything had to be in the present. To me the sound of the film was definitely the present, we were never to go back in time.'[23] In just over two months the script had been constructed and the dialogues begun.

When it came to casting, Resnais immediately thought of Emmanuelle Riva, whom he had just seen performing at the théâtre de la Michodière. It was to be her first film role. He did a short, silent 16-mm screen test. 'The effect was extraordinary,' Resnais recalled.

'I immediately showed it to Marguerite, who felt the same thrill as I, the same thunderbolt and lightning.' So the production team engaged Riva. Now they had to choose the Japanese. For financial reasons there was no question of flying out to Japan; Alain Resnais had to select his hero from photographs. When he first went to Japan to look for locations, he asked to meet the actor, Eiji Okada, at the earliest opportunity. 'Without realizing it, I'd chosen the most cultured actor in Tokyo. That first evening I invited him out to dinner. The first thing he asked me was, "How is Marguerite Duras's work different from existentialism?" I felt reassured.'

They didn't have much time. Resnais asked Marguerite for two kinds of continuity: the film continuity as such and the 'background' continuity. He wanted to know everything about the story – the one that would unfold on the screen and the one that wouldn't. He also wanted to know everything about the three characters: the French woman, the Japanese man and the German man – their youth and their future beyond the end of the film. As requested, Marguerite created three biographies.

> The woman could have been a prostitute. But the profession would eventually have bored her. She would have chosen it out of pique. And yet she wasn't piqued, she was in despair. She has no illusions, although she's always ready to completely delude herself. She wants, but that's not all, to please the man so that she can indulge in physical pleasure with him. She is the be-all and end-all in feminine wiles.[24]

Resnais 'saw' this woman being drawn before his very eyes. He then asked Marguerite to make a kind of commentary to go with the pictures that would illustrate the story. From Japan he wrote, 'Tell me how she remembers Nevers.' 'And so,' Marguerite recounted, 'we invented Nevers as it had to be seen from the other side of the world.'[25] Resnais knew what he wanted and how he wanted the narrative to develop. Bombarded with questions, Marguerite replied straight away.

Production had not envisaged Marguerite going to Japan, so it was alone that Resnais set off on 28 July 1958 to sort out the locations. The continuity girl, as they were then called, joined him a few days later. When Resnais was about to board the plane he confided to

Dauman, 'I'm sure I'm going to come to the conclusion that this film is impossible, quite impossible.' Production gave him a two-month deadline to find locations and complete the continuity shots of the Japanese scenes. He couldn't speak a word of Japanese, knew no one and wasn't sure whether it was safe to eat raw fish in a country where there had been nuclear fallout. And yet he worked wonders in the studio and on location, delighting the Japanese team with his precision, professionalism and courtesy.

Every day Resnais sent his impressions to Marguerite, who assimilated them and then gradually added scenes to the film script. As they couldn't speak to each other, they communicated via the written word. Both benefited from the distance that separated them. 'At first Hiroshima scared me,' Duras explained, 'and then it began to fascinate me. For it is up to you – who have forgotten – and up to others who have forgotten to read between the lines in order to raise the subject from its "ashes". Thousands of pages have been written on Hiroshima. How was I to go about it? Thanks to Resnais I saw that Hiroshima could be brought back to life."[26]

Marguerite had nine weeks to write the script. All Resnais had said was, 'Write literature, don't worry about the camera.' But Duras didn't have time to write literature. She didn't know how to write film scripts and didn't have a clue how to begin. Resnais was reassuring and told her just to get on with it by doing what she pleased. 'Go on, this is an opportunity to make a low-budget film,' he kept saying. He thought it was going to be a flop anyway. 'If we get just one screening, we'll have done it,' he wrote from Tokyo. 'All I ask is that you do it as you see it. Forget about me.' In an internal memo for production, where the use of 'we' shows the extent of their collaboration – which must be emphasized, for Duras later fell out with Resnais – she summarized it as follows:

We have endeavoured to bring Hiroshima back to life through a love story. We hope it will be unusual and 'full of wonder' and that having happened in a place so accustomed to death people will believe in it a bit more than if it had occurred anywhere else in the world. We have endeavoured to make Hiroshima the common ground for two beings who couldn't be further apart geographically, philosophically, historically, economically and racially, where the universal elements of eroticism, love and misfortune are shown in a more truthful light than elsewhere. While we may have failed, I feel it was worth attempting.

In the minds of both scriptwriter and filmmaker the film was never to be a Franco-Japanese co-production. If anything it was to be anti-Japanese. That would be an unprecedented feat, Duras thought, adding, '*Madame Butterfly* is out of date. And so is *Mademoiselle de Paris*. We have to bank on the egalitarian function of the modern world.'[27]

In Resnais's letters, everything was the way Marguerite imagined it would be.

Dear Margot

... There are piles of wood in the streets of Hiroshima as in Autun. And rivers like the Loire and bells that ring in the mist and brackish canals that run alongside the house as in Nevers ...

And the temple ruins on the hillside and patches of grass beginning to appear and souvenir shops and people having their photographs taken in front of the cenotaph and the blackened stones and the fish market ... And newly planted trees that seem unable to grow. And temple stones replaced by reinforced concrete. And thousands of lotuses in place of the ornamental ponds where before 6 August giant carp lived. And a town hall with its charred and blistered façade.

In Paris, she'd jump for joy when she realized that what she'd visualized could be adapted to what Resnais was going to film. Dauman remembered that she'd clap her hands like a little girl whenever a letter arrived, and drag him into a dance with her in a state of exaltation.

Resnais needed Marguerite's voice and her intonation, so he asked her to make tape-recordings of the script. Thereafter she communicated as much through the intermediary of tape as through writing. Having seen Okada's films in the downtown cinemas, Resnais asked Duras to rethink the Japanese. 'Picture,' he told her, 'an actor who can slap effectively and kiss like a Westerner.' She imagined him to be tall, with an almost European face, well-defined but hard lips, an international type. 'It is crucial, absolutely crucial, for his charm not to be exotic,' she told Resnais. 'His charm must be instantly identifiable as that of a mature man.'

'Fine,' Resnais cabled back. 'Send me the next instalment.' Faithfully following the continuity, she sent him scenes every day: 357 in all.

Two days before they were due to start filming, production noticed they were a third over budget. Resnais cabled Marguerite and told her he'd decided to go ahead anyway, but that she should bear in mind that he'd have to make some sacrifices. 'I've always said it was more interesting to shoot an interesting subject on a shoestring than a detective film with a normal schedule. Now I have to practise what I preach.' Marguerite made some modifications. Eiji Okada spoke his lines into the camera. Resnais told her some of the lines didn't work, and Marguerite went back to the drawing board.

Emmanuelle Riva was due in Japan on 20 August. They had a week to get the continuity editing done. Resnais conveyed his despair to Marguerite. 'Tell Riva she must be word perfect. That way we can knock a few days off the shoot. Remind her to get a good leg-wax.' In Paris Marguerite worked with Emmanuelle Riva. In Japan Resnais waited impatiently. 'I shan't forget these strange days in my room,' he wrote to Marguerite, 'with only your voice for company and the two articulated wooden dolls that represent Okada and Riva. They remind me a bit of the time I spent in a Dominican convent. No mystical ecstasy there either. Act 4 however very moving. Let's hope the spectators...'

The shooting with Riva went like a dream. Resnais returned from Japan with his rushes. The early filming in Nevers was never part of the original film script. Marguerite had written the Nevers love affair as a separate story, without having taken chronological order into account. 'Do it as though you were describing the frames of a finished film,' Resnais told her. They began shooting in Nevers in December 1958, having made several visits to locations. Gérard Jarlot was always at Marguerite's side, helping her with ideas and suggestions, which were often taken on board.

Resnais had wanted one of the episodes in the film to take place in wartime France so that the heroine, when she meets the Japanese, will be haunted by the memory of her old flame. Marguerite came up with the idea that the heroine, just before the end of the war, loved a young German soldier. Nevers is a town the size of the love affair. 'Their love is watched like nowhere else,' Duras declared in a text she wrote before they started shooting.²⁸ An imaginary Nevers where an unforgivable love was born. Fear and pleasure were indissolubly mingled. 'In Nevers,' Duras wrote, 'the only adventure was waiting for death.' Masochism and shame became the only way to achieve pleasure. Duras insisted on the theme of the night, the dark night of the Occupation, the perpetual night of the cellar the young woman would be locked up in after her crime of love, the darkness that stretched over the world after she had made love for the first time.

Bernard Fresson played the German soldier. Just before he dies, she smiles and says, 'You see, my love, even that was possible.' When he's been killed, she lies on his body for a day and a night. And when he's loaded into a lorry and taken away, she still desires him, crazily, obscenely desires the dead man. And then they shave her head. We retain the image of Emmanuelle Riva's gentle gesture as she offers her head to the scissors. After she'd been shorn, she waits, she doesn't stir. Is she afraid they're going to cut off her head? Marguerite Duras, who watched as they filmed in Nevers, found this scene unbearable. She screamed and fainted.

It's difficult, on seeing these images once again and on rereading the pages describing the events in Nevers, not to think of her wartime experiences with Delval. Until the end of her life Marguerite was convinced, though she had no proof, that Delval was a German passing himself off as a Frenchman so that he could work as a spy. Was she referring to herself when she put these words into the heroine's mouth: 'I'm morally suspect, you know' and 'I lie and I tell the truth'? Was she referring to her own badness when she made Emmanuelle Riva say, 'I went mad about being bad. I felt I could make a veritable career of being bad'? And the head-shaving episode, wasn't it very reminiscent of what happened to her friend and neighbour Betty Fernandez after the Liberation? In *Hiroshima*, Nevers has to be seen in the light of Marguerite's need to clarify certain episodes in her own past, and Resnais was able to tune into her imagination and to integrate it brilliantly into the story.

Yet Resnais was worried. He was wondering how all these different threads were going to come together to make a film. Superstitious, he kept saying to Marguerite over and over again, 'We're not really making a proper film.' He started on the editing with Henri Colpi and Jasmine Chasney, who hadn't been there for the filming. Marguerite would often go and watch them work. Meanwhile production asked her to come up with a title and to write the summary. She suggested *Hiroshima mon amour* and wrote the following note: 'It is impossible to speak of Hiroshima. All we can do is speak of the impossibility of speaking of Hiroshima. The action takes place in the summer of 1957 and the spectator should emerge from the evocation of Hiroshima cleansed of a good many prejudices and ready to accept everything we are going to tell him about our two heroes.'

And that is the problem posed by the film: that of verisimilitude, of credibility. Is it a proper film or a spurious documentary? Resnais was full of self-doubt. While he was editing, he decided he should hold some advance screenings. He invited a few friends, who, at the end of the screening, all admitted to finding the film interesting but thought it might not be suitable for general release. 'Which meant, I understand your film but I'm not sure other people ...' Resnais translated, adding, 'In fact, it was the music that structured the film and clarified its intent.'

HE: You saw nothing in Hiroshima. Nothing.
SHE: I saw everything.

When the editing was finished, Resnais could no longer see his film, no longer hear anything. The number of people he consulted increased. In all, thirty-four people watched the first version. Needless to say, opinions varied – long, too long, the pacifist message not strong enough, not enough personal testimonies, and so on and so forth. As for Marguerite Duras's script, most found it displeasing, but some found it intriguing: 'To begin with the highly pitched tone was disorientating,' recalled Frédéric de Towarnicki, one of those who saw the film before the final cut, 'then it became an astonishing score where the dialogue was transformed into melodic lines that projected a kind of lyrical and cadenced matter on to the screen.'

Alain Resnais cut the film by thirty-five minutes, reducing it to one hour and five minutes. Still it had no cohesion. He decided to re-edit the whole thing, and the running time was reduced by a further one minute and twenty seconds. Resnais decided it was take-it-or-leave-it time.

The Cannes Film Festival board of selectors suggested to the minister and the festival committee that *Hiroshima mon amour* should represent France. But the film was considered 'inappropriate' and rejected by five votes to four – on the grounds that it might shock the Americans. It was the same old story. *Night and Fog* had been rejected because it could have offended the Germans. As Resnais said, 'The film became a martyr. Had it been entered, it would not have been as lucky.'[29] The filmmakers René Clair, Roberto Rossellini, Jean Cocteau, Henri-Georges Clouzot, Claude Chabrol, François Truffaut and Louis Malle all expressed their enthusiasm. Breaking from conventional narrative structure, *Hiroshima* took on the time of affective memory and drew us into a charred territory where love is a crime and self-knowledge impossible – Durassian themes par excellence. As in *Moderato Cantabile*, the spectator must piece together the jigsaw of memory. The theme of the inner exile of the characters, who are forever separated even in the act of love, fuses the sequences together. 'You are killing me. You are good for me.' This was the first time Duras painted war as an attractive source of punishment, of evil, and also of pleasure.

Marguerite said repeatedly that had she not been commissioned to write *Hiroshima*, she would never have written about Hiroshima. But did she actually write about Hiroshima? Did she not – by situating her characters in a place called Hiroshima – continue to write again as always on love condemned to death? Reality is always better than fiction. When Resnais arrived in Hiroshima, he took a tourist bus to the site. Over the loudspeaker Gilbert Bécaud was singing a love song that mingled with the guide's commentary ... 'You saw nothing in Hiroshima.' That line was to travel the world. In a radio interview in 1969, Marguerite Duras explained, 'What I think she meant was, you will never see anything, you will never write anything, you will never be able to say anything about the event. And it was really from my powerlessness to speak about it that I made the film.'[30]

Resnais was so faithful to Marguerite's script that, stopwatch in hand, he based the length of his tracking shots on 'the *moderato cantabile* rhythm of the Durassian sentence'. But the film's strength lies mainly in the *mise-en-scène* and editing. 'It must have been a blow to her modesty for I can assure you that Alain Resnais is the true author of his films,' says Dauman today.

The film was exclusively premiered in Paris for six months, then

London and then Brussels. In France alone there were over 250,000 viewers, an exceptional number for a supposedly difficult film. It beat Fellini's *La strada* in Italy, was a triumph in Germany, a sensation in Tel Aviv and was awarded a prize in Athens. Several South American countries and even the USA bought the distribution rights. It was voted best foreign movie in New York, Los Angeles and Chicago.

In the credits Gérard Jarlot appears as literary adviser. In the foreword of the book *Hiroshima mon amour* published in 1960, Marguerite wrote, 'I deliver this book to be published dismayed that I am unable to complete it with an account of the almost daily exchanges between Alain Resnais and myself, Gérard Jarlot and myself and Alain Resnais and Gérard Jarlot.' Resnais confirmed Jarlot's crucial psychological role – in saving Marguerite from indiscretions and in publicly poking fun at her narcissism – and her professional reliance on him.

CHAPTER 11

Roots and Revolt

~

A photograph taken at the time shows Marguerite on a beach, with wind-blown hair, wearing pedal pushers rolled up to reveal tanned legs. She's relaxed and smiling, with a twinkle in her eye. Next to her stands Gérard Jarlot, hands in pockets and with feigned nonchalance, as though posing for eternity. Marguerite was still living with Dionys, still cooking for the friends who'd turn up at the flat in the evening to set the world to rights over a Vietnamese dish. Jarlot divided his time between his family – the wife and children he adored – and his studio flat in rue de Rivoli. 'We each had our own life, but people knew we were together,' Marguerite would say. Theirs were the drinking sessions, the lovers' trips to the seaside, the holidays in Saint-Tropez or Italy. 'I'm crazy about him,' Marguerite confided to a friend. As a reporter, Jarlot travelled a lot; he often had to set off at a moment's notice to go and cover a story. And so Marguerite waited for him, night after desperate night. She became completely engrossed in him. Her friend Madeleine Alleins was surprised to find her shut up at home waiting for the phone to ring. 'She became submissive. And in exchange he wanted her protection in the literary world.'¹ Jarlot's friends understood the situation, and had done for some time, and the Saint-Germain-des-Prés bistro jet set knew: he was a womanizer, a seducer who boasted of the quantity and the quality of his female conquests. Marguerite was the last to know.

Jarlot was accepted by the gang. Monique and Robert Antelme appreciated his nonchalance and humour; Louis-René des Forêts his charm and lightness, and Alain Resnais enjoyed discussions with him and admired his enthusiasm and intelligence. Michel Mitrani was completely taken in by both the adventurous and the Saint-Germain-des-Près intellectual Jarlot – who, having seen existentialism for what it was, hungered for knowledge, and could discuss Kierkegaard and Eastern philosophies well into the night. But Gérard Jarlot was a liar. His wife did not mince her words: Gérard was a mythomaniac, a compulsive liar, he lied about everything and nothing, and he had no idea he was lying. When this finally dawned on Marguerite, she went crazy.

He lied all the time, and to everyone, about the reality of his life. Lies reached his lips before the words to tell them. He never felt a thing. He never lied about Baudelaire or Joyce, or when it came to boasting or getting people to believe in his adventures! Oh no. He lied about the price of a pullover, a journey on the underground, the time of a film, an appointment, a conversation, a whole journey, even the names of towns, about his family, his mother, his nephews. Things that were of no interest whatsoever.[2]

This was confirmed by Louis-René des Forêts, who added, 'But Marguerite was just as much of a liar as he was. They lied to one another. It was an incredible relationship. He was the very per-sonification of the lie, but I liked that. I remember we'd planned a trip to the Dolomites. Marguerite and I were to meet Jarlot in Rome. It was bucketing down. We waited for him for days. He never turned up and never called.'[3]

Jarlot didn't care about anything – not truth, not love, not death – he respected only womanizers and writers. Marguerite to him was a lover but also a writer he loved and admired. They wrote two screen-plays together: *Une aussi longue absence* in 1961 and *Sans merveille* in 1963. Both were filmed, the first by Henri Colpi and the second by Michel Mitrani. Jarlot's two novels, *Les armes blanches* and *Un mauvais lieu*, published by Gallimard after the war, were adapted for the screen by Marguerite but, despite their best efforts, both scripts were eventually put away in a drawer.

They enjoyed working together. The different stages of the manu-script for *Une aussi longue absence* – which Marguerite later disowned because she said it was so bad – reveal the extent of their collaboration. Jarlot often provided her with a point of departure, a real-life story, as for *L'amante anglaise* and *Une aussi longue absence*. Gérard Jarlot wrote, Marguerite corrected. He revised, she tightened it up and found the logic. A shared style was fleetingly born: short sentences, repetitions, refrains, linguistic innovations.

Marguerite was prolific, her self-confidence had returned. Neither Dionys nor Robert ever again laid a finger on her manuscripts. They saw the books once they were published. Jarlot was not a mentor. He admired her, reassured her but never criticized her. Marguerite at last felt 'her' men weren't supervising her. And for the first time in her life she was financially independent, money seemed to be coming at her from all directions, thanks to the sale of the film rights for *The Sea Wall*. She who had always shared everything with Robert and Dionys was at last going to be able to realize a childhood dream: to buy herself a huge room of her own, a house in the country. A place for all kinds of adventures and above all for what Marguerite wanted most – solitude. The kind of solitude that has you trembling, the solitude that makes you down a litre of red wine so that you can sink into the sheets. The solitude that brought tears to her eyes as she watched a fly struggle for hours against the windowpane and then die, the solitude when, shivering, she got up at dawn to consign to paper all that had filled her night.

In Neauphle Marguerite found the house destined to be hers, giving her at last, at the age of forty-four, the joy of having a roof over her head and nature all around her. No typhoon, no tide, no crabs to gnaw at the foundations of the house. The childhood nightmares hadn't gone, but Marguerite could at last shut herself away and have the illusion she was safe. 'I love Neauphle. I had no homeland, now I do. A homeland to laugh in, which is how it should always be.'[4] (It was also her wish that the house should belong to her child after her death, and today her son lives in it.)

Neauphle is a country house, not far from a trunk road in what used to be called Seine-et-Oise. It has what estate agents would call character. It's a house with a lot of presence. It had a history and Marguerite decided she'd reconstruct it. She went to the town hall in Versailles to research the names of previous owners and delved into archives back to when it was built. There had been peasants living there in the Revolution; during a famine, wheat had been planted in the front garden; and it was seized by the Germans during the Occupation. Having arranged the house to be attractive and welcoming, she then steeped it with the presence of her characters, thus making it the natural arena of her inner world. 'It's a bit like I was born here,' she would say in *Les lieux de Marguerite Duras*, co-written with Michelle Porte. 'I've made it so much my own that I feel like this house has belonged to me since ... since before me, since before my birth.' The windows overlook the gardens, the lake, the forest and the nearby school.

To Marguerite, the village was an extension of the house. She went out all the time, day and night, with Jarlot, long nocturnal outings to cafés, drinking in bars until she collapsed. One day they were downstairs making love in the middle of the afternoon. They hadn't drawn the curtains. A group of village youngsters were watching. She looked up and saw them, and she never forgot them. For a long time she said she felt like killing them.

Jarlot loved the house. He even suggested moving out of Paris to live with her, the two of them all cosy in Neauphle-le-Château. How dreadful! said Marguerite. Every weekend and all through the holidays she threw the house open to her long-standing friends – Robert and Monique Antelme, Dionys and his wife Solange, Edgar Morin, Louis-René des Forêts and the others ... all the others. An excellent gardener, Dionys took charge and planted peonies and old roses and created a delightful garden that he later abandoned, after an argument. 'The roses continue to grow. There are ninety thousand roses at the moment and it's killing me,'[5] wrote Marguerite, who never had green fingers. There were also numerous cats in Neauphle, stray cats after food. And cushions, lots of cushions on the sofas; lots of tables; dried flowers, wilted flowers – here, as in rue Saint-Benoît, you didn't, on principle, throw flowers in the bin – embroidered mats, odd lamps from the flea markets Marguerite loved browsing around. Blue wardrobes where she stored manuscripts and then forgot about them. Lights were left on all night, beds left unmade all day, the out-of-tune piano could be played by anyone who felt like it. From the outside the house looks like a farm, but inside it was like a holiday home; everything was light, from the rattan furniture – a touch of colonial exoticism – to the pastels of the fabrics. Everyone chose a room: the piano room, the fireplace room, the dining room, they were all interconnected. You could hear the birds in the forest, the shouts of the children coming out of school, the hum of traffic from the trunk road. In spring you could see the peonies burst into bloom, in winter you could walk along the Mauldre through the fog. 'Over there, you have thousand-year-old trees and saplings. Larches, apple trees, plum trees, a walnut, a cherry. The apricot's dead. Outside my bedroom window, there's that fabulous Atlantic man rosebush. A willow. Japanese cherry trees, irises. And under the window of the music room, the camellia Dionys Mascolo planted for me.'[6]

And yet, towards the end of her life, Marguerite would stop going to Neauphle, except as a visitor. She'd spend an afternoon or evening there and then leave. It was as though she was frightened of all the presences she'd filled her house with. Then Marguerite preferred the seaside, the huge expanse of the beaches at low tide, the grey sand, the sea merging with the sky. She first fell in love with Deauville when she was a student, driving to the Normandy coast in 1924 in her convertible Ford Cabriolet. She found Deauville a strange place with its nineteenth-century buildings, its empty streets, the sea pounding the sides of the enormous hotels and the uncultivated plots of wasteland. She just loved that part of the coast, the limpid light and the row of hills. In 1963 she eventually bought a flat in adjacent Trouville when she was still living with Jarlot. It was a seaside apartment without sea views. If you wanted to see the sea, you either had to lean out of the window or go out. But you could hear it, it beat like a pulse, said Marguerite, who would go down and gaze at it. She'd lived by the sea as a child, and her characters often wander along the beach at night. In her books, Trouville – where as a student she first experienced a European sea – is turned into a wild, intemperate place battered by winds and tides. 'I'm terrified of the sea, I'm more frightened of the sea than anything else in the world ... My nightmares, my bad dreams all have to do with the tide, with the invasion of water.'[7]

'For me there was no greater or more exquisite happiness,' Marguerite would say, 'than when I was involved in politics or involved in the politics I was committed to.'[8] Happiness in 1960 was commitment to the independence of Algeria. The declaration of the right to insubordination gave concrete expression to the intellectual resistance already engaged in by those working on *Le 14 Juillet*. It was the happiness that comes from feeling the strength of unity, from envisioning a revolutionary future, from fighting to protect the right to freedom of thought. Marguerite had rediscovered the virtues and joys of collective thought and action to which she was fully committed. The Manifesto of the 121, which was one of the most important acts of intellectual resistance against 'French Algeria', was very much the declaration of a group. During the Dreyfus affair (1894–1906), there had been politicians, organizations and representatives of public opinion who sided with the intellectuals. No such thing happened in 1960. The whole nation had been plunged into a state of unrest that no governmental or intellectual body, no political organization, no moral or cultural institution was addressing.[9]

Before the manifesto was drawn up, Marguerite and Dionys had aided and abetted those fighting for the cause of Algerian independence. They both hid FLN funds up the chimney in rue Saint-Benoît, carried suitcases and lodged people wanted by the police. The pro-FLN activist Madeleine Lafue-Veron, at the time a barrister practising in Paris, under surveillance and for a long time accused of undermining national security, remembers that whenever she had a 'favour' to ask of Marguerite, this was promptly carried out. Her apartment was a crossroads. 'We had a lot of funds in the rue Saint-Benoît, which had to be delivered around Paris. I was a porter. I remember the terror of being followed and searched,' Marguerite told Luce Perrot.

There were numerous discussions around the drawing-up of the manifesto. The third issue of *Le 14 Juillet* had published the results of a questionnaire devised by Schuster, Breton, Blanchot and Mascolo and sent out to intellectuals. It was already a call to resistance. Maurice Blanchot finally came up with the title of *Déclaration sur le droit à l'insoumission dans la guerre d'Algérie*, as his letter of 26 June 1960 to Dionys Mascolo confirms: 'Insubordination, the actual word can appear limiting. We could add to it and say quite bluntly: the right to insubordination and desertion in the Algerian War. But I think insubordination should suffice. Insubordination means the refusal to carry out military duties. And on the basis of this, the principle can be expressed through different behaviour...'[10] The text was circulated in France and then in the rest of Europe. Until the end of August it was passed from person to person, with the list of the original signatories where Marguerite's name appeared alongside that of Tristan Tzara, Alain Robbe-Grillet, Jérôme Lindon, Simone de Beauvoir and others, as well as the core group.

'It was brilliant. Wonderful. You couldn't not sign it without falling behind, falling way behind with history. It affected everyone, even those who didn't sign it,' Marguerite declared in 1985.[11] The manifesto led to repressive measures. Those referred to as 'propagandists of desertion' were forthwith banned from the airwaves and screens of the RTF (French broadcasting service), and from subsidized theatres. André Malraux, the minister of culture, published a circular announcing that state funding would not be granted for films involving any of the artists who signed the manifesto. The measures, regarded as despotic, backfired.

The unrest peaked in the lead-up to the Jeanson trial, due to be heard by a military tribunal on 5 September 1960. Francis Jeanson, author of a book published in 1955 entitled *L'Algérie hors la loi*, and a contributor to *Les Temps modernes*, had set up an underground network that arranged accommodation, assistance and raised funds for the FLN. The Jeanson trial stoked the fires of passion and was the cause of violent confrontations. People would queue for hours to attend the sessions. They went to court as one might go to the theatre. The accused did not deny the charges brought against them but wished to broaden the debate to include the whole conflict. Among the character witnesses called by the defence were Jean-Paul Sartre, Claude Roy, Nathalie Sarraute, Claude Lanzmann and Jérôme Lindon.[12] Unable to attend, Marguerite had a letter delivered to Roland Dumas, lawyer to the signatories, reaffirming her support for the Declaration of the Right to Insubordination in the Algerian War.

The events had rekindled the resistance fighter in Marguerite, which was how she saw herself. Her hatred for de Gaulle, already very much in evidence during the Liberation, had been thoroughly reinforced. In her eyes de Gaulle was not only a dictator but also a liar. On the subject of the Algerian war, history would prove her wrong. As far as she was concerned, though, she was right. She saw de Gaulle as the man who had liquidated the Resistance, the man who in 1945 had disbanded the patriotic militia. In her eyes he was

not the man who brought peace to Algeria but a rational Machia-
vellian who, concession by concession, mindful of his own personal
agenda, lied to everyone including himself for the sole purpose of
staying in power.

When, through lack of funds, the magazine *Le 14 Juillet* folded,
they needed a new paper to express new truths. At the beginning of
1961 therefore, the concept of a *Revue internationale* was born, the
idea being that there should be an Italian, a German and a French
edition. In Italy Elio Vittorini, Pier Paolo Pasolini, Italo Calvino,
Alberto Moravia; and in Germany, Martin Walder, Günter Grass and
Ingeborg Bachmann agreed to join their French counterparts already
working on the project: Maurice Blanchot, Dionys Mascolo, Louis-
René des Forêts, Maurice Nadeau, Roland Barthes, Michel Leiris
and of course Marguerite, who put her all into getting the magazine
off the ground. Despite the passionate aims and obvious ambitions of
these committed and earnest European intellectuals, the magazine
Gulliver only survived one issue, and that one issue only came out in
its Italian version – as a supplement to a newspaper that agreed to
distribute it just the once. Lack of financial backers and intermediaries
meant the magazine died before it had had time to live. But the
discussions and subsequent debates in rue Saint-Benoît were the
precursors to the anti-establishment spirit of 1968. They were in a
way like the opening credits.

Once more, Marguerite was short of money. She was living from
hand to mouth but still unable to make ends meet. Gaston Gallimard
suggested she publish the script of *Hiroshima* in book form. Embarrassed, she wrote back on 23 December 1959 that 'the idea of making
it public bothers us a little, especially given the film's success. It would
be like revealing a secret, a love affair, the moment it was over.' In
the end financial considerations swayed her.

Having been approached by several filmmakers after the success of
Hiroshima, Marguerite and Gérard Jarlot wrote *Une aussi longue
absence*, based on a real-life event that had taken place the year before.
A woman thought she had seen her husband, a former Buchenwald
deportee, walking down the street. The film tells the story of the
confrontation between a woman and a tramp whose memory she tries
to jolt. Jarlot wrote the story and Marguerite set to work describing

the effects of the war on the body and mind of a woman who refused to accept that the man she loved was dead. She immediately thought of Henri Colpi to direct the film. He and Jasmine Chasney had edited *Hiroshima*. On 10 March 1960 she called Colpi, who accepted. On the morning of 11 March she found a producer in the shape of Raoul Lévy, and the evening of the same day she had Resnais encouraging her.

The script set out to describe the one thousand and one little tricks used by the woman to bring back to her a man who had lost all sense of time: the warmth of an embrace, the softness of her voice. The more she besieges him, the more he locks himself away in his fortress without a past. He, the river man, the mud man, the garbage and scrap-iron man, living in a makeshift hut on the banks of the Seine, needs nothing and no one. Unreachable in his imbecilic joy, he doesn't even feel the need to pretend he recognizes her so as to change his life, have a roof over his head, an identity, a name once more. Nothing and no one can stop his desperate withdrawal and his contentment at being no one. 'The object of the film,' said Duras, 'was to show that remembrance and forgetfulness cannot coexist.' The final manuscript of the screenplay reveals just how far the two authors collaborated. Jarlot took charge of the final film script, Marguerite the lines and psychology of the characters.

Henri Colpi didn't use the whole script. Alida Valli and Georges Wilson gave brilliant performances in the title roles, and while it bears the nostalgic hallmark of French neorealist cinema – with its overindulgent effects and meaningful music – it is still a pleasure to watch today. Apart from *Combat*, which found it pretentious, boring and overrated, the film was praised by the critics, who focused on the elegance of the script and the sound performances of the actors.

Colpi remembered that Marguerite was never there when they were shooting and seldom there when they were editing, and that when she was there she never said anything. Looking back on the film, she said it was a commission and that she had been a technician and not an author. Although she enjoyed the film's success – it was joint winner with Buñuel's *Viridiana* of the Palme d'or at the Cannes Film Festival – she wondered about the ease with which she could knock out a script rather than devote herself entirely to her own writing.

Next, she accepted an invitation from the British theatre director Peter Brook to adapt *Moderato Cantabile* on condition that she could write it with Jarlot. She completely rebuilt the novel's matrix. Required to give the story a unity of time, she decided the meeting between Chauvin and Anne Desbaredes would take place over five days. She gave the woman found dead in the café at the beginning of the novel an identity and a past, but most of all she worked on Anne Desbaredes, that phantom of femininity who haunts the café and seduces Chauvin. Anne Desbaredes wants to leave her milieu, her husband, her house, even her town. 'I shall go and live in a town where there are no trees or wind. Here it is always windy and all, or virtually all the birds are sea birds, found dead after a storm, and when the storm has passed, the trees can be heard shrieking over the river as though their throats had been cut. It keeps you awake at night.'[13]

Duras chose the town of Blaye as the setting for the film, because it is near the Gironde estuary and the docks are vast. Blaye is the provincial town *par excellence*, where everyone is home by eight and gossip is rife. Anne Desbaredes gambles with her honour. She has nothing else to do. She's the laughing stock of the town. Chauvin drives her out but she returns. She's immune to what people think of her. Shameless and bestial, she gives herself to Chauvin. She goes looking for men everywhere – in the factories, the streets, around the port. To Chauvin she says, 'I don't think I was destined to be happy for long periods of time but just for fleeting moments and with specific men. I've only been aware of it since I've known you.'

It took eight drafts to reach the point where Marguerite was satisfied with the adaptation of her novel. She had had a tendency to gloat before getting down to a task, but as this was her first adaptation of one of her books, the altering of the storyline and the need to endow the main characters with certain attributes initially struck her as insuperably difficult. Marguerite's novels don't tell stories. Like a puppet-master she positioned her characters and then built the story around what could take place between them – her novels have atmospheres rather than plots. People are always on the verge of things. Everything could happen but in fact nothing happens.

The film was not released for another two years. Marguerite distanced herself from it despite her admiration, regard and friendship for the leading actress, Jeanne Moreau. She blamed the director for what she considered to be a disaster. Peter Brook understood nothing, she was heard to say on more than one occasion. It was her reaction to this film that encouraged her to move round to the other side of the camera.

Marguerite steered clear of psychoanalysis, although she read Freud's *Interpretation of Dreams* several times and was close to Jacques Lacan, who was at the time a friend and regular visitor to rue Saint-Benoît. Although she didn't deny the existence of the unconscious, it was a term Duras never used, for to have made of it a psychoanalytical model would have been to demean and caricature it. 'Symbols' abound in her work but, for someone who always confused the issue, who perverted the very notion of meaning, who reinvented her own life as she went along, and who – making use of many influences, encounters and books read – tinkered with rather than constructed her own writing, they are too easy to decode. Marguerite was a sponge. She had written in the style of Beckett for Lindon, Sartre for *Les Temps modernes*, and for a time Hemingway and Dos Passos for Gallimard. Writing is a dangerous art, composed of abandonment and darkness. Duras, the impudent Duras, she who would later say everything and anything, was already dual. But she had decided to bury the civilized, civil historian Duras, she who boasted, who obstructed, to allow to the surface the Duras who decoded, dreamed, meditated, waited. The medium of the real, her friend Madeleine Alleins called her. Writers are all repairers of the inner shadow, people who have consented to empty themselves.

Highly respected and valued in the literary circle Marguerite said had rejected her, in 1960 she was elected to the panel of judges for the prix Médicis. She sat on the panel for six years in the company of, among others, Alain Robbe-Grillet, before resigning along with Nathalie Sarraute and Claude Roy because 'the institution is more concerned with the prize than the book'. She was proud that Claude Ollier and Monique Wittig had won the Médicis prize, but it didn't make up for errors, she said after she resigned.[14] Marguerite was now very much a part of literary society. She was highly acclaimed by the country's top critics and fashionable in the world of avant-garde cinema. She had a very high opinion of her work and friends and editors couldn't criticise, couldn't even comment. It was between her and herself: 'I write to move myself from me to the book. To alleviate myself of my importance. For the book to take some of it in my place. To massacre, ruin; damage myself in the publication of the book. To popularize myself. To lie in the street. It works. The more I write, the less I exist.' She wrote more and more. Six books in four years, plays, film scripts and novels.

Should we see in her next novel *Ten-Thirty on a Summer Night* a hint of the jealousy beginning to sour her relationship with Jarlot? At the beginning of the book a couple find themselves stranded after a storm in a hotel in a small Italian town. With them is their child – a little girl, timid, fragile and anxious as though already aware of the fate of her parents' love. Duras describes the dank smell of the earth after the rain, the movement of the clouds, the atmosphere in the hotel, the rumbling of the storm. And then – a Duras hallmark – the crime, which is needless to say a crime of passion. Duras also borrows the theme of the eternal triangle from the corniest of middle-class comedies and with a masterly hand transforms and steers it. There is no infidelity here between a man and a woman but an exchange between two women. No break-up, just a hint of sadness. It was the first time a book by Marguerite Duras dealt not with the beginning of a love but with the couple agreeing to end it without there being the bitter aftertaste of defeat and humiliation.

As in *Moderato Cantabile*, the heroine turns to drink to satisfy her desire. Her unquenchable desire. To fall – in slow motion, Duras's heroines fall into a state of inebriation, only to pick themselves up damaged, broken, without memory or bearings, always on the edge of pleasure there next to the precipice. Duras's heroines always feel guilty. Guilty for existing, for being so dependent on alcohol, guilty for being desired or for no longer being desired – it all boils down to the same thing. They don't know how to let themselves flow with the world. The men in Duras's oeuvre are only looking for sunny women, eager for fulfilment, for serenity. Only natural then that they should turn away. 'On her face you see that she senses, that she knows she was once beautiful but that now she is less so. You can see in the familiar way she passes her hands over her face that she knows, that she accepts that she is forever defeated.' Interviewed, she said that for her the main theme of the book was the end of love and the dignity of the woman as she confronted the discovery. How do you deal with a situation like that? she was asked. 'You don't prevent love from being lived, to love is still the best thing down here on earth.' 'So do nothing, even if it causes pain?' 'That's right. But there's a way to dull the pain and that's to become an author.'[15]

The idea of making *Ten-Thirty on a Summer Night* into a film was mooted the moment the book was finished. The screenplay was planned and Marguerite got on with the job of adapting it. She wrote three versions. The crime was committed at the beginning and the marital problems were more advanced. 'It could be a silent film. It could be stripped of idle chatter. Just a few words crucial to the action could be spoken. The essential would never be spoken. The language would be as rarefied as the air we breathe.'[16] She came up with a title: *A Man Had Just Killed Himself*. Duras wanted there to be no ending – it would be as though the end had been 'sliced off with a razor'. The project was abandoned in the end. The book eventually made it to the screen in 1967 in a production by Jules Dassin starring Melina Mercouri and Romy Schneider.

Ten-Thirty on a Summer Night was reviewed afresh. It has to be said that Marguerite Duras's output was so prolific that some of the critics were resorting to sarcasm – Piaf sings the same old song, Duras writes the same old book.

From October 1960 Marguerite received a monthly stipend from Gallimard, which she had asked for 'so that I can stop churning out all this cinema stuff. I've had enough.' At the end of the year, *The Sea Wall* and *The Sailor from Gibraltar* came out in paperback with a print run of 60,000 copies.

Why do you write, Marguerite Duras?

> Every interview I give, I'm asked that question and I've never yet found a satisfactory answer. Doesn't everyone want to write? The only difference between writers and the rest is that the former write and publish, and the latter only ever think about it. It is in fact the only correct dialectic definition of a writer: a man who publishes. There are loads of people who spend their lives toying with the idea of writing a novel but who never take it any further.[17]

Marguerite spent several months working on a book called *Of Course the Builder Will Come* and then changed it to *The Afternoon of Mr Andesmas*. Andesmas is the contraction of three names An/telme – des/Forêts – Mas/colo. Was it Marguerite's intention to gibe at the three men who'd been criticizing her for publishing too much and for speaking too often in the newspapers? Probably. For Marguerite didn't need her tutor-fathers or big teacher-brothers any more. Everything inspired her.

This was the first time that a place provided the opportunity and the excuse for a novel. The summer before, Marguerite and Jarlot had stayed in a remote house on the Riviera between Saint-Tropez and Gassin. The intensity of the light and the wildness of the area made a great impression on her. When she returned to Paris she decided to try to write about the things that made the place, as some *nouveau roman* writers were doing. And then the character of Monsieur Andesmas appeared, a tired, paunchy old man with a wheezy body. He is extremely rich but alone, convinced he is about to die and that his only link with life is his love for his daughter. A dog, a crazy little girl and then a sad woman interrupt his melancholic musings. All three visit him but Andesmas can only wait for his daughter who will not come.

The Afternoon of Mr Andesmas describes – through the use of inner monologue – the last days of an old man rejected by all. Andesmas thinks out loud and goes on ad nauseam. But it is to us, the reader, that he speaks, for he talks also of us, of what we shall all become – tired, doddery old men, forever moaning and therefore abandoned and alone. 'There was a time, and a long time at that, when I was oppressed by the silence that millions of men were steeped in,' Marguerite said. 'It struck me that the role of the writer was to give the silence a voice, to imagine what the silence would say if it were able to break through the paralysing wall.'[18] But the book is more than just the description of people's inability to communicate. Forest, madness, young girl: it pulsates with Marguerite's obsessional themes.

When she'd finished the final draft, Marguerite sent it to Robert Gallimard with the note: 'I'm fed up with this book and yet I'm deeply attached to it.' As was her habit, she wrote the blurb herself and tried to tell Gallimard when best to publish it. Once again the critics were divided.

Duras worked quickly, too quickly for some. She was in a frenzy of activity, producing more stage adaptations, film scripts by the score, newspaper articles, and was never averse to a spot of producing for the radio. She didn't know how to be selective. She loved being loved. The popular women's magazine *Elle* voted her 'the writer who has the best understanding of love today', and she was proud of it. She knew she was doing too much but justified the commissions she took on because of the pleasure they gave her and the energy she drew from them for her own literary writing. She read the complete works of Henry James before working with Robert Antelme on a stage adaptation of *The Aspern Papers*. At the beginning of 1961 the play was a sell-out for the théâtre des Mathurins. Next, James Lord, dissatisfied with his work on adapting James's short story 'The Beast in the Jungle', asked her to help him. She cut, pruned and transformed the short elliptical tale into a tragic poem on mystical love. To the technical side of the writing, she added rhythm and depth by reconstructing the mechanics of the narrative. 'What attracts me to Henry James? Patience maybe, which is always impatience become patience,' she said in *Le ravissement de la parole*. The adaptation was performed in September 1962 at the Athénée and its success was attributed to her by the press.

At the time, there was a feeling that whatever Duras touched would work out well and please people. Duras was in fashion. *The Viaducts of Seine-et-Oise* opened in February 1963 at the théâtre de Poche Montparnasse. Samuel Beckett went to the opening night. 'It's wonderful,' he said as he came out. The play was awarded the prix de la Jeune Critique.

Offers were pouring in from the world of cinema too. Jeanne Moreau was about to acquire the rights to *The Sailor from Gibraltar*, which she would direct and star in. Marguerite Duras and Gérard Jarlot were co-writing a script for Michel Mitrani entitled *Sans merveille*, the story of a modern couple who love one another although each is unfaithful to the other. Should one or should one not tell the truth? 'We have no secrets from each other. We are like a glass house to each other.' The screenplay was a platform for Marguerite and Jarlot's own emotional upheavals. Marguerite thought she could allay her jealousy by writing about it with the person concerned; and Jarlot accepted the challenge in the hope that he could get Marguerite to understand a man could love a woman even while he was being unfaithful to her. Mitrani said the idea for the script had come from both of them.

Marguerite and Jarlot were spending many nights in bars. In a nightclub that was popular with petty crooks, they'd often hide in the back room which was separated from the dance floor by a two-way mirror. Marguerite enjoyed watching without being seen. Wine, whisky, the two of them drank a lot. Jarlot would start; Marguerite would soon overtake him. Behind the bed in his bachelor flat Jarlot kept a stock of brandy. Marguerite would pinch a bottle and walk around with it in her coat pocket. She didn't drink in secret, she even bragged about it to her friends. Day and night. Monique was alarmed but when she warned her to be careful, Marguerite just laughed.

How could she get Jarlot to be faithful? By sharing in his drinking and by writing together, Marguerite thought. She showed him a few pages of an erotic text she'd written. Should she throw it away and give up or start again? Jarlot told her it was beautiful and she should finish it. This would very much later become *The Man Sitting in the Corridor*. The text, in its 1962 draft, began as follows:

A man was sitting in the house, facing the door to summer. He was watching a woman, concealed on the gravel path, a couple of yards away, naked in the sun. She raised her legs, presented them to him spaced apart, parted them, parted them more with a gesture of furious immodesty and in such a way that her body swelled, became one long wound, contorted until it became ugly. Then she froze in that position, of an insane defecation, of an insane desire to give birth to one's sex.

The bees and their honey and the silence of summer surrounded their abode.

The sex steamed briefly in the sun. Then the man saw it feed on the heat, saw it slowly dry out, saw the source of honey run dry.

And only then when it was done when he knew it was feasible for before it would have hurt did the man move.

It was first on the mouth that he did it.

She shut her eyes.

The jet broke on her teeth and splashed her hair with its dew. Then he made his way down her body, flooded her breasts, already slow to come. When he reached her sex, his strength returned, he crushed himself into her heat, mingled with her come and foamed.

At last he'd run dry.

The man stayed where he was for a while, watched the body steam in the heat then, when she could have been thought to be asleep, placed his foot low down on her belly to assist her in her difficult undertaking.

He pressed down.

Marguerite had three copies of the text typed out – one for Gérard Jarlot, one for Madeleine Alleins, and the third she 'forgot' in a cupboard for a few years. In 1969 she had it delivered anonymously to Éditions de Minuit.

And then suddenly she took the whole of the end. She closed her mouth around the rim that marked its growth. Her mouth was filled with it. Its softness was such that it brought tears to her eyes. There was nothing as powerful as this softness save the order not to damage it.

Ordered.

On her tongue she had May, April, the spring of a man but couldn't allow herself to take any more except by caressing it, cautiously, with her tongue.

What we normally have in our minds, she had in her mouth. In her mind she devoured it, drew nourishment from it, filled her mind with it.

The crime in her mouth, her teeth ready, she couldn't allow herself to do him anything but good. And so she licked. And between two kisses, named her love, insulted her love, yelling words, words. Yelling words of encouragement...

With reasonable sweetness she grows impatient again to swallow the man's thin and sterile milk, to endlessly slake her thirst on it.

No one was supposed to know the identity of the author. Jérôme Lindon skimmed through the piece, convinced it was by Marguerite. She retrieved the text and years later modified it slightly before Minuit published it in her name in 1980. There is no communication between the man and woman. Desire finds gratification in violence. In the first version, the woman can only reach orgasm if the man intensifies his blows.

The hand strikes. Each time more selective, it's reaching a speed and mechanical precision. An animal couldn't do it better. By itself, her face yields to the blows better and better. It moves automatically on the neck ... Thanks to the hand it becomes vaginal. It's done. Memory has left the room. Intellect banished. Blows resound. Blows given, blows received. Strike like time. All one can do is receive blows. All the other can do is give blows.

In the final version, with the blows come fear, then screams and finally silence. And so the man and the woman reach orgasm. Duras does not pass judgement on their relationship; she describes it in great detail and analyses it wonderfully. Is it an echo of life with Jarlot? She really was hounded by violence and was beginning to wonder if she wasn't inviting it herself. She remembered her mother's blows, her brother's blows. Now it was the lover's blows. 'I couldn't have written it if I hadn't experienced it,' she said.

I love you. I kill you. Duras and Jarlot beat each other up but didn't separate. Marguerite introduced Jarlot to Mitterrand and they discussed politics for nights on end. With a shared fascination for crooks and outlaws, the three of them wandered the streets of Paris together, and Duras arranged for Mitterrand to meet a gangster recently freed after serving eight years for armed robbery. She was the last to know Jarlot was cheating on her. Was she really under the illusion over the years that Jarlot, through the erotic and symbolic power of writing, was choosing her rather than the others and that he would eventually give up doing the rounds of the women? In *L'homme menti* she wrote, 'Women were the mainstay of this man's life and many women knew this the moment he went up to them, the moment he looked at them. The man just had to look at a woman and already he was her lover.' For a long time their writing together served as a screen. For years he'd been scribbling away at a projected novel, tearing it up, then starting again. He was getting desperate. Marguerite asked to see what he'd written, annotated it and encouraged him. 'She helped him a lot to change and improve the novel *Un chat qui aboie* [*A barking cat*],' Eva Jarlot confirmed. On Marguerite's insistence, he showed it to Gallimard, who turned it down. Blows also abound in Jarlot's novel *Un chat qui aboie*, where the main character can only make love if – to her evident delight – he beats his beloved.

Thanks to Marguerite's perseverance, Jarlot returned to *Un chat qui aboie*; Marguerite gave him precise instructions that allowed him once and for all to organize the narrative. Jarlot entrusted the new manuscript to Louis-René des Forêts, who gave it his full backing when it was presented to Gallimard's reading committee. The novel was at last accepted. It came out in September 1963. In *L'Express* Jarlot admitted to having described what he knew best – himself, 'that is to say a mixture of horrible things: sadism, masochism, egoism and cruelty.' His novel is a burlesque portrayal of a weak seducer who is completely surrounded by fickle, hysterical and alcoholic women. The Médicis judges – of which Marguerite was still one – awarded him the prize on the fifth ballot after discussions that were so heated that some members were asked to send in postal votes. The prize marked the beginning of a period of bitter arguments between him and Marguerite – for he now saw himself as her equal. Jealousy finally killed their love. Sexual jealousy on the part of Marguerite, literary jealousy on the part of Jarlot.

During this time Marguerite was working on the dialogues for a television play, *The Rivers and the Forests*; a novel then called *Vice-consul de France à Calcutta*; and with Louis Malle on the film adaptation of *Ten Thirty on a Summer Night*, which would never see the light of day. She started co-writing, with the young film director Marin Karmitz, a script that was to deal with alcoholism but turned into a poetic meditation, *Nuit noire Calcutta*. And she accepted an offer from an American producer who also invited Beckett, Ionesco and Genet. 'People over there realized intellectual films could make money, that the public had evolved,' she commented. 'So you see, we're doing it the American way.'[19]

The producer paid for her trip to New York. Together with her friend the painter Jo Dawning, she set sail aboard the *France*. Awe-struck, she discovered 'her America', an America she loved and passionately defended. The American project ended abruptly but Marguerite did not for all that abandon the cinema.

On her return from the USA, she called Alain Resnais and asked him to come round to her place immediately. 'Read my screenplay, we start filming in two weeks,' she told him peremptorily. After *Hiroshima* they had sworn to make another film together before long.

She locked him in her flat for two hours. All Alain Resnais remembers today is action set in a hotel, the sound of tennis balls, and a depressed girl. It was quite obviously an adaptation of 'Les chantiers', published in 1954, a preliminary draft for what would later in 1969 become *Destroy, She Said*. Resnais was not convinced – it was a text and not a script. Before he left he said, 'Write the way you usually do. That will give me an idea of the images. Don't write a lot. Leave it to me to sort out.' Marguerite never forgave him this rejection and was always jealous after that of Resnais's collaborations with other scriptwriters. '*Muriel* is trash,' she declared publicly as she came out of the screening, 'like a Cocteau!' She became quite aggressive towards him and went as far as to accuse him of having stolen the subject of *Hiroshima*. Then she accused him of having pocketed the profits that should have come to her following the film's success. A copy of the 1966 summer issue of the magazine *L'Avant-Scène*, where Alain Resnais's face appears on the front cover, is testimony to the strength of her feelings for him. Marguerite has scrawled all over Resnais's face, writing the word 'trash' on his cheeks and brow and the word 'impure' over his hair.

Resnais pointed out that the quarrel between them had been one-sided and that the accusations she levelled against him had been made in public but never to his face.[20] She claimed that she should have received 50 per cent of the takings from *Hiroshima* – 22 million francs. She had been paid one million when the film was released. 'I thought it was a gesture from the producer.'[21] Alain Resnais has a different version of events: ' "Sign nothing," I told her. She told me she needed money immediately.' Anatole Dauman confirmed that she had agreed to sign the contract for one million for *Hiroshima* and she had said, 'It isn't a gold contract but a golden contract, for it gives me complete freedom, a freedom that was denied me with *The Sea Wall*.' 'Afterwards she told me she'd been bloody stupid.' Two days after the film was released, Dauman had a visit from Marguerite. 'She had a face like thunder. She insulted me. Called me a thief. I gave her four million. After that she was all sweetness and light.'[22]

CHAPTER 12

In the Dark Room

~

Once Jarlot's novel had been accepted, Marguerite withdrew to Neauphle, where she took refuge in her room overlooking the lake. She
started work on a text initially commissioned by Peter Brook, who
was offering her a stage 'so that I could do anything, whatever came
to mind'.[1] And so she began to write a conversation between two
people, for two actresses she loved, Loleh Bellon and Tatiana Moukhine. 'As I write I hear their voices. I don't know where I'm going.
It's great fun.' Only the two first names would survive. For the piece
soon became a story, for a long time called 'L'homme de Town Beach'.
Loleh would become Lol. In her solitude and emotional angst Duras
allowed the pale-eyed Lol to come to her. Gérard Jarlot turned up
and persuaded her to go with him to Trouville, where they had been
so happy. There by the sea Marguerite Duras finished, in the summer
of 1963, *The Ravishing of Lol V. Stein*.

The emptying of the self that Duras wanted so much to achieve
had at last begun. Handing in the manuscript to her editor Robert
Gallimard, Marguerite had written on a sheet of paper torn from an
exercise book, 'It's done. I cannot reread it; I've had it. The animal is
out, I love her.' The galley proofs were delivered on 24 December
1963. She made few changes, which was unlike her. Only the last page
was crossed out. An ambulance with its siren blaring was supposed to
take Lol away. Instead Marguerite left her in a field of rye waiting,
exhausted, for night to fall.

How do you escape the night? That is the question that nags at the heart of the book. The night during which Lol watches powerless as Anne-Marie Stretter seduces her fiancé, the night of love, the night of writing. The character of Lol is perpetually running away: from common sense, from the definition of love, from social order, from all attempts at categorization. Lol runs away from her fiancé, her husband, her lover, her reader, even her author. She utters enigmatic sentences or howls, people are beaten up, there are policemen downstairs. Hallucinations, fantasies, phantoms pass through her. It speaks, as Lacan would say, it speaks all the time. When it's not coming out of her mouth, it's coming out of the body. Lol lives in fear and trembling. She suffers from permanent lethargy and sleepiness. 'To speak the emptiness, the transparency of Lol,' wrote Duras in the margin of the first page of one of the early versions. And added, 'She alone, the so-called Lol Blain, she was no one. At the edge of being she had never sunk into illusion.' Everyone is frightened of mentioning the fateful night her fiancé left her. She's been waiting ten years to return to the scene of the crime of love, to try to understand how she could have stood by and watched the man to whom she was promised walk away from her into the distance. And yet Lol knows there's nothing to see in the casino where it all happened. A mighty calm has covered everything, engulfed everything. 'No trace, none, everything's been buried. Lol along with the rest.'

It wasn't the broken engagement that sent her into a state of madness. 'Crazy she was,' wrote Marguerite on the second draft of the novel. In the margin, she added, 'Nothing should be clear.' 'She was of course mentally ill,' she said in 1976, 'but named from the outside.'[2] Marguerite Duras knew from the outset that the novel would lead her a long way from the traditional narrative, far from the accepted laws of psychology, far from common sense. The different drafts of the book with their many annotations testify to the intensity of the work and mental effort required of Marguerite to reach the end of the ordeal of truth she had inflicted on herself. In all there were nine complete versions of the novel before this major character of her oeuvre could be born: Lol V. Stein.

Initially her name was Manon. Manon actually existed; Marguerite met her one Christmas evening in a psychiatric hospital in the suburbs of Paris where she and some friends had gone under the auspices of a charity to hand out presents. Manon immediately caught Marguerite's attention. She was beautiful and serene but stared blankly in front of her. Marguerite visited her again after the festivities and asked to take her out. She took her for a walk and brought her home and listened to her talk for a whole day. 'I knew her. And then I never saw her again. She became Lol V. Stein. I didn't need much. A look.'³ But Manon is not Lol. Marguerite Duras borrowed some of her characteristics: her way of keeping her distance from the world, her ethereal gaze, the gentleness in her almost imperceptible madness. Manon was the character's point of departure. Marguerite found herself listening to someone considered to be mad but who made sensible comments. She was impressed by this woman who'd agreed to go into the psychiatric hospital because she felt abnormal.

Then she lost sight of Manon. Duras found her another first name, Loleh, after Marguerite's friend Loleh Bellon, one of her favourite actresses and Claude Roy's wife. She gave her the surname Blair – Loleh Blair – and then a body. 'She wanted to be thin, and she was gloriously so. A skeleton with a boney face, the body she wanted.'

The narrative gradually fell into place. At the centre there was Lol, 'certifiable but not mad,' Duras specified in a preliminary note.⁴ Lol Blair was outside social conventions, definitely elsewhere. She neither inhabited her body nor her name. What was she hiding? Why did she lose her mind? Lol is the younger sister of Anne Desbaredes from *Moderato Cantabile*; like her, she is permanently listless and sensuous. She is also the daughter of Maria from *Ten-Thirty on a Summer Night*; she's inherited her emotionality, her frantic search for love and manic desire for pleasure. All three are fearful and tormented, and experience intense bursts of great joy and deep pain. They belong to no one – not to a father or a husband, even less to a lover. Men pass through their lives but never possess them. Maybe God sometimes visits them. 'Then one day that sick body stirs in the belly of God,' wrote Duras in the final version of *The Ravishing of Lol V. Stein*. Marguerite always left a bit of herself in every woman she created. Here, it was the terror of her adolescent sexual experiences. Lol was also ravished, captured by herself, separated from her own body, obliged to withdraw into herself. She had to find a way to be reborn into the world and to believe again in the idea of love despite the fact she was tainted.

When Marguerite Duras began writing the novel she put her relationship with Jarlot on hold and locked herself away with Lol. Would she find the words? *The Ravishing of Lol V. Stein* is not only one of Duras's most daring books but it is also a treatise on writing. What is a word? Where do we put ourselves in this total immersion in a language in which we live? Can the writer reduce the distance between feelings and words? Lol can't find the word to prevent the irrevocable. In fact she very much doubts there is a word. But the writer has a duty to find it, or to invent it.

As the word doesn't exist, she falls silent. It would have been an absence-word, a hole-word cut into its centre of a hole, of the hole where all the other words have been buried. We would have been unable to say it but we would have been able to make it ring out. Immense, boundless, an empty gong, it would have kept back those who wanted to leave, it would have convinced them of the impossible, it would have made them deaf to every other word except itself, in one go it would have named them, the future and the instant.[5]

When reading *The Ravishing of Lol V. Stein*, it's impossible not to be reminded of Nathalie Sarraute's work, from which Marguerite Duras always distanced herself; it's impossible not to think of the mystical tradition Duras never claimed to follow even though her friends say she was an avid reader of St Teresa of Avila and St John of the Cross. For during the ball Lol experiences ravishing, beatitude, separation from the real. Then she faints. When she 'returns', she cannot find the words. Nor can her loved ones. They would only have found bad words, false words. To make the long journey to reason, Lol will need her best friend Tatiana, who witnessed the events at the ball. And she will in turn ravish the lover in order to find a place in the world. Lol isn't trying to become the woman who is loved. She just wants to watch the friend and the lover embrace there in the rye field at the back. By the end of the story, Lol no longer knows who she is. What body does she inhabit? What's her name?

Jacques Lacan asked Marguerite Duras where Lol V. Stein had come from. She told him she didn't know.

'Symbol will best extricate us from the immediate meaning,' Lacan writes. 'Ravisher is also the image imposed on us by the figure of a victim, an outcast, whom we dare not touch, but who makes us their prey.'[6] Lacan refers to Duras as the decoder of sublimation, who through writing can instantly tap into the unconscious. 'Her quest can be compared to a mystic's asceticism.' 'She strives for ecstasy,' Matthieu Galey added, in *Arts*.[7]

Marguerite never knew how she finished the book. She remembered the intensity of the fear that gripped at the end. She let go of the manuscript as she would have let go of a strange and evil object. There were times during the writing when, like Lol, Marguerite wondered whether she might not be going mad and she was sure some of her friends thought she was mad. She finished the book at the end of her first detox. She who had written so much of her previous books while drinking at night, was suddenly face to face with herself. The fear she felt as she wrote merged with the ordeal of having to find the strength to live without alcohol. 'I was in a kind of relationship of trust with myself. Not only was it the book I most wanted to write, it was also the most difficult.'[8]

Marguerite had not yet decided to break with Jarlot. The lover in the novel was for a long time called Gérard. 'I love you but I don't like you, understand,' Lol told him. *The Ravishing of Lol V. Stein* was the last common ground between Marguerite and Jarlot, their final collaboration. At the end of her detox Marguerite decided to leave Jarlot and live alone. His affairs were making her miserable, and her own jealousy was making her life hell. 'All he ever learned about himself had come from women,' she wrote in *L'homme menti*. 'At night in bars I saw him blanch as though about to faint when a certain woman went up to him. And as he looked at her, none of the others existed. Each was then the one and only. And that's how it was until the day he died.'

'You know he's cheating on me. He said he'd stop, but he hasn't.' The film director Michel Mitrani noticed Marguerite's look of defeat when, one evening, she asked to see him urgently. 'He's cheating on you with a stripper, it's not as if she's an intellectual,' said Mitrani. 'So, he prefers a nice arse to an intelligent woman,' Marguerite responded.[9] 'I'm not really being unfaithful – she belongs to any man who looks at her,' said Jarlot. Marguerite asked him to break it off and Jarlot agreed, but it started again. She threw Jarlot out, became extremely aggressive and thereafter only ever spoke about him as a traitor. Love had turned to hate. Jarlot felt bad and was sinking into a depression; Marguerite later admitted that she too went through a period of despair. They would never meet again. But Jarlot was hounded by Marguerite's hatred, he confided to Alain Resnais, 'Marguerite's dangerous, she's a witch.'

'In the age of the twist, Freud and whisky, to say you don't like a book by Marguerite Duras is to admit to being a cretin. There are still a few of us cretins around, who prefer intelligence to madness, lucidity to alcoholism, self-control to pathological ravishing,' is how André Ducasse expressed himself in *Le Provençal* when *The Ravishing of Lol V. Stein* came out. The critics were as usual divided, but the novel, published in 1964, sold 9282 copies in the first year. The expatriate US director Joseph Losey wanted to buy the rights, but Duras refused. She made her own film adaptation of *The Ravishing of Lol V. Stein*, which was never finished.[10] At this time she was also working on television and radio programmes. Above all, her interest in the theatre was growing and she loved working with actors. A turning point was to be the birth of *Whole Days in the Trees*. Firstly, because it was the first time her life and that of her mother was to be played out in the theatre – a cruel and distressing experience. And secondly and crucially, because it was when she met Madeleine Renaud.

Madeleine Renaud was to play the Lady of the Trees, Marguerite's mother. Marguerite, was stunned the day she arrived in the middle of a rehearsal – there was her mother, as large as life, on the stage of the Odéon. Samuel Beckett had encouraged Madeleine to take on the role, telling her it was an opportunity not to be missed. Marguerite entrusted her mother to Madeleine, who proved to be patient, gentle and careful. One day she asked her for a photo, and in the family album Marguerite found a photo of her mother looking young, beautiful and voluptuous. Madeleine also wanted to know how she dressed – in a sack, not a dress, Marguerite told her – how she walked, what she smelled like. Marguerite went along to rehearsals but said nothing and Jean-Louis Barrault, the director, asked her nothing. He saw Marguerite as a poet rather than a writer, and she had absolute confidence in him. 'Duras is a child,' he said, 'not a big child but a child who's grown up.' As the rehearsals progressed she understood that her play was slipping away from her and becoming Madeleine's.

'*Whole Days in the Trees* is Madeleine Renaud and not me, I'm not responsible for the play, she is,' she told the critics. 'The text is essentially a kind of shambolic mess, which is what I love about it, it's a kind of fantasy flea-market, anything. And Madeleine takes to it like a duck takes to water, and she takes absolute control of it, she remoulds it.'[11]

Critics and public alike applauded Madeleine. The play was revived ten years later, when Bulle Ogier was an unforgettable Marcelle, the big dope of a girl, generous and clumsy, who has to bear the brunt of the mother's harshness and the son's egoism. Duras attended every rehearsal. The focus of the play had shifted with the years, and although the mother's intense love for her son was still an overriding theme, the spotlight also fell on the tender and fragile relationship between the son's lover and the mother. There soon followed a radio adaptation, to which Marguerite added West Indian waltzes and jazz, and then the play became a film. The adaptation involved Marguerite in a huge amount of work. A forty-page notebook of drawings, cuttings and technical notes testify to the film director's meticulous work, planning everything shot by shot – camera positions, viewing angles, actors' moves.[12] The film, after its first televised showing, was then screened in six cinemas and quite well received. It won the prix Jean Cocteau and was presented at the New York film festival in October 1976. On that occasion Marguerite – with tears in her eyes – again spoke of her mother. 'No, she didn't die after her last visit to her son, after her final return to Europe. She died much later when she was over eighty, far from her chosen homeland of Indo-China. Her last words were for my older brother. She only wanted him at her bedside, only her son. She asked for him, only for him.'[13]

Duras always rejected the idea there was a difference between the stage and writing. The theatre came naturally to her. She accepted its codes, its sorrows and its joys. She couldn't live without the atmosphere of the rehearsal. She loved the smell of the boards, the weight of the stage curtains, the light, like a servant, always there in the auditorium. It wasn't long before she was trying her hand at directing. She knew how to make actors move and taught them to speak her distinctive hoarse, broken, sparse, repetitive language, which was so often like a long wail. 'Listen to the music behind the words,' she'd say. She loved fragile actresses who trembled on the verge of hysteria. She knew nothing about the theatre and yet had an instinct for the essentials – the way to position an actor, how to play on the audience's emotions through the use of half-lights and beautiful, haunting music between acts. In short, theatre to her was more like life than a caricatured reproduction of reality. Performance was a vital act, a propitiatory ceremony that each time acted out the essential. And she loved actresses – Loleh Bellon, her favourite; Madeleine Renaud, of course; but also Jeanne Moreau, Delphine Seyrig and Bulle Ogier. With them she was humble, always full of admiration, keen to communicate and to give. This was summed up by Jeanne Moreau when she said, 'You, Marguerite, you allow yourself to be dispossessed, it's your vice. Some people are miserly. You on the other hand, are the opposite, and that is such a great pleasure.'[14] In her eyes actresses were not so much characters as mirrors on to which the spectator could be projected.

Marguerite also wrote plays for the sole pleasure of playing with words. It was in this spirit that she wrote *The Rivers and the Forests*, performed on 14 May 1965 at the théâtre Mouffetard. The title was a friendly dig at Louis-René des Forêts, to whom the play is dedicated. The subject of the play would appear to be the small talk (the traffic, dogs) between passers-by until suddenly something happens – a man is bitten by a small dog. That's all. The action takes place between the Café Flore and Les Deux Magots. The two women in *The Rivers and the Forests* confide in each other, swap useful addresses and their recipes for dog. Chihuahua, for example, 'makes a very cheap dish. Very good served with chickpeas ...' The intellectual Duras was making clumsy puns. The critics did not understand – they searched for hidden meanings and grammatical refinements. But Duras wrote anything, for fun and with no ulterior motives. 'There's no trick,' she explained after the single performance of the rather dreary play. 'I just fancied writing a comedy.'

Three years later, she again tried her hand at writing a play in a similar vein. *Shaga* was a kind of comic repertoire of accepted ideas, a kingdom where an unknown language was spoken. 'Hambo, hombre, yo oyo, kaback itou kaback.' In the land of Shaga, speech is a sound, conversation is a meaningless drone. To invent the exotic-sounding language, Marguerite Duras took various courses at the

Institute of Oriental Languages. Only one French word is used – *terminer*, to end. 'Staga moa. Yumi une moa.' You get used to anything, even to Shaga, and by the end of the performance the audience felt it had picked up a few words. Duras, who at the time claimed to be a disciple of Alfred Jarry, was cocking a snook at theatre. Some saw the play as heralding the events of 1968. Duras was celebrating the era of emptiness by applauding gags and destroying meaning. Barthes was right: only Duras finds words wholly irresponsible in all possible contexts.

'Actually, I still have a fondness, a deep-seated preference for the novel. It probably comes from the wilder side of my nature.' This statement, made in 1965 when she was fifty-one years old, came as a bit of a surprise. At the time, Marguerite seemed so completely immersed in the world of the theatre and her many film projects and television adaptations. At the invitation of the Vittorinis she spent the summer in Livorno, and returned to Paris at the end of August to complete the play *La Musica* in time for the opening of the autumn season and to begin work on a new adaptation of *The Square*. She was also after money. Despite Claude Gallimard having doubled her allowance, 2000 francs a month was not enough and she claimed to have serious financial problems. Compared to most Saint-Germain-des-Prés writers, Marguerite was living it up. She had three houses, two employees – a housekeeper in Neauphle and 'a gem' of a woman who did the housework in rue Saint-Benoît – and a fast and expensive English car. Marguerite accumulated traffic fines of over 20,000 francs a year, which she'd ask Gallimard to pay. She was still off alcohol, and every evening she went out to bistros where she drank soft drinks only. ('It's hell,' she said, 'this no alcohol.') She wore her hair short and dressed in men's jumpers and straight skirts. Very sensitive to the cold, she wore a sheepskin-lined jacket virtually all year round. She smoked Gitanes and worked all day, but never to a timetable. Those days she couldn't face her desk she made cushions, and when she wasn't repairing her lamps or knitting socks for the children of friends, she painted and drew in India ink. She dreamed of working with her hands, of jobs that would leave her physically drained, her brain emptied. Catering, for example. She could see herself the owner of a restaurant in the suburbs specializing in wedding receptions and banquets.

She told her friends that at night when she went up to her lonely bedroom and got into her empty bed, she wept. She hankered after a well-ordered family life – she'd have loved to have had a large family – and missed the chaos, exhaustion and excitement of life with Jarlot. She was finding alcohol more difficult to resist, and told Dionys she was living in constant fear.

She shut herself away in the house in Neauphle and set out on a strange inner journey. The memory of a woman obsessed her, although Marguerite had already captured the person who had frightened her so, screaming and running around the fringes of Sadec's white district, in *The Sea Wall*. She was young and puny and had a baby concealed in her arms. Passers-by averted their eyes. Then like a dog she would follow them. To women she offered her revolting, filthy, wailing baby. She had a sore on her foot, eating into her heel. The mother in *The Sea Wall* takes the beggar in and accepts the child. 'I knew the woman personally,' said Marguerite. 'I was ten. I was terrified of her.'[15] Twenty-five years later, Marguerite Duras went back in search of that pain. Night and day the nomadic, violent, wailing witch pursued Marguerite, who would immortalize her in *The Vice-Consul*. A beggar has left her mother a child who is going to die. Half woman, half animal, the beggar travels the land, not in search of the child she abandoned like an overripe fruit, but in search of the mother who's thrown her out.

The book took her eight months to write, she said, working at her desk without a break from five in the morning to eleven at night. The idea had come to her before the writing of *The Ravishing*, and for a long time the draft had developed alongside *The Ravishing*, until Lol appeared. The beggar woman had to wait her turn. The book went through innumerable metamorphoses and several restructurings. Believing it to be finished, Duras agreed in 1963 to publish a few extracts.[16] At the time, it had evolved on two levels: a woman living in Neuilly was inventing a story inspired by an abandoned private house. She made enquiries and discovered that the house belonged to a man who was Vice-Consul of France in Calcutta. A beggar woman prowled the street of Calcutta. The two stories had nothing in common. What held them together was the literary gamble.

As usual, Marguerite was inventing nothing. The Vice-Consul existed. His name was Freddy and they'd been friends at university. He'd joined the diplomatic service and been posted to Bombay. Marguerite's friends had met him during one of his brief stops in Paris between postings. He described to Marguerite the blue palms, the sultry air and the muggy ennui of the white community. The Neuilly house existed too. On one of her walks Marguerite had come across a nineteenth-century house, 10 avenue Saint-Nicolas, with its shutters always closed, its neglected garden where only the lilac survived. She had made enquiries of the neighbours, but no one knew the identity of the proprietor.

Marguerite gradually abandoned real places and the problems of the novel's structure to give the narrative a focus and to bring to life the one she called her little girl. 'How do I not return? You have to lose yourself. I don't know how. You'll learn, I'd like a suggestion how to lose myself.'[17] Thus begins *The Vice-Consul*. The characters are all lost, geographically, physically, emotionally and psychically; all silent, shut away with their shameful pasts, withdrawn with their secrets. What happened to Anne-Marie Stretter twenty yeas ago when the motor launch snatched her away from her married life? What terrible mistakes did the Vice-Consul commit in Lahore? In Calcutta, where the body is sapped by the heat, nothing matters. 'You think love is something we make up?' the Vice-Consul asks. No one answers. So he screams.

The novel with its two parallel stories became more focused as a result of a commission Marguerite accepted. Marin Karmitz was to produce, in collaboration with writers, a series of thirty-minute films on people suffering from various psychiatric disorders. The first was alcoholism, and Karmitz thought of Marguerite. In the middle of her writing chaos, Marguerite jumped at the opportunity to work on this commission and returned to Neauphle to write the script and dialogues. The action was supposed to take place in France but Marguerite found herself returning to the story of the man who was vice-consul in Calcutta, a city she knew nothing about but which in her eyes symbolized the weariness of being. 'I have to completely invent Calcutta – the heat, the fans everywhere screeching like frightened birds, his love for a young woman he met.'[18] Slowly Marguerite transformed the commission. To reassure the producers, she wrote a piece to make them think she was telling the story of a man who drank because he was bored, and who continued to drink even though he wasn't bored any more since he'd discovered his vocation as a writer. Happy, he drank to celebrate being reconciled with himself before giving up. Marguerite described wonderfully well the physical and sensual levels of alcohol in the man's body. She had accepted Karmitz's commission because the subject of alcoholism fascinated her. She worked on the script night and day in a creative intoxication that both elated and terrified her.

> Tonight, it's me who writes
> Alcoholic, what a joke, I can stop when I want
> With a trembling hand she confides
> the other's the alcoholic, the one we don't see
> It's only for ourselves we drink.[19]

Marguerite drank more and more so that she could give a better picture of the alcoholic groping for words. She tried to describe the heaviness that surrounded the Vice-Consul, the feeling of perpetual suffocation. She began to despair. Hadn't everything already been named for all eternity? She gave up on the script and returned to the book. In her notebook, she set herself tasks: she had 'to write every day, to find the link between all the things I've been writing about, to begin at the beginning, to stop drinking, to be sensible'. She imagines Calcutta as the mother of India and the mother of the dead. It's a bad city that smells bad, that stinks of slime and the sweat of men. Marguerite then returned to the story of the writer who drank, and created two women to meet the needs of her script. In scraps from her personal diary, we discover how Duras conceived her characters, identified and grappled with each one, gave up, reeled, then set off again. She summoned her characters and spoke to them as though they were physical entities there with her in the room in Neauphle.

> The heart of the Vice-Consul comes towards me. I have to embrace his vertigo. I, Vice-Consul of France in the face of happiness, say I don't care.
> Let me make myself understood, the man who suffers in Calcutta, I am near him. Let me be left in peace, let me be left alone, let me be left

to see what I want to see, say what I want to say ... The idea can be invisible ...

Why am I here? What's my problem? Not knowing why I am here ... the futility of the effort and its vital importance ... I'm dying. What is dying in this room?

... Further

I'm drunk and I'm near him. Empty. Dizzy.

A man doesn't sleep in Calcutta.

What a past. Folly weighs on my shoulders.

It's killing me because I don't know how to use my strength and experience; it's killing me. The idea? Because suddenly it smells bad, it's oozing, it's decomposing. Is this sudden despair not a sign that the Vice-Consul's heart is slowly entering me? Yes, it's beating.

Duras delivered her script on time to Marin Karmitz. 'We worked together a lot during the shoot,' he said. 'I filmed in her apartment in Trouville using her objects. She stayed close by. She watched to see what I did. She was there all the time.'[20] She told him she'd had some bad experiences with the film industry. Karmitz explained what he was doing as he went along. And so it was the shooting of the film – called *Nuit noire Calcutta* – that triggered her desire to become a filmmaker. 'She lost her fear of things technical. She saw that making films could be easy.'

Marguerite took Marin to Trouville Casino. Her bets were small but every time she lost she made a fuss. She showed him Normandy, the markets, the estuary, tree trunks left lying in the middle of fields, and talked to him of her brother, her mother. The film shows an abandoned town, shots of the sea, slack and leaden, waves of sand. It looks like Duras. The writer is brilliantly portrayed by Maurice Garrel. He haunts bistros, walks the streets alone at night, tries unsuccessfully to pick up young women. The film exuded melancholy. And it used a technique that Duras as filmmaker would later use and abuse – that of dissonance between the soundtrack and the images.

When *Nuit noire Calcutta* was selected for the Tours festival, Karmitz asked Marguerite to come along and help support it, but she never responded. The film was booed by the public but fiercely defended by Peter Brook.

By the end of her life Marguerite had forgotten all about *Nuit noire*

Calcutta. Of *The Vice-Consul*, she said it was her finest book, the most difficult and the most daring because it described the magnitude of a misfortune without ever revealing what had caused it. She invented her Calcutta using a map to plot the beggar woman's wanderings. The areas she crosses all exist. The book is built around the beggar. 'Without her,' Duras explained in a radio interview when the book came out, '*The Vice-Consul* would not exist.'[21] 'He, rich, decadent, generally inflated. She, poor, ragged, distended with poverty. Each diametrically opposed to the other. Never meeting. Yet through the misfortune of life, so close. The fact that they are in a nonexistence of an identical place, albeit for a few seconds, makes it the book I want to do,' she wrote in a note.

She took a break from writing to spend a few days with Ginetta and Elio Vittorini in Italy. It was the last time they walked together, drank Campari, argued, danced, discussed communism, the last time she ate his spaghetti *al pesto*, expressed her opinions on Togliatti and the latest decisions of the Italian Communist Party. She decided against returning to Paris but was also frightened to return to Neauphle, to the anguish, the shrieking. From Livorno she went to Venice and locked herself away in a hotel bedroom with her bottle of whisky and her manuscript. In Venice it rained. The panic she felt as an adolescent when she saw lepers returned to haunt her in this unsettling town that smelled of death. Venice is there in *The Vice-Consul*, for Anne-Marie Stretter used to live there. Marguerite lost heart. During the day she followed people around; at night she drank and wept, shedding tears over Anne-Marie Stretter, the Vice-Consul, the forests of Malaysia. In her diary she wrote:

I'm sitting at my table, searching for a sentence, yes, a little drunk, I'm searching for a sentence that won't come. Yesterday the sentence was spiralling fragmented inside me. Today it won't recreate itself. It was long, quickened by the pitch of a song, a refrain; it was like a lament, regular, intoned. Words I remember were caught up in it: slime, death, fan, frightened birds, thief, I'm searching for the sentence. It is such exquisite pain not to find it tonight. It will return tomorrow like a bitch to her master after the shame of the night hunt.

Duras at last made progress thanks to the smells – the stench of the slime from the riverbanks, the faint morning scent of oleanders in the gardens of the French embassy, the sickly spermatic smell, as she called it, of the Vice-Consul, always tired though he did nothing. In the first draft he had a wife, but in the final version she is allowed only the briefest of appearances in order to put the spotlight on Duras's favourite heroine – mother and whore rolled into one – Anne-Marie Stretter, that urbane, respectable married woman and mother of two who drives a young man to suicide.

Marguerite Duras said that Anne-Marie Stretter really existed, but she is obviously the synthesis of two women. One was the wife of an administrator who lived in the remote corner of Siam where Marguerite spent her holidays. When she was little, she and her mother had been to visit her out in the sticks where she lived. It had taken them three days in a motor launch to get there. The little girl had been struck by her beauty. The other woman was Elizabeth Striedter, whom Marguerite as a teenager had visited every day for several years. She was the mother of one of her classmates at the lycée Chasseloup-Laubat in Saigon. Beautiful, the perfect mother and a gifted musician.

Later, in 1977, thanks to the film *India Song*, this woman emerged from the mists of the past. After having seen the film, Elizabeth Striedter's granddaughter wrote to Marguerite informing her that her grandmother was in a rest home outside Paris. She suggested she visit her. As there was no reply from Marguerite, Elizabeth Striedter wrote to her:

> Madame
> You are right to remain silent.
> Your imagination has turned the young woman I was into a fictitious image that retains its charm precisely because of the mysterious anonymity that must be preserved. I am personally so deeply conscious of this that I had no wish to read your book nor to see your film. Private memories and impressions that retain their value by staying in the shadows, conscious of the real, become unreal ...

Elizabeth Striedter died on 8 October 1978, aged ninety-one.

In Venice Marguerite sank into a deep depression when she was creating Anne-Marie Stretter. She cabled a friend, telling her of her wretchedness and fears. The friend sent a doctor. 'The doctor came, no, it's not the alcohol. What then? I am ageless. I am loveless. I don't care about anything. I just want to know why I keep crying.' Deeply depressed, she finished the book in Neauphle. *The Vice-Consul* has no ending, the author leaves the narrative unresolved. But the characters wouldn't leave her memory. All it took was a short melancholic tune, the time of a waltz, and they resurfaced in her later work.

The Vice-Consul was typeset at the end of October. A huge number of changes were made to the first two sets of proofs, with the whole of the beginning having to be rewritten. '*The Vice-Consul* is the starving child, the animal-girl who walks the swamps of Burma,' Marguerite announced on the radio.[22] With a print-run of 25,000 copies, the book came out in January 1966 – three months after Alain Robbe-Grillet's *La maison du rendez-vous*. Same faraway, sultry and wearying oriental city, same interminable receptions, same trivial games of death and the past against a backdrop of mirrors disappearing into infinity: The literary press often compared the two books, especially as it was no secret that the two authors were friends. The comparison irritated Marguerite intensely and she decided it was time to dissociate herself from the *nouveau roman*. She announced that she didn't understand the *nouveau roman* at all, had never been a party to it and condemned its sometimes caricatural linguistic experimentation. She accused it of going around in circles and of being a fairly skilled rereading of American surrealist literature. 'It's even a bit tiresome. Personally, it's not a literary movement I believe in.'[23]

The Vice-Consul had bad reviews, and Duras was livid. She might have looked like a shy, sensitive, fragile writer when she appeared on television, but with the press she was beginning to practise the art of self-glorification and turned on anyone who didn't acknowledge her. To a Swiss newspaper she said, 'The French press didn't understand it. It didn't bother me ...' She kept journalists waiting for months and only agreed to give interviews on the understanding that she drew up the questions and answers. Duras held forth. Duras was only interested in herself. Already.

Gérard Jarlot died on 22 February 1966. He was struck down in his prime just as his talent as a writer was being acknowledged. And what did he die of, this eternal youth of forty-three? A heart attack, stated the obituary. A heart attack, while making love, his friends were told. Jarlot was found dead one afternoon in a hotel room in Saint-Germain-des-Près. A young woman had called the police from a phone box. When Marguerite heard the news she went mad. Mad with grief for the man she still loved, and mad with jealousy for the woman she blamed for his death. She tried to find out who it was, she even went to the police thinking they'd help, but it was to no avail. Jarlot's friends wondered whether he hadn't anticipated and planned his death – a Don Juan-style death, suicide through love. He knew he had a heart condition. He'd already had one attack and been warned that lovemaking, alcohol and cigarettes were bad for him. 'With madness we destroy time, in other words we kill death. The same can be said of poetry, love if need be, alcohol and drugs … with all of those things we kill death,' he had said when he won the Médicis.

'He was a wonderful man, in every sense of the word accomplished, exhausted from always dying without it killing him, demanding as much from death as from passion,' wrote Marguerite.

Elio Vittorini had died ten days earlier. In Elio, Marguerite lost a trusted companion, maybe her only real friend, a comrade in arms, a brotherly man always so attentive, so close that without even looking at one another, they'd react in the same way. A mentor too, a former master in ethics, in humility and in courage.

The Vice-Consul had left Duras empty, cleaned out. For the first time in her writing career she had no plans for another book. She was looking for other ways to calm the despair that constantly plagued her. That was when she decided to make films. 'Nothing would relax me more than to go round to the other side of the camera,' she wrote in a notebook.[24] She didn't want to work for anyone else; she was fed up with selling her author's rights to filmmakers who didn't understand the spirit of her books, or producing scripts for films she'd never see. And so Duras decided she would make films. It was also a way for her to get closer to her son, who had just turned eighteen. 'My son never talks about my books. What he loves is the cinema. It's maybe because of him that I'm getting involved. He can join the crew.'

Jean Mascolo was second assistant on the film La Musica, made with Paul Seban. Duras had met Seban when they'd been shooting for a TV programme. He'd just co-produced two shorts which she'd liked enormously. The contract clearly stated that Seban and Duras would be co-producers, but when she was interviewed before work on the film even started, Marguerite referred to it as 'my film'.

Her film maybe; her script definitely. *La Musica* started off as a stage play commissioned in 1964 by British television within the framework of a series entitled *Love Stories*. It was published by Gallimard, then performed in Paris on 8 October 1965 at the Studio des Champs-Elysées. For the French premiere Duras had already changed the play considerably and had had a hand in the stage production. She had asked that the production 'be cinematic. With strong lighting on the faces similar to medium and high-angle shots of faces in total darkness.'[25] The idea of film was already there.

The plot of *La Musica* – which Duras would later call sentimental – is not new. '*La Musica* is my tarty side,' she told me and laughed, adding that she could write three or four stories like that a year.[26] Two people are back in the provincial town where they had lived for twelve years. They are there to get a divorce. Everything is over between them. Tomorrow will see them set off on new emotional or professional adventures. Separated for ever.

Duras dusted everything off for the film version. She looked at the characters in practical terms and created new scenes. It took some time to find the right location. Hunting for an old-fashioned hotel in a sleepy Normandy town, Duras and Seban travelled the length and breadth of the region and visited hundreds of hotels, unsuccessfully. 'Paul, I don't hear *La Musica* here,' she would say. Eventually Seban came to a decision and told her it had to be the Castel Normand in Deauville.

Shooting in Evreux and Deauville began on 7 May 1966 and lasted a month. Sacha Vierny was the director of photography; Delphine Seyrig played the Evreux woman. She was quick to grasp the role, and became the very epitome of the tall, lanky provincial woman, the depressed younger sister of Lol V. Stein, who, like her, aimlessly wandered the streets and woods in an attempt to calm the fever in her soul; a woman obsessed with the cinema, like Suzanne in *The Sea Wall*. 'A profound woman but as light as a feather,' Marguerite stated.[27]

Delphine Seyrig staggered as she walked, had the look of a drowsy doe about her as she draped her body on a sofa, and a way of gently modulating her words with a voice so husky it made you tremble. Duras had met her through Alain Resnais, who had launched her in *Last Year in Marienbad*. Marguerite hesitated before taking her on. She really wanted Anouk Aimée, who was coincidentally in Deauville filming *A Man and a Woman*. Marguerite suggested they wait, but Seban insisted on using Seyrig. Marguerite would not regret it and the film was the beginning of a long and close friendship. 'When Delphine Seyrig moves into the camera's field, there's a flicker of Garbo and Clara Bow and we look to see if Cary Grant is at her side,' Duras explained. 'And so, we find it depressing that the future of the cinema looks to be in such a mess.'[28]

The male lead was played by Robert Hossein. Seban thought of him immediately. At the mention of his name, Duras exclaimed, 'What a dreadful thought, no, anyone but Hossein!' But Seban persisted and in the end she had to climb down once more. Hossein takes over the story:

The first time she saw me, she said, 'Listen, I'm going to make you intelligent.' My ratings were good and things were going well for me. She treated Seban like a technical adviser and me like a kid. She'd tell me I wasn't concentrating hard enough. She treated me like some kind of bazaar Don Juan or Casanova for bimbos. So I called her Christiane Rochefort [a rival writer[29]]. It drove her mad, but it made her laugh. There was this one take she made me redo at least fifty times. Still, I adored her. If I had a problem I'd go to her. I was extremely impressed. She crushed my instinct. She brought out ranges of emotions, she knew exactly what she wanted. She was very good.[30]

Duras felt too much attention had been paid to objects in *Hiroshima mon amour* and wanted *La Musica* to be a film without objects but with faces. A theatrical film. A cinematic play.

A production still shows her with the technicians, happy and cheerful. She was there, omnipresent, polite but firm, imposing her compositional vision and directing. Seban soon realized he'd been dispossessed. 'I had explained about lenses, tracking shots, I'd made sure she had a detailed shot-by-shot shooting script as I knew

directing was difficult to share. I'd picked out some remarkable tech-
nicians. But it wasn't working. She knew that to divide was to rule.
And that's what she did.' The atmosphere became highly charged, as
Michelle Porte confirmed:

> I'd seen in the papers that she was going to make a film. I went and rang
> her doorbell. I didn't know her. She suggested I work with her on the
> filming of *La Musica*. I wasn't given any special responsibilities, I was
> just there, that's all. She'd said, 'We can't pay you, but you can have free
> lodgings at my place at Les Roches Noires.' The tension between her
> and Seban was unbelievable. He kept to the script, she didn't. He played
> at being the professional technician, she didn't. When she spoke, and
> she was often right, the technicians complained about her behind her
> back and said she didn't know what she was talking about.

The permanent tension was mentioned in an article written on the
shoot for *Arts*.[31] 'They could never agree on how to interact. When
one was satisfied, the other insisted they start again. They each shot
their own shots. "What's yours? 3? Then I'll do 7. We'll see when it
comes to editing," Duras would say, playing for time.' 'I asked
the producers Ploquin and Dorin three times to let me go,' Seban
confided.

> But they wouldn't. In the end she went along with my obstinacy. Shoot-
> ing was extended and to the great despair of the producers the lights
> were switched back on. We made up at the end-of-shoot dinner. But
> then she tried to claim everything for herself. She even wanted 'film
> produced by Marguerite Duras' added to the credits. Then she dis-
> appeared, didn't even want to present it with me.[32]

It was referred to as her first film in the book that accompanied
her 1992 retrospective at the National Film Theatre. With Delphine
Seyrig, it was the beginning of the story. With Robert Hossein, it was
definitely the end. 'Marguerite asked for me again but I wasn't free.
She saw me as a sailor working in the docks, a brute. Pity. She was
the only one who could tame me ever so gently.'[33]

When it came to scripting *Ten-Thirty on a Summer Night*, relations
with the veteran director Jules Dassin were much more harmonious

than with Paul Seban. Dassin and Duras wrote the synopsis together. She imagined the locations, atmospheres and smells; she produced numerous drafts, which were reworked by Dassin; and she wrote biographical notes on the two heroines to help the actresses, Melina Mercouri and Romy Schneider. She went on location and was delighted to discover that Melina was the absolute embodiment of Maria. 'I think, I am even sure that the way she plays Maria is so close to what she's like body and soul in real life,' she stated in *Vogue*.[34] It was not an opinion shared by the critics, who gave the film a very chilly reception, criticizing Marguerite Duras for having sold her soul to the cinema and for having agreed to turn her book into a vulgar melodrama with Mercouri at the centre exceeding the bounds of vulgarity.[35]

Marguerite developed a sensual, intellectual and emotional attachment to Melina that did not dim with the years. Duras often fell in love with her actresses: Delphine Seyrig, Melina Mercouri, Jeanne Moreau. 'I started to have friends when I had you as a friend. You were my first adult friend,' Jeanne Moreau told her. 'With you I learned what friendship was and acquired other friends.'[36] Marguerite offered herself and the actresses gave. Marguerite loved their bodies, their voices, the way they walked, the faces her camera revealed to her and for her. The cinema to her was the art of the loving abduction. She used the camera to steal beauty. With the help of this instrument, it was possible at last to look at a face. The human face became the subject, the very essence of the film. 'In the theatre, you don't have the face, the face eludes you, not in the cinema.'[37] Duras was a voyeur. And the cinema was also the perfect opportunity to satisfy her passion for news items, and her romantic schoolgirl side that got a thrill out of slumming it in the seedy parts of town.

She wrote the script and dialogues for Jean Chapot's first film *La voleuse*, based on a real event in Germany which had been the talk of the town for months. A woman, played by Romy Schneider, confessed to her husband that before she met him, she'd had a child by another man. The baby had been entrusted to a working-class family, and now the birth mother wanted it back. The adoptive father, played by Michel Piccoli, threatened to kill himself if the child was taken away. The mother decided to 'steal' her own son from the adoptive family. Duras identified with the thief. 'Collaborating with Duras was not easy,' Jean Chapot admitted. 'Whereas I wanted to show thief and victim, she concentrated the focus of the film on the thief.'[38] The film was released in November 1966. Duras had stolen the film from Chapot – the press hailed it as a Duras film: 'Jean Chapot's first film heralds the birth of a new *auteur*. But is Marguerite Duras the author or the *auteur* here?'[39]

Duras was obsessed with the desire to solve what appeared to be gratuitous crimes. She loved looking for and finding skeletons in people's cupboards. Particular stories haunted her; for example, that of the couple who got rid of a cousin by cutting her up into pieces, which had inspired *The Viaducts of Seine-et-Oise* in 1959. In 1967 she returned to the story and completely rewrote it in the form of a dialogue-novel. It became *L'amante anglaise*, a short treatise on perversion and a wonderful detective story. She claimed 'to see' the crime, to have witnessed it almost. Duras 'dislocated' the characters, introduced distance between what they said and what they did, and allowed doubt to creep in over the identity of the criminal. She created suspense by inventing a narrator who, armed with a cassette recorder, settled himself in the bistro of the village where the crime had been committed so that he could eavesdrop on people. The reader suspects one character after another, each of whom is subjected to an interrogation, which is a cross between an examining magistrate's and a psychiatrist's.

Duras loved Agatha Christie. Like her she was fascinated by the prosaic nature of crime and by the apparent ordinariness of the criminals. What fascinated her was the destruction of the self through the death inflicted on another. 'It's too easy to forget the suffering experienced by the criminal,' says Pierre in *L'amante anglaise*. She called them Claire and Pierre Lannes. It was inevitable that Claire would commit a crime. It could have been her husband she killed; instead it was the deaf and dumb cousin. She said nothing to explain what lay behind the murder. And so Duras put herself in Claire's position. 'I am searching on her behalf for the reasons behind the crime,' said Marguerite.[40]

In real life 'Claire' was sentenced to five years in prison. When she was released, she returned to her village. Duras followed her there. The woman lived alone and talked to no one. Then one day she disappeared. In the eyes of the world 'Claire' was mad but not in Duras's eyes. 'They will look and find nothing and call it madness, I know.' The crime was her safety valve. Like many of Duras's heroines, Claire is part clairvoyant, part visionary and part witch, experiencing the odd hallucination, living in a state of perpetual dislocation. She skulks in the forbidden zones of the mysteries of life.

> I have had thoughts on joy, on plants in winter, certain plants, certain things, food, politics, water, on water, icy lakes, the bottoms of lakes, the lakes at the bottom of lakes, on water that drinks, that takes, that encloses, on that particular thing, water, a lot, on animals that crawl, continuously, without hands, on things also that come and go a lot...

Like the starving little animal in *India Song*, Claire survives the chaos of the world by roaring incomprehensible words. Weak and simple-minded, both are the envoys of the gods of madness, the forest-women, fish-women, women barely out of the slime of the unconscious, who have come to turn upside down our petit-bourgeois way of thinking and reasoning.

Marguerite Duras made so many last-minute changes to *L'amante anglaise* that several sets of proofs were needed. The book came out in April 1967 with a print run of 10,000 copies. The reviews were enthusiastic, stressing the depth of the writer's psychological analysis and her talent for giving a voice to people who lived their lives in almost perpetual silence. 'Marguerite Duras,' said one critic, summing up, 'touches a damaged area that is in all of us.'[41]

In December 1968, thanks to the director Claude Régy and the actors Madeleine Renaud, Claude Dauphin and Michael Lonsdale, *L'amante anglaise* became the most memorable of Marguerite Duras's plays. 'Crime,' said Régy, 'is first and foremost the potential for crime we have within us.' Régy's objective in staging the play in Paris, in the théâtre de Chaillot, was to confront the audience with the intoxication of murder, 'our longing to be the criminal, to speak to the criminal, to know him, to understand him, to identify with him'.[42] The actors were motionless. The action had to be mental, internal. Envisaged as a clinical examination, an experience in an enclosed space, the play subjected actors and audience to the test of truth. It was a triumph of Duras's power to fascinate. She would never again venture this far into the analysis of behaviour. The reviews were unanimously favourable.

Duras did not let up. She continued with her radio work, travelled the length and breadth of France giving talks on literature and poetry to secondary-school pupils and introduced them to the work of Henri Michaux – whom she described as the greatest French poet – by reading to them, for hours on end, extracts from *Un certain Plume*. She pleaded long and hard for poetry readings to be given in factories as well as salons. She joined in cultural activities, and attended several workers' councils. A radio journalist accompanied her when she spent two consecutive evenings persuading the women of the Pas-de-Calais mineworkers' council of the absolute necessity for literature, and read some Michaux, an extract from *Moby-Dick* and a piece by Aimé Césaire to a spellbound audience.

In May 1967, she accepted RTL's proposal to go to the Cannes Film Festival as their special envoy. Conscientious and enthusiastic, she supported Bresson's *Mouchette*, Losey's *Accident* and above all Antonioni's *Blow-Up*, which she predicted would get the Palme d'Or, and it did. Marguerite captured the atmosphere of the festival, and with a critic's practised eye wrote and spoke about everything, not just the films. She was starring in her own film which she constantly projected:

> Cannes is there. White stones and films. A bit like Calcutta. It's built like a theatre. And from where I am on the fourth floor, that's what it looks like, with the sea for a stage. The news is bad. Buy a paper, open it, and you're confronted by the horror of Haiphong razed to the ground. It's been eleven days since the military took over in Greece. And yet there are still American marines on the beach having their photos taken with the duty starlets.[43]

From Cannes she wrote an incensed letter to Robert Gallimard telling him she hadn't found her latest book in any of the bookshops in town. Robert apologized, as did Claude, and set in train an inquiry to find out from the distributors Hachette how this could have arisen. On 22 May she responded to Claude Gallimard:

> I had high hopes of this book. But the critical figure of 10 to 13,000

copies will once again not be exceeded. My snowball of readers has been destroyed. Success must be snapped up and capitalized upon immediately. If we don't give the public what they want, if we drag our feet, we ruin what is a natural relationship. And then it's too late.

But what I'm after is, in short, special treatment. Which is perhaps not very nice of me. But I knew *L'amante anglaise* was a book that could reach a wider readership than either *Lol V. Stein* or *The Vice-Consul*. I'm sorry.

'People are stupid but there's nothing new in that,' she kept saying. France was bored and so was Marguerite. Her hatred of General de Gaulle had not diminished. She tried to drown her disenchantment in alcohol. The world was a gigantic swamp ruled by the betrayal of the revolutionary ideal. She still claimed to be a communist, 'a real communist,' she said, to distance herself from the hyenas of the Party she abhorred. Although Dionys Mascolo finally moved out of rue Saint-Benoît in 1967 (he had just become the father of a daughter and gone to live with the mother, Solange), they still met regularly; and with him and Robert Antelme she continued to dream of a utopian communism.

CHAPTER 13

The Street and the Camera

~

The popular revolt of May 1968 was like a miracle. On 5 May, with Dionys and Robert, Duras joined the intellectuals and artists demanding a boycott of the ORTF, got people to sign a petition and was generally militant. When the demonstrations first started, she was down in the streets singing at the top of her voice, confronting the police and joining the barricades. Cheerful, laughing, a kid again. The joy of the Liberation was back, the streets were packed with people, there was hope and a desire for togetherness. She occupied the Sorbonne, spent nights on end listening to students talk, called for civil disobedience and believed, while the dream lasted, that the government might resign. They were going to change the world. Duras, like her friends from the defunct *Le 14 Juillet*, thought the revolution had come. In a demonstration she was always nervous of being knocked down and trampled so she took her 'bodyguards' with her – Blanchot, Mascolo, Marin – and ran breathless through the streets. She didn't bother going to bed, spent her time outside and watched things unfold. The events of May 1968 were for her the exploration of the wild place, the expression of the fundamental chaos inside each one of us.

In mid-May, she and Maurice Blanchot, her constant companion throughout that blissful month, were among the founding members of the students' and writers' *Comité d'action*. Committees were set up and a secretariat established. There were some sixty writers, journalists, students and television reporters in the room. The next day they were down to twenty-five – the television reporters and journal-ists had disappeared. The debates were less heated, more audible. Marguerite along with Blanchot, Antelme and Mascolo was there every day. The *comité* consisted of some twenty regulars and others – students and teachers – who'd drop in. Some listened and then, slamming the door behind them, left never to return, disgusted at the fuss the members made as word by word they pored over the contents of revolutionary tracts. First they rejected what was being proposed, then they were suspicious, then the text had to be completely rewritten. Some found the procedure quite exasper-ating. Maguerite persevered. She proved to be a skilled negotiator and was delighted to uncover the contradictions of leftism. She was revitalized by the contact with these brilliant young people who didn't recognize her but who bullied and admonished her. She who saw herself as a high priestess discovered the joy of being anonymous.

Her contribution to the revolution was to offer her services as a zealous little soldier of the French language. She came up with a couple of the slogans that turned up as watchwords or on walls around the Latin Quarter. 'We don't know where we're going but that's no reason not to go,' was one of hers, as was 'No prohibiting', if we are to believe Mascolo. But she didn't care, she was relishing her part in the collective as an activist, not an author.

There were unsuccessful attempts to sabotage the *comité*, but it kept on meeting until the end of August. Then the members were stuck in an attitude of political and metaphysical refusal. They had survived everything: the elections, the return to order, the summer doing nothing. Having been brought together by fate, they continued to debate philosophical issues from the ruins of a failed revolution, determined to pursue their dream of a world where Marxism was finally free of Stalinist crimes and where some of the aims of sur-realism had at last been realized. Their debates had become incom-prehensible to all but the core group of Marguerite, Maurice Blanchot, Jean Schuster, Dionys Mascolo and a handful of others. What mattered was unlimited revolutionary demands. Marguerite lived them all intensely, putting the needs of the group first, self-effacement, a systematic smashing of values. She wanted a change of identity: 'I'm fed up with Duras,' she said. And a change of country –

to leave France for the USA; and a change of profession – to give up writing for good.

Some still laugh about it today. What did they think they were playing at? To them, 1968 wasn't even a backdrop for an operetta; it was more like studio space for students who were nothing but self-important rich kids. But Marguerite believed in it. On 13 September 1968 she wrote to Henri Chatelain, a young man who'd become a close friend, 'Les Evènements. I was there night and day. May will never come round again. I am suffering from angst and ennui. So much so that I am seriously thinking of leaving France. The tragedy of Prague killed me. [The Soviet invasion in August had put an end to Czech liberalization.] I dream of a time when I won't be writing.'[1] Marguerite became very caught up in her beliefs. She wasn't a follower of the far left, not interested in working in a factory or in the country. In her view leftism was nomadism, leftism was freedom of thought. To define and fix the left is to eradicate it. It all happens inside you. To be politically committed means being able to recognize the wildness, the power to refuse, to express it and not allow it to be hijacked by any other party. The power of the individual lies in the ability to refuse what exists, so as to subsequently redefine the world. Marxism was dead; it was not a question of finding an ideology to replace it but of creating reasons for living and ways of hoping.

Marguerite found the post-'68 disillusionment difficult to deal with. For a year it was the dark night; she later said that she felt she was suffocating, that she wouldn't get over it, she wanted to die. Writing would once again save her from the void. 'When I began to write again, I wrote against myself, I wrote without a routine, against Duras, because I couldn't stand myself any more. Sometimes you have to take a risk, I'm in the dark,' she confessed in January 1970.

Marguerite felt weak and from this weakness a painful book was born, *Destroy, She Said*, which had as its point of departure 'Les balles', the short story written in 1964 for the film she wanted to make with Resnais. Marguerite had been upset by the filmmaker's rejection but she had taken his comments on board and turned a philosophical conversation into a story of disenchantment and depression, where the characters discuss their view of the world in front of a tennis court. Then 'Les balles' was abandoned in favour of 'La chaise longue'. After the events of May 1968, Duras added the theme of destruction – of love, of politics, of words. Having lost interest in everything, the heroine, Elizabeth Alione, is in a deep depression that trails her through the corridors, gardens and dining room of a hotel that may be a clinic. A dangerous, wild forest, a place of attraction and perdition, surrounds the hotel. '*Destroy* is not a novel at all,' Duras told Alain Vircondelet. 'It was born of me and my despair.'[2] Meditation, incantation, lament, chant, poem, it's a sacrificial ceremony. The convalescent heroine takes her medicine and appears to do as the doctors tell her. But there is no cure for Marguerite and Elizabeth's condition. At night Elizabeth Alione's sleep is shattered by dreams, and by day benumbed by drugs. She stares into the void. She has lost a child, it was stillborn. There is no drug to take away Elizabeth Alione's pain; is there, Marguerite?

Destroy, She Said is a quartet. Elizabeth is weak, listless, open; Alissa is hard, beautiful, aggressive, sensuous, a slave to convention. Max Thor and Stein are intellectuals, voyeurs, hunters and destroyers. Each drowns in the other's desire. Max in Stein's, Elizabeth in Alissa's. The two men, both Alissa's lovers, are very taken with Elizabeth, their new prey. Then the world collapses and the atmosphere becomes untenable. Everything loses its meaning – life, death, writing. What's the point? *Destroy, She Said* celebrates the cult of the void set against a background of voyeurism and latent homosexuality. 'For me,' Marguerite confided, 'writing is to arrive with the crisis at the end of the crisis. I write quickly so the crisis doesn't leave me.'[3] Everything is written against a background of absence. Duras dug even deeper into the language, abandoned the continuity of sentences and brought out such words as 'madness', 'desire', 'Jew' and flogged and fretted them in an attempt to exhaust their meaning.

Marguerite found *Destroy, She Said* obscure and difficult to talk about: 'I can see nothing in it, I tried to show a future world, post-Freud, a world without sleep.'[4] But having written the book, Marguerite found she could sleep again, and with that came a degree of peace.

Without her informing Gallimard, the book was offered to Minuit. Jérôme Lindon, after an eleven-year wait, was delighted to welcome her back as an author, but he didn't like the title *La chaise longue* and asked Marguerite to change it. She came up with the word 'destroy' and Robbe-Grillet added 'she said'. '*Destroy, She Said*, a fiendishly Durassian title, greeted with enthusiasm,' according to Robbe-Grillet.[5]

Marguerite wanted her book to be a political tool. 'I think it is necessary to destroy. I'd like all notes destroyed, all curiosities, for us to pass through an immense bath of ignorance, of darkness.'[6] The writer must be a tireless agent in the fight to destroy the bourgeoisie and old social laws. *Destroy, She Said* was only a beginning. The struggle must go on through the publication of other writers.

At the beginning of January 1969, she suggested Gallimard start a series specializing in politics. Robert wasn't against the idea but asked her to be more specific. Marguerite was losing patience. The revolution couldn't wait and she'd already promised some young writers. She wrote to Robert and Claude Gallimard:

Last Monday I spoke to you of a political – anti-establishment style – series for which the book I have just written will be the first.

For political reasons I must act fast. And I don't have the four or five advance titles you say are required to launch the series.

I have nothing but this very short book which I might not even sign. And this overwhelming need for freedom, which means I could work under no one but myself in this series.

I've signed with another editor – it's done.

After twenty years it's only to be expected that our emotional ties should go through a difficult patch. Let's just say I'm having a crisis. Which is another reason why I signed.

'Claude reacted like a jilted lover,' Robert Gallimard said. He reminded her that he very much admired her work and that he'd been a loyal friend. It was too late. Marguerite had had enough of being Gallimard's woman writer, associated with Robert Antelme and Dionys Mascolo who both still had important positions in the publishing house. She didn't want to be just an author; she wanted to be an editor as well. From time to time she sent manuscripts to Gallimard recommending they publish them, but not a single one was accepted. Why? She didn't know what they wanted.

We see so little of each other that I have no idea what kind of new writing you're looking for or whether you're even looking. All I know is that I can't go on being only a writer *writing your books, from this point of view I'm fed up with myself.* I'd like to bring others in, to get others to write, to open up the profession, to *give a meaning to writings which, kept isolated,* only have *a limited meaning.*[7]

In March 1969, *Destroy, She Said* was published by Minuit. 'The most important novel to reach me this year. A book that must be read in a way that is radically different from our usual plodding tendency for reference and explanation,' wrote Philippe Boyer in *La Quinzaine littéraire,* summarizing the favourable reviews.[8]

The idea soon came to Marguerite to make a film of the book. The moment it was published, she started work on the script. Eight days later it was finished.[9] Marguerite's dream was about to come true; she was going to make her first film alone. She would claim authorship of everything: production, direction, script, dialogue. She even worked out a budget, which amounted to 1,343,600 francs, 250,000 of which were for the actors. Nicole Stéphane and Monique Montivier produced it. The film was to be a partnership, and they would film over fourteen days. Marguerite started on the casting and – ever the romantic schoolgirl – began by phoning the stars of the big screen. Within the hour they were all there.[10] Rue Saint-Benoît was like a parade ground. Marguerite auditioned. She was relying on her intuition, had the odd tantrum and regretted her decisions next day. Marguerite thought she was an expert but she was groping in the dark. 'If you can't find anyone, I'll do it,' said the actor Michael Lonsdale and became part of the great Durassian legend. But in the end Daniel Gélin, Henry Garcin, Nicole Hiss and Catherine Sellers were selected. They filmed in the garden of a house belonging to a wealthy banker who wouldn't allow the crew into the house. To learn to make a film Marguerite made a film. Michael Lonsdale remembers that one afternoon at the beginning of the shoot, she went over to him and Gélin who were sitting in the grass and said, 'Just be patient, my darlings, I don't know where to put the camera.'[11] There was a convivial atmosphere and Marguerite discovered the joy of working communally. 'It is so exquisite to do something together, it makes solitary creativity look like a bad habit.'[12]

But Marguerite ran out of inspiration and didn't know how to finish her film. One day she happened to be listening to Bach's *The Art of Fugue*. Music would do her work and define the tone and tempo of the film. The natural light of summer was used. You never know the time or the day. The characters wander through the gardens. The surrounding forest is omnipresent and menacing. 'The forest is whatever you want it to be, it can be Freud, death, truth, everything.'[13] And from the forest comes the music. The air trembles. The film, made up of sixty shots, alternates between static shots and close-ups of faces scrutinized by an inquisitive camera that tracks weariness, disgust, fear, waiting.

Dedicated to the youth of the world, the film was supposed to be unconditionally political – to destroy society in the name of revolution, to destroy the very notion of love in the name of another way of loving. The lines are packed with political allusions. Stein's, for example, are inspired by Bakunin's 1870 speeches in Lyon: 'Nations suffer but begin to understand it isn't necessary.' Slogan film, propaganda film, *Destroy* also saw itself as a prophetic film, calling for a new kind of political optimism. 'I am endeavouring in this film to place the revolutionary front in the inner life,' she wrote in the programme note. The two main themes are politics and love. In a TV programme devoted to her at the end of the shoot, Marguerite explained that she'd interviewed dozens of prostitutes in search of a new definition of physical love. The lesson she learned was, 'Make love with anyone. Mating is all that counts. Availability is all that counts.'

Destroy was released at the beginning of 1970 and screened on the artistic and experimental circuit. While it didn't attract much interest from the general public, it did provoke a great deal of discussion in intellectual circles influenced by psychoanalysis. Debates were organized to 'decode' it. During the debate of 5 February 1970, for example, Philippe Sollers for *Le Nouvel Observateur* saw it as a determined attempt to turn upside down and reinterpret Engels's book *The Origin of the Family, Private Property and the State*. 'A very sexual film too with that exquisite ending where the climax happens so suddenly, where the noise and music are like a kind of terminal orgasm, a kind of final release.'[14] Most mainstream critics were less kind, typically describing it as gloomy, venomous and vertiginous. Why did she make films? Duras was asked. 'Because I want to see and

279

hear outside what I could see and hear inside. I wanted to see if it was communicable.'¹⁵

Duras had no intention of explaining, commenting or enlightening. She said what she thought, soliloquized out loud, transcribed what went through her mind and avowed her part of darkness. And then she published what is regarded as her most unreadable, most obscure book – *Abahn Sabana David*. She herself admitted that having reread it, she did not understand it. To the end of her days, she fiercely protected this book from the critics and refused to explain herself.¹⁶ It had exhausted her; grappling with the text had threatened her mentally and drained her physically.

In *Abahn Sabana David*, the game isn't being played with tennis balls but with bullets. It's a question of life and death. The shots are fired at point-blank range and the revolver is omnipresent. The first version was called *Les dieux de Prague* and described the recent terrible events in Czechoslovakia. Gradually Marguerite Duras changed her focus to Judaism. What is a Jew? Who is a Jew? Why is one a Jew?

A man goes by.
'We call him Abahn the Jew, Abahn the dog,' said Sabana.
'Jew? And dog?'
'Yes.'
'Who do we call Jew in Staadt?' asked the man.
'The others.'
'Who do we call dogs?'
'The Jews.'

The book is dedicated to Maurice Blanchot and Robert Antelme. Later it would become a film under the title *Jaune le soleil*.

The class struggle is mixed up with dog breeding, and the mindlessness of the *Lumpenproletariat* with the life of Bach. In the total rejection of meaning, in the demolition of her own style, in the despair of alcohol, in the disillusion of revolution, Duras wrote without rereading what she'd written, not understanding what she'd written; like a strong swimmer who continues to crash through the waves thinking she can reach the horizon. She was worried that she was sinking into the state of madness she was so good at describing and with which she'd been familiar for some time. When she wrote – or rather when *it* wrote, for she had decided to surrender herself physically and mentally to whatever was besieging her, not to control the flow of the narrative or coherence of her visions – she felt even worse. Due no doubt to the alcohol and the anguish of being alone. She felt forsaken by her friends, as though dead. Photos reveal a tired face, wrinkles, grey hair and eyes tiny behind the big glasses. Not quite an old woman but a woman who has – temporarily – given up looking attractive.

Marguerite was not at all well when she started work on *L'amour*. She was suffering from stiffness all over and thought it was probably psychosomatic. *L'amour* started out as a continuation of the story of *The Ravishing of Lol V. Stein*. Lol's fiancé returns to the scene of the break-up. Since the ball, the town of S Thala has fallen into ruins. The characters are stranded on a sandbank, surrounded by the nauseous movement of the sea.

The sea in *L'amour* is omnipresent. That viscous mass that breaks, advances and engulfs, the sea from which we came, the sea she watched in Trouville night after endless night of insomnia, the sea that so terrified her, which she'd been trying to describe ever since she wrote her first book, *La vie tranquille*. 'She is alone lying in the sand in the sun, decomposing ... her hand still buried next to the white bag.' The name of the town where *L'amour* is set – S Thala – is in fact Thalassa (the Greek for 'sea') the other way round. Duras said it took twenty years before she realized it. S Thala doesn't exist; Duras invented it. To her the sandy place, the wild stretch that appears on no map, was also the waiting place for the future, the open place Rilke spoke of (Duras was avidly rereading him at the time), the place 'that we only recognize from the animal's face'. The world of love had definitely been destroyed. 'We have to wring the neck of the Balzacian real and Stendhalian passion.' It was also a desperate attempt to destroy the book as it was being created. She would say of this book that it flowed through her and that she was content to just let things happen. Her only guide was the sea, the sea with its movements, its tides and its seagulls. At the end of her life she remarked that she should have either begun or ended with that book.[17] '*L'amour* is a book that contains a hundred books, all the books I have written and me. And others too that others could have written.'[18]

What happened when she wrote was too harsh, too traumatizing, too exhausting, too dangerous. The desire to write beat down on her like a shower of hailstones – impossible to avoid and difficult to master. 'It's like a crisis I handle as best I can. It's more reassuring when I write about it. It's a kind of subjugation. When I'm writing I'm frightened; it's as though everything were crumbling around me. Words are dangerous, physically charged with powder, poison. They poison. And then that feeling that I mustn't do it.'[19]

And so Duras gave up writing and fled the madness that lay in wait for her. She moved into films the way you take refuge in the mountains when there's the threat of a storm. She needed people around her to calm her, to reassure her. The cinema was more of a biological need than an aesthetic choice. There was too much talk going on inside her, it was spilling over from everywhere, her voices, her characters. She tamed her visions by exorcizing them with a camera and for a limited period of time found in the unity of a film crew what she needed to recharge her batteries and quieten her down.

Duras had had a radical change of heart and even held conflicting views on the subject of the cinema. At the start she thought making a film would be easier than writing a book. After *Le Camion* (1977) – which according to her was her most successful film – she even said there was no difference between films and books, only between the people who made films and those who wrote books. But she soon discovered it was extremely complicated and in fact never abandoned the belief that only with writing was there a genuine confrontation with the self, that only writing met the absolute demand and involved the supreme risk. To her a film was matter and a book was spirit. A film could translate emotion but a book was emotion. To her, the act of writing gave her direct access to creation; a film would never be more than a material object, the product of technical and mental processes whose status was ambiguous. But for all that, cinema was not the lesser of two evils. It was an ideal setting for the celebration of beauty, a place to dream, to play with sound, a chance to manufacture time that could be folded and unfolded at every possible opportunity, a way of approaching the mystery.

Marguerite Duras was to make nineteen films altogether, four of which were shorts. First in black and white – *Destroy, She Said, Jaune le soleil* and *Nathalie Granger* – then with the strange colour-wash of *India Song* and *Son nom de Venise dans Calcutta désert*. She tackled every kind of style: the traditional narrative, poetic ode, experimental film, aesthetic documentary, philosophical dialogue, comedy and so on. She even made films with no images, just sound and a script – but black, nothing but black. For ten years filming was her main activity and writing merely accompanied filming. Duras made text-film, filmed text, film of text, call it what you will but it didn't exist before her. To her making films was undeniably also a way of writing. 'Marguerite Duras didn't just write bullshit ... She also filmed it.' In 1986 Pierre Desproges voiced an opinion others had been whispering for a long time.[20] And Marguerite Duras also produced her own kind of cinema, cast herself in *Le camion*, lent her voice to *India Song*, and saw herself as the madwoman in *Savannakhet*, the murderer in *L'amante anglaise* and the prostitute of the Normandy coast. She tried to quieten her own anxieties by creating characters who shared her spiritual lethargy and quiet despair. Chief puppet-master of a broken world where mirrors no longer reflect images, where the ground can't be seen, where bodies are dislocated from voices; through the use of syncopation and distortion she launched a new style of film. She created an imaginary universe, which had its own codes and secrets. However Duras did not destroy the notion of cinema, as she had hoped to; she did not wreck a particular kind of cinema she constantly criticized and called shameful; she did not revolutionize the history of cinema as she claimed to have done. She was a part of it: today her films belong to the post-1968 intellectual and artistic period and are extremely dated.

In an unpublished piece, she confessed, 'Cinema just happened to be there, easy to do, so I did it. That feeling still of prostituting myself. That niggling shame at talking on what I know nothing about ... making films had made me vulgar, depraved.'[21] Aware that she had not really left her mark, Marguerite Duras swung between this kind of avowal and the proclamation that her genius was going to revolutionize cinema. She frequently used the medium as an instrument to satisfy her passion for writing rather than as a means of expression in its own right; to this we should add being part of the city, the rejection of solitude as she approached old age, the desire to be with young people, to recapture the feeling of community that had reigned in rue Saint-Benoît.

For with Duras, films were a family affair. Dionys Mascolo was one of her lucky actors and their son Outa contributed to virtually all her films as either an assistant or a stills photographer. Making movies is not just a question of shooting; it's also a question of inventing a way of living and sharing. The more shooting she did, the more Duras worked on the tribal mentality. It was a special tribe, with its own mores and language, which put up with poor pay and long hours. At the time there were many who wanted to be admitted, to be seen to belong to the circle, and who were ready to work for nothing, happy just to watch Marguerite directing. Jean-Marc Turine for example, the author of *Le Ravissement de la parole*, later a friend of Marguerite's. 'In 1970,' he recalled,

> I wrote a screenplay of *Lol V. Stein* and sent it to her. She very politely turned it down. Afterwards I met Delphine Seyrig and talked to her of Duras. In January 1971 I got a call from Duras. She asked, 'Have you been to university?'
> 'Yes, but I studied philosophy.'
> 'It doesn't matter,' she said, 'we shoot in a week. If you're free, come down. There's no money in it but you'll get free board and lodging. It'll be like living in a commune.'[22]

Mascolo took Turine to Neauphle, where with no time to prepare he was thrown straight into the excitement of the shoot. At the time, Duras was unassuming and modest. She corrected the actors when they didn't understand the text and would start over again until the dialogue felt natural. Mindful of the wellbeing of each, she prepared tasty meals and saw to the needs of actors and technicians.

One day Luc Beraud, who was first assistant on the shoot, introduced her to a young man who was just starting out as a filmmaker, Bruno Nuytten. She immediately suggested he should take photos of the film. Rather than enquire about his professional experience, Marguerite asked, 'Are you Vietnamese?' She'd guessed right. 'She instinctively approaches the confusion over our origins that sets us apart within the family and holds us spellbound throughout her work,' said Bruno. 'That's what she was like, intuitive, directive, owner of people and their stories, but also generous, inspiring confidence.'[23]

Marguerite understood that Nuytten wasn't ready to shoot yet. But she adopted him. 'We were instantly members of the same family.' Nuytten became Duras's principal director of photography, Outa's friend, the man to whom she would dedicate *The Lover*, the friend of Marguerite's friends. The whole crew camped at Marguerite's house; ate, talked and slept at Marguerite's house. Collective management was in fashion but with her it was never simply a slogan. Everyone had their say on the film they were working on. Marguerite would listen and take their suggestions on board. 'She wasn't manipulative but she loved charming people,' Nuytten explained. The shortage of money, communal life, the intensity of shooting, the feeling that together they were inventing a new type of cinema, contributed to creating an atmosphere that all those involved would remember with nostalgia. And Queen Marguerite reigned over the tiny world. She eroticized all her relationships and specialized in the casting of beautiful and intelligent young people, whose talents she, in her imaginary universe, took the credit for. Nuytten, Benoît Jacquot, Turine and all the others fell in love with her. Marguerite had a gift for forming emotional attachments where she played the role of initiator, bringing out into the open the dark areas of each one's story and bringing love into the world, transforming the men into little brothers with whom she had incestuous relations. For her filming was always a test of truth, a wild psychoanalysis, a rare moment of intensity and interaction. Everything that took place had to benefit the film.

Duras discovered filmmaking by making films and by not being afraid that she couldn't do it.

When I talk about films, a lot of people think I 'miss the point', that when I talk about films I don't really know what I'm talking about. I think everyone can talk about films. Films are there and we're making them. Nothing pre-exists in films. Most of the time we feel like making them because filmmaking doesn't require a particular gift. It's a bit like handling a car.[24]

But although Duras learned on the job, she also knew how to pick her technicians and actors. For her third film, *Jaune le soleil*, Ricardo Aronovitch was in charge of lighting, and Michael Lonsdale,

Catherine Sellers, Sami Frey and Gérard Desarthe took on the leading roles. Already Duras was aiming high and she was rarely wrong. The majority of actors who worked with her remained loyal. But while she admired the talents and skills of some, she also thought anyone could become an actor overnight. She made Mascolo appear in *Jaune le soleil*, delivering his lines while in the middle of gardening, despite having pleaded that he would rather prune his roses than represent the worker calling for the class struggle.

The translation to the screen of the book *Abahn Sabana David* as *Jaune le soleil* gave the characters faces and voices. But as it wasn't their stories but their exchanges that Duras wanted to capture, she didn't want the actors physically prominent. 'I want to create an impression of having filmed without electricity. For there to be no lighting effects, for the whole film to bathe in a uniform light that favours no one person.'[25] 'This film is a film on speech. The role of the image is therefore to carry speech.'[26]

What stood out was the mythical figure of the wandering Jew, personified by Sami Frey. Marguerite selected and developed all the passages in *Abahn Sabana David* that dealt with Judaism. While they were working on the film, she wrote in a notebook, 'The Jews, they see and judge in its entirety the time in which they live. Their defence is political thought. By judging the world, they cease surrendering to it, and are thereby liberated from it.'[27] The main theme of the film remained the Jews – the Jews as the future of the world, the Jews whose status she claimed to have the honour of sharing. Outa once said that his parents' views on their origins were so strong that for years he thought he was Jewish.[28] The film made little impact at the box office and was soon forgotten.

Duras was living permanently at Neauphle and the world came to her rather than the other way round. The house was a refuge, the place to which she had invited her female characters: Lol, Tatiana, the beggar woman, Anne-Marie Stretter. She could make them appear and disappear at will but already they haunted the house like ghosts. She spent many a long hour at her worktable on the first floor. From the window she could see the lake and would gaze at it for hours. All around lay the forest, which scared her just a little.

It was in her house that the family filmed *Nathalie Granger*. Dionys

Mascolo acted, Outa took the stills, Valérie (Mascolo's niece) was the little girl and Solange (Mascolo's wife) was in charge of editing. But Marguerite had also taken on two of the most beautiful stars of the international screen, Lucia Bose and Jeanne Moreau, who had accepted the parts immediately. This 1972 film was a pause, an interval in her debilitating urge to destroy, a necessary breathing space. A woman's film on women, *Nathalie Granger* is probably the only one of her films to be quite conventional in its construction, its progression and its interpretation. It hasn't aged and still exudes a mellow, sensual and melancholic mood. In a preliminary note, this is how Marguerite described her main heroine: 'She sees her solitude spread all around her, contained by the house. Like the cat, she's restrained by the place. But this recreated solitude is desired by the woman, it is like a deep breath.' The film is also the exploration of a place, a residence. What is a house? How do you live in it and feel at home? The camera slowly explores a place where two women live in close harmony. The house itself is disconcerting. 'Just walk in somewhere, anywhere,' Marguerite suggested. 'Anywhere is terrifying. Wherever it is, we ask ourselves: how could anyone live here?' In the script, external events – gangsters hiding out in the area, a washing-machine salesman keen to sell his wares – disrupt the tranquillity of daily life.

Duras put the finishing touches to her screenplay and planned the sequences shot by shot. She worked swiftly, leaving nothing to chance. She studied each frame for a long time before shouting, 'Action!' Once she was satisfied and the camera was running, she discarded nothing, not even the accidents. At the beginning of the film, for example, the two women are supposed to clear a table. They do it slowly, extremely slowly, more slowly than had been foreseen in the script. But Marguerite captures the slowness of the gestures, their repetitiveness, the mundaneness of an everyday action that is never normally filmed. Do we go to the cinema so that we can spend eight minutes watching two women, however sublime they may be, clearing a table? Yes, we go for that too, says Marguerite. The shot is indicative of the spirit of the film: the attention paid to the materiality of things, the respect felt for the most mundane of gestures, the desire to praise banality.

Duras steered a course between hyper-realism and fantasy. 'When I say magic, I say cinema in general, let's say a cinematic life. Because

287

cinema is bizarre. You put a camera there, nothing happens, apparently nothing, and at the cinema it's fantastic, someone's going to appear on that path and people will be frightened.'[29]

The light in *Nathalie Granger* is very beautiful, thanks to Ghislain Cloquet, one of the great masters of black and white, whom Nuytten had suggested she take on. It's an end-of-winter light, a little sharp, slightly misty. On the terrace there's a black cat, broken toys, a little girl faltering over the piano, women draped on the divan: Jeanne Moreau in a tight sweater, Lucia Bose, depressed and unemotional, staring into space. The spectator has the feeling of penetrating into the house as into a living organism. Slowness of time, everyday gestures and already that tracery of sounds that would become the hallmark of a Duras film: the voice from the radio reading the news merges with the discordant notes of the piano, the murmur of women and Gérard Depardieu's loud voice.

It was Marguerite who gave Depardieu his first cinema role. She had spotted the rather strange, half-tough, half-rough man during a rehearsal of a play by Claude Régy where he was doing bit parts. He had pleased her as much as he had scared her. She offered him a job immediately and wrote him into the script at the last minute, as the washing-machine salesman. From the start of the shoot Marguerite had been talking to the crew about the strange bloke who was going to join them. Every day for the sake of suspense she did a countdown, he'll be here in five days, four, three. On the due date, she had the camera set up behind the front door and forbade anyone to leave the house. She had told Depardieu to arrive in a small van. When she heard the engine, she called: 'Action!' She opened the door abruptly and ran and hid behind the camera. 'And then we saw this strange person arrive,' said Nuytten, 'a huge young golem pitch and roll across the street in Neauphle. He was flirting with the ground. It was Gérard Depardieu.'[30]

Marguerite was claiming to have visions. Before they had started shooting, she saw a man returning from the fields and a woman bending down to pick up a child asleep under the larch. The woman looked at the child for a long time and complained about the heat. This scene, though it was never filmed, was the film's point of departure. From that spot she filmed the house. 'The book is the house. The house is the book.' Marguerite had started off by trying to write the book, but she couldn't. Then, one day, the visions came to her and the script began to flow. Once the film was finished, she returned to the book, giving it too the title of *Nathalie Granger*. The sleeping child became a solitary and aggressive little girl who kept herself to herself and was always punished. The woman in the fields became a mother who didn't know how to deal with her daughter's wildness and didn't know whether she should send her away or not – an allusion to her experiences with Outa.

Marguerite took everything she experienced, saw and heard, and transcribed it. She was ever watchful. Whenever the actors asked what rhythm they should adopt as they walked in the house, she'd find it by improvising a few arpeggios on the piano. These then became part of the film score. When it came to assembling a story, everything was useful and life had to 'enter' into the film. While preparations for filming were under way she happened to hear on the radio that two local men had murdered three people for no apparent reason. Arrested after a chase as they tried to escape to the south of France, they did not appear in the least contrite. Marguerite inserted the news item at the heart of the film and made the young hooligans little Nathalie's brothers-in-violence. *Nathalie Granger* is a very fragile film, interwoven with numerous silences. At the end of the shoot the film snapped. Marguerite stopped the film there, abandoning the scripted ending.

More and more Marguerite loved producing images, finding echoes in words, and then creating mysterious discords between these images and words. She spent several years on this building site of unbroken creativity, shielded from her visions by the human warmth of the close-knit film crew she had built up. When her house wasn't filled with the crew Marguerite shut herself away to listen to music. Of the ghosts that visited Marguerite in the night, the most persistent was Anne-Marie Stretter, who begged to be brought to life. She had come to claim her dues. In the end Marguerite acquiesced and gave her satisfaction. She depicted the love and fascination she had for her, which was part disgust, part admiration and part terror, in a cycle of films that would bring her international recognition – the first was *Woman of the Ganges*. Anne-Marie Stretter, with her skin so white, has a husky voice, a weary gaze and walks like a doe. She is the woman of the Ganges, the dancer in *India Song* and the grave robber in *Calcutta désert*.

With Marguerite it was always the same story: desire prowls and catastrophe threatens. She repeated herself ad nauseam; she had a few obsessions but little imagination. Taking names from a map and people glimpsed in childhood, she created an epic where the slowness of the action and the deepening of desire intensified the mystery. Duras said the films she made were lean. In *Woman of the Ganges* there is no camera movement at all but one hundred and fifty-two static shots. When she was filming, she didn't know what she was looking for, and told the crew as much. The film would be created at the editing stage. The film was shot in front of where she lived on the beach at Trouville, in a place devoid of geographical landmarks. It is neither Calcutta nor Venice nor Lahore. Benoît Jacquot joined the small team of 'boys' living in the apartment of Les Roches Noires as it had lived in Neauphle.

Marguerite was in a rut. She played cards, drank and appeared to have lost interest in the shoot. She asked Jacquot to go down to the beach to take shots of sand and sky. Nuytten just filmed. We'll sort it out afterwards, said Marguerite. Bruno Nuytten regarded the film as a rehearsal, a series of experiments for another film.

Woman of the Ganges consists of the images shot in Trouville in twelve days and quickly edited, and what Duras called the film of voices heard over the images (but recorded elsewhere). The voices are not a commentary on the images, and speak words that bear no relation to them, thus accentuating the impression that the spectator is being deliberately ignored. When we read, we rediscover ourselves. When we go to the cinema, we lose ourselves. Duras wanted to lead the spectator astray. With this film, she had at last arrived in 'the area before books',[31] the place of madness and anguish that she wanted to reach. The film was well received at the Digne festival and picked for the New York film festival.

Overwhelmed by all the women's voices that besieged her, Marguerite was frightened that she was going out of her mind. So she carried on. Instead of shouting alone in her house in Neauphle, she sent for the crew, re-established her little community and produced film after film. 'Neauphle was a real factory at the time,' recalled Benoît Jacquot. They were all low-budget films, made in a couple of weeks or so. And so that she could shoot at a moment's notice she always had to have on hand two or three people in permanent residence: Bruno Nuytten, her continuity girl Geneviève Dufour and Jacquot.[32] Jean-Marc Turine, one of the boys who'd been around since *Jaune le soleil*, had become a lodger. A friend of Outa's and a reader of Marguerite's manuscripts, he too has never forgotten the intensity of communal life in Neauphle, where eating together was mandatory. Everyone went to bed very late and got up very late except for Marguerite, who rose at dawn to write and prepare excellent meals.

To work with Marguerite meant being on the same wavelength and sharing the same vision: Marguerite couldn't bear people not 'following' her, not being as passionate as her. 'She was our mother. We'd ask her to hold our hands to cross the road,' said Turine. 'She was in a permanent state of seduction,' Nuytten added. 'She talked for hours,' Benoît Jacquot recalled. 'She regarded herself as the guardian of a treasure, considered herself a cut above the others and felt a need to express her ideas on everything and anything before her captive audience of friends.'[33] 'In her eyes she was an exceptional person,' explained Michelle Porte, 'had absolutely no modesty, was already saying she was brilliant.' Crazy fun, hard work and collective happiness is how Geneviève Dufour fondly remembers that time. In her late fifties, Marguerite invented a new way of being together that was less intellectual than life in rue Saint-Benoît; more affectionate, more creative too, with people some thirty, forty years younger than her: people her son's age, who were her son's friends. She admired the young, saw them as role models and thought that in the wake of 1968 she could invent a new type of social contract. After the depression brought on by disappointment, she recharged her batteries from this group of young people who venerated and protected her from the creative madness that overwhelmed her.

India Song was originally a commission for a stage play.[34] Duras's starting point was the intense emotion she had felt when, at the end of shooting *Woman of the Ganges*, she had the idea of introducing new voices into the finished film. Through this dislocation of image and sound, she discovered a new source of sensations, a mental territory where the world was hidden and where meaning vanished. She had since *Lol V. Stein* been trying to fathom the unspeakable. Duras set fire to the darkest recesses of our perception; she pushed back the boundaries of a reality she considered wanting and too flat; she expanded our field of comprehension. It isn't so much what lies inside each one of us that interested her but what is in front of us, maybe out of reach. If at all possible, this had to be conquered. Hence she was much more influenced by surrealism than by psychoanalysis. Who is it speaking when we speak? Often, no one. Speech therefore wallows in the hullabaloo we call conversation.

India Song is an odyssey of the senses, an initiation ceremony, a suspension of time, the *mise-en-scène* of a transient world. Everything will soon crumble – social conventions, lies about love, the rule of money and hypocrisy. At the end of her life Duras would say that *India Song* was her only film. She confessed that she had been moved to tears the first time she heard Carlos d'Alessio's waltz and that she sobbed when she heard the Vice-Consul shout. She never watched the film again. 'What is portrayed in *India Song* is me. Entirely me.'[35] She had glimpsed India when she was seventeen, and seen Calcutta for two hours during a stopover. But apart from this fragment of a souvenir, she created an India she wanted us all to share.

Before starting out, she wrote a synopsis.

This is the story of a love affair which takes place in India in the thirties, in an overpopulated city on the banks of the Ganges. Two days in this love story are presented. It is the season of the summer monsoon.

Four voices – facelessly – speak of this story. Two of the voices are those of young women, two are men's.

The Voices do not address the spectator or reader, they are totally independent. They speak among themselves and do not know they are being heard. [...] We never know who the Voices are. But just by the way each of them has forgotten or remembers, we get to know them more deeply than through their identity.

The story is a love story frozen in the culmination of passion. Around it is another story, a story of horror – famine and leprosy mingled in the pestilential humidity of the monsoon – which is frozen too in a daily paroxysm.

The woman, Anne-Marie Stretter, wife of a French ambassador in India and now dead – her grave is in the English cemetery in Calcutta –

might be said to be born of this horror. She stands in the midst of it with a grace which engulfs everything, in unfailing silence – a grace which the Voices try to see again, a grace which is porous and dangerous, dangerous also for some of them.

Besides the woman, in the same city there is a man, the French Vice-Consul in Lahore, in Calcutta in disgrace. It is by anger and murder that he is connected to the horror of India.

There is a reception at the French embassy, in the course of which the outcast Vice-Consul cries out his love for Anne-Marie Stretter, as white India looks on. After the reception she drives along the straight roads of the Delta to the islands in the estuary.

When Dominique Sanda pulled out, Duras turned to Delphine Seyrig to play Anne-Marie Stretter. She has red hair, a bared back, a very low-cut black dress, a swan's neck and those tender glances for the Vice-Consul. In *India Song* we see nothing of Calcutta, all we see is a woman dancing in the drawing room of the French embassy and that is enough, for Delphine fills the screen. The place is not important. Calcutta is the dustbin of all the colonies in the world. In Calcutta, it stinks of leprosy and oleanders, for at night the leprous beggars lie in the cool of oleander beds. Anne-Marie Stretter puts out water for them. She is the only white woman to do so. The others shut their eyes.

Imagining it all, Marguerite refused to look at photographs of Calcutta. What she 'saw' was the Ganges, the tamarind and banyan trees. She 'felt' the presence of the stagnant, viscous and filthy water. In July 1972 she completed a first draft in the form of a play for Peter Hall. Then she began nervously to fill an exercise book with a narrative. But the vision of the film soon swept aside both the play and the narrative. Anne-Marie Stretter emerged from her visions. 'I hear her voice, I see her body, her walk especially when she's in the gardens, wearing shorts to go and play tennis, you see, I see her there, I see the colour of her hair, red, her fair eyelashes. Eyes a little weary, very clear eyes, you know, very clear eyes in the sun,' she explained.[36] But why film her? Probably to get rid of her, to kill her off. For the whole of the film is steeped in death – the Vice-Consul's, of course; Anne-Marie Stretter's suicide, and not because of a broken heart but because she wants to die while she still has all her faculties; the death of a world decaying from the inside.

Marguerite filled four whole notebooks with shots, shooting scripts, sketches with camera positions and actors' moves. At the beginning of the first notebook was this note: 'In reality everything is empty; it is in the mirror that they appear.' Everything is dependent on the split between actors and characters and the dissonance between soundtrack and images, which makes one tremble inside, giving a delicious feeling of unease, a nostalgia for the burning of love. *India Song* takes place in a time postponed. Duras said she hated films that told a story, psychological thrillers, what she called direct films. This kind of film bored her in advance, as did the idea of one producer who wanted to work on a screenplay of *The Ravishing of Lol V. Stein*. 'It's pointless to shoot the novel,' she said in a handwritten note to the crew of *India Song*.

No film can do the written version justice. What we are shooting is a filmed interpretation of one episode from the book, that of the ball. The ball scene is *literally* begging to be interpreted. The camera must be the voyeur. It moves towards holes of light, around reception rooms. Everything is sealed. It's impossible to get out. The camera rushes around from hole to hole, turns, stops, takes a breath and then sets off again, searching again: no, it can't get out, it's an inner space, it's the inside of the body of the book. The noise diminishes. The camera's stopped moving. We hear a sound, panting and then nothing more.[37]

The film, produced by Stéphane Tchalgadjeff, cost 254,542 francs. Due to insufficient funding, the two-month shoot had to be delayed. In mid-May Marguerite sent an SOS to Alain Peyrefitte, who was then minister of culture, and he responded quickly with an advance of 250,000 francs from the National Film Centre.

Marguerite spent months searching for the right location where the metamorphosis from writing to image could take place. One day, following her nose as usual, she stumbled upon the Palais Rothschild in the Bois de Boulogne. It was a place she talked about for the rest of her life, she was so impressed by it. She used to tell the story of how Goebbels had lived there and how some of the Rothschilds' staff, unbeknown to the Germans, had remained in the palace, living in secret rooms, and working for the Resistance. The Rothschilds decided never to return there after the war. When she chose to shoot there, everything was in an advanced state of neglect and dilapidation.

Some of the sequences were shot at the Trianon Palace in Versailles, and in two apartments – one in rue de l'Université, the other in rue Lauriston; both were due for demolition. The tenants had left everything behind, even the piano. Marguerite left them in the state they were in. Anyway, she hadn't planned on taking on a set designer; she thought she'd just add a few accessories: a fan, incense, perfume burners, bunches of flowers, cushions, a photograph of Anne-Marie Stretter dead, cigarettes. That was all.

Shooting on location began on 13 May 1974. Marguerite pre-recorded the voices in a studio. During the first day's shoot in rue Lauriston, she asked the technicians to record Carlos d'Alessio's music while they were playing the soundtrack of the dialogues. She who so loved technical challenges had to concede in the end that it wouldn't work; she would have to choose between the dialogue and the music. There was no contest. In the music of *India Song*, Carlos d'Alessio had given her the most wonderful present. She sensed immediately the force of its emotional impact. 'The presence of the melody must be very strong, played all the way through and thus fill the time – always long – needed for the spectator to leave behind the commonplace he's inhabiting at the start of the show.' Before saying 'action', she wrote in her notebook, 'think of white images.' When the film was released she advised her friends to watch it with their eyes shut.

'*India Song* is not entirely my film. It was a team effort. In fact I'm still discovering the significance of some of the scenes,' she stated when the editing was done.[38] The atmosphere had been electric all through the shoot. Bruno Nuytten speaks of it in terms of an initiation to an erotic ritual. Marguerite had treated him and his electricians with the same sympathy she'd felt for the person of the Vice-Consul, the disgraced man who fired on beggars and shouted his love and despair.[39] During each take Delphine Seyrig was rocked as though drugged by the music that came from the small transistor and by the polyphony of recorded voices.[40] Marguerite put them all at their ease and gradually and naturally introduced her actors into the story.

All of them – actors, technicians, author – believed in Anne-Marie Stretter struggling in a poverty-stricken India. The Rothschilds' park was turned into a garden in the colony. A huge quartz soft-light attracted moths in their hundreds. The white light of a Parisian summer took on the colours of the monsoon. So where in India did you film? Marguerite was often asked when the film was released. Sometimes you see nothing on the screen. At times you hear nothing either. Marguerite made a number of sound recordings which she would then deliberately blur. She wrote seventy-two dialogues, each made up of about thirty sentences. From time to time one word emerges clearly but most of it flows past mingled with different sounds: she took a tape-recorder to churches, cellars, corridors and cafés.

Marguerite loved voices, yet she used the cinema to rid herself of them. In the film, Lonsdale could hear his voice as a deaf person might. Eight days before filming was due to start, Marguerite asked the future Vice-Consul how he was intending to give the impression of aloofness, of perdition. Marguerite was short of ideas and worried. Lonsdale thought about it. All of a sudden Marguerite had an idea: 'What if you shouted?'[41] The scene where he shouted and sobbed went smoothly. 'I had a load of pain to get rid of and felt like shouting,' Lonsdale said.[42] The Vice-Consul's shouts still cut through us today and his pain is so acute and so poignant that the spectator can only feel for him.

No actor in *India Song* is aware of the others; they are barely aware of themselves, as though about to die. With the exception of the Vice-Consul's, the voices in the film are never raised but constantly soft. Marguerite had thought of asking Gilles Deleuze, François Mitterrand or Edgar Morin to do the main voice, which she called the author's voice. In the end she got Dionys Mascolo to do it. Viviane Forrester played the beggar woman with a voice that was always on the verge of breaking. Together the voices form an echo chamber, a sensory labyrinth; they speak to one another but never reply; as for the actors, when their voices are heard on the soundtrack, in the image they have their mouths shut.

The music gave the film its rhythm and tone. You cannot think about the film without Carlos d'Alessio's melody coming into your head. Composed during an impromptu dance on an old, out-of-tune piano, it flows through the film, supplying it with blood. 'It was the music I heard play on liners in the middle of the ocean when I used to return from the colonies once every three years.'[43] Carlos and Marguerite were on the same wavelength and were extremely fond of each other. Marguerite never needed to explain anything to him.

I asked him to write the music for a film of mine, he said yes, I said for no money, and he said yes. Then I made the images and words fit in with the blanks I was leaving for his music and explained that the film was set in a country that neither of us knew, colonial India, a twilight stretch of leprosy and starvation belonging to the lovers of Calcutta, that we had to completely invent together. We did it.[44]

Marguerite felt quite lost at the end of the shoot; she had no idea what she was going to do. Everyone else returned to the merry-go-round of life and she was alone again. The end of summer was unbearably hot, depressing and lonely. In Neauphle she tried to rest but the voices had returned. 'Things are not at all good,' she told a friend, 'I'm having difficulty returning to reality.' Marguerite was already contemplating an *India Song* encore. She wanted to return to the scene of crime, to smash down the door of reality, to peer into Anne-Marie Stretter's grave.

'*I have to make a living, I am alone* and I am no longer young and I *do not want to end up destitute*,' she wrote to Claude Gallimard. 'I'd rather blow my brains out than end up back in the poverty I knew as a child. I have to stand up for myself. I am no saint, any more than the next person is. I cannot bring myself to believe that what Bataille has suffered these last years (he was nearly down to 50 francs) is normal ... If my books don't sell here I'll go abroad.'[45] She began having strange dreams. She dreamed she was being robbed, that her Trouville apartment was taken from her, and for good measure even the sea view was stolen. Then it was her identity papers, her money and her bag. She wept but no one was taking any notice of her. Marguerite woke up sobbing. The nightmares continued. She regularly dreamed she was being fleeced, or that a tide of reinforced concrete was moving towards her ready to suffocate her. She was having difficulty coming to terms with the fact that the film was finished, couldn't talk about it, felt embarrassed. 'Let me tell you something for nothing,' she told a journalist who wanted to interview her. 'I blame myself for being so stupid, yes, for always having been so stupid. Let me be, I hate this film that no one will see.'[46]

She was surprised and relieved by the reaction to the film. *India*

Song became a cult movie, and is still shown the world over. It was the only film by Marguerite Duras that was a commercial success. By June 1975, 180,000 people had been to see it. It was screened at the Cannes Film Festival in May, not in the competition but as part of the official selection. André Delvaux, a member of the international jury, declared, 'This film is the culmination of its author's poetic and cinematic oeuvre. This film I know has mesmerized the whole festival. Had it been entered it would without a doubt have won the Palme d'Or.' Others concurred. '*India Song* is the huge event of the festival, the only film that is like no other,' Henry Chapier wrote, 'and, without a doubt, the only film that will linger long in our memories when we recall 1975.' It was a triumph, and won the prix de l'Association française du cinéma d'art et d'essai. Marguerite, previously so much maligned by the professional bodies attached to the film industry, with the notable exception of *Les Cahiers du cinéma* and *L'Avant-Scène*, saw herself being recognized for the first time. The critics had constructed, each in their own way, their own film. Marguerite had sent them off on an initiatory journey where her own language – a strange mumbo-jumbo of sounds, music, voices and slow pans – was at last comprehensible.

A few critics compared Duras to Vicki Baum (author of romantic blockbusters) and her film to an Emmanuelle (a soft-porn series) against a background of a gaunt India. *Télérama* was outraged that the film should compare the moral deprivation of the rich to the physical deprivation of the poor. 'I'm fed up with such categories as the rich are disgusting, the poor are not disgusting,' Duras responded. 'We have two women in the same region of the world, in the same geography, going towards their doom. The beggar is killed by society and Anne-Marie Stretter kills herself. I can't say I like one better than the other.' In the interviews she gave, Duras deliberately took a political stance – to her India represented the deprivation of the whole world, and all around India there was war. The film was a call for the founding of an egalitarian society and not a charming poetic flow. 'I haven't exposed a millimetre of film that wasn't political.' Loud and clear she declared that her films were different: 'It means we won't be conned by the established cinema, the mouthpiece of a capitalist society. *India Song* is unequivocally the end of the capitalist world.'[47]

CHAPTER 14

The Duras Cult

~

How much longer would we have to wait for this famous revolution and the advent of a classless society? It won't be long now, said Marguerite, who, hope having returned, was going through her most militant period, prophesying the emergence of a European proletariat freed from Marxist dogma. Young revolutionary forces were about to seize the reins of power and liberate humanity from lies and inequalities. Marguerite talked, yelled, declaimed and proclaimed. Like a fortune-teller she predicted the glorious future of a post-capitalist society. She became the priestess of a desperate, poetic and incandescent leftism, and began to spout a feminism that met with a response from her circle of male admirers and, of course, female admirers. Marguerite announced that whole generations of men would have to disappear before women could breathe at last. And yet, when it came to men, she was spoilt! Dionys, loyal friend that he was, had just published a wonderful article on *India Song*, comparing Marguerite's approach to Rimbaud's. 'A film that touches us with the brilliance of its sublime audacity, a harmonious work and so near to perfection.'

Dionys became one of the few men Marguerite could tolerate. Every weekend he came to Neauphle with his wife – Solange Leprince, who edited *India Song* – and her daughter Virginie. As the gardener, he experimented with grafts, cultivated old roses and constructed mazes of greenery. Thanks to him the Neauphle garden was magnificent.

The moon was full. It was late evening after dinner. D. was in the
garden, he called me, he told me he wanted to show me what happened
on a clear night to the whiteness of white flowers in the full moon. He
didn't know whether I had ever noticed it. In fact, no, I never had. In
place of the beds of marguerites and white roses there was snow, but so
dazzling, so white that it threw the whole garden, the other flowers and
the trees into darkness. The red roses, become very dark, had almost
disappeared. There remained this incomprehensible whiteness that I
shall never forget.[1]

Marguerite talked about herself, a lot about herself, especially about
herself, only about herself. Those who were her friends at the time
can confirm it. She had locked herself into a narcissistic cage, which
excluded the interlocutor, and she soliloquized on her daring, her
talent, her genius. How was she to survive her success? By creating a
myth. She began tinkering with her personality, the Duras that was
hers. At the beginning she did it just for fun, but, relentlessly, without
realizing it or really wanting it, Marguerite became increasingly distanced from Duras. Marguerite herself founded the Duras cult. Soon
she began to speak of herself in the third person and referred to
herself as Duras.

Henceforth she no longer feared madness, she abandoned herself to
it. She welcomed all the characters that lived inside her and spoke to
her, all the feelings that came to her and overwhelmed her. Marguerite
was super-clairvoyant. When she went out in the street, she would soak
everything up until she was ready to faint. When she saw a fly crash into
the windowpane, she became that fly. When she came across bloodied
linen in an old chest of drawers, she followed the flux back through time
and felt the blood flow. Distancing herself further from reality, she
spent more time with characters she'd created than with her friends,
unless of course her friends joined her on the dreamlike road.

Bruno Nuytten returned to the location of *India Song*, the Palais
Rothschild, so that Marguerite could exorcise Lol V. Stein and Anne-
Marie Stretter. When they were filming *India Song*, she had never
dared enter the Palais; they had filmed only the façades and front
steps. Six months after they'd finished shooting she telephoned
Nuytten and said, 'Bring your camera, we're going to film inside the
house.'[2] The producers, Pierre and François Barat, managed to raise

130,000 francs. The idea of a new film became a reality. On the first day of filming Marguerite held Nuytten by the hand, by the belt, by the shoulders, by the waist, and a look of terror on her face went with him into the house. Her whole body shook. She had brought a cassette player with the soundtrack of *India Song* and a torch. He went first with his camera. 'What she really wanted was to go inside Anne-Marie Stretter's tomb, and I actually felt as though we were going to open a grave. She was genuinely terrified. She guided me with her light, and with her torch described the ruins of *India Song* for me, and Anne-Marie Stretter's dust.' During their travels, they came across a trap door that Marguerite refused to open, so convinced was she that Germans were still torturing Jews in the cellar underneath. She could hear the screams. Possessed by her past, Marguerite mingled her story with Anne-Marie Stretter's. She asked Nuytten to film soundlessly in the mad hope of not rousing from her eternal sleep Anne-Marie Stretter who lay there.

We never see a human figure in *Son nom de Venise dans Calcutta désert*. Of the actors all we hear is their voices. All Duras had done was copy the soundtrack of *India Song*. Repetition? Technique? It was the first time in the history of cinema that anyone used the soundtrack of a previous film while shooting new images. Technically, it looked like a permanent experiment in backlighting. It was experimental on several levels: lighting, sound, rhythm, structure. There were seventy-eight shots only, of which thirty-seven were static frames. *Son nom de Venise* does not so much illustrate *India Song* as challenge it – it pushes *India Song* into the dark. Through her ambition to challenge the concept of cinematic narrative, Duras first invented, then destroyed. 'I told myself I was going nowhere or into a kind of no-man's-land of the cinema. It was up to me to carry out a destruction whose meaning eluded me.'[3]

With limited time and limited funds, Duras completed the shoot in eight days, with a very reduced crew. It was at the editing stage that Duras created her films. It was painstaking work. Four versions were needed. Desperate, Marguerite was ready to give up. She worked in a painful, intellectually elated but physically exhausted frenzy. She had that feeling again that she wouldn't come out of the experience completely unscathed.

The film was released in June 1976. The reviews admired the

sensual camera that caressed the ruins, the overwhelming feeling of a love lost for ever, the clever way the heaviness of the wait is described. 'We could hear *Son nom de Venise dans Calcutta désert* in the shots of cracked and scratched walls, from which hung scraps of wallpaper that exuded the pink smell of leprosy,' wrote Jean-Louis Bory, and *Les Cahiers du cinéma* spoke of pictorial perfection. But only a limited public went to see the film, which is still a pleasure to watch today.

Teetering on old age, Duras said that *Son nom de Venise* was without a doubt her most important film. She only regretted that she hadn't gone further into the process of destruction. 'The real destruction would have been to kill myself.'[4]

Despite the recognition she was enjoying, Marguerite felt isolated. Her book *Abahn Sabana David* had sold only 4600 copies, and *L'amour* 6000. Yet she did what she wanted, made film after film and was funded from the public purse. It wasn't long before she was working on her next project, *Vera Baxter*, the film adaptation of her stage play *Suzanne Andler*. She was given an advance of 40 million francs. For once, things were properly organized and the crew paid at the beginning of filming. What a luxury! Marguerite hired a cook and then moaned all the time that her own soups were better. And so every evening she did the cooking, just as she had when there was no money.

From then on, no more producers would grow fat off her back (as she thought they had, but there were those who had actually lost their fortunes and reputations there). She became an excellent administrator of her own talent, constantly recycling Duras. It was no longer creation but reproduction. She conveyed through images what she had written in books or wrote books based on her screenplays. 'At the end of a fortnight, you were supposed to know all of Marguerite's books by heart, all the characters and the feelings they had,'[5] Nuytten said. And so she filmed – continuing to challenge the cinema as a means of expression, and continuing to grow desperate at not being able to get back to her writing. She made films because she couldn't write any more, and filming gave her a sense of her own existence.

She had a following that eagerly awaited her films: fans of her books, of course, but also a section of the feminist movement that saw her as their mother-mentor. The films Duras was making at that time were very much a part of her feminist activism. *Vera Baxter*, for example, was a captive of her fidelity, the eternal woman, around since time immemorial, raised to believe you love only one man.

A thousand years ago, it is said that there were women in the forests that fringed the Atlantic. Their husbands were nearly always a long way off, fighting for their lord or on a crusade, and they were sometimes alone for months waiting in their huts in the middle of the forest for their men to return. That was how they ended up talking to the trees, the sea and the animals of the forest. They were called witches. And they were burned. One of these women, it is said, was also called Vera Baxter.[6]

Duras accompanied her opinions as a committed feminist with experimental images. She made no secret of her antipathy for petit-bourgeois films. Hers became progressively more static, with an abundance of static shots. The camera stayed in one position and endeavoured to capture that place where each one of us is deaf and blind – the place of passion. Duras's films became more and more dreamlike, poetic and autobiographical. She found a particular tone and a way of expressing the despair of love. How do you love? How far do you go? What happens between a man and a woman when they live together as a couple? Where is the unbearable found? What can a woman put up with?

Baxter constantly commits adultery. His wife accepts it. One day he walks out unexpectedly. Terrified, Vera waits for him. He returns and sells his wife for a lot of money. He throws her out of the marriage so that she can become desirable. On her husband's orders Vera becomes an adulteress. The film is a satirical and feminist poem on the death of the bourgeois couple. The ending is deliberately enigmatic. Duras pushes the spectators to their limits seeking to unnerve them, to question them.

And yet, a year after its release in 1976, Duras claimed that *Vera Baxter* had failed. She could feel something was wrong but couldn't put her finger on what it was. It was while filming *Le camion* that she finally understood. No man had gazed upon Vera Baxter, and without a man to desire her, Vera Baxter didn't exist. The women's pseudo-physical community described in the film couldn't work. Feminist ideology was preventing Duras from telling her truth – desire doesn't circulate among women. She later published a modified version of the story as a screenplay. But it was too late, the film couldn't be reshot and she eventually disowned it.

While Marguerite was producing an interminable succession of filmed images, she still didn't want to give up the theatre. And so it was with great enthusiasm that in 1976 she accepted a television proposal to film *Whole Days in the Trees*, whose recent stage revival had been a great success. To film theatre is not a problem, said Marguerite. It's just a question of not cutting corners and of making an adaptation rather than filmed theatre. Duras observed the chronology, preserved the dialogue, but added silences to increase the dramatic intensity. The film was conventionally shot without betraying any of her principles. Scrutinizing Madeleine Renaud's face in the splendour of age, capturing Bulle Ogier's poignant awkwardness, she filmed with humility and respect the final conversation between devouring mother and delinquent son, wonderfully acted by Jean-Pierre Aumont.

Again the soundtrack had pride of place. The lighting in the film *Whole Days in the Trees* was intentionally played down so that the spectator wouldn't become engrossed in the images but in the proliferation of words. Marguerite explained to her director of photography, Nestor Almendros, that she made films to be listened to, not to be looked at! She filmed to capture the meanings of words, the resonance of speech. This quest was to be relayed by the actresses who agreed to practise concentrating solely on the music of her words. 'Marguerite's writing was as precise as mathematics,' Bulle Ogier explained. 'She would bring me to the meaning through the beat of the lines and it was our feelings that expressed her writing.' 'The text was not to be spoken. We had to find the toneless tone of her voice,' added Madeleine Renaud, who was searching for what she called the non-voice of the voice. Claude Régy, Marguerite's theatre associate, friend, accomplice and confidant, confirmed, 'She loved actors but couldn't bear them. She wanted only her inner voice. Her own thought had to go through the actor and on to the spectator who would then take it with him elsewhere.'[7]

Delphine Seyrig, Catherine Sellers, Bulle Ogier and Nicole Hiss soon found the right way to deliver Duras. For Madeleine Renaud it was more difficult. She had to break away from talking Marivaux, forget the language of Beckett and show infinite patience and humility before an authoritarian Marguerite, who made her start the same sentence over and again. 'I understand nothing of your silences,' she would often say to Marguerite. 'When will you be able to send me the next line?' Marguerite would laugh at Madeleine's impatience, her energy, her radiance. Duras and Renaud admired each other's work, but their relationship soon turned to one of distrust and aggression. The two monsters observed but never really met, trusted or liked each other. Anyway how could Marguerite have loved a woman who reminded her so much of her mother? In the film Madeleine is the mother, her mother, all mothers in her oversize coat, eccentric hat and cotton stockings. Literature, cinema and theatre had come together to describe the emptiness, the futility of existence, the absurdity of human relations.

Marguerite didn't feel loved enough, respected enough, worshipped enough. Although she spurned honours and public recognition, she complained at her lack of fame. She would tell her visitors that she was a star in the USA and a nobody in France, and threatened to leave the country that didn't want her. 'I don't know where I am, I only know I'm not there! I'm not really socially integrated and live among strangers. My main relationship with the state is through the inland revenue and television.'[8] Shutting herself away in Neauphle or rue Saint-Benoît, Marguerite started to go out less and never again set foot in the cinema. The world she was living in was shrinking.

Television was about to play an important role in her life. 'That bloody television,' she called it and watched it eagerly, angrily and scathingly. She had a love-hate relationship with the medium, especially with the eight-o'clock news, which she would never under any circumstances miss. Afterwards she would go over it with her friends over the phone as though she'd been in direct communication with the world's heads of state. A fierce and inspired critic, she could describe the presenters' complicitous smiles, the compulsory lies and unchallenged reports. Television gave her the illusion that she was summoning the world to her place and thereby able to continue the struggle against the oppression of the workers. She declared that she belonged to a wild, natural leftism, but that she was now against any kind of political activism except that of non-work. She admired her son for doing nothing. She would have loved to take a break from herself. But she was obsessed by her image, her identity. And who is she, this Duras? she wondered. That was the subject of her film *Le camion*. She, she again, always she. She who wrote the text that would be spoken, and who would now also play the lead.

Duras had short hair and wore big glasses in *Le camion*. She filmed herself as she was at sixty-three with deep lines at the corners of her mouth, her face tired and worn, no longer the perfect oval it had once been, her skin cracked and puffy. She made no attempt to improve her appearance with special lighting or make-up to erase the ravages of time and alcohol. No, we see her as she was – an old lady whose body has deteriorated, but whose eyes are still very much alive. She looks calm, patient, as though she has all the time in the world. She describes herself as 'a small, thin, grey, banal woman. She is nobly banal. She is invisible.'

Who is it? It is of course Duras but it is also the character she has created, a woman hitching a lift from a lorry driver. She speaks to us and we listen to her. The old lady's a writer. As a child, she used to live in the colonies. As a director Duras liked to blur the issues. The spectator asks himself, is Duras the actress speaking her lines or giving us snatches of her autobiography? She holds forth endlessly. The lorry driver couldn't care less. As far as he's concerned she's just another old nut going on about the world and saying nothing in particular.

Duras had mulled over three projects before arriving at the definitive version of *Le camion*. The first was theoretical: how – through cinema – can you kill cinema and at one and the same time belief in anything? The second wanted to surpass the very notion of cinema and invent a revolutionary art of refusal that would forever ruin what she called 'digestive cinema'. The third featured a woman – Duras did not specify either her age or her identity – waiting at the side of the road. Marguerite thought first of Suzanne Flon, then of Simone Signoret to take on the part. Both refused and Marguerite abandoned the project. Six months later, she thought of herself. And during a bout of insomnia the idea came to her to film it as the story of a film that was going to be shot. As an epigraph to the book of the film,

Duras gave the grammatical definition of the conditional tense, which expresses a possible or unreal fact, a tense used by children when suggesting games. *Le camion* is a game and, like all games, it is both playful and serious.

The film was shot in three days in the freezing cold. On the first day Bruno Nuytten filmed inside the lorry with a camera chained to the outside. Marguerite hated the idea. In the evening she said to the crew, 'Let's go home, it's more comfortable at my place in the warm sitting around a round table, we can pretend it's the steering wheel of a lorry.'[9] The dialogues were shot in the attic; the room would be the cab of the lorry, the bedroom of a brothel and an enclosed space, she explained.

For the first time Marguerite was at both ends of the camera. Her most important role, she told the crew, was her role as a director. She was making a film. But is it a real film or a hypothetical film, this story where two characters discuss a film that doesn't exist? 'It should've been a film. The shoot should've been quick. It shouldn't have cost a lot,' says Marguerite's voice at the beginning of the projection. Marguerite wanted to shoot in black and white but the producers – Pierre and François Barat – insisted it would never sell. And so Marguerite gave in and agreed it should be in colour. The film was bathed in the beautiful whitish light of a winter's afternoon. All through the shooting, Marguerite was happy, cheerful and confident. 'For the first time in my life, there was no particular logic bothering me. I let myself go completely and paid for it later. I suffered the most terrible insomnia, and would tell myself: OK, not good, you've lost your marbles. Now I realize I hadn't; I was going all over the place? so: I went all over the place.'[10]

Le camion was made in a spirit of joy. Duras felt she had found a new cinematic form and no longer missed writing. With *Le camion* she said she was at last equal to her books. Through her double identity as author and actress, she had finally managed to unsettle the spectator. Is that really Marguerite Duras talking to us? Is she talking about herself? The woman in *Le camion* looks slightly deranged, talking about her obsession with revolution and her admiration for the working class. She knows she's run out of elsewheres, of dreams, of hopes. And she delights in the knowledge of the nothing her experiences over the years have taught her. Rather than weep, she laughs. 'She says: let the world go to its ruin, it's the only policy.' 'Of course it's me,' Duras told Dominique Noguez. 'Doesn't it sound like me?'[11] The woman on her way to nowhere, no longer quite sure where she is, with no social or family ties, is Duras – 'disconnected from everything in this society, even from the most crucial relationship, but with what? With the whole? Sometimes I say God.'[12]

She could never have made the film without Gérard Depardieu. He accepted the role without knowing anything about it. She asked him to read the script but not to learn it. Reading, his eyes would sometimes stray to the wrong line – Marguerite's too, for that matter – and he got confused, got lost. So much the better. At the editing stage all the slip-ups were kept so as to accentuate the rejection of psychological realism. In any case, 'Depardieu can't read, can't write! He's illiterate, everyone knows that.'[13] An extremely intelligent illiterate who exuded sensitivity and warmth, and whom the actress Marguerite looked at longingly and lovingly all through the film.

Le camion is about the impossible relationship between a man and a woman. She wants to get closer to him, but he's not listening. He wants nothing to do with what she is. And yet she tells him important things about God, childhood, how to survive the world, dead planets. He's afraid, he's not used to such free words, he won't listen. He can only tolerate well-ordered speeches given in the name of a party or union. He is locked into definitions and what he says never connects with life. She, on the other hand, is in the fissure of words, in the ambiguity of meaning. When she's not talking, she's singing with her eyes shut. 'I've never met a character as amiable as her,' said Duras after the film had been released. We understand why. Thanks to the lady in *Le camion* Marguerite discovered that speech and writing can merge. The lady from *Le camion* spoke and Marguerite Duras was at last writing again. The soundtrack was to have been music by Bob Dylan and Joan Baez but the rights were so exorbitant that Duras chose Diabelli's variations on Beethoven, which she had already used in *India Song*.

Later she said that the film had allowed her to express her political opinions without fear of what people would say. For the first time she publicly admitted to her anticommunism without fear that she'd be accused of being reactionary, and refused to come out in favour of either the left or the right. She no longer believed in the idea of actual revolution. Utopian hope was all that was left. Duras thought everything she said was brilliant. Duras was a loudspeaker. Duras thought she was connected to the collective unconscious. It spoke Duras and Marguerite allowed it to speak. She spoke with an immodesty that she flaunted like a libertarian act.

The screening of *Le camion* in Cannes in May 1977 sparked off a fierce debate; partisans and detractors fell into two irreconcilable camps. During a long press conference, Duras refused to speak as a filmmaker. In her eyes the film was nothing less than a political act. And so they spoke of politics. 'In Moscow as in Ethiopia it's the return of Hitlerism. The same can be said of Argentina and East Germany.'[14] When the film went on general release two weeks later, she prophesied the end of Marxism, which she accused of misplaced phallocracy, of semantic terrorism, of being the prime example of the error of political ways. In her eyes the very notion of hope had become a political error. Instead she celebrated the void, sang the praises of nothingness.

Afterwards, Marguerite was politically desperate and psychologically depressed. She had nothing to make her feel she wanted to get up in the morning. Once again she moved back to Neauphle, saw fewer people, kept chickens, ducks, birds, made jam, caught her breath, went at her own pace; no fixed schedule, no demands, no one watching her. She shut herself away for weeks, disconnected the phone, let herself go and abandoned herself to alcohol. It was the only lover she was faithful to all her life. In her yearning for sensory derangement, alcohol remained her favourite road to pleasure.

It was her mother who had first encouraged Marguerite to drink. 'Where I come from,' she used to say, 'in the north, when girls were thin like you we gave them beer to drink.' And so Marguerite, when she was very young, began to drink beer to please her mother. She didn't put on weight but she gradually got used to alcohol and it soon became a need. When she arrived in Paris she was a moderate drinker but, all the same, one who needed to drink. It was later that she got into the habit of drinking more and regularly, with the comrades after the Party meetings and during those crazy postwar evenings in her apartment in rue Saint-Benoît. She drank cheap whisky, gin and rum, happily mixing them. Alcohol made her talk, gave her wings to dance, to kiss men on the mouth. In those days the Saint-Germain-des-Prés set drank a lot and often – especially the men; it was not so common among the women. In fact, it was regarded a scandal if a woman drank. But Marguerite wasn't a scandal at the time. She just loved alcohol, that was all. Her friends didn't notice. Only she could see she'd become an alcoholic. 'And so I started drinking like an alcoholic. I could drink the others under the table. I began to drink at night.'[15] And she'd begun to drink in secret.

Then came the meeting with the man who loved drinking. Day and night they drank together, collapsing, swearing, fighting, making love. And she had to increase the dose when her mother died. Whatever the hour of the day or night, Marguerite never went out without her flask of whisky. She refused to see a doctor. 'By the time they tell you you're drinking too much, it's too late. You drink too much. It's such a scandalous thing to say to anyone ... In a hundred per cent of cases you take it as an insult. You say, you must have something against me to tell me this.'[16]

Marguerite was drinking more and more and eating less and less, and she was permanently tired. One morning she noticed she was coughing up blood. She told no one. Next day it started again. She panicked and finally went to see a doctor, who diagnosed cirrhosis of the liver. That was when she was fifty. She agreed to be treated, but she refused to go to a special unit. All by herself she found the strength to stop.

It lasted on and off for ten years. In 1975 she started drinking in earnest again. At first the odd glass of white wine with the others, from time to time two glasses of champagne; then she increased her ration, went back to red wine and drank alone in Neauphle. She was drinking so much she didn't want anyone to see. She shut herself away and lived according to the rhythm of the alcohol. It induced the pleasure of regressing, in which she wallowed. Marguerite became its consenting prey. She recklessly surrendered herself to it. And so she discovered the sweetness of time suspended, the ability to do nothing for hours, insensibility, where the body is at peace and the anguish is eased. She drank cheap wine, supermarket plonk that she bought by the crate. She drank, spat blood and drank again. Marguerite was on self-destruct. Apparently so popular, she felt she had no one to turn to. And if she did happen to drink too much in front of friends, she would implore them with 'If you love me you haven't seen a thing and you won't say a word.'

After having worked as Marguerite's assistant on her first film, Michelle Porte spent a lot of time in Neauphle and built up a relationship with her based on trust. 'One evening [in 1976] she phoned me,' Michelle remembered. 'She couldn't get her words out. Frightened, I jumped in my car and dashed over to Neauphle. She was prostrate, confused. She was taking pills for hypertension and washing them down with whisky and wine. She couldn't walk, couldn't breathe properly.' She agreed to let a doctor examine her, and the doctor drove her straight to hospital. She was there five weeks, then returned to Neauphle, held out for a few weeks more, and then started drinking again. 'I have written in alcohol, I had an ability to respect intoxication that sprang no doubt from my horror of drunkenness. I never drank to get drunk, I was withdrawn from the world, unreachable but not drunk.'[17]

At the suggestion of her friend Claude Régy, Duras started work on a stage play, searching for a role that Madeleine Renaud would find challenging. The image of her mother returned to torment her. Régy made regular visits to Neauphle, where an exhausted Marguerite, worn down by alcohol, would show him pages of a dramatic poem on her mother, a restructured rewriting of *The Sea Wall*, which was a mixture of the daughter settling scores with the mother and denunciations against colonial injustice. Her memory was playing tricks on her and preventing her from constructing the narrative. She almost abandoned it on several occasions, and worried she might be repeating herself: 'I'm sick of my bland little music,' she told Régy, still lucid and still able to laugh at herself. Régy encouraged her, supported her and persuaded her to persevere.

Two months later, she handed him *Eden Cinema*. Thanks to the Renaud-Barrault Company it opened on 25 October 1977 at the théâtre d'Orsay, directed by Régy. Once again it was the story of the mother, of her mother of course, but also of all mothers. And Madeleine was once again cast as the mother, an often silent mother, a defeated mother, a sick mother. 'There is no one else who can play the part of the mother.'[18] But the mother – the subject of the story – never speaks directly about herself, Marguerite wrote in the margin of the manuscript.[19] Madeleine, through the intensity of her presence, was again brilliant. Bulle Ogier, diaphanous, fragile, transparent, supported the cruel and loathsome mother. Carlos d'Alessio's music helped intensify the play's nostalgic mood, which many spectators found deeply touching. Duras and Régy had similar ideas on theatre. To them theatre should never be life reproduced; it should never provide the illusion of a nondescript reality. 'It's like opening a book and bringing to the theatre the material that creates the dream as we read a book.'[20]

Eden Cinema was intended to be the sequel to The Sea Wall. The Eden Cinema in Saigon was real, and Marguerite sometimes claimed that her mother had worked there as a pianist, which is how she is employed in the play. Duras took the opportunity to settle a score with René Clement, who, in the film, had betrayed the truth by giving the impression that, after their mother's death, the brother and sister did not leave Vietnam but settled on the concession like vulgar pioneers of the American West. In the play, Marguerite underlined the criticism of the colonial institutions, which she felt had been too tame in The Sea Wall. She drew attention to how they had ground her mother down and gave her a speech that in The Sea Wall had come from the brother's mouth, shouting and defending herself. The mother accuses the officials of having killed the children of the plains, of having robbed the whites, of controlling the whole country, of trampling the dignity and honour of a whole nation. The tirade lasts a quarter of an hour.

Marguerite herself was frightened by her violence. She even hesitated over whether to keep her mother's murderous threats. In the end – for the sake of truth and out of consideration for her memory – she decided to leave them in. 'The violence existed, it rocked our childhood. My mother told us that the whites who'd robbed her – and the peasants of the Prey-Nop plain – of hope, should have been massacred, done away with.'[21]

Marguerite said her mother had been unfulfilled. She was convinced she'd never experienced pleasure with her husband and that once she'd been widowed, abstinence from the physical side of marriage had come as a relief. Wasn't it in order not to be like her mother that Marguerite flaunted her appetite for lovemaking? It was rare for a woman at that time to admit to such feelings, but Marguerite had listened to her body since adolescence. She could talk for hours about a man's physical beauty, his grace, his attractiveness, his virility, in the same way that a womanizer praises a pretty woman. She would say that, at the risk of turning life upside down, only desire could and should rule life, and that she possessed the science of love, screaming out at the height of passion. Whoever has not experienced such physical passion has experienced nothing, she would say with a knowing look.

Although Duras felt old, ugly and wrinkled, 'not functional' to borrow the phrase she used to describe herself at the time, she was given a true story of desire, sex and absence by a friend immediately after *Eden Cinema*. She gradually turned it into a script. For months a man had been having an erotic telephone relationship with a woman who refused to meet him. He made unsuccessful attempts to get her to lift the ban. The woman told him she was ill. One day the telephone calls came to an end. What had happened to her? Duras was intrigued. She arranged to meet the man in question, whose name was Jean Meunier, and he confirmed that what Marguerite had been told was true. She asked him to describe the evolution of the relationship into a tape recorder.

Duras then set to work using the transcript of the tape. A first version appeared in February 1978 in Minuit's magazine, fourteen tight pages written in the present tense and in a telegraphic style. Voices played a predominant role for it was through the voice that love grew. The woman, F., controlled the game and would throw the man into a panic with her phone calls and appointments arranged but never kept. He would turn up and wait. She told him she'd seen him, knew what he was like, what he looked like, what he was wearing. He, on the other hand, had to use his imagination. One day a woman brought him two photographs of F. The man was disappointed, tried to return them, to forget the face he'd seen. He didn't want any pictures of her.

The phone calls started again and the voice obliterated the memory of the photographs. He was finally left with a 'dark image' of the woman who, while professing to love only him, continued to hide from him. The piece ended with a question Marguerite put to 'J.M.':

would he agree to see F. now? He hesitated for a moment and then replied yes.

At this time, Duras accepted an invitation to Israel from the Ministry of Foreign Affairs. She was bowled over by the country; she loved the inhabitants and some of the landscapes, which had a major influence on two shorts she made the following year. She successfully presented *India Song* in Jerusalem and *Le camion* in Tel Aviv. André Rougon, who was the cultural attaché in Haifa, remembers that the ministry had warned him of the writer's extremely fragile state. He had been asked not to leave her alone, and not to put her up at a hotel. And so André Rougon took the withdrawn and anxious Marguerite Duras into his house. She knocked back the whiskies without a break and said very little. During a trip to Galilee he suggested they take, she appeared to be overwhelmed and deeply moved by the beauty of the villages and the transparency of the light. In Caesarea she had a kind of revelation; she immediately fell in love with the sensual and mystical place. She lingered there a while and told André Rougon she would one day return to film there. *Césarée, Césarée,* a short film on creation, reproduces the intensity of her emotion.

Since its founding, Marguerite Duras had defended the state of Israel. Until the end of her days, she professed fiercely held pro-Israeli views, defending the state's policies despite the fact that for a long time it would not even acknowledge the existence of the Palestinian people. Alone against the opinion of all her friends, she supported Begin during the Lebanese war. She felt she had become Jewish on discovering the camps. To her, being Jewish meant being pro-Israeli in spite of everything. And she remained an unconditional ally of their most repressive policies. No argument could get her to change her opinion. Her trip to Israel served to confirm her impression that the Jews were still besieged, still in danger. The land of Israel was for her the refuge, the salvation of the survivors of the Holocaust.

On her return from Israel she started to think about making a film of the telephone story, suggesting to Benoît Jacquot that they make the film in the form of a dialogue. As was her habit during the preparations, Marguerite and Jacques Tronel walked and travelled day and night all over Paris and the suburbs. For days she walked around the cemetery of Père-Lachaise, lingering at the tombs of the generals of the Empire. She would visit the recumbent figure of Victor Noir with its extraordinary bronze sex, polished by a zealous populace, and speak to him of his beauty and courage. Preparing a film with Marguerite Duras meant being on call night and day, said those who were still part of her tiny tribe. She wanted to film the images in her head, images born during her walks. Her hunt for locations became a pretext for dreamlike strolls. Tronel accompanied Marguerite around the streets of Neuilly in search of a place she'd just conceived of which had to be at the end of a deserted alleyway. Like a couple of private detectives, they discreetly questioned the locals and pushed open rusty iron gates and discovered neglected parks in a secret Neuilly. They both abandoned themselves to the fearful delights of these excursions. Marguerite hardly said a word. She walked. She dreamed.

Then, all of a sudden, she stopped. She locked herself away in rue Saint-Benoît and in two months quickly wrote the script for *The Navire Night*. She tried to take on the production herself but it was too much for her, and she managed to get 600,000 francs from the Office de création cinématographique. *The Navire Night* was produced by les films du Losange, Eric Rohmer and Barbet Schroeder's production company. As usual the small production team was put up at Neauphle. She undertook to do the casting, choosing Bulle Ogier, Dominique Sanda and Matthieu Carrière. She told them she didn't want to make a film that cut corners. Then two weeks into the shoot, she announced she wanted to make a film without images! To her the characters of *The Navire Night* were invisible. The solution was 'to make dark engraved images. Unborn images. The unfinished image. I want to drive home the power of the text.'

As was her habit, Marguerite drew up a very precise shooting script and then had a radical change of heart. The film would be a conversation between Benoît Jacquot and herself; and the actors, reduced to extras, would walk around the couple, occasionally reopening the conversation. Shooting began on 31 July 1978. The first two days she stuck to the schedule and filmed without enthusiasm. On the evening of the second day she looked at the rushes. They were a disaster. It was not a film; it was speech backed up by images. In her diary she wrote, 'Film a failure.' She abandoned it and decided to distance herself from it as much as possible, as though the film were

315

a living person capable of doing her harm. She went to sleep relieved. At last, she'd finished with the cinema! She who had tried so hard to kill it off had at last managed to kiss it goodbye. The following morning she informed the crew the film was a disaster and that their only option was to use up the rest of the film trying to shoot the disaster. She told the actors to forget their lines and proceeded to film them as in a silent film. The camera caught Dominique Sanda being made up and Bulle asleep between the spotlights. Marguerite filmed the film in the process of being filmed. She deconstructed it by covering it with words and then overloading the soundtrack. She filmed the actors' faces in such close-up that they ended up unrecognizable. Insisting on doing it her own way, she soon had the camera upside down to film anything that came her way – the night, the air, the spotlights.

Marguerite was running out of steam. She didn't want to lose face in front of her supportive crew. But even Marguerite was never satisfied with *The Navire Night*. When the shoot was over, there was no special press night. In a short letter of explanation sent to a handful of journalists, she said, '*The Night* is the name we gave a kind of drifting. I'd like it to live alone.' For future audiences she wrote a tract that was handed out at the entrance of the only cinema to screen it:

> Every night, in Paris, hundreds of men and women take advantage of the anonymity of the unallocated telephone lines that have been around since the German Occupation to speak to each other, to love each other. These people, orphans of love and desire, are dying to love; to escape the abyss of solitude. These people who scream in the abyss at night all make appointments to meet up. The appointments are never kept. What counts, is to make them. But no one goes. It is the cry sent from the abyss, the scream that triggers pleasure.

Before becoming a novel, *The Navire Night* metamorphosed into a stage play, once again directed by Claude Régy. 'It was all too quick; Marguerite wasn't well, the actors lost track of where they were or what Marguerite wanted, and she kept changing the text and the direction,' he confided. This was corroborated by Michael Lonsdale. 'Marguerite would turn up at rehearsals at the théâtre Edouard VII and ask, "Can someone go and get me a bottle of Ricard?" One of us would go even though she never produced so much as a coin.' Marguerite was drinking all the time and becoming more and more aggressive. Marguerite constantly rewrote bits of the script and unsettled the actors even more with comments like, 'Desire is the virgin forest. And the virgin forest is in the film. If it is anywhere in the theatre, it is in the audience.' To give the impression they were speaking over an abyss, Claude Régy asked the actors to speak from the edge of the stage. At Marguerite's insistence the actress Marie-France was decked out in a skin-tight imitation panther jumpsuit and heels so high she kept tripping. She was very uncomfortable and had no idea what she was doing there. Two days before the dress rehearsal the three actors were still forgetting whole sections of the text. And so Claude Régy decided he'd have to be prompt. But so that the audience wouldn't know it was his role, he sat in the auditorium and shouted out the lines. 'I hadn't told a soul, and friends who came to see the play all thought I was some lunatic!'

The first night coincided with the film's release. Few spectators subjected themselves to both experiences. The film was a flop and the play a fiasco. Peter Handke understood her well – having seduced her readers, Duras was throwing them out. Many were those who, like him, had loved Duras very much and then abandoned her because they felt she had lost interest in them. 'For me, a spectator reader, there was nothing left: zero space.'[22]

The Navire Night was published by Editions Mercure de France in 1979, a few months after the film was released. Before publication, Marguerite submitted it to the protagonist of the story, who read it carefully. 'While it's all true,' he told Marguerite, 'I don't recognize any of it.' The story had been completely rewritten and the careful reader will spot bits from *The Vice-Consul, Nuit noire Calcutta*, fragments of *Anne-Marie Stretter*, not forgetting very dated commentaries on the politics and importance of psychoanalysis. *The Navire Night* appears to be the story of a disquieting love affair. It is in effect a literary exercise where the author constantly interrupts any pleasure the reader might be gleaning from the 'story'. Numerous 'apparitions' come to break the suspense. There is the unexpected appearance of a banker, personal financial adviser to the president of the Republic, a real working-class mother and a false middle-class mother from

Neuilly, not forgetting the stone head of a woman with only half a face and the haunting presence of a lizard-skin wallet.

Jean Menier found the publication of the book very disturbing. He had just got married, but when he read *The Navire Night* his desire to see F. was so strong that he asked Marguerite Duras to spell out F.'s name in future editions of the book so that she would recognize herself. Marguerite thought the initials sufficed, and she was right. In the week after the film's release, F. called J.M., or rather he received calls where there was no one at the other end, save a breathing presence he knew to be F., 'because it was already her way, during their affair, of letting him know she still loved him, and so much that she thought she'd die'.

Along with *The Navire Night*, Mercure de France published other Duras titles. *Césarée* and *Les mains négatives* were more recent versions of the commentary Marguerite had written for two shorts created out of shots not used in the film of *The Navire Night*. The idea of making a film from offcuts greatly appealed to Marguerite, who, in life as in literature and films, did not like throwing anything away and hated waste. Her way of always recycling her work, of always reiterating the same themes, was also an attempt to annihilate the actual subject, to wear out the words, to empty them from the inside. In her films, the way she used and recorded words was always more important than the images. Duras was no longer interested in the actors, nor in what might be happening between them, but in the way their words and the range of their different voices could touch and unsettle us. Writing, in her view, contains everything, including films. A single word contains all the images. For the word possesses the power of proliferation and its own energy, which the image does not possess.

The title of her first short film, *Les mains négatives*, 'negative hands', refers to imprints of hands found in prehistoric caves, usually outlined in blue or black. Marguerite had seen some in Altamira twenty years earlier during a trip to Spain with Dionys Mascolo. They had made a deep impression on her. In *Les mains négatives* people shout that love has been around for thirty thousand years. The images show black-skinned men emptying the dustbins of Paris in the small hours of the morning. No whites, just blacks. The shouts of love seem to be addressed to this black population, rejected, despised, humiliated, employed in the most menial tasks. The text says, 'You who have an identity, you who have a name, I love you.' And we hear Marguerite, in her husky alcoholic's voice, sing in winter the intensification of her desire, Marguerite who is already in the winter of life.

In *Césarée* it is Berenice, 'Queen of the Jews, repudiated for reasons of state', who shouts. She too has been struck down by the dangers of forbidden love. Same dissonance between image and soundtrack; images of statues in place de la Concorde, hieroglyphs on the Obelisk, the gardens of the Tuileries, while the words spoken by Marguerite on the soundtrack describe Lake Tiberias, the lights of St John of Akko, the olive groves, orange groves and wheat of Galilee.

They weren't having a good summer in Paris that year. The weather was cold and misty. In any case, Marguerite had always hated summer. A static, unchanging season, it often made her anxious and fearful. Marguerite preferred the autumn.

When they were at Auditel in Paris editing film, she'd arrive in the morning and then leave immediately for the bistro and knock back three or four glasses of white wine at the bar. Then she'd give the boss empty Evian bottles so that he could fill them with white wine. At the bistro, when her film editor and friend Geneviève Dufour begged her to eat something, she wiped each potato chip with her handkerchief. She couldn't eat fat. Her body could tolerate only alcohol.

In Neauphle she wrote or sat around doing nothing. Listened to herself, lost herself, let herself be haunted. At night Marguerite would take herself off to one of those big cafés that stay open till late, where men with faces furrowed with fatigue stand drinking at the bar until they drop into the sawdust. Billiard tables, jukeboxes, waltzes for the lorry drivers. And sometimes, before knocking the tables over, some sing, after their tenth glass of wine. Others, like Marguerite's friend Coco the Italian, might dance alone for hours in front of the jukebox. Marguerite would go home at dawn, exhausted but feeling better. At the end of her life she would look back at that happy period with nostalgia.

How was she to go on living? By writing. So that she would be forced to write, she accepted a commission for a thirty-minute film. In her solitude she imagined an interlocutor to whom she felt disposed to tell a story. Her friends speculated on the identity of the man –

maybe Benoît Jacquot or Michel Cournot – but Marguerite never said. An epistolary novel began to take shape. 'I'd like you to read what I've done, I feel like giving you fresh, new writings, fresh despairs, those that are my life now.' She was writing in confusion, about confusion. She no longer knew anything, except that she was trying to write. She'd challenged writing too much to be able to return to the narrative. She'd have liked to, but didn't know how any more. In any case, she couldn't understand life, her life. She surrendered.

Leaving her rose garden, the thieving blackbirds, the thin white cat that frightened her, she went to her apartment in Trouville. She needed the sea, the immensity of the beach, the sweetness of the air, the grey expanse, the noise of the gale. In Trouville she continued to write to the unknown man without ever posting the letters. 'For me, to write to you is to write this because of what connects me to you, this love so violent.' She wrote about the sea, wanted to be merged with it. She started to drink at dusk, let the sound of the sea into her room, drank again and wrote. *Aurélia Steiner* is a narrative that deliberately heads for a fall. 'I am perhaps going to write you a thousand letters, give you letters about my life now. And you, you will do with them what I want you to do with them, that is to say, what you will.'

Aurélia Steiner is the name of a woman who died in the gas chambers, the name of her daughter born in the camp, the name of a seven-year-old child who lives with an elderly lady where her mother left her when the police came to arrest her, the name of a young woman who now lives in Melbourne or Vancouver. Aurélia is also Marguerite, the narrator, who has taken refuge in the bedroom filled with the sound of the sea. 'I have been alone in this house for years. Everyone has left it to go to more peaceful areas of the world.' The name Aurélia Steiner belongs to no one. Since the death of the mother in the camp, it has echoed through the world. By writing the three stories about Aurélia Steiner, Marguerite Duras was returning to her feelings of guilt for the Jewish people.

The first Aurélia was born as a tribute Marguerite wanted to pay to Sami Frey's mother, who, during the war, on hearing the police on the stairs, said to her son, 'Quick, go to the neighbour downstairs, I'll be down to fetch you in a minute.' Sami was five. His mother never returned from Auschwitz. The second emerged from the story in Elie Wiesel's book *Night* of a thirteen-year-old boy due to be hanged because he had stolen some soup in the camp. And the third Aurélia was the woman who gave birth to a daughter in the camp and then died a slow death lying in her own blood next to the child. 'I lost a child, a brother, I lost friends in the Resistance, in camps, but I got over these individual losses better than I got over the general fate of the Jews. And it is that emotion that returns when I speak of the problem and that is what I have tried to convey in *Aurélia*.'[23] Mystical poem, tender incantation, philosophical meditation, *Aurélia* is also a song and a lament without beginning and without end, a deliverance and a death, a chant that Duras tossed down on paper, not wanting to reread it. She continued to hear her shout but couldn't get rid of her.

Having with words given her a life, Marguerite wanted to give her a face. Almost as soon as she had finished the *Aurélia Steiner* cycle she set about adapting it for the screen. She left Trouville and returned to Neauphle, where she had seen a young girl who looked like Lewis Carroll's Alice. She phoned Pierre Lhomme, a director of photography she liked and respected; Pierre Lhomme filmed the girl but Duras was disappointed with the rushes and gave up on the idea.

'Aurélia Melbourne' was made into a film commissioned by the city of Paris. It was only a small budget so Marguerite decided it would be a quick shoot – four days, very little film and a reduced crew. First she walked around searching for locations, but with no preconceived ideas. She filmed the sky, the sand and the holes in the sand. *Aurélia Melbourne* was systematically filmed against the light. There is no Melbourne and no Aurélia, but fragments of the history of the Holocaust, a mewing cat, shots of the beach in a misty light. Everything is in everything. Marguerite declared that she was both the leprous cat and Aurélia Steiner, and declared that the cat was Jewish.[24]

Marguerite decided to go straight into the shooting of the second film – *Aurélia Steiner Vancouver* – with the same crew, but this time in Honfleur, and in the harsh midday light. She soon felt the need to leave the sea to film 'a river' that had to flow through Aurélia and engulf the town. Marguerite returned to Paris and filmed the Seine. The waterway acts as the axis of the film. The presence of the water creates a disturbingly strange atmosphere. The end of the journey is made by water. Water is more enduring than stone. Funeral barges can glide over it quietly.

CHAPTER 15

Yann

~

After making the *Aurélia* films in 1979, Marguerite returned to Neauphle exhausted and broken, and continued to drink. 'It was terrifying,' she was to say later.

No one can replace God
Nothing can replace alcohol
So God is irreplaceable.

Marguerite was convinced the reason she drank was because she knew God didn't exist. She had never been a believer, not even as a child. She looked at believers as people suffering from a kind of infirmity, a kind of irresponsibility. But reading Spinoza, Pascal and the fourteenth-century Jan van Ruysbroek led her to understand the faith of the mystics. 'They utter the cries of non-belief.'[1] Aurélia Steiner cries out, calls for God's help. At the time Marguerite talked constantly of God: 'we lack a God,' 'I don't believe in God, it's an infirmity, but not to believe in God is a belief.'[2] Alcohol put her in touch with her spirituality. 'God is absent but his empty chair is there,' she said in 1990.[3] She got drunk to find 'the insanity of logic'. Friends claimed to have seen Marguerite guzzle several litres of whisky while reciting passages from Ecclesiastes. 'Alcohol was invented to help us tolerate the void that is the universe, the swaying of the planets, their untroubled rotation in space and their silent indifference to the site of your pain,' she wrote in *La vie matérielle*.[4] Alcohol sent her into regions she had never yet reached and of which she saw herself as the ruler. It gave her the illusion that she could hold herself together and not be bombarded by a present she thought was destroying her. 'I have no story, I have no life.'

In Neauphle she continued to write fragments of letters, whenever she was able, to her stranger. She'd reached the stage where she wasn't sure whether she was actually writing them or just imagining them. It didn't matter. It was the idea of the epistolary relationship that kept her alive. 'I must stop drinking at night, I must go to bed early so that I can write you long letters and not die.'⁵ One night she called Michelle Porte and told her she'd had enough of living. When Michelle went over to see her, a wild-eyed, staggering alcoholic opened the door. She wouldn't last another year, she said. Michelle reassured her, looked after her, and Marguerite got back on her feet. She started leaving the house again, taking trips in her old Peugeot 203, going to see the colour of the wheat, visiting cemeteries, singing Piaf at the wheel, breaking out of the Neauphle–Trouville routine. She resumed cooking, inviting friends round, entertaining her son's friends, giving interviews to students. She, the queen of narcissism and the high priestess of self-proclaimed genius, was a great listener and a terrible nosy parker. All those who had seen her participate in debates in France or abroad were astonished at her ability to turn the tables on people when it came to the question and answer game, 'And what about you, what do you think?' she'd reply to questions put to her. It wasn't an affectation, but a genuine desire to know. Marguerite was insatiable. She fed off others, asked friends indiscreet questions, telephoned them in the middle of the night, encroached on their love-lives and generally meddled in everything. 'I used to talk quite freely about myself and in total confidence,' said one of her young men, 'the way I would have talked to my mother, or more precisely to a mother.'⁶

For fifteen years or so, hundreds of letters from admirers and fans had been delivered to rue Saint-Benoît. There were people who had worshipped Marguerite for years. They talked like her and could quote from her books at length. Marguerite was not averse to the adoration felt by some of these young people but she didn't go out of her way to encourage it. She would often open the letters but never answer them. Now for some months she'd been receiving letters from a young student in Caen, beautiful letters, a delight to read, and had started to wait for them. That summer she was invited to present her latest films at the Hyères Film Festival. A young filmmaker in Hyères told her he had friends in Caen who on a Saturday danced all night to *India Song* and drank Camparis like the protagonists of *The Little Horses of Tarquinia*. 'I've received a lot of letters from someone in Caen,' she told him. 'Do you know Yann?' Of course he knew him. She asked him to describe the young man, to tell her about him. He gave her information without realizing he was being manipulated.[7] A few months later, Marguerite went to Caen as a guest of the university film club which was organizing a debate on *India Song*. When the debate was over, a group of young people invited Marguerite Duras to join them for a drink in the local bistro. At two in the morning, as she was about to leave, one of them offered to walk her back to her car. 'It's me,' he said. He talked to her of Anne-Marie Stretter and Lol V. Stein, told her to drive carefully and saw her off into the night as she headed back to Neauphle.

A few days later, she decided she'd write to him. This was in January 1980, in Neauphle. She'd just been to see a doctor and told him she wasn't well, but she couldn't bring herself to tell him she was an alcoholic. He diagnosed depression and prescribed antidepressants. The cocktail of alcohol and antidepressants triggered three days of fainting fits. In the middle of the night at the end of this ordeal she was rushed to hospital in Saint-Germain-en-Laye. She was there for two months.

When she was discharged she wrote to Yann again, telling him she was finding it difficult to go on living. 'I told him I'd been drinking a lot, that that was why I'd been in hospital, that I didn't know why I drank so much.' She confided in him, out of the blue told him everything there was to know about her life. The young man was all of a sudden confidant, brother and companion in despair all rolled into one. Did he embody the stranger to whom she had been writing all these months, never posting the letters? Probably. Fiction had again become reality. She had imagined a man, and suddenly there he was, waiting. But now that she was trying to establish a relationship with him, he didn't reply.

Marguerite returned to her battle with alcohol. For six months she didn't touch a drop. She was irritable, irascible and sometimes downright nasty. And yet she hadn't lost her energy, her appetite for living or her penchant for telling stories. Michèle Manceaux, her friend and neighbour, thought she could make a story out of everything she saw, and transform reality into a succession of visions. 'She expanded my life the way she expanded everything, from the particular to the general, from the everyday to the metaphysical. And I had the privilege of witnessing the metamorphoses,' wrote Michèle Manceaux in *L'amie*. Marguerite started having friends to stay again in Neauphle. Her passion for politics returned as she ranted against 'Soviet fascism' and raged against the invasion of Afghanistan.

Marguerite began work on new projects. When Serge Daney approached her with the idea of producing a special issue of *Les Cahiers du cinéma*, she was very enthusiastic. She wanted to take advantage of it to return to her native land, her childhood, and intended to include photographs of her mother and brothers. She thought of mixing writing and pictures, of offering the reader a treasure trail rather than a straight narrative. She began by recording long conversations with Serge Daney, who then had them transcribed and returned them to her to be rewritten. The special issue came out under the title of *Green Eyes*. Marguerite had created a polyphony of images, texts, conversations, stolen letters and confidences that gave it a tone of nostalgia, sadness and warmth. Later it would become a book published by *Les Cahiers* – a slightly cruel and mischievous self-portrait of a filmmaker who wanted to revolutionize the cinema knowing full well that she would never succeed.

Marguerite was feeling better. She was eating normally and indulging in one of her favourite hobbies – going out in her car. She decided to spend the summer in Trouville, hoping that there, near the sea, she would be able to write a new book. She had no particular project in mind; she just hoped it would happen.

When Serge July called and offered her a column in the newspaper *Libération*, she jumped at the chance. July went to see Marguerite at Les Roches Noires, Trouville, to discuss it. He wanted her name and her vision of the world but had nothing precise in mind. He didn't want a political editorial or a cultural review, or news in a journalistic sense. Marguerite saw an opportunity to get back in touch with everyday writing, with the subjective journalism she had always passionately defended. July wanted a regular contribution, and she agreed

to write one amusing article a week for three months. And so throughout the summer she made small talk, chatted about the weather, about
everything and nothing: the colour of the sky, the stupidity of tourists,
the ridiculous rituals of sun worshippers, the price of ham sandwiches,
Iran, Afghanistan, Brezhnev, Uganda, and especially the thin grey-
eyed child she watched every day from her balcony in Les Roches
Noires, who would feature in her book *L'été 80*. Beside herself with
joy over events in Poland, she even thought of going to Gdansk. The
shipbuilders' strike had sounded the reveille for revolutionary hope,
she wrote.

And she got carried away, did Marguerite, and wanted her friends
involved in these sudden passions of hers, her crushes as they affectionately called them. They were all young, beautiful and sweet
towards her. Admiring but protective, seeking her company – because
life with her was droll, light-hearted. When you were with her,
said Henri,[8] you felt like confiding, going for long walks, dancing,
laughing, listening to music, watching the lights, living at night, being
aware of the world all the time.

Although disfigured by alcohol and no longer inspiring desire, Marguerite could still dream that one day a man would come, but she
told a friend she'd given up hope of ever meeting anyone. Even Yann,
the young man who'd struck her as being bashfully enamoured of
her, had given up. But then one day he telephoned. He, the sweet
and elegant young man, the mystical poet, the philosopher who loved
Campari, the frail boy with the melancholy smile, dressed all in white,
who knew her books and films off by heart and who had so tenderly
talked to her of them one night.

His name was Yann and she gave him the name Andréa. He was a
cheerful person who loved laughing and walking. His movements
were slow, his hands long, his voice fairly high-pitched. He looked
after you. Whoever you were, man or woman, you always felt safe
with him. He was unassuming and patient, thin, lanky, with an air of
astonishment.

It was the beginning of September 1980 when he rang and asked
if he could come over. 'Why?' 'For us to get to know one another,'
he replied. Marguerite was extremely lonely at the time. No, I've got
work to do, she said, and I don't like new people. He called again but

Marguerite had gone to a film festival in Italy. He kept on trying until she returned. Before hanging up, she said in a whisper, 'Call me back in two hours.' Then she murmured, 'When are you coming?'

'Tomorrow morning. The bus gets in at ten-thirty and I'll be at your place by eleven.'

She waited for him on the balcony outside her bedroom and saw him arrive. 'You were a sort of tall, thin Breton and struck me as elegant, though very unobtrusively and unconsciously – one can always tell.'[9] He knocked. She didn't answer immediately. 'It's me. Yann.' Still she waited, she didn't make a sound; then she made up her mind to open the door. 'You never know a story until it's written.'[10] She kissed him.

They talked. Late that night he asked for the name of a hotel. She told him it was the height of the tourist season. Her son's room was free; he could sleep there. 'When I heard his voice, I knew it was madness. I told him to come. He left his job; he left his house. He stayed.'[11] Bulle Ogier remembered Marguerite phoning her the next day. 'I've just met an angel,' she told her. The angel stayed a few days. First she showed him how to watch the sea at night. In the morning she always calmed down. 'I'm in the dark room. You're with me. We're looking out.'[12]

In the dark room she gave him herself. Together they discovered a territory no lover of Marguerite's had ever dared go to, which they travelled the length and breadth of, by night and by day, in the delirium of alcohol, in the ecstasy of passion, in the shouts of pleasure that come from suffering and waiting. He told her she was brilliant, adorable, confessed to wanting to write. He thought she could do everything for him. She told him she could do nothing for him. A few days later Yann left.

Marguerite waited for a letter, a phone call. Nothing. In desperation she wrote a story about a wounded mother whale. She couldn't go into the dark room alone. She loved him so that she could suffer at his hands, even though she knew he only loved men; perhaps because of that too, because of that evening when she thought he might change; she was already crazy about him, because the actual idea of this love had given her back the power and desire to write.

Yann hesitated before returning to Trouville, as though he knew that only the impossible could happen. But he did return, never to

328

leave again. The following year she wrote *L'homme atlantique*. 'You will think that it was I who chose you. You. You who are always wholly with me, whatever you do, however near or far from my hope you are.'

Yann came suddenly into Marguerite's life. He was from the outset an actor in her imaginary theatre, the one who already knew, who was there to authenticate what she saw. She devoured him lovingly, took away his gaze. Thereafter, she would be the one to look at the world for him. She took away his name, his nights, his time, his loves. Yann became Marguerite's chauffeur, confidant. He would inspire her to write about and film their love, the impossibility of their love. Yann would protect her, put up with her. An often silent presence, he accepted the blows, the insults, Marguerite's nastiness – oh, why am I so nasty? she'd sometimes ask him quite distraught. Yann is the only one to know the story and today he keeps himself hidden away.

In Trouville and in Paris Yann would disappear from time to time, sometimes for whole nights, sometimes for a week, and not get in touch. Marguerite would be frantic with worry; she'd call friends and get them to go looking for him in station hotels and dangerous areas. She'd even phone the local police station. Yann didn't leave – he escaped. And then returned. 'He doesn't want me to die and I don't want him to die, that's the nature of our relationship, our love...'[13]

From the start of their affair they'd shut themselves away in alcohol. The first time he came to see her, the American, as she sometimes affectionately called him, brought a bottle of wine. They drank it, and Marguerite asked him to go and get some more. All night they talked and drank. 'I don't think he could see I was dying,' she would say later. Marguerite had been proudly telling people that for weeks she'd had some Italian vermouth in a cupboard and not even opened it. Yann ended up going to supermarkets to buy wine by the crate.

At the end of autumn, they both left for Neauphle. Marguerite grew jealous of Yann, of the lovers he might have, of his homosexuality, which he lived with an all-consuming passion. She couldn't tear him away from it, and this was insulting and exciting. 'In the morning when I hear you come downstairs always late, cheerful and charming, words of vomit come into my head like "gay boy," "poofter", "queer". That's it, that's him. And then you appear, a charming young man, and I ask myself, what's he doing here?'[14]

Alcoholism fuelled her jealousy. Marguerite was also jealous of her own writings, the characters she'd created. Yann would encourage her by agreeing to live with her characters as though they were there with them. It wasn't Yann and Marguerite but Yann, the Durassian ghosts and Marguerite who all moved in together. Yann would alleviate the suffering that writing caused her, the physical and mental anguish to which Marguerite was prone. A month after meeting Yann she told an interviewer, 'You know, I don't always understand everything I say. But what I do know is that it's absolutely true. You can't be on all fronts at the same time.'[15]

Nobody could understand her, not even Yann, who thought he did. 'Our hell is exemplary. You don't understand anything I say. Not a thing. Not once did you understand me. No gay man can understand what a woman who has a homosexual lover says. I myself am upset. There is something secret, religious about this.'[16]

Marguerite's relationship with homosexuals was complicated. She regarded homosexuality as a strength, and her friends were for the most part gay. She felt a mixture of admiration and aggression towards those able to reject the sexual norms. At the time she believed a woman is closer to a homosexual than to a woman and that the possibility of sex always exists between them. The homosexual's non-accepted desire for the woman only arouses the woman's passion for the man who fundamentally wants nothing to do with her. 'He penetrates her in order to have an orgasm. He does not make love to her. All it is – love with a gay – is a parody of love. At least that's what he thinks ... I don't think gays ever make love. A woman's gay lover can only feel horror and contempt as he penetrates her.'[17] She had a growing intolerance for homosexuality when it was lived as a difference, as another way of seeing the world. While she accepted a gay lifestyle, she also rejected it. To her a homosexual was a heterosexual who didn't know he was a heterosexual. She also nurtured a deep hatred for men who rejected the idea of having children. Two months before meeting Yann, she declared to a gay magazine, 'I see homosexuality as a form of violence wanting a confrontation with itself, therefore as a longing to undertake the redistribution of current violence. A homosexual's apparent gentleness is an invitation to violence.'[18] Many of her homosexual friends heard her make savage remarks against 'bloody gays', as she used to call them. Marguerite found it very painful that Yann could love her but that it was impossible for him to love her physically. There were times when she found it so painful that she would ask him to leave and never return. Three months after they met, she declared, 'I see passion as heterosexual, sudden, intense and brief. When a man penetrates a woman, he touches her heart; I speak of the organ. Unless you have experienced that, then you cannot speak of passion, only of sexual games. You have to rediscover nature.'[19]

One night they made love. She asked him to stay with her unto death. In July 1982 she wrote to Yann:

> The passion that binds us will last as long as I live and for the length of the life that to you looks long. Nothing will be any good. We can expect nothing from one another, no children, no future ... You are gay and we love each other ... Nothing will be any good. There's no point you going back to doing the rounds of the Tuileries, to back-rooms, to carriage entrances, to circling the place Saint-Martin. Nothing will be any good. You will love me for the rest of your life. Because I shall be dead long before you, in a very few years, and because the huge age gap between us reassures you and neutralizes your fear of facing a woman.[20]

All Yann wanted was 'to help' her write as long as she lived. And while she wrote, he had the 'right' to go off elsewhere. He'd come home in the early hours, exhausted. In the morning, next to him, writing, she'd watch him sleep. Trouville was their special place, the place where they met, the place of the dark room, the walks in the wind, the persistent roar of the sea. As an old lady, it was there she found peace and a degree of serenity. 'Trouville. It's my home now. It's taken the place of Neauphle and Paris. It's where I got to know Yann.'[21]

At the end of October 1980, Marguerite read Robert Musil's *The Man Without Qualities*, which she found extremely moving. As a postscript to Musil's unfinished novel, she wrote *Agatha*, a book about incest, a last conversation between a brother and a sister just before they separate. In the book we find echoes of her own family history in the Dordogne house where Marguerite stayed as a child and in the portrait of the mother – 'she who taught us to be so wonderfully reckless' – and the brother – 'you were very handsome without ever wanting to appear so, and this gave your beauty an elusive childhood quality.' Agatha was the second in the family, and she referred on more than one occasion to her incestuous relationship with her younger brother, the pleasure brother and sister shared, a pleasure so strong that all they wanted was to begin again.[22]

Incest was the subject Marguerite had particularly strong views on. She forbade those who knew nothing about it to make any kind of judgement. The older she got, the more she saw it as one of the most perfect forms of love. Reading Musil had been a painful reopening of the wound left by her love for her dead brother. 'Without the relationship with my brother, I could never have written *Agatha*. The book is a combination of my having read Musil and my childhood with a young brother who was a silent, wild, and beautiful, adorable but not very bright little boy. If I hadn't experienced it, the depth of my love for my little brother, I would most probably not have written the book.'[23] She superimposed on to Yann – who played the brother in the film – the image of the dead little brother, her love, her treasure, her splendour. For, needless to say, *Agatha* also became a film, with the title *Agatha ou les lectures illimitées*. It was shot in Trouville and Marguerite did Agatha's voice. '*Agatha* is my first film on happiness, filmed in happiness,' Marguerite confided.

This is corroborated by *Duras filme*, a documentary by Jérôme Beaujour and Jean Mascolo which shows a cheerful, humorous and funny Marguerite. With her salt-and-pepper hair cut short, her face puffy from alcohol but her eyes sparkling, and wearing lipstick, she looks as though she's walking on air. The small, closely knit crew is like a bunch of schoolkids playing at making technical improvisations. Marguerite is using films to play hookey, to fill time and to give her new lover something to do. Marguerite is behind the camera and is using it to control and dominate the leading actor, Yann Andréa, who is not finding his debut into films easy. Marguerite bosses him around. 'Walk like this, look at me, never pretend, only look at me, I am me, the camera is me.'

Early in April 1981, the film barely finished, Marguerite and Yann took the plane to Montreal, where she was due to give a series of lectures. She visited Cap Tourmente, which reminded her of landscapes from her childhood. When French Canadians asked her questions, she would jokingly and seriously come out with such definitive statements as 'in *Le camion*, I play at God', 'I like only my films', 'I am a rare being, a free being who speaks beyond the reach of the censors.' Yann, always there at her side, smiled. 'If I say I am brilliant, if I have the impudence to sometimes say that what I write is brilliant, then it is certainly not through vanity. It is indeed a form of modesty. What I say about my books is what I would say if they were not mine. Sartrian humility and intellectual guilt are abhorrent to me.'[24] Duras delighted and shocked her audiences. She spoke only of herself, always of herself. She boasted she was in fashion and that it was her provocative rejoinders that kept her there. She claimed people saw her as embodying political marginality, subversive power and the ability to say all. The more people mocked her conceit, the worse it got.

On her return from Canada, the presidential election campaign in France was just starting. Asked about François Mitterrand, she replied, 'I love Mitterrand's despair, his dislike of power, his doubts.' 'Are you making him out to be a failure?' 'Yes, that's all that interests me.' 'Are you going to vote for him?' 'I don't know, I probably won't vote.' 'Not even for Mitterrand?' 'If he's the only candidate I will, yes.'[25] She drew a psychological portrait of him: 'He's fairly vague about politics. He drifted into it. But he's a very good man. I used to criticize him for having an historic rather than ideological approach. Today I think it's an advantage. He is essentially pessimistic like all of us. With him it will be the end of lies.' Mitterrand was elected president in May 1981.

François Mitterrand invited Marguerite to join the delegation going to the USA to celebrate the bicentenary of the Marquis de Lafayette's October 1781 victory at Yorktown. On the eve of Marguerite's journey, Michèle Manceaux dropped in at rue Saint-Benoît.

Marguerite was in the kitchen sewing. In the ceiling there was a naked bulb, an old sink, not a kitchen gadget in sight. She was getting ready to leave next day with the president of the republic. She showed me the waistcoat she was making to wear to the reception hosted by the president of the United States. She showed me her luggage: every single article of clothing had been rolled into a bundle and tied with a ribbon;

we used to do that in Indo-China, it's very good, it stops everything from creasing.[26]

Marguerite was happy to see Mitterrand again, and had nothing but praise for him.

During the trip, in her hotel bedroom with Yann, she drank until she dropped. On their return to France, they both moved to Neauphle. 'She was ashen,' said Michèle Manceaux. Her hands shook all the time. She couldn't walk unaided. She rarely went out now. When she was in Paris and when she walked down the rue Saint-Benoît she'd hang on to Yann's arm, he literally carried her – she, his little made-up doll; he, her little pet.

In January 1982 Minuit published *L'homme atlantique*. Marguerite had written it the previous year during one of Yann's absences. At the end of her life she said it was one of her most important books. 'I've forgotten where we were, at which end of which love, at which new start of which other love, into which relationship we had strayed.' The sense of the pain of loss was so strong that people were moved to tears by the book.

L'homme atlantique also became a film, starring just one actor – Yann Andréa. It was a forty-two-minute film made from offcuts of *Agatha*, and as there weren't enough images, Marguerite filmed blackness. The only voice we hear is hers. She says: 'I don't love you the way I did that first day, I don't love you any more.' She goes on, 'I'm in a relationship between living and dying. It's a film, just a film, a book, a small book.'[27]

The film, watched by a select audience, was enthusiastically reviewed by critics, who praised the way Duras had violated the rules of the cinema. *L'homme atlantique* is steeped in a great anguish that overflows on to the blind screen. It was the first time she had filmed black, a colour she considered to be deeper than any other. Black, absence of light, horror. 'Waterways, lakes, oceans have the power of black images. Like them they move.'[28] Black is behind the image in all Duras's films. The black of the film is connected to the black of writing, to what she called the inner shadow, that which makes a living being. 'I think I have sought in my films what I sought in my books. In the final analysis, it was a diversion and nothing more than that. I didn't change my job. The differences are ever extremely small.'²⁹

Marguerite then made *Dialogue de Rome*, a short film commissioned by Italian television, a poetic meditation against a backdrop of war and apocalypse, a conversation between a man and a woman who want to separate in a civilized fashion. In Rome, Marguerite filmed images of the city but any kind of movement left her exhausted. Yann had disappeared again, and she was alone and unhappy. Was the subject of the film inspired by what she was going through with Yann? It would appear so. In despair Duras filmed the hopeless hurt of love. She had no ideas and no script. She filmed so that she could have a sense of being alive. The film suffered as a result – it was long, long-winded and obscure. She wanted to film Rome, but in the middle of the shoot she realized it would be impossible.

She couldn't sleep at night. She'd go up to her hotel room late at night with several bottles of *vino blanco* – so as to 'be numb and forget' she told her film-editor friend. She waited for some sign of life from Yann but none came.

Back in Paris, she edited the film in a trancelike state of anguish. She drank nonstop. 'People drink because they're lost,' she said.³⁰ She had nothing left to lose. What else could she do? Die? Write? She went back to Neauphle, where she wrote what became *Savannah Bay*. 'You're somebody in writing. You're less so in real life.' Marguerite thought she wasn't anybody any more.

When Yann returned, Marguerite was in a pitiful state. In a panic, he asked Michèle Manceaux if she knew of a doctor. Marguerite said she didn't want to see anyone, she just wanted to be left to die quietly. Michèle contacted her friend Jean-Daniel Rainhorn, who would become one of Marguerite's friends. 'My Moldavian Jew,' she called him, a genius. A meeting was arranged in the Café des Sports in Neauphle. They discussed everything except her health. She talked to him of Israel, 'a wonderful country where you only find Jews'. She drank continuously. He asked no questions, didn't suggest examining her. Before leaving, he told her it was up to her to decide whether or not she wanted to go into detox. He went to see her several times and didn't rush things. 'Sometimes she wanted to die, sometimes she'd ask about the hospital she'd be going to.' She began to drink less. She wanted to finish *Savannah Bay*, but her hands were shaking so much that she was finding it difficult to write. So she dictated and Yann wrote or typed. When she finished the manuscript, Yann delivered it to the offices of Minuit, and Jérôme Lindon phoned her next day to express his admiration. For a few days she felt better.

Savannah Bay is a wonderful story about a granddaughter winning the heart of her grandmother. The grandmother is a woman who is lost, whose life has come to a standstill, and who expects nothing more from either life or the world. A former actress whose tours had been triumphant, this now absent old lady, a phantom among the living, is one day visited by a young woman who wants to know about her mother. The mother who, the night after bringing her into the world, was driven by love to commit suicide by drowning. The old lady locked herself away the day her daughter died and has never seen her granddaughter until now. She lives near the spot where her daughter killed herself. All the granddaughter is to her is the daughter of her dead child. But the granddaughter gradually draws her grandmother out of her morbid lethargy and brings her out of her bewilderment and madness.

Marguerite's legs were so swollen she couldn't even go out into the garden. She'd stopped washing her hair and wouldn't change her clothes. She was turning into a tramp – joked, boasted about it to Michèle Manceaux, the only person, apart from the doctor, Jean-Daniel, who was still allowed into her house. Her friends thought she was lost. They watched the disaster, powerless to do anything about it. She later remembered that period of her life with nostalgia and tenderness. It pleased her to feel disgust for herself. She thought she was rather brave.[31]

Marguerite left for Trouville. She worked in a jubilant mood on what would become *The Malady of Death*, though at the time the text was called 'A scent of heliotrope and citron'. She wrote pickled in six to eight litres of wine a day. She experienced altered states, saw everything except her head change shape. 'I was never drunk, I was tight,' she claimed. The sea did her good. From time to time she'd go out and look at it. But even those outings grew less frequent, and she couldn't walk without stumbling. Yann wanted to take her back to Paris to have her looked after. When she had written ten pages, she agreed to leave Les Roches Noires, but only to go back to

Neauphle. She couldn't drive any more. Those days were over, the sense of control and the exhilaration of speed. With no driving licence, Yann took the wheel.

Every morning Marguerite vomited up her first two glasses of wine. The third stayed down. Alcohol was the only thing that could control her shakes. She'd stopped eating, occasionally swallowing a drop of vegetable soup. She'd stopped going out, except to the supermarket on the corner where she went every three days to buy cases of cheap Bordeaux. 'We drink unaware of drinking, we've stopped counting the bottles.'[32] Every morning Yann woke up wondering whether she'd died in the night. 'I've reached that age where people die, why should I want to prolong my life?' Marguerite told Yann. But still there were moments of great joy when she wanted to go on living. She called Yann. There was no need to explain. He understood, and settled himself at the typewriter. Her voice would be faint, a whisper in the night, especially after hours of silence. Yann was always ready. He typed fast. She remembered nothing. Not even the adjective in the sentence she'd just finished. Yann recorded it all. It became writing. The book was growing, Yann pointed out, like a wild plant. Yann could have wept as Marguerite dictated. When the manuscript was twenty pages long, she announced that it would be called *The Malady of Death*.

At last Marguerite agreed to go to a clinic for treatment. Yann kissed her, got her another drink and called Jean-Daniel, who arrived in Neauphle the next morning. He was appalled at the state she was in, concerned there might be a risk of senility, an embolism, a ruptured liver. Marguerite could see the doctor's fear. Having agreed to go for treatment, she withdrew her consent. After all she'd rather die peacefully at home. Then, giving in to intuition, to hope, she did a U-turn, as she so often did, and said, 'I choose the hospital.' She locked up the house carefully on leaving. Jean-Daniel put her in a taxi. She was crying. She was drunk. With her was Yann. Michèle made Jean-Daniel promise he'd have her instantly discharged from hospital if the tests showed it was already too late. The taxi dropped Marguerite and Yann off in rue Saint-Benoît. A couple of days later, on 21 October 1982, Jean-Daniel arrived to pick her up and take her to the American Hospital.

Marguerite was soon refusing the so-called cold-turkey treatment.

She said she'd rather die. She bellowed for a drink, threatened, said she'd do anything, tried to run away. She complained that the room was too expensive, the food was bad, the nurses incompetent. Detoxification would be harsh, and the doctors were unsure whether she would survive it, because she was in an advanced stage of cirrhosis. Without the detox programme Marguerite would have been dead within months. The hallucinations started on the third day. She told Yann she could 'see' calves instead of cars when she looked out of the window, fish in bottles of water and nurses in dinner jackets. She became increasingly delirious. 'I know you went to Boston last night with a Portuguese nurse,' she screamed at Yann one morning. 'There's no point in denying it, so tell me the truth.' The doctors sent her for an encephalogram – was it health-related atrophy of the brain or an extraordinary bit of playacting? The examination revealed nothing abnormal.

Marguerite drank milk, slept curled up in the bath, dreamed. She regressed to her childhood, thought she was back in Indo-China, in her mother's school, wept like a child who'd been chastised. The doctors stopped the treatment, the drugs, the tranquillizers, everything. For twenty-four hours Marguerite hovered between life and death. 'It's not funny having to die,' she told Yann in the middle of the wait. She knew what was happening in her body but her mind continued to wander. She was regularly visited by a captain's wife and a Chinese man. (The former would become the heroine of her novel *Emily L.*, the second would be immortalized in *The Lover*.) Marguerite abandoned herself to her visions – black tortoises, hundred of birds perched on the tips of branches. She suffered but accepted her fate. Weeping, she turned to Yann and asked him, 'Why me?' Marguerite saw herself as the toy of destiny, the instrument of an unnamed superior power, who might have been God or not, it didn't really matter. 'God is never, under any circumstances, shown except in the form of an empty black box,' she told Yann. She wasn't afraid of death. Sometimes, she was afraid God did not exist, and when she was very old, she chose to pretend he did exist. Towards the end of her life she only ever read Ecclesiastes. 'All my books speak of God,' she would say laughing, 'and nobody's noticed.'[33] Madeleine Alleins, her friend of fifty years and incisive interpreter, is also of the opinion that her whole oeuvre is permeated with a mystical urgency, a continual wish to approach God and a constant need for spiritual fulfilment.

At the end of three weeks, Marguerite came out of detoxification, exhausted. Only writing had any kind of meaning for her still. Before leaving the American Hospital, she presented a woman with her book *Outside*, a collection of articles, saying, 'You'll see, it's good.' Back in rue Saint-Benoît the first thing she asked Yann for was the manuscript of *The Malady of Death*.

The following day she had an appointment with her hairdresser, who didn't recognize her. When Marguerite explained where she'd been, the other women in the hairdresser's stopped talking, and the hairdresser asked her to keep her voice down. Why should she? She had nothing to hide.

Michelle Porte went to visit her. Physically she thought she looked well, but all she could talk about was the hallucinations she kept having, which were on the increase. She really could see things: monsters, mythical animals – it was like hearing her innermost imagination speak. Each vision was an opportunity for embellishment, an abandonment to words she found beautiful. Michelle Porte spent an afternoon listening to the story of a blue fish beached on the carpet.[34] The doctors couldn't understand the cause of the hallucinations; her brain had not been affected. One night, Yann found Marguerite in her nightdress and high-heeled boots, armed with an umbrella, trying to kill the animals in her room – cats, lions and hippopotamuses. In a very beautiful letter about this painful period entitled *M.D.*, lovingly recorded by Yann, he wrote, 'I'm not trying to find out whether you believe it or not, or whether you're pretending or not, I know that fear has merged with the pleasure of telling, that dread has become confused with lying, that everything is logically jumbled up in your mind and that you are the only one to know it.'[35] When Marguerite asked him to kill the horrible creatures, he took the umbrella and lashed out. Marguerite was reassured. Michelle Porte preferred to tell her that personally she couldn't see anything. Marguerite didn't insist. Dionys told her she was delirious, and that none of those things existed. Marguerite just shrugged.

Little by little the nightmarish visions receded. The dead dog behind the radiator vacated the apartment and the powdered man waiting for her in the drawing room vanished without trace. Marguerite began to take little trips. Yann took her to see Balzac's house and she walked along the banks of the Seine. While she convalesced and got her wits and strength back, she corrected the proofs of *The Malady of Death*, and set to work planning a stage version. In an exercise book she wrote how she visualized it: 'We would hear the sea without seeing it. The girl who sells herself for sex would be stretched out in a pool of sheets. The actress taking on the role would have to be beautiful and unusual.'[36] Marguerite worked on projects, stopped the medication and no longer needed Yann to get her around the apartment.

The Malady of Death was a sequel to *L'homme assis dans le couloir*, originally written in the early sixties, then revamped and published two years earlier. In it she returned to her adolescent love and to the only genre that really dazzled her: poetry. *The Malady of Death* is an incantatory poem on the absence of desire. It is also the odyssey of a great love between a man and a woman. It is the dawn of humanity and they are shut up in a bedroom together. He has paid her to be there. To do what? The body of the woman is manipulated by a man who does not know where to penetrate. The sheets can also represent a shroud. It is said of a man that after making love he experiences the *petite mort*, the 'little death'. The man of *The Malady of Death* is a carrier of the big death. Because the man doesn't like women and because unbeknown to him he is the carrier of a disease, some have seen the book as prefiguring AIDS. Maybe ... Marguerite was witch enough, through writing, to pick up consciously or otherwise on events that were stirring but – for want of a name – did not yet exist. But *The Malady of Death* is also a long address to the man she loved and who had chosen to live with her. 'One night you are asleep on top of my parted thighs. There against my sex you are already in the moisture of my body. There, where she opens. She lets you do what you want.'[37] It is the death knell of an old lady's sexuality. *The Malady of Death* puts homosexuality on trial; it is not the *mise-en-scène* of a death wish, as Peter Handke portrayed it in the film adaptation.

When the book came out, Yann read it out loud to her. 'It's a very beautiful piece,' she said at the end, adding that it was a book for him, a private act, a gesture for him alone. In large print *The Malady of Death* is some sixty pages long. Nothing repeatable is recounted. 'Where are you going with this book?' she was asked, and replied, 'I'm going towards the unknown.'

*

'We're starting to see some progress, she's beginning to sound more like Duras,' wrote Michèle Manceaux,[38] who spent Christmas Eve with Marguerite, Yann and the two doctors who had saved her. Marguerite had bought nobody a present, though everybody had one for her. In front of an embarrassed Yann, Marguerite turned on Jean-Daniel, the friend who was at her side all through the detox programme and who had saved her life. 'Doctors are lucky to get the chance to treat writers.' And she went on, 'You've been particularly lucky. Thanks to me medical science has made great strides.'

A film made by Michelle Porte between 22 August and 22 September, during the rehearsals for the stage version of *Savannah Bay*, shows Marguerite with all puffiness gone from her face, features relaxed and her eyes, behind the large spectacle frames, bright and sparkling. During the rehearsals she showed considerable energy and her attention never strayed. She never tired of going over the lines with the actors, listening to the music of the words and reworking any passages that weren't clear. Yann always sat next to her, solicitous, shy, protective, knowing the lines off by heart and coaching the actresses. Marguerite was rediscovering the theatrical space, the tiny area where the fiercest of passions are confronted, and learned again the infinite patience required during rehearsals. She saw to everything – lights, moves, costumes. She was funny and cheerful and made people laugh. She was alive again. In the empty theatre, humming Piaf songs to herself and dancing, she seemed to grow visibly younger.

Marguerite said she originally wrote *Savannah Bay* for Madeleine Renaud. Since *Whole Days in the Trees*, Madeleine hadn't so much performed the role of her mother as she'd become her. She had carried on in *L'amante anglaise* – crazy, aggressive and unpredictable. In *Eden Cinema*, the mother was still there, a silent, wild and pathetic presence. Madeleine had had enough of playing Marguerite's mother. She had asked her on more than one occasion to write her a part tailor-made for her, and, for a change, in the style of a comedy. Marguerite gave her a tragedy in the guise of a comedy. It was to be Madeleine's last appearance on stage. Madeleine Renaud, eighty-three years old and brilliant, with her feral gentleness and repressed authority, surpassed the role of the actress and in the face of her imminent death offered her great age, the strength of her presence and her innocence.

To Marguerite Duras there is no theatre that is not tragic. The theatre must be the bare bones of passion, and must represent the unbearable. Her absolute model was Racine's *Bérénice*. The set reinforced the feeling of eternity, of timelessness. 'I believe in the sacrificial dimension of the theatrical ritual,' she declared, 'in a space that has its roots in the archaic and where every actor risks his own death, so that the characters he creates can remain enigmatic.'[39] Everything can be exposed in the theatre. To her exhausted actresses, a few minutes before the first performance, she simply said: 'You must structure the invisible.'[40] The audience wept on the first night. Leaving the theatre, they did not know whether *Savannah Bay* was a myth or a true story. Madeleine had peeled the words, to use Marguerite's expression, and uncovered their flesh; she took something from them, not their meaning but their significance. Madeleine Renaud was Marguerite Duras's ferry-woman: physically she had assimilated the text so well that you ended up forgetting that someone had written the words for her.

Marguerite was annoyed by Madeleine's success – after all, *she*'d written the lines. She complained about the media's lack of interest in her work and would have liked another column in *Libération*, but July never called her back. When she did get some space in *Libération*, she stated, 'I think the press is quite right not talk about my books. There comes a time in a writer's life when the critics no longer have a role; what I mean is that they stop following us and, though they wouldn't know how to admit if they had to admit it, they have become redundant.'

Marguerite only talked to herself. Did other people still exist? Marguerite had friends, a few, nearly all young men, like Jean-Pierre Ceton, whose book *Rauque la ville* she wrote the preface to, having arranged for Minuit to publish it, and with whom she was planning to write a new erotic book. With him, she went to restaurants, walked the streets of Paris at night. She liked to go out with a friend behind the wheel for a nocturnal spin around Paris and her favourite suburbs and afternoon trips in Normandy. Amazed friends described outings in an old banger with Marguerite, who would comment on everything she saw in a most hilarious way. Marguerite talked, she couldn't stop talking. But to whom was she talking? Today her friends say she was inventing life, creating life, giving life. The more she felt death recede from her physically, the more she freed herself from conventions and taboos. 'Why am I so nasty?' she asked me on several occasions. 'Nasty ... I can be so nasty.' How many insults did she hurl at Yann in front of us, how many cruel remarks with the power to humiliate? He took it with his nervous laugh, and would sometimes go up to his room – but always calmly – shut the door and listen to Schubert. Marguerite fed Yann, clothed Yann, spoke for Yann and chose every-thing for Yann, from the menu at the restaurant to his Saint-Laurent shirt – having first checked with the head of the firm, Pierre Bergé, that she could get a discount. And from time to time he'd disappear. How many of her companions at that time were spared the phone calls in the middle of the night from a panic-stricken Marguerite wanting the police contacted so that they could search the streets and hotels for Yann? When he returned, Marguerite couldn't even find the words to ask him to stay. And there were times when he was there but never opened his mouth. On those days Marguerite would have liked to see the back of him.

Marguerite had successfully removed Yann from the real world and incorporated him into the fabric of her imagination. And in the master–slave dialectic she preferred to be the slave – at least that's what she said, although we don't have to believe it. 'I can't live without her,' he said. 'She's a drug; I'm her main focus, the focus of all her attention. No one has ever loved me like that. Her writing about it, about the passion, it doesn't kill me, I'm no longer me, Yann, but she's made me exist to the power of a hundred.'[41]

And where was Duras? 'I am a writer more than a living being,' she said at the time.[42] Since her detox she had finally understood that her mother and little brother were dead, that she was alone in the world with her son and that she wasn't scared of dying any more. 'When I die,' she said to Yann on 5 January 1983, 'it will hardly be a death since most of what defines me will already have gone. Only the body will be left to die.' All that remained to be done before her physical death was to actually kill herself writing a few books, for, as she said, 'with each book the author murders the author.'[43]

She was happier and gave the impression she was finding life easier. Ostentatiously she would offer you liqueur chocolates, begging you to eat them so that she wouldn't have a 'relapse', but in fact she was drinking again. Oh, but only in the evening! Oh, but only a tiny wee sip! Oh, but such a small glass, first of champagne – 'Can champagne really be classed as alcohol?' she asked, and she wasn't joking – then a few glasses of good-quality white wine, before moving on to more generous helpings of rosé. 'Despite the treatment, it's something you can always go back to. Tonight. For no reason. For no other reason than alcoholism.'[44]

After detoxification she had to physically learn to write again, to shape the letters, to form a word, to leave gaps between them. It took a few days to master the movements, and left her with a 'fragmented, disjointed' little girl's handwriting.

CHAPTER 16

The Lover

 ~

The book that brought Duras international fame was thought to be the story of her life. In her view writing was the opposite of telling a story; yet readers of *The Lover* believed in the story. They took *The Lover* at face value; this was the main reason for its success. When the book first came out, she kept repeating that it was fiction and not an autobiographical account. In the end she gave up and agreed to remember herself as a fourteen-year-old girl who one day, on a ferry in Indo-China, in a large black car . . .

At the back of the cupboard in Neauphle Marguerite had one day found a stash of manuscripts she thought she had lost for ever, like the school notebook in which she'd written the Leo story just after the war. When Outa in 1983 suggested they write the captions for a book of photographs from the family album, Marguerite started rummaging in her cupboards again. She came across an old text and some family photographs, photos of her as a young girl and as an adolescent. 'The photo without which we couldn't live already existed in my childhood,' she wrote in *La vie matérielle*. 'Why has the absolute photograph of my life not been taken?' she wrote by way of a commentary for the future album. 'The absolute photograph is maybe the one that can't be taken, the one that recognizes nothing that is visible. It doesn't exist and yet it could have existed.' And so Marguerite changed projects. She left the captions for the family photos at the planning stage, took up another notebook, still called her text 'The absolute photograph' but began to write what would become

The Lover. The descriptions of the childhood photographs can be found in the first third of *The Lover.* They are like stages as the book moves nearer the meeting with the lover. An armistice in the turbulent story of her hopeless desire for Yann, *The Lover* is a dialogue with the reader – 'let me tell you again' – where the desire to explain herself is greater than the desire to tell a story. She recorded her intentions in a notebook:

> The story of my life I have more or less written ... what I am doing here is different. Here, I'm talking about specific elements of that particular story, and above all of those about whom I have hidden things ... things I have buried, facts, feelings ... They are all dead now, the people who inhabited the houses of my childhood. And they died for me, for everyone and for me. And the impropriety of writing disappeared ...

In *The Lover* Marguerite Duras crossed the river of memory to the other bank. It is no accident that the meeting with the Chinese is on a ferry between the two banks, on turbulent waters so yellow and murky that no one can see the bottom, on waters that frightened her so much that she thought they might swallow her up. Marguerite rediscovered the little girl, scrawny and yellow and so ugly that her mother thought she'd never attract a man, so badly dressed that she herself couldn't imagine holding someone's attention, so slow and so backward that her brother insulted and beat her, so terrified of herself, of others, of God and the world that she wanted to hide under the stairs in the hope she'd be forgotten.

Marguerite journeyed back down into her memory. The brownish-pink hat was recorded in the postwar exercise book: 'the faith I had in my mother's good taste was such that although I'd never seen anyone in a hat like it, and although Leo eventually told me just how much it upset him, I still wore it in secret from Leo but for the whole school to see.' For the novel Marguerite made some improvements to Leo, whom she would no longer name and who would for ever be known as the lover. He hadn't had smallpox and was no longer rickety or ridiculous. His skin was soft, his gestures slow, his eroticism was oriental. Marguerite dreamed out loud of what could have been, of what should have been, the story of her adolescence. Marguerite invented this gentle and patient lover, affectionate and tender.

A year after its phenomenal success, Marguerite Duras would say she didn't like the book. The only sections that she could tolerate were those that related to the war, and she regretted she hadn't developed them more. The evolution of the manuscript in fact reveals her hesitations. In the second draft she had the book begin with the war and the description of Marie-Claude Carpenter. The book was then entitled *L'amant: histoire de Betty Fernandez*, and described Marie-Claude Carpenter's salon and its regular visitors as the winter of 1942 drew to a close – Henri Mondor, André Thérive, P. H. Simon, Robert Kanters and the Khmer poet Makhali Phol, whom the young Marguerite had very much admired. In the final version Marguerite Duras in part abandoned the war, but kept Ramon and Betty Fernandez, who appear like ghosts from a past to which she at last had no wish to return. They remain fixed, frozen, like bad extras who have inadvertently strayed into a photo-story. Therein probably lies the secret of the book, in the movement the author creates between one element too many – Ramon and Betty Fernandez – and the one element that is missing – the Chinese.[1] To give her narrative some coherence, Duras invented the missing photograph that would become the heart of the book.

It is not the Chinese who is at the heart of the book, though millions of readers thought he was. For Duras, the subject of *The Lover* is writing. 'Nowadays it often seems writing is nothing at all. Sometimes I realize that if writing isn't, all things, all contraries confounded, a quest for vanity and void, it's nothing.'[2] But if *The Lover* is seen as a love story between a rich Chinese and a very young, destitute girl in the colony, then it is also because that's what Duras wanted. True to her method of putting the reader in the position of actor, assembler and decoder, she was offering a variety of possible interpretations. The leads were numerous, the openings countless. *The Lover* is an experimental construction site designed to awaken the reader's imagination. This could be why it was so successful, for the reader is the main character and, in reading, rewrites the story.

What Marguerite wanted to say – unconsciously or otherwise – was that the ultimate taboo was not to have slept with a Chinese but with a collaborator; and the memory-screen itself was hiding the inadmissible: to have slept with one's own brother. 'The absent Chinese is the enemy soldier,' wrote Alain Robbe-Grillet. '*The Lover* is an important book even though it has sold two million copies: let's not be petty here ... Marguerite Duras is a fool, but she's a great writer ... and without being aware of it she has some very intelligent creative urges.'[3]

The Lover is not an autobiography. We must believe Marguerite when she writes: 'The story of my life does not exist. It is not to tell my story that I write. Writing has taken from me what was left of my life. It has emptied me and I no longer know what – in what I have written about my life – is real, and what I actually experienced.' By the end of her life Duras had convinced herself and others that she had loved the Chinese. Writing had wiped away the distaste, obliterated the shame of the mother selling her child, and exaggerated the relationships. She adjusted what she had been through and thereafter what Marguerite Duras had written in *The Lover* became more real to her than her own recollections. Because the lover is a source of money, the violence inflicted by the brother and mother is eliminated. Through the elegance of the writing, the little white prostitute becomes the love doll of the Chinese man. In *The Lover* Marguerite Duras protected her mother's memory, defended her honour, swore that her mother didn't know that her daughter was sleeping with someone. Yet, in reality, the mother had not only authorized the affair but kept it going for financial gain.

Duras wrote the book very quickly, in just under three months, still intending it to be part of the photograph album. When Yann Andréa had finished typing it up, he convinced Marguerite it would be better as a novel and persuaded her to give it to Editions de Minuit. There, Irène Lindon read it and called Yann and Marguerite to tell them how moved she'd been. Her father, Jérôme Lindon, went over to Marguerite's place and told her it was neither a preface nor captions but a book. She listened and agreed to publish it. The book came out at the end of the summer of 1984. The reviewers hailed it as 'absolute literature' and spoke of the grace, the radiance, the inner drive that carries the words.[4] 'Duras has not manufactured a book,' said one critic. 'She has lived a book the way people live a religion.'[5] The initial print-run of 25,000 copies – a first for this publishing house, which had never printed more than 10,000 copies of a book – had sold out by next day.

On 28 September, Marguerite was interviewed on the television programme *Apostrophes*. For an hour and ten minutes, a playful, serious, light-hearted and profound Marguerite Duras talked openly about alcohol, writing, the Communist Party, Jean-Paul Sartre and her adolescence in Indo-China. She managed a few silences, looked intent, and gave the impression that what she was saying came from deep inside her, that it was neither a performance nor an attempt to please or sell. Next day there were queues outside the bookshops. Minuit's distributors had to meet orders of 10,000 copies in a day. Requests for the translation rights were pouring in from all over the world. For the first time the US magazine *Newsweek* devoted a whole page to French writing. Duras was no longer just an author, she had become a publishing phenomenon. Some booksellers remembered customers rushing to buy several copies of *The Lover* as though supplies were about to run dry.

Duras was also a social phenomenon. People started sending her their life stories – Jérôme Lindon recalled that sacks of mail would be delivered to their offices every day. People started to speak like Marguerite with long silences, and, to her great joy, people in Saint-Germain-des-Prés began dressing like Marguerite too, in roll-necks, waistcoats, ankle boots. She was the only topic of conversation – in the papers, on television and radio. It was too much. She was almost embarrassed.

At the beginning of September there were rumours that Duras might get the prix Goncourt. One of the judges, Michel Tournier, phoned Jérôme Lindon and asked why he hadn't been sent the book. Lindon told him he never entered the books he published for literary prizes. Tournier went out and bought the book and called Lindon again when he'd read it. Would Duras accept the Goncourt? Marguerite pretended not to care. She was at Les Roches Noires in Trouville, and had no plans to return to Paris. She was sulking because she hadn't won with *The Sea Wall* in 1950. But she didn't say no. She sent Lindon the terse reply: 'Proust got it.' In the third ballot the prize was awarded to her. Two hours after hearing the news, Marguerite declared, 'Everyone wants to imitate Mitterrand, in other words, to do as they please, and according to them, in all areas as entrenched and out of step with current affairs as the Goncourt.'[6]

From that day on, Marguerite stopped acknowledging the book as hers. She distanced herself from it once and for all, saying that she had been mistaken, for she had thought the book would make the reader angry with her. It bothered her to be reconciled with the public. In her eyes the triumph of *The Lover* was the result of a gradual evolution; until then her work had had a small but passionate and loyal following, but the style of the book had allowed her to reach a wider public. 'It is a book so immersed in literature that it appears to be without literature of any kind. It is unseen, like the blood in the body.' What she called 'the popular elements' had played a part – alcoholism, eroticism and colonialism, which people found intriguing, fascinating and appealing. Moreover the book was cheap, 49 francs, and short, only 142 pages. By the end of November the book had sold 450,000 copies.

Jérôme Lindon and Marguerite Duras held a reception at the Renaud-Barrault theatre on 26 November. It was a strange ceremony where the Paris intellectual and artistic set came to pay homage to Queen Marguerite, surrounded by her court, in a space filled by her presence. Sitting there, hands stretched out, rings sparkling brilliantly, Marguerite Duras revelled in her triumph as famous actors and anonymous fans came up to kiss her. Henceforth she would believe only in the myth she had created. With *The Lover*, Marguerite had given up the story of her life in favour of the novel of her life. Having already adopted the strange habit of referring to herself in the third person, she would now, ironically or narcissistically, call herself *la* Duras. 'If you only knew how fed up I am with me,' she confided one day to a friend.

In December Duras did a series of five long interviews with Dominique Noguez where she covered her career as a filmmaker for the video edition of her oeuvre.[7] She appears visibly moved as she listens to Delphine Seyrig and Bruno Nuytten remembering the shooting of *India Song*; affectionate and touched as she and Carlos d'Alessio recall the role of the music; quite amazed at herself at times. 'I wrote *The Ravishing of Lol V. Stein* and *The Vice-Consul* in the same year, that took some doing,' she commented in the afterword, full of admiration for herself. '*Le camion* is a great joy, even I'm in seventh heaven whenever I see it again. *Le camion* is quite brilliant. It's probably the most brilliant thing I've ever made.'

The next year, 1985, Duras was reunited with the theatre through her adaptation of Chekhov's *The Seagull* and a request from Jean-Louis Barrault to restage *La Musica*. Although she had no hesitation in saying that *La Musica* was an extremely easy piece – 'It's my tarty side, I could write as many *Musicas* as I liked' – she chose to rewrite it for the new cast of Miou-Miou and Sami Frey. In a short explanation handed out to the spectators at the théâtre du Rond-Point, she stated:

> There are exactly nineteen years that separate *La Musica 1* from *La Musica 2* and during most of that period I have wanted to write this second act. For nineteen years I've been hearing the husky voices of this second act, voices exhausted by their sleepless night. Nineteen years of never going beyond the youthful first love, scared. Eventually you end up writing something.

In the 1965 version – the play and then the film starring Delphine Seyrig and Robert Hossein – the couple meet in a hotel where they talk until three in the morning and then, exhausted, go to bed, separated for ever. In *La Musica 2* Sami Frey and Miou-Miou experience their night-long ordeal right up to the bitter end. They repeat themselves, contradict each other, get closer. Through their words they realize they are forever linked. So why get divorced? They know that when day comes it will separate them. They both have someone else in their lives, projects and plans for the future. He clings desperately to their last few moments. She is already a long way away from him, out of reach, withdrawn inside herself.

There was a lot of coughing during the dress rehearsal. 'Children should be taught three things: respect for their parents, respect for others, and not to cough in the theatre,' said Marguerite to console the actors. The presence on the first night of the minister of culture, Jack Lang, inspired some members of the press to sarcasm, but many reviews were good: 'The words look like nothing, she sublimates our state of mind'.[8] 'The pure stuff of life ... a great theatrical moment'.[9] If the critics sang Duras's praises, she despised them; if they ignored her, she was unhappy. 'It strikes me as quite extraordinary that we still tolerate from the old theatrical guard – and God knows there are enough of them – a critical view based on the same forty-year-old criteria of psychological plausibility, of what shouldn't be said and shouldn't be done, criteria founded solely on their concerns for their reputation.'[10]

Duras had become a star. She was asked her opinion on everything under the sun. A women's paper even suggested she take over the horoscopes! Unfortunately she turned them down. She wrote a wonderful article on infidelity for *Le Nouvel Observateur*, and an article on the right, entitled 'La droite la mort' (The right, death) for *Le Monde*.[11] She continued to profess her boundless admiration for Mitterrand (too boundless to be seen as having no ulterior motives) and her loathing for Chirac, which was so strong it was becoming comical. 'Mitterrand, as choice as amber, sharp and clear, with words of precision ... Chirac, Boy Scout, old-fashioned talk and absolutely useless.' Duras was parodying herself, making herself look ridiculous. Those who had expected most of her held it against her. But Jérôme Lindon continued to protect and defend her.

Luc Bondy and Peter Stein requested permission to perform *The Malady of Death* at the Schaubühne theatre in Berlin. Peter Handke, who had just presented his film adaptation of the play at the Cannes Film Festival, was to take charge of the translation and to play the leading role. The film was badly reviewed by the critics and judged to be clumsy, pedantic, unfinished.[12] And so Marguerite Duras worked on the stage version and sent it to Berlin. Two days later she telephoned Stein and Bondy to tell them that she wanted to pull out. At their insistence, she reread her text, and started it again three times. What she was writing disgusted her. 'I was hollow inside, I had become the opposite of a writer. It wasn't the book. It was a betrayal of the book, I'd lost faith in myself, I was lost.'

For a long time Duras had been contravening the rules of polite society. With the publication of *La Douleur* in April 1985 she was risking the rules of love and friendship. A harrowing and breathtaking book, *La Douleur* would never have been published had Robert Antelme been consulted. When the book came out he was in hospital and unable to respond. Marguerite knew Robert would be shocked to see his life exposed in this way. She did not take him into account – Marguerite never took anyone into account except herself and maybe God, in other words herself.

The first version of *La Douleur* had been published anonymously in February 1976, in the feminist magazine *Sorcières*. Under the title 'He didn't die in the concentration camp', the author describes her

husband's slow recovery after his return from deportation. Robert
Antelme's attention had been drawn to the piece by a friend who had
come across it by accident and immediately recognized Robert's story.
Robert had been astounded to read the article.[13]

Why, forty years after the event, did she decide to publish this
book? It is dedicated to Nicolas Régnier and Frédéric Antelme,
Robert and Monique's son. Was it to pass on her side of the story to
her ex-husband's family? Robert's friends and family rejected the
book. She sent it to his wife with the following dedication: 'To
Monique in memory of life, of him, of the love of him, of love.'
Monique didn't even acknowledge receipt of the book. Among her
friends, Dionys made no secret of his anger. 'It should have been an
opportunity to describe the sublimity of the love between her and
Robert. She didn't take it. She kept his first name and called him
Robert L. That kind of conundrum is unhealthy.' L. was the initial
of his Resistance name, which was Leroy.

There was a certain logic in continuing, after the publication of
The Lover, to expose her life in order to reconnect with it. *La Douleur*
is not literature; it's the memory's construction site, a revisiting of her
past.[14] 'It was instantly too late. My returning to the texts was from a
kind of fear that it might soon be too late, that I no longer care or
that I might die without seeing them again,' she explained.[15] Marguerite had actually forgotten the texts. She vaguely remembered that
she had put them away somewhere. What she found wasn't the diary
of Robert's recovery but the meticulously kept record of her moral
and metaphysical distress. If God existed, then why had he allowed
the camps to exist? The publisher Paul Otchakovsky-Laurens
observed how emotional Marguerite was as she reread the notebooks
before copying them out for publication:

One day she phoned me and said, 'Come over, I've found something
incredible.' Evidently extremely moved, she showed me an exercise
book that was falling apart. The pages were covered in writing. But the
pages were torn and the writing faded. Nothing had been changed since
the end of the war. As we talked we had the idea of adding later pieces
that had already been partly reworked. But she never touched the first
part of *La Douleur*, the one that opens the volume. To me it's a sacred
text. When I left Marguerite's place I photocopied it and put the original

in a cupboard in my office. As I walked away that evening, I was terrified the building would burn down.[16]

Marguerite wrote in the name of truth – of her truth. In the first section she accuses Henri Frenay of not having done enough for the camp deportees before the Allies arrived. In her view they should have sent in the paratroopers. 'But it hadn't been possible because Frenay didn't want the credit to go to a resistance movement ... So he let the Germans shoot them.'[17] Henri Frenay reacted badly to the publication by P.O.L. of *La Douleur*, and with Jacques Benet, Robert Antelme's comrade in the Resistance, wrote to Marguerite asking that corrections be made to future reprints, 'so enormous were her fantasies, the falsehood of this huge blunder exploited as though it were a historic truth to gratify the public's baser instincts'. Marguerite Duras replied:

> What I wrote was instinctive on my part. I copied it out as I had written it, in the intolerable pain of the wait. I left it there as I left my comments on de Gaulle. Had I examined the validity of all my assertions, of my 'injustices', there would have been no book. I should like to point out that I also did not censor the torture that I myself inflicted on the informer against the Jews – in 'Albert of the Capitals'. I think that people have understood that in this state, in the state I was in, I must be forgiven an error or two. And that's probably what people have done ... I have received no letters accusing me of injustice during the pain I was suffering – but if I can remove the sentence – even though it is too late – I shall do so out of friendship for you.[18]

But she didn't remove the sentence; it was still there in the paperback version of *La Douleur*. Should we, in the name of pain, accept errors and false interpretations? *La Douleur* is not a war history, nor is it an objective witness account. 'Many things described in *La Douleur* are true,' Dionys confirmed. 'Some of them are exaggerated. 'It's a little bit our story,' Mitterrand commented, 'but I wouldn't have written it in the same way. *La Douleur* is not the most scrupulous of her books.'[19] In Marguerite's eyes the fact that she hadn't spared herself and that she had admitted to having tortured, gave her the right to manipulate the truth. Hardly a fair exchange! To the end of her days she would say she wasn't afraid of being judged by her actions. 'No one has the right to judge me. To gossip about me. I am answerable to no one, I was there, confronting the inexplicable.'[20] She maintained that during the torture sessions, God was 'working' through her, that God had chosen her to carry out the hideous crime, and that she was therefore forever safe from the judgement of men ... and therefore sacred, made sacred in the cellar in rue de Richelieu where she waited patiently for the body to drop to the ground like a limp doll.

Strange as it may seem, when *La Douleur* came out, the press did not comment on the confession in 'Albert of the Capitals', with the exception of *La Quinzaine littéraire*, which was shocked. The critics then said they'd been so distressed they'd been unable to find the right words.

On 29 May 1985, when the Cannes Film Festival came to a close, her new film, *Les enfants* – previously entered at the Berlin Film Festival in February – was given a limited screening in Paris. It was greeted by general indifference.

It had all started in 1971 when Marguerite published, in an excellent series from Harlin Quist, a stunning short story, a funny but nasty little tale written for and from the point of view of children. Obviously influenced by Lewis Carroll, the book, entitled *A. Ernesto*, describes the thoughts and feelings of an irresistible little boy who doesn't want to go to school because there you're made to learn things you don't know. Ernesto is seven, has the body of an adult and the easygoing mentality of a professor of philosophy. When he eventually decides to go to school, the teacher tells him, 'The world is all messed up, Mr Ernesto.'

The book was not at all successful in France. But the friends to whom she had given a copy loved it so much that they wanted to work on a screenplay. Among them was Jean-Marc Turine, who, in 1978, suggested to Marguerite they make it into a short film, but Marguerite had not given him the exclusive rights. Without applying for permission, Jean-Marie Straub and Danièle Huillet made it into a short. The focus of the narrative is the child Ernesto who learns without needing to be taught. 'How can you teach a child what he already knows?' asks the teacher. *En rachachant* (by reclaiming) is the expression that gives their film its title. And it is true to the spirit of the book.

When she saw the film, Marguerite returned to the book, which she now thought was too 'innocent'. She decided to transform it and began by integrating into the narrative her memories of her readings of Ecclesiastes, which she gets Ernesto to speak. She first called it *Les enfants d'Israël*, then *Enfants du roi*. She wasn't yet sure what she wanted to do with it. Then Jean-Marc Turine returned from a long trip to Africa and asked what stage the project was at. 'The three of us – Outa, you and me – are going to work on it together,' she told him. 'I've just been granted 500,000 francs from the ministry to shoot *The Malady of Death*, which I no longer want to do.'

Marguerite completely reworked the book and during the next two years, she, Outa and Jean-Marc Turine produced six versions of the script. Having killed Ernesto off in the early versions, the authors brought him back to life to have him speak. For he knows everything, does Ernesto. Everything there is to know about anything. 'Everything about God, America, chemistry, knowledge, Marx and Hegel and the large mathematical organizations on the planet. Ernesto is a hero.' (As the incarnation of *fin-de-siècle* metaphysical despair, five years later, Ernesto would become the hero of *Summer Rain*, a title taken from Ecclesiastes.)

Marguerite approached Gérard Depardieu to take on the role of Ernesto but he refused. So Axel – a brilliant actor with Claude Régy and friend of Marguerite and Outa – played Fortune's fool, while Daniel Gélin and Tatiana Moukhine played the parents and André Dussolier the teacher. During the shoot, the faithful group of regulars reformed. Carlos d'Alessio composed the music, Bruno Nuytten was put in charge of photography and Robert Pansard-Besson saw to the production. The film was shot in Vitry-sur-Seine, a suburb of Paris, with the main action taking place in the classroom.

The *in camera* atmosphere soon became static and the words dislocated and awkward. Despite many video rehearsals, they were finding it difficult to convey the comedy of the language in a film. Marguerite was tired and had no idea what she was doing. She said she no longer understood anything about films – neither the continuity of the narrative nor the logic of the characters. 'It's a complete shambles. I can't follow a film these days. The psychology is beyond me, and as for detective films, I just can't watch them any more. I gradually lose the plot, it disappears, I have no idea what I'm watching.'²¹ She ended up making a conventionally constructed film where only the words were disturbing. Production problems and an argument over copyright – Marguerite demanded that Turine's and Mascolo's names appear in the credits – had a negative effect on the atmosphere during both the shooting and the editing stage and eventually affected the film's release.

Duras did not go to Berlin to present the film but in the press release she described it as 'an infinitely desperate comic film whose subject connects with knowledge'. *Les enfants* was awarded a minor prize in Berlin but divided the critics in France. 'A philosophical film you can't make head nor tail of, pretentious and incoherent,' said the critic from *Le Figaro*, who wondered if the projectionist hadn't got the order of the reels mixed up.²² 'A poignantly melancholic and ironically luminous fable,' according to *Le Matin*²³ and 'a hilarious and desperate burlesque,' in the words of *Libération*.²⁴

Then a legal ruling put a stop to its being screened. Summoned on more than one occasion to appear in court, Duras went along shaking like a guilty child, afraid she would be thrown into prison. Through her lawyer she was informed of the date the film would be released. She tried to challenge it – 'It's the worst release date of the year' – failed, and finally lost interest in the fate of the film. Having decided she wouldn't do any interviews, she did at the end of the summer agree to one long interview with *Les Cahiers du cinéma*, where she conceded defeat. '*Les enfants*? I have to remind myself the film exists. It's as though I've just put out the rubbish.'²⁵

With her continual passion for news items and her hunger for the tragic, Marguerite Duras had, right from the start, taken a keen interest in the case of Christine Villemin, a woman accused of murdering her son Gregory. Like everyone else, Duras first saw her on the television and in photographs. She found her a solitary being, like a servant who'd been thrown out, and she felt compassion for her. She wanted to send her books in prison but thought they might never reach her. It was at that point that she really started thinking about her. Literary commentators will always claim that by taking her over, Marguerite did not actually intend to attack her as an individual, but to create a fictive character that had nothing to do with the real Christine Villemin. That is all very well, but Marguerite Duras knew what naming her could do, that words can kill or incite to murder. She hadn't invented a new Anne-Marie Stretter, another Lol V. Stein. No, this woman was alive. Marguerite became obsessed by her. For quite some time she talked only of her, of her husband and her child. Her name, her face, her eyes, her story, her sexuality haunted Marguerite Duras's imagination. In her view Christine Villemin had been created by God to commit the ultimate crime.

On 13 July 1985, *Libération* asked Marguerite Duras to write an article on the tragic event that had become an ongoing saga that summer. Marguerite hesitated, wondering what on earth she could find to say about it. She felt that while there had been reports on the Villemin affair there had been nothing on 'her', no 'story', no 'novel'. She wanted to meet Christine Villemin to find out what her life had been like before. She couldn't stand the legal farce that was being played out around the drama. Then she hit upon the idea of visiting the various scenes. The scenes will speak, she thought. And so she travelled to Lépanges, in Vosges, with a journalist from *Libération*, Eric Favereau, and Yann Andréa. Her request to interview Christine Villemin was turned down, but by now Duras was hooked. She really wanted to meet this woman, whose every expression was being scrutinized and whose slightest gesture was being interpreted by the press. She thought that if she saw her she would understand. So she insisted. And again Christine Villemin refused. If she wouldn't speak to her, would she at least agree to see her, just see her, without having to say a word to her? Duras asked her lawyer. Strange, the way Marguerite wanted at all costs to see her but not necessarily communicate with her. Would innocence show through? Was Christine Villemin about to be paraded like a freak, the way nineteenth-century psychiatrists studied hysterics without ever looking them in the eye or saying a word to them? Marguerite Duras did not see Christine Villemin and very much held it against the lawyer, who in her eyes represented social stupidity and 'ancient' justice. Yet from this non-meeting she began to visualize a scenario. Since Christine Villemin was refusing to see her, Duras would have to capture her another way. She would not escape that easily.

'I shall never see Christine Villemin. It's too late. But I saw the judge and he is probably the person closest to this woman.' Thus began the article published in *Libération* on 17 July. It was the 273rd day of what was being referred to as the Vologne affair. The appeal court had just freed Christine Villemin, pointing out that there were no witnesses nor any established motive for infanticide. The news headline in *Libération* read 'The right to innocence' and announced on the front page the article by Marguerite Duras, titled 'Christine Villemin, sublime, obviously sublime.' (She claimed she had crossed this out before submitting the article and criticized Serge July for having restored it without consulting her.) 'The moment I saw the house, I shrieked that the crime existed, and I believe it. Beyond all reasonable doubt.' Marguerite Duras might not have seen Christine Villemin but she did see her house. And the fact that she'd seen it gave her the right to have a feeling that became a certainty that was 'beyond reasonable doubt'. Marguerite believed she had psychic powers. They frightened her, and her first instinct on her return from Lépanges was to write nothing about Christine Villemin. Having spent forty-eight hours at the scene of the crime, sniffing the atmosphere from the midst of the pack of journalists, she returned to Paris and declared she was giving up. But at two in the morning she had begun to write, using as her starting point what she imagined to be the woman's pain. Duras took herself to an imaginary country where love between men and women no longer existed, where maternal love had disappeared, where a man could beat his wife because she'd ruined the steak and where a child's life had become meaningless.

From the vision she moved on to identification – Christine Villemin is me. She could be me. I am beyond all reasonable propriety. I turn order upside down. Only incomprehension fascinates me. Supreme intelligence is to be found in the darkest recesses of our selves. Maybe Christine Villemin satisfied the most abominable desire a woman can have. Maybe? Duras never actually accuses Christine Villemin of being guilty, though she implies it. Duras would love Christine Villemin to be guilty. She feels the desire: 'One night that might fall on her, Christine Villemin, innocent but who killed maybe without realizing it, the way I write without realizing it . . .'

In her attempts to sweep aside self-righteous conventionality, had she gone beyond what she really thought? I don't think so. She was playing with fire and knew full well what she was doing. She tried to lure Christine Villemin into her universe so that she could turn her into a modern tragic heroine. She turned her into a wild, fickle,

nomadic runaway woman. Christine V. became the older sister of
L'amante anglaise, the woman who did nothing all day except sit on a
bench, staring up into the empty sky, as she allowed the most abominable of crimes to foment. Marguerite Duras led the narrative into
the world of fiction. It no longer related facts but told a story, mainly
hers. She could turn anything to good account if it fed her imagination, and had no hesitation in trampling on a person's dignity or
pouring scorn on the presumption of innocence. Although she cared
so much about integrity, and when it came to political practices, loved
to assume the role of moral arbiter and to right wrongs, she was
herself guilty of failings which in her contemporaries she considered
to be the most reprehensible – the violation of an individual's rights,
the desire to place oneself outside the law.

Two years earlier, in the preface to *Outside*, a collection of her
articles, she wrote, 'There is no journalism without ethics. Every
journalist is a moralist. It is absolutely unavoidable.' So where are the
ethics in the article 'Christine Villemin, sublime, obviously sublime'?
Serge July himself decided to publish an article next to Marguerite
Duras's and entitled it 'The transgression of writing'. In it he endeavoured to justify the nature of the piece as 'probably not the truth, but
a truth even so, that is to say that of the written text. It is obviously
not Christine Villemin's truth, nor is it really Marguerite Duras's
truth but that of a "sublime, obviously sublime" woman, floating
between two languages; on the one hand that of the writer, and on
the other, the very real largely unspoken one of Christine Villemin.'
Marguerite Duras came across it when she was reading the paper.
She was outraged.

Maybe Serge July had thought he was protecting himself against
accusations arising from the article, but it had the opposite effect. A
veritable avalanche of indignant letters crashed down on *Libération*,
and other papers took up what had now become the Duras affair.
Villemin herself sued for damages. Women writers were called upon
to give their opinions. Françoise Sagan expressed her indignation.
Simone Signoret said the article was confused and ambiguous, and
others were disturbed by this kind of condemnation and shameless
complacency at others' misfortunes. The day after the article was
published, Duras bumped into François Mitterrand in a bookshop in
the Latin Quarter. Mitterrand cornered her and said, 'Well, you don't

beat about the bush, do you!' 'No, that's right, I don't,' she replied. 'Apart from a few exceptions, I never consider a crime as being either good or evil but only ever as an accident that happens to the person committing it. Forgive me, but I never pass judgement.'[26] Mitterrand left after having agreed to see her again the following week to do a series of interviews.

Marguerite Duras was badly affected by the violence of the reactions to her article and made aggressive comments about some of the letters the newspaper passed on to her. Convinced she was right, however, she concluded that her piece had reached so deeply into the collective unconscious that it had become painful.

For Duras, true pleasure could only be achieved against a background of crime. Christine Villemin became the embodiment of all humiliated women whose only way to understand the world was through crime. Marguerite Duras saw her as a heroine of whose rehabilitation she would have liked to take charge. And so she started on a novel about herself and Christine Villemin, though this project would never see the light of day.

The whole affair left Duras bitter and aggrieved. The article in *Libération* had damaged her reputation and her image. 'It was an opportunity to accuse a writer of a moral offence.' For a few months she felt ostracized from society. 'I might have written too much but they on the other hand have shouted too much.' Soon after the end of the affair, during a conversation, Marguerite Duras admitted she had gone too far. 'Maybe I did fly in the face of caution. It was certainly an aberration on my part, a fit of writing, an excess of writing as a reaction to the worst thing a person can do: to kill.'[27] Yet until the end of her days, Duras thought she had been misjudged and misunderstood. She felt not the slightest remorse, but became quite agitated when she recalled the hatred her comments had stirred up. She saw herself as a martyr to truth, a truth so disturbing that it could not be heard.

In January 1994, Christine Villemin lost her case against Marguerite Duras and Serge July. The judges ruled that legal news gives a journalist the right to publish information on a person brought to trial and to illustrate his or her article on that person without obtaining prior consent.

Michel Butel, in preparing to launch a new magazine, *L'Autre Journal*, had the idea of having Duras and President Mitterrand in conversation. He told each of them separately that the other was anxious for a meeting. His little trick worked and a deal was soon struck. During the interview, held in rue Saint-Benoît, Mitterrand kept having lapses of memory. An embarrassed Marguerite Duras tried to set the record straight and then gave up correcting his mistakes on the chronology of the Resistance.[28] At the end she asked to see him again. Mitterrand accepted because she was the ex-wife of Robert Antelme, whom he greatly admired and because her style amused him, the way she suddenly changed the subject.

The second meeting took place at the Elysée Palace on 23 January 1986. Marguerite arrived unprepared and just said whatever came into her mind. They covered Africa, the war, animals, childhood, plants. Seduced by Marguerite's easy manner, Mitterrand dropped his politician's wooden language and frequently spoke in the first person.

Marguerite wanted to continue with the interviews, and kept pestering his secretariat because she wanted to make a book of them. She came up with a title, *Le bureau de poste de la rue Dupin*, decided on the number of pages, 204, and even the number of characters, 298,000. Gallimard offered her an advance of 200,000 francs. But Marguerite couldn't get another appointment with Mitterrand, though he would not commit himself to saying either yes or no. Something urgent had come up and Mitterrand's cultural adviser was entrusted with the delicate mission of asking Marguerite to wait – she ranted and raved and demanded an explanation. Three years later, she still hadn't given up on the idea of finishing the project.

Mitterrand found Marguerite charming, admired some of her books – especially *The Little Horses of Tarquinia* and *The Sea Wall* – acknowledged that she had energy and enthusiasm but had no confidence whatsoever in her ability to stick to the facts. He also believed that, because she wanted at all costs to play the role of *agent provocateur*, she hindered true political debate through the way she asked questions. In addition he was very wary of her narcissism and the way she systematically brought everything back to her. He didn't want her to assume the role of official biographer collecting the thoughts of an incumbent president. And so Marguerite did not see Mitterrand again. She continued to send him her books, all of which he read immediately, and courteously acknowledged receipt of.

She took her activities as a journalist with *L'Autre Journal* seriously, and found her editorial responsibilities rejuvenating. She loved being part of a team, regularly gave advice, took her thoughts on political issues straight to Michel Butel and never hesitated to wake him in the middle of the night when she had an idea.

On 7 April 1986, in the presence of the minister of culture, François Léotard, Duras received, from the hands of Mohamed Al Fayed, the Ritz-Paris-Hemingway prize worth $50,000. She had already amassed substantial funds through royalties and selling film rights, and a large part of this money had been used to buy apartments in Paris. She invested the prize money too in property.

Marguerite's editorial aspirations, which she had periodically expressed to Gallimard and Minuit, were fulfilled when she was allowed to edit a series called 'Outside' for P.O.L., the publisher Paul Otchakovsky-Laurens. The first two titles she had chosen came out in May 1986. 'She used to tell me she wanted to encourage young writers,' Otchakovsky-Laurens said. 'She wanted to publish and protect them. I gave her carte blanche.'[29] 'The public doesn't read the author but the book,' Duras claimed.[30] She published such young and up-and-coming writers as Catherine de Richaud, Nicole Couderc and her protégé Jean-Pierre Ceton, before the experiment ended. 'We didn't fall out,' P.O.L. would say, 'we just didn't have the same taste. She never asked for a penny.'

Blue Eyes, Black Hair, the sequel to *The Malady of Death*, came out of the rewriting of an abandoned stage adaptation. *The Malady of Death* was set in a bedroom, and so is *Blue Eyes, Black Hair*, which she dedicates to Yann Andréa. Four years separate the two texts. *The Malady of Death* came out of her horror of homosexuality and the pleasure the horror inspired. *Blue Eyes, Black Hair* describes the armistice of desire: how can a woman live with the fact that the man she desires is a homosexual? They are in bed, motionless and naked in the room where love is impossible. He doesn't even want her to touch him. Around them the actors read their story.

She tells him to come. 'Come.' She says it's like velvet, like vertigo, but also, you shouldn't believe it, it's a desert, an evil thing that leads to crime and madness. She tells him to come and see it, that it's a revolting, criminal thing, cloudy, dirty water, the water of blood, that he will one day have to do it, just once, to rummage in the commonplace, that he won't be able to avoid it all his life.

The woman is a writer. The story is universal. The woman thinks that through his repulsion for this love she might get him to see her distress at no longer having orgasms with him. They have been living together for five years, in the impossibility of ever loving each other, in the inability to leave each other. She seeks pleasure outside the bedroom – on beaches where men make love to women they don't know, they don't see; or in hotel bedrooms where a man awaits her who beats her so she can have an orgasm more quickly. But it is always to him that she returns, exhausted, at the end of the night.

Blue Eyes, Black Hair, by depicting a point in the relationship between Yann and Marguerite, attempts to exorcise it. Is it possible to love without making love? The word 'homosexual' never comes up in the text. Duras wants to destroy the word. Before she'd used it often. Now she was finding it false – for homosexuality is more than just sexual. It was also the first time Duras was venturing so far into the analysis of female sexuality. She describes in great detail the physical sensation of the penis penetrating to the back of the vagina, the secretions of pleasure, and outlines the ideal male member for all the different stages of female love. *Blue Eyes, Black Hair* is a love song to female sex, a hymn to pleasure. It is a battle, lost in advance, from which, however, the woman comes out victorious, for although the man cannot penetrate her, he nonetheless has to lie down beside her so as not to weep. She knows she will die soon. She is certain he will be there at her side until she draws her last breath. The proximity of death and the impossible dialogue with God add a tinge of great sadness to the narrative.

Although she worried about how the readers would react, Marguerite Duras had no qualms about publishing the book. Two years after *The Lover* she changed her style radically and shattered the image she had created of herself. The attractive young girl who had surrendered herself to the expert hands of the man with skin like rain had gone, replaced by a howling old woman who clamoured for sex from a disgusted and depressive young homosexual. Interviewed on the radio when the book came out, she made no secret of the fact that it was partly autobiographical. 'People always write books about themselves. Invented stories are not my thing. I don't have the words for that.'³¹

Duras wrote about Yann. And she wrote to Yann. 'I'd like you to write and tell me you don't love me, to sign the letter, to record. Write: I don't love you. Sign it and date it. At the bottom of the letter, add: I cannot love a woman.'³² Yann did not sign. Duras turned her friends and her lovers into actors in her own theatre. Duras decided everything, even her readers' reactions. Yes, sir, Comrade Duras! There were those who were fed up with her play-acting, her need for impropriety, her imitations of herself, the same words that kept coming back – love, lover, shouts, tears, sea, night. Love had to be terrifying; cries were howls or shrieks; the sea was devouring and cruel; and the night interminable and cold. Was the writer who had been called the Callas of French literature becoming the slightly senile Castafiore?

In a piece entitled *La pute de la côte normande*, first published in *Libération*, then by Minuit, Marguerite Duras described the circumstances in which *Blue Eyes, Black Hair* was written. Yann is no longer referred to as 'the young man', he is called Yann. For two hours every day he types *Blue Eyes, Black Hair*. And while he's typing he doesn't shout. The rest of the time he shouts, at her, at himself. And then he leaves. He goes to the large hotels in search of beautiful men. Sometimes he finds them, not dark-haired men with blue eyes, but barmen. When he returns he shouts. Whatever she says, he shouts. It stops her from writing. But soon she can't live without his shouts. Yann made the book. Not only did he type the innumerable different drafts, not only did he put the bundles of paper into some kind of order, but he inspired her, he supported her. Although he appeared servile, it was Marguerite who was afraid of him, not the other way round. She was afraid of his shouts, his absences, she was afraid he would die. And all he could say was, 'Why the hell d'you write all the time, all day long? Everyone's deserted you. You're insane; you're the whore from the Normandy coast, a stupid bitch, you're embarrassing.' Marguerite wrote the book to appease him.

With *Blue Eyes, Black Hair* she felt she had at last captured Yann

Andréa. There in the pages she'd caged him, she'd revealed everything about him, his most secret obsessions, his most private gestures, his craziest desires. She exposed him in the same way she'd exposed her ex-husband Robert Antelme a year earlier. By writing his name on paper in black and white she could at last distance him from her life. By writing about him, she had regained the upper hand. For a while. The book was well reviewed – 'a book even more beautiful and pure than *The Lover*, childhood far into the night and into madness'.[33] A year later she distanced herself from it and regarded it as a failure: 'There's a kind of Barthes-like essayism about the book.'[34]

Quillebeuf is a small port on the border between Evreux and Seine-Maritime, where tankers sail past. Yann and Marguerite spent many summer afternoons there in the peace of the Hôtel de la Marine bar. One day Marguerite suddenly saw some strange people arrive: they all had slanting eyes, crew-cut hair, same face, same body, same Asian appearance. A moment later these Koreans were all around them sitting at nearby tables, but Yann couldn't see them. Marguerite's alcohol-induced hallucinations were back. The Koreans were staring at Marguerite and Yann, smiling cruelly. Marguerite was afraid; Yann was sarcastic. Why Koreans? You're just being a pathetic racist. Marguerite said he must be right, but she was trembling like a little girl. Yann gave in and suggested they go to the café to get away from the Koreans and their cruel stares. 'And I followed you into the café. I always followed you wherever you went.'

That's how the novel *Emily L.* begins. Waiting in the bar of the Marine Hotel we have Emily L. and the Captain, two characters from the bottom of the ocean, Captain Ahab's grandchildren, R. L. Stevenson's distant cousins, stateless people whose only frontier is the horizon and whose only homeland is the intoxication of whisky. But the Koreans have surrounded the Marine Bar. Marguerite looks to Yann to protect her, but Yann is staring into space. Marguerite tells him her fears. Yann is not listening. And so Marguerite weeps. 'I don't love you any more. It's you who love me. You're not aware of it.'

Once more Yann and Marguerite were drinking six to eight litres of wine a day. They'd given up eating, yet they'd put on a lot of weight. They looked revolting. 'I loved finding myself revolting. I could see myself falling apart. The disintegration was really great.'[35]

Thanks to alcohol they had no idea whether love was too close or too far away, whether it was still there or not. All they knew was that in alcohol they were together. Duras's strength at seventy-two was amazing. She knew death was fast approaching, accelerated by alcohol. But that didn't stop her. She knew she had to leave Yann so that she could continue to write; that if she were a long way away from him she'd rediscover the sky of Indo-China and her youth. Marguerite wanted to write something for a young girl she'd just met. She scribbled a quick note that said 'My advice to you, the little girl, just you: first. Go to Vietnam and see where we were all a little born. So that you can play at being born everywhere.'

The hallucinations were back, clouding her vision, inhabiting her imagination. Those nightmare characters were preventing her from creating fictional characters. And yet she created Emily L., the woman with rings on her fingers, her body broken, wrecked by alcohol; Emily L., crawling from bar to bar, the forever wilted aquatic plant, the woman who stooped so low to improve her chances of side-stepping death. Emily L. – younger sister of Virginia Woolf and Emily Dickinson – is a woman as engaging as Lol V. Stein and as fascinating as Anne-Marie Stretter. She writes poetry, which she finds interesting yet allows to be swept away by the wind. Her husband, the Captain, is jealous when she writes for he notices that she distances herself from him. Try as she might to explain that she puts into her poems all the passion she feels for him, the Captain doesn't believe, doesn't see, doesn't understand. The Captain cannot read what Emily writes. And one day he burns the only poem Emily wants to keep, a poem about winter light, written after the long silence that followed the death of their little girl. Emily searches everywhere for the poem. The Captain never tells her the truth. And she never writes again. They set off to sail the seas. She begins to drink. She becomes a ragdoll with broken nails, a poor little bird trembling and thin, exhausted by alcohol, broken by life's misfortunes, forever separated from writing.

'Emily L. is a genius,' says Marguerite. 'She's the woman I like best in the whole world, an old alcoholic with holes in her shoes. Too bad those people who haven't seen her for what she is. If they had seen, it would have changed them. It changed me, I drag Emily L. around with me.'[36] Emily is her sister. When Marguerite is afraid, she can even hear her heart beating. Emily L. escapes death by living in the oblivion of the words she has written, waiting for a lover who is out of reach, on the bridge of a ship, drunk, eyes half-closed, tossed on the sea, waiting for death. Marguerite Duras puts the reader in a state of absolute readiness, of return to innocence. Maybe that's what the Duras effect is – to get us back to square one, to get us to start again from the beginning. Maybe that's how Duras can be of use to her readers – in getting us to believe, as Marianne Alphant put it, 'in daily sudden appearances'.[37]

Writing the end of *Emily L.*, Marguerite Duras knew Yann didn't love her. She had a feeling he was about to leave her. Illness would change all that.

A few months before *Emily L.* in 1987, Marguerite Duras had brought out a non-book, a monologue, a long string of meditations. A motor-way of words, as she put it, that spoke of the colour of the sky, a recipe, the beauty of something she'd read or a fit of the giggles. It wasn't a novel, though in parts it was close, nor a diary like *L'été 80*, nor a collection of articles like *Outside*, nor a book of interviews like *Les parleuses* or *Les Lieux*, and it had no beginning and no end. The book was called *La vie matérielle.* In it Marguerite was addressing Jérôme Beaujour. Talking, in order to untangle the inextricable – childhood, the mother, sexuality. Duras admits to having always been out of step with herself, to having done everything wrong in life, to having always been one train, one fashion, one joy too late. She would so desperately have liked to have been like others, tried but never succeeded. 'I have no chance of finding a model for my existence. I wonder what people base themselves on when they talk about their lives.'

In a long passage she touches upon the 'problem' homosexuality has become. 'A homosexual's passion is homosexuality. What the homosexual loves like a lover, a homeland, a creation, a land; is not his lover, but homosexuality.' Duras now saw all men as homosexuals. To her, heterosexuals were homosexuals who didn't know it or who were waiting to metamorphose. She was accusing her gay friends more and more of being filthy queers and old queens.

Duras had a ravaged face, a body that was completely wrinkled, an incredibly vicious streak, a desire to charm, and her only weapon was the fact that she saw herself as Duras. 'Duras who is idolized.' The duress of desiring Duras. Durable Duras. Caricaturable, pastichable Duras – Marguerite Derange. In a series of four television programmes broadcast in 1988 she showed how she could be fragile, lost, bucolic, mocking, cursing, bad-mouthing.[38] Duras the wounded diva, a genius and also, as she kept reminding us, a 'friend of the President'. In *La vie matérielle* she bombards us with such truisms as 'A woman and a man, say what you like, they're different.' Who can resist Duras?

Marguerite Duras only went on return journeys between herself and herself. If she spoke to you, it was to talk about herself. To her Paris was like a huge glass cage with watchtowers everywhere. She'd go no further than the newspaper kiosk at the end of the road to see if there was anything about her. She'd confined Yann Andréa to his room, where he took refuge in music. They rowed more and more in front of others, over nothing – the state of the cooker, a recipe for chicken curry or the name of a journalist. There was an exhibitionist side to their relationship. Everything that happened to Marguerite was interesting because it happened to her. So if they argued, she thought you were lucky to be there, to see her, to hear her. In fact you only wanted to flee, but you didn't dare. Modesty was nothing but a form of hypocrisy, she argued. 'My character? Ask people what they think. I have a difficult character. My son says I'm unbearable. Maybe. Like him. I shout like him. I think men have loved me because I was a writer. A writer is a foreign land; it's the writer who calls rape. He calls it the way we call death.'[39]

She agreed to take part in a television interview with the director Jean-Luc Godard. 'We are both kings, savages, beasts,' she said. Refusing him the film rights to *The Lover*, she questioned him on the future of the cinema. Their artificial dialogue was a great moment in television history. Godard pretended to be asleep; Duras kept telling him not to yawn. Duras reprimanded Godard, 'Don't start talking drivel again.' Duras, with that eternal smugness where she was concerned, said, 'What we do is useless.' And she wrote in the margin of one of her notebooks, 'I'm not sure I could put up with Duras.'

CHAPTER 17

Eyes Wide Open to Nowhere

~

Marguerite had emphysema, she was short of oxygen, and the attacks were fuelling her anguish. She withdrew further from the world. Physically she was finding it difficult to walk downstairs and out of the building, and her intellectual isolation was also growing. Age, time and illness had changed her relationship with Yann, who over the years had become her protector, her nurse, more of a presence than a lover or a companion. Marguerite could see the future fading. She'd had enough. What was the point? Yet she would fight to survive until she drew her last breath. On 4 December 1986 she wrote, 'If I live to be very old I shall one day stop writing. It probably seems unreal, impractical and absurd.'

In October 1988 she was admitted to hospital with breathing difficulties. They operated on her. She was in a coma after the operation. In June 1989 they said she was too far gone and called for her son to inform him that it was all over. Outa kept putting off the decision to 'unplug' her. Intuition, he said, a premonition. Drunk, he wandered the streets of Paris all night. Next morning, the hospital woke him with the news that the temperature chart showed an improvement – Marguerite Duras was on the mend.

After she came out of the coma, she loved saying she was a special case, that it was a miracle she was alive. Medical science hadn't saved her life, *she* had by wanting to live. Her belief in her own strength and her fundamental solitude always gave her energy just when she needed it most. Marguerite had had to be self-reliant from the age of seven. Her intelligence had protected her from physical harm. The second skin of words she'd sewn over her body had protected her from dying. She would say that during those nine months she forgot everything, her past.

Yann was wonderful. He never left her side. When Marguerite opened her eyes, there he was. She spoke his name, Yann, without emotion, as though she'd seen him only the day before. At least she thought she spoke it, but no sound came from her throat. She'd had a tracheotomy and lost her voice. But from her eyes Yann could see she had started talking again. She asked him for paper and scribbled a few words – she wanted the page of the manuscript she'd been working on the night before she was rushed to hospital. 'There's a badly constructed sentence I want to rewrite.'

Marguerite was the sleeping beauty. In the enchanted forest of the coma, time had stood still. The book she would finish a few months later, and call *Summer Rain*, was her Prince Charming who had woken her up. When she left intensive care she had lost a serious amount of weight, had no voice and was once more haunted by visions. She lived in an imaginary world filled with new male characters. Her fantasies revolved around sexuality. She described lots of rapes of which women were always the victims.

Little by little, she got back on her feet with a string of new projects for stage, screen and books. She summoned Claude Régy to her and suggested a stage adaptation of *Emily L.* Régy went to Normandy and found the locations in Quillebeuf where the story is set. She wanted Omar Sharif to play the Captain. She also wanted to engage her downstairs neighbour from rue Saint-Benoît. The project was prepared, written, presented and approved by the théâtre de Bobigny. Then she abandoned it. She said she wanted to finish *The Malady of Death*; she picked it up again and rewrote it, this time with less violence. She called it *Le sommeil* and it was about a woman who, in the relaxed atmosphere of summer, was trying to come to terms with the fact that the man who said he loved her was gay. No hysteria, no scenes, it was more like the mood of *La musica*. But she ended up hating the text and abandoned it.

Duras seemed to want to settle scores through some of her writings, to see just how far she could take them, whether they could be transformed or whether they would have to be consigned to oblivion.

She worried she wasn't leaving things open, in suspense. She started rereading some of the texts she had written to see if they were reusable or re-adaptable. She came across a play she had written at the beginning of the sixties, *Un homme est venu me voir* (published by Gallimard in the collection *Théâtre II*), asked Claude Régy to take on the production, contacted an actor for the leading role, and then once again gave up.

Duras finished *Summer Rain* a few months after leaving hospital. For a time she thought she had stopped herself from dying so that she could finish the book. 'It was probably the opposite,' she said a year later; 'maybe by becoming seriously ill I was trying unsuccessfully to kill the book.'[1] She dedicated it to Hervé Sons, the doctor who saved her life. She did not make many changes to the twenty-five pages written before her coma. 'It was there, inevitable.' *Summer Rain* follows on from the film *Les enfants* and is one of the few instances of a Duras film becoming a book. She had for a long time been incorporating foreign words into her language. In *Emily L.* there are scraps of English. In *Summer Rain*, we come across Spanish, Portuguese, invented words, fragments of foreign languages that give her French a new ring.

As in the film and children's story, the hero is called Ernesto. He's somewhere between twelve and twenty years old, and extremely intelligent. He's never learned anything and yet he knows everything there is to know about the world. He's directly connected to the origin of the world, to the whys and wherefores. He knows of the nonexistence of God. He philosophizes constantly. His family members understand him; everyone else is a long way behind. The action is set in Vitry, the suburb of Paris where the film was shot, an ocean of concrete with many empty houses, an abandoned motorway, a curve of the Seine, shacks where the homeless sleep, a local library barred to unruly children and almost certainly to Ernesto's parents – long-term unemployed, nothing in the eyes of the world. As usual, Duras disrupts the main story so that she can introduce the theme of incest and a dialogue with God.

Summer Rain is an echo chamber in which Duras transcribed the voices that reached her, though she didn't necessarily understand what they were saying. When questioned about the contents of the book, she replied, 'But you know all that, it's stories about Ernesto ... I had nothing to do with it, he did it all, all of it ... He's very strong, is Ernesto. Very. So much so that he invented Duras and I got to keep the name.'[2] Duras parodied herself, acted the clown, said anything that came into her mind.

The book had a mixed reception. She told an interviewer that while she was in a coma she had kept her biological link with writing and that ever since she'd been trying to make her life 'logical'. Every night she tried to go to bed at five in the morning and to get up two hours later to write. She was getting herself into condition 'so that she could rediscover the state of entry into that crowded place'.

Duras went out at night with Yann driving through the suburbs. They took roads that led nowhere, stopped off in refreshment areas, came home at dawn and shut themselves up. Duras would see no one except her son and his girlfriend, would see nothing – not a single art gallery, not one museum in six months. She returned to her self-absorbed state. Still Duras talked about everything and found what she said brilliant. She was an expert on China, Romania, the Berlin Wall; she had an opinion on everything because she watched television. She never saw anyone, but she communicated through the intermediary of the newspapers – they had all given her a column. She kept the crowds entertained, wrote about the new microwave she'd bought, her car, the Saint-Laurent jackets for Yann; in an interview with Mitterrand she confused an aircraft carrier with a submarine.[3] She did sometimes hit the target. Five years before mad cows came on the scene, she announced, 'We in Europe eat sick, disabled, decalcified animals, walking mush with no muscle that stumble with each step.'[4] 'Life these days I feel is not compatible with God. There is nothing sacred about him any more.'[5]

From time to time, journalists would tell her she was narcissistic, but Duras had an answer for everything. 'There's some truth in it, I suppose. But there's no one more courageous than a writer ... Do you think it's because I'm narcissistic that my books have sold all over the world? My books sell because I say my books sell all over the world. So, where's the problem? You'll just have to put up with me the way I am.'[6] Some still idolized her, while others who had once had nothing but praise for her were growing tired of her facetious remarks. Some loved her so much that they wanted to touch her. Marguerite saw herself as a kind of living idol. She described how one election night, a bloke had come and wanked against her ... 'The President of the Republic,' she added, 'finds me irresistible.'[7]

Robert Antelme died during the night of 25–26 October. Marguerite didn't go and see his wife and didn't go to the funeral.

Duras was bored. She talked too much to be able to write. She couldn't see well enough to sew pyjamas and make lamps, and her legs could no longer take her shopping, though she did the odd spot of cooking. She saw very few people – you had to insist – but when she did invite you round, out would come the macramé cloth and, in breakfast bowls, she would serve up her most excellent leek soup, the best in Europe, she said, if not the best in the world. And here – a true piece of literature – is her recipe:

> People think they know how to make it, it looks so simple, and is all too often neglected. It should be cooked for between fifteen to twenty minutes and not for two hours – all French women overcook their vegetables and soups. Moreover it is better to add the leeks once the potatoes are boiling; the soup will be greener and much tastier. Also it is crucial to weigh out the leeks carefully, two medium leeks to one kilo of potatoes should suffice. This soup is never good in restaurants. It is always overcooked (reheated), too 'long', it is sad and dreary, and belongs under the – much needed – collective name of 'vegetable soups' used in provincial French restaurants. No, you have to want to make it, to make it carefully, and to avoid 'leaving it on the stove' otherwise it will lose its identity. You can serve it as it is, or with a knob of fresh butter or fresh cream. You can also add some croutons just before serving, but in that case you will have to call it by another name, make one up, that way children will be more willing to eat it than if you saddle it with the name of leek and potato soup. It takes time, sometimes years, to rediscover the flavour of this soup, forced upon children on the pretext that the soup will make them grow, make them good, and so on and so forth. There is nothing in French cuisine that compares with the simplicity, the necessity for leek soup. It must have been invented (but did she know it?) on a winter's evening in the West, by a local young middle-class woman, who, that evening, had a loathing for greasy sauces – and probably more besides. The body gleefully swallows this soup. No, there

374

is no doubt about it, it isn't cabbage and bacon soup, nourishing or warming soup, no, it's a refreshing low-fat soup, the body gulps it down, is cleaned out, flushed out, the finest greenery, the muscles soak it up. Its smell spreads fast and strong through a house, simple like the food of the poor, the work of women, the bringing in of the animals, the vomit of a newborn baby. You might not want to make anything, and then, yes, want to make that particular soup and between the two wants, there is always the same very narrow margin – suicide.[8]

Jean-Jacques Annaud's screen adaptation of *The Lover* would allow Duras to finish the project she had been working on for a few years, to return to her childhood, to the skies of Indo-China and to the hated-adored mother. The story had begun much earlier, in the spring of 1987 to be precise. Duras had called her friend and former film assistant Jacques Tronel, who was then working with Claude Berri, to ask for his advice. The Americans had offered her a pittance for the rights to *The Lover* – should she accept? That same day Jacques Tronel talked it over with Claude Berri, who suggested he buy the rights for his own production company. An early meeting was arranged. Duras and Berri fell into one another's arms. Duras was toying with the idea of making the film. Berri didn't object. Why not? Then Duras changed her mind, said she was old, too tired. So they discussed bringing in a director – Roman Polanski, Stephen Frears? Both declined. Michael Cimino accepted, signed, and then later pulled out.

In the meantime Duras was making progress and, on Claude Berri's advice, had produced a screenplay. Jacques Tronel suggested that Marguerite should read *The Lover* out loud in front of the camera. The recordings were made in a small studio belonging to the production company. Jacques Tronel asked her questions and then filmed. Claude Berri came along to encourage her. When they looked at the tapes they saw that right from the start Duras was finding it difficult to read *The Lover* and stay calm. She admitted it herself: 'Every time I start to read *The Lover* it's as though the lights go down.' She burst into tears when the little brother died. The further she got with the reading, the more unworkable she felt the project was. 'Is the greatest enemy of the film not the novel?' she said to Berri. 'A film can be made, but not a commercial film, no, that's not possible.' And anyway,

375

should they only be telling the story of the lover or of the family as well? Berri let her talk. During the recordings Marguerite rewrote her life, rewrote the book, dreamed out loud. She recalled the sweetness of the coconut cakes the old ladies sold where the ferry arrived, the sweltering heat on the road to Saigon, the colour of the metal lamps in the yard of the boarding school where, at dusk, the half-caste girls danced.

Claude Berri suggested Marguerite should appear at the end of the film.

'I don't see the point,' she said.

'But it would authenticate it,' Berri explained.

'OK if I must,' said Marguerite.

When the recordings were done, she told them, 'I can't build a script. I can't do it the way you want me to.'

'So write the one you feel like doing. And then we'll see,' he told her.

Marguerite set to work. She did not want the film to be her story, rejected the chronology, objected to the erotic background and was thinking about a film on writing; because, for her, the story of *The Lover* was that of a child who discovers, thanks to the Chinese man, that she wants to be a writer. On 20 August 1987 she finished work on the first continuity script. Meanwhile Berri had contacted Jean-Jacques Annaud, who, having initially refused, now agreed to direct the film. He too began to work on adapting the book and doing the groundwork to the story of a young girl who, against the exoticism of a colonial backdrop, has her first emotional experiences in the arms of a young Chinese, to the great scandal of the colony. They were obviously not on the same wavelength and not preparing the same film.

Then Marguerite went into hospital. Annaud carried on. He had fallen in love with the project and with the story of the young girl. Claude Berri gave him the script Duras had been working on and persuaded the scriptwriter Gérard Brach to work with Annaud. Together they produced a script based on the novel and on Marguerite's script. Annaud went off to Vietnam on location. While Marguerite was in a coma, the project continued without her.

In the autumn of 1989, soon after her amazing recovery, Marguerite called Annaud. She wanted to see him. He arrived in Neauphle-le-

Château with hundreds of location shots taken in Sadec and Vinh Long. Marguerite's eyes sparkled as she looked at the photographs of landscapes from her childhood. Next day she phoned Claude Berri: 'He's a nice boy. And he speaks well of the film. You'd think it was his, the way he talks.'

The honeymoon period lasted another few weeks. In public Marguerite said that their collaboration was fertile. Slowly it dawned on Annaud that Marguerite wanted him to be the cameraman – *her* film was already written. 'So, you like my script?' she asked him.

'No,' he said, 'I prefer the novel, it's more inspiring.'

'And what did it inspire you to do?'

'To write a screenplay.'

'But it's my film and you're the one going to rake in the cash with my film.' Duras pretended to laugh it off.

Annaud continued to visit her in rue Saint-Benoît. He fed off her memories, took notes and, one day, handed her the script he had co-written with Brach. At page 10 she stopped: the Chinese man's car is crossing a boggy pothole. 'The pothole was never boggy, it was muddy.'

She read no further. Three hours of haggling over the pothole. Annaud told her it was an unimportant detail since they'd be shooting in the dry season.

'So, don't you check anything? If it's dusty, why let them write boggy?'

'And at that point we moved into phase two, that's when the insults started,' Annaud explained. 'She felt she'd been dispossessed. I knew her secret and she held it against me. The chaos in which she worked was getting worse. One day she said to me: "See those flowers in the dining room? Know who sent them? Adjani. She'll take the role and so will Suzanne Flon." '9

Annaud went to see Claude Berri. 'Marguerite was obviously not falling for Annaud's charm,' he admits. 'We'd signed. I had the film rights but there was the question of moral rights. She could have turned against the film. I waited for her to give her consent.'10

The negotiations were long, complicated and punctuated by several temporary peace treaties arranged between Trouville and Quillebeuf. Gérard Depardieu and Thierry Lévy demonstrated that they were both skilful and tactful. From the wings Yann Andréa supported the peace process, concluded only after it had been agreed to make Marguerite a cash payment. She was given 500,000 francs in case of default on the rights, and a further 500,000 in case of default on the script, plus 10 per cent of profits, not forgetting the money for the initial purchase of the rights to *The Lover*, which came to 1.5 million francs. Financially it was an extremely good deal. In exchange Marguerite agreed to acknowledge that her adaptation did not correspond 'to the conception of a film based on *The Lover*'. She signed the following: 'I have stopped all writing work and will not stand in the way of the production.'

And so Marguerite Duras began to detest her book. She was angry with herself for having agreed to write the last page which mentioned the phone call from the lover. She regretted having dressed up the truth. The adaptation that was being prepared for the 'multimillion-dollar cinema' distanced her from the book. Before falling out with Annaud, she told him, '*The Lover* is a load of shit. It's an airport novel. I wrote it when I was drunk.'

Another book was already brewing that would undermine the first. She wanted to return to the myth of the lover. She would rewrite this new novel four times. Before being published as *The North China Lover*, it had several different titles: *Love in the Street*, *The Scent of Honey and Tea*, *The Lover's Cinema*, *The Lover's Story*, *The Lover Rewritten*. Although when the book came out Marguerite Duras denied it, it began as a reworking of the film script. The condition of the various manuscripts shows this. We can see where Marguerite cut, crossed out, added, stuck bits of paper on to the actual script, thereby gradually transforming the script into a novel. In May 1990, when the book was finally finished and put together, Marguerite received a telephone call informing her that the lover had been dead for some years.

Duras spent a year writing the novel, cocooned in the love story between the Chinese man and the child. She rediscovered the light of her childhood, the gentleness of her little brother, the smell of the earth of Indo-China after the rain, the cruelty of the mother, her pathetic madness and her body against her own small body in the night surrounded by the beating of wading birds' wings and the rank smell of wild animals. She kept her promise to open the door, to return to her childhood, to be at peace with herself, and, with the passage of time, to lay down her arms and give her life to her love, her torment, her certainty, her wonderful misfortune – her mother, Marie Donnadieu.

Duras returned to her original idea for the film script, using the matrix of *The Lover*, with long tracking shots of frozen images, of scenes that had marked the little Donnadieu girl for ever. Duras created a series of separate scenes; it was up to the reader to link them. 'As my books are known worldwide, I shall only leave M.D.'s *mise-en-scène* and not the bulk of the family problem,' she wrote in the margin of the last chapter of the manuscript. The gold lamé shoes became black, the dance club was called the Cascade and no longer the Source. It was the same but very different, an adolescence rewritten for CinemaScope. Duras was making her film through the visual writing, the numerous dialogues and stage directions. Wanting us to believe she was talking about a real lover, Marguerite invented one who was tall and handsome. On the other hand she left in the mother's madness and her willingness to sell her daughter for a fee, the beatings from the brother, the beatings from the mother, and the girl's vocation to be a writer born while the affair was going on.

> They cry.
> 'And one day we'll die.'
> 'Yes. Our love will be in the casket with our bodies.'
> 'Yes. The books, they'll be outside the casket.'
> 'Maybe. We can't know that yet.'
> The Chinese says:
> 'Yes, we know it. That there will be books, that we know.'

With the desire to write came the desire to die. Writing distanced her sadness. Thereafter the young Marguerite Donnadieu saw her life as outside herself. 'I think my life has begun to reveal itself to me,' Marguerite wrote in the margin of *The North China Lover* manuscript. With that, she separated herself for ever from her story. Through her writing she became unreachable.

It was a heavily crossed-out and corrected manuscript that left Trouville for Jérôme Lindon in the autumn of 1990. She heard nothing from him for two months. When she enquired, Lindon told her he was working on her script and that he would return it to her.[11] And so he did. A year and a half before her death, Marguerite Duras still wept whenever she told the story of the manuscript of *The North China Lover*, sobbing, 'Do you realize he had cut, rewritten, crossed out in red as though it were a piece of class work?'[12] Jérôme Lindon never denied that he was disappointed with the manuscript and that he'd made corrections. 'It wasn't up to scratch at all but she wouldn't accept it. The fact is, she wasn't sure. She needed reassuring. Maybe I was wrong to tell her so. But the desire for truth was part of the respect and admiration I had for her, for her and her work.'[13] At first, though Marguerite Duras was badly affected by Lindon's reactions, she thought he might be right and that the manuscript needed reworking. But then came her anger, indignation and finally hatred. She telephoned him to inform him it was over between them for ever and that she had decided to put the pages he'd taken out back in. 'He said: All you have to do is put them back. I said no. It was the end, for good. He wrote again and again. But to no avail.'[14] It was an annotated contract that was returned to Jérôme Lindon – she considered that her text had been 'completely mutilated' and that the editor had set out to 'spirit her manuscript away'. The text had in effect been reduced from 213 to 154 pages. 'There are huge numbers of changes and sentences or words deleted on almost every page. *The book you returned to me is not the one you received from me.*' She warned him she was off to see 'her friend Robert' at Gallimard, where they would help her 'legally escape from you'.

From that day on Marguerite felt only bitter hatred verging on paranoia for Jérôme Lindon. She accused him of all manner of evils: of tampering with her title, of wanting to rob her, of having been shocked by her erotic manuscripts, of being a castrator of texts ... She immediately signed a contract with Gallimard.

Before the final falling-out there had been numerous minor skirmishes, not over her own manuscripts but over the actual notion of editing. Duras had criticized her editor for not taking enough risks, and for only liking well-written and grammatically correct literature.[15] She also found it intolerable that whenever Yann dropped off a new manuscript, Jérôme Lindon would rush it straight to the printers without another word. This overly swift transformation from manuscript to book-on-bookshop-shelf made her feel dispossessed.

For despite the fame, the Goncourt prize, the millions of copies sold, Marguerite remained the eternal worrier, the anxious little girl who both feared and wanted, each time she handed over a finished manuscript, approval and gratitude. Critics soon learned to expect, on being sent her latest book, an apprehensive late-night call from Marguerite asking, 'What did you think of it?' Overblown pride, extreme narcissism, studied performance? All of these, but also with each book the excruciating certainty of always being outside a closed door. 'I think I have given literature an author named Duras,' she wrote in an exercise book. The comment was for her, to reassure her, to convince her that she was indeed the one people believed. In the hall of her apartment she pinned up a double-page spread from *Le Monde* that featured a graph showing the sales figures for *The Lover*. Next to it she put a photograph of penguins on ice floes with the handwritten caption: 'The readers of *The Lover*'.

In December 1990, Jérôme Lindon requested 6 per cent of the author's royalties plus half of Gallimard's editor's share of the royalties for *The North China Lover*. He declared that his work on the manuscript had not 'gone unheeded'. However, his request that Gallimard return the manuscript was unsuccessful. An amicable agreement was reached in April.

The book was well received. Duras would say that it was one of her most important books along with *Lol V. Stein* and *The Vice-Consul*. To the almost instant accusations of a pastiche or a remake, she retorted:

I have not rewritten *The Lover*, I have written another book. The narrative does not have the same epistolary form. In *The North China Lover*, the memory of the lover has vanished. He's been replaced by the new lover, also from Manchuria, with the same name and the same homeland. When it comes to love stories I go looking for lovers in Manchuria. And in the bachelor flats of Cholon or in Vitry on the hillsides that slope down to the Seine.[16]

Now she felt she'd finished with the story of the lover. 'I think it's the last time I'll be writing about this story. But there are times when I don't know.[17]

At the end of the book, there are three pages of suggested images –

insert shots, Duras called them – which could one day be used to punctuate a film based on *The North China Lover*, hers, not the one that was due out in a few months, Jean-Jacques Annaud's *The Lover*. She felt she knew in advance what that would be like. Annaud had gone to Vietnam to shoot reconstructed scenes, whereas all she had to do to recall her native land was find a loop of the Seine. Before the film's release she'd seen photographs in magazines of the actress they had chosen and felt she was far too pretty for the part. In a note added to *The North China Lover*, she wrote, 'Some Junior Miss France would bring the whole film down. Worse: it would make it disappear. Beauty doesn't act. It doesn't look. It is looked at.'

With a budget of 150 million francs, *The Lover* had taken seven months to make. It was a success in France and abroad. In Vietnam it was considered a masterpiece. Its so-called erotic scenes were censored, but pirated videocassette versions of the original were available. Duras claimed she never saw the film. But one evening in the Le Duc restaurant, where Claude Berri had given her open house, Marguerite bumped into Annaud. She went over to him, kissed him and whispered in his ear, 'I went to see your film. It's wonderful.'[18]

At the theatre, a play based on her interviews with Mitterrand, entitled *Marguerite and the President*, was a big hit.[19] But she found the cinema more attractive. 'In literature, I have no family, in the cinema I do.' Thrilled with a retrospective of her films organized in November 1992 at the French Film Theatre, she went to all the showings, delighted to see certain films again that she thought had been lost for ever. The cinema was packed. 'You see, it's the young who love me,' she said to the organizer. She made friends with the spectators and held impromptu debates. She confessed to no longer liking her film *Les enfants* very much, judging the form to be too timid, but had a particularly soft spot for *Whole Days in the Trees* and of course for *India Song*.

Duras had new projects she was working on. She wanted to shoot two of the short stories in *La Douleur* – 'Aurélia Paris' and 'The Crushed Nettle'. She wrote a commentary for a short called *Le dernier client de l'hôtel* – a conversation at night between lovers in the gardens of Chambord. She wanted to make a ten- to thirty-minute film on

Lol V. Stein – with Lol very old, caked in make-up to look like a whore, carried through the streets of Trouville in a sedan chair by young Chinese men. She felt like making accidental, light and spontaneous films. She wanted to work like a guerrilla, and dreamed of roaming the streets of Paris by night doing impromptu shoots with a crew reduced to a minimum. She wanted to do only spontaneous filming. In *Green Eyes*, she wrote, 'We are always looking for places to film and there are so many places just looking for a camera.' The film she wanted to start work on there and then was one based on *L'été 80*. She had already chosen a title, *Le jeune fille et l'enfant*. Set in a holiday camp, it was to be the story of a 'different' child and a camp counsellor. She wrote: 'It will be very gruelling, very dangerous.'[20]

But she would never make any more films. From out of the project, however, was born the book *Yann Andréa Steiner*. It returns to *L'été 80* – to Trouville, to the sky, the grey-eyed child, the counsellor, the story of the shark – and incorporates her meeting with Yann Andréa, to which she adds the story of Theodora, which she had made up for Yann, basing it on a drawing discovered in Auschwitz, made by a deportee. Georges-Arthur Goldschmitt had brought her the drawing after he read *L'été 80*. It shows a tree, a bench and on the bench a young woman in a white dress waiting for the train the Germans had promised would come. She's been waiting for a long time.

'Now,' says Duras, 'I'm going from me to me. That's narcissism.' She went from Yann to her, from her to Yann, from the beach in front of her to the skies she never grew tired of describing. Out came the same old obsessions – love, literature, the pain of the Holocaust that never fades, the charm of childhood, the terror and joy of incest. 'The girl said people were always writing books on the end of the world and the death of love. But she saw that the boy didn't understand. And this made them both laugh, made them both roar with laughter. He said it wasn't true – people write books on paper.' 'When Duras is in front of paper she likes solitude, love, death, mediocrity as well as power in the hands of the mediocrity,' wrote Jacques-Pierre Amette.[21]

Marguerite Duras loved herself. She loved what she wrote. She loved Yann through what she wrote about him. She gave him the name Steiner from a character in one of her plays, *Un homme est venu me voir.* All Yann had to remind him that he had had a life before Marguerite was his first name. Marguerite had vampirized him and Judaized him. She had exposed his life, his sexuality, recounted his conversations, his fantasies, his cruisings, his fear; written about what he liked to eat, to drink, how and at what time he liked to go to sleep. She had drained him. And now she was putting him on show. When the book came out, they had their photographs taken together – Yann and Marguerite in a street in Trouville; Marguerite and Yann in a self-service restaurant on the motorway, her usual stop between Trouville and Paris; Yann in Neauphle behind the window watching Marguerite in the garden; Marguerite and Yann side by side gazing at the sea. Marguerite declared to *France-Soir,* 'My passion for Yann is reborn every day.' 'When I see him walk through the apartment in the morning for his black coffee, I get the feeling of never really having seen him before,' Marguerite explained. 'Old and alone she was before she met him,' she wrote in the book. What did he want? Why did he stay? There's horror in Duras's love, terror, the desire maybe to be killed by him before dying of natural causes; a fictional death, death by a destructive passion that would halt time, a death like those at the opera. 'All my women friends and acquaintances were charmed by how gentle you are. You were my best visiting card. But your gentleness made *me* think of the death you must unknowingly dream of inflicting on me.'[22]

In *Under the Volcano* Malcolm Lowry said that the hardest thing for a writer, because he had so little time, was to live long enough to finish his work. Duras had run out of time. She knew it, and wrote in a notebook, 'There are times when you're frightened of dying before getting to the bottom of the page … you recognize the signs, you know how you want it to end but still have to get the text there. You must get there, complete the journey and sometimes it's … I think it's because of the nature of the activity that the thought of death is always there.'[23] She didn't care about dying; what really bothered her was that she'd have to stop writing. 'When you're not writing, you have to pass through a forest that never closes in around you, but because there it's *the forest that closes in,* you can't get out.'[24]

The forest was in effect closing in. Marguerite would write nothing more. Admittedly she would publish another three books, one of which, *Ecrire,* sounded like a legacy, although it was a collection of comments, conversations and film interpretations. Marguerite would never again have that close relationship with paper, the relief, the physical release, the feeling of shattering the mirror, as Thomas Mann put it. 'Living becomes the passion of dying,' she wrote on a torn-out sheet of paper.

Only death interested her, physical death, the memory of the dead. A walk among graves had inspired 'La mort du jeune aviateur anglais' (The Death of the Young English Airman). Was it purely fictional, a war story, a local village tale? Even Duras couldn't remember. Looking into the camera of Benoît Jacquot, who had come to visit her in Trouville, she made it up as she went along. Starting with a name on a gravestone in a Normandy village, she took the bones of a story about a twenty-year-old Englishman killed during the war by Germans in the forest of Vauville. 'La mort du jeune aviateur anglais' is a poem on the innocence of life, an ode to the brother who died. And it is above all a meditation on death. Marguerite always loved going to cemeteries – old cemeteries, of course, not the new ones, the kind she called supermarket cemeteries, which looked like golf courses and where the wreaths were made of plastic. She was deeply moved when she came upon the grave in a village cemetery. She was haunted by the memory of her dead brother. She imagined his body being tossed into a communal grave and getting mixed up with all the other bodies. Knowing that she was going to die, maybe she felt guilty that she hadn't been to visit his grave in the Saigon cemetery nor that of her father buried in the land of his childhood. And so she said, 'Any death is death ... Anybody's death is death undiminished.' She talked to her friend Benoît Jacquot and his camera while Yann transcribed. Yann took charge of everything, and negotiated rights and titles with Gallimard. 'La mort du jeune aviateur anglais' is neither a book, nor a song, nor a poem, nor thoughts. It is perhaps a lament, an attempt to establish a dialogue with death. 'Never before had I been so deeply moved by the idea of death. So completely captured. Enthralled.'

Can writing keep death at bay? Marguerite didn't think so and pre-pared to welcome it peacefully. Writing can numb the idea of death, by preventing thoughts from straying too often in that direction. But she was lucid when she wrote, 'It's finished, the decisive period is over.'²⁵ Death was no stranger; she had kept a watchful eye on it when she was in a coma. She knew she hadn't shaken it off completely.

Marguerite was nondenominational. She didn't believe in God even though she had spent her life trying to communicate with him. 'God, which is to say nothing, God, a word I use for the sake of convenience.' But she believed in the earthly reality of Jesus Christ and Joan of Arc. 'I, who do not pray, say so. And there are evenings when I mourn the fact so as to get through the inescapable present.' And she did cry a lot. She never left her apartment in rue Saint-Benoît. She rarely slept, had stopped reading; she watched television, tidied and untidied her library, looked through family photos. 'I can say what I like, but I shall never know why people write and how it is people don't write. In life, there comes a time, and I think it is total, that we cannot escape, where we doubt everything: that doubt is writing.' Marguerite couldn't write. At the end of shooting *La mort du jeune aviateur anglais* in Paris,²⁶ Marguerite confided to Benoît Jacquot, 'I haven't told everything.' He suggested they do an immediate shoot in the Neauphle house. He could see she wanted to be looked after. In the film, Marguerite makes a touching figure and looks beautiful in the soft light chosen for the close-up shots of her face, lacerated by wrinkles, looking more Chinese than ever; her deep eyes are bright, the husky, panting voice comes from the depths: 'Everything wrote when I was in the house writing. Writing was everywhere. It is also possible not to write, to forget a fly. To only watch it. To see how it too struggles so desperately, recorded in an unknown sky and for nothing. Well, that's it.'

Marguerite seemed very preoccupied by a book Frédérique Lebelley had written about her, which was due to come out in 1994.²⁷ She showed me the manuscript and told me she thought it was bad. On the other hand she loved Christiane Blot-Labarrère's book about her. 'It's extraordinary to quite suddenly rediscover a sentence you are the author of. When she quotes from my work, the inking changes. When Christiane Blot-Labarrère says the sentence, she is teaching it me, offering it me. I'd forgotten it.'

Read and reread the texts again, she said to me. Give them to be read. Offer the reader his own reading. Try to talk about writing. At the time she talked to me a lot about the death of the fly she was happy to have captured on paper. But she always came back to her mother – 'I'm left with my mother, why hide it from myself?' – and all the time showed photographs, returned to her childhood.[28] Yann was there in the apartment, but he'd go off to his room and leave us alone. She often had need of him for a date or some other detail, to jog her memory. She would tire quickly, hold me back, laugh, kiss me like a child. Marguerite's an ingénue, said one of her friends.

What I remember most about her, apart from her writing – the only proof she ever existed – was the gentleness of her presence, the way she had of taking me in her arms, of saying, as I left, 'Take care of yourself.'

Dionys visited from time to time; Outa regularly. Her friends Henri and Serge took her to Trouville. They were among the last to be allowed to see her. She cut herself off from the world, didn't answer the telephone; Yann screened her calls and gradually stopped the visits even from the oldest friends. He'd laugh and chat but he wouldn't pass you over to her. Was Marguerite still there? What was it he was protecting? Her, or her myth? Marguerite wasn't a prisoner. She waited calmly for death. Yann became the guardian and, in the eyes of some of her friends, the gaoler of the wait. No one could talk to her apart from Yann, Dionys and the two nurses who took turns at her bedside. Yann would go out only if he had a mobile phone with him and would call the nurses every fifteen minutes. He never went beyond rue Saint-Benoît.

Outa managed to get his father and mother in the Neauphle house so that he could photograph them together. The portraits he took of his mother are so beautiful and sad they make you want to cry. The last time Dionys went round to rue Saint-Benoît, a month before she died, she opened the door, looked at him for a long time, then took him in her arms and said, 'You and I were very much in love.' It was Dionys whom Yann would summon to close her eyes.

Marguerite didn't want to die. Yann had had to call the emergency services out on more than one occasion, but each time she came back to life. She hung on. Yann said she talked all the time and if you listened carefully there were moments when she was lucid. And some of the things he felt were so important that he decided to record them there in front of her. She joined in the game. And thus was born her last book, *No More*, which caused quite a stir when it was published.

The book was begun on 20 November 1994 and ended (in its non-expurgated Italian version) at 13.00 hours on 28 February 1995.[29]

In this last monologue, Duras speaks only of death, of her imminent death, of which she is not frightened, for after death there is nothing. 'The living must smile who support each other.' She returns to her childhood, the sweetness of her native land, her lifelong unhappy love for her mother.

'It would appear I have genius. I'm used to it now.' She does battle for the last time; she doesn't want 'to throw herself' into death but to control the moment. She gets ready to go – eyes wide open to go nowhere.

For Yann the last words:

I love you.
Goodbye.

NOTES

~

PREFACE

1. Interview between Marguerite Duras and Suzanne Koapit, *Réalités*, March 1963.
2. Frédérique Lebelley, *Le poids d'une plume*, Grasset, 1994.
3. *The Lover*, translated into English by Barbara Bray, Flamingo, 1986, p. 23.
4. Ibid., p. 11.

CHAPTER 1 A Child of Indo-China

1. Marguerite Duras and Michelle Porte, *Les lieux de Marguerite Duras*, Minuit, 1978, p. 52.
2. In 1887 the Union of Indo-China was created. It consisted of Cambodia, Laos, Annam, Cochin-China and Tonkin; the last three territories formed French Indo-China. An alliance between republican opportunists and certain sectors of the business community soon made of Indo-China a colony to be exploited. The slogan was: 'Today, to civilize people means to teach them to work so that they can earn and spend money' (quotation from the president of the Lyon Chamber of Commerce in 1901). Cochin-China was given special treatment: in 1899 a governor general was appointed, seconded by a lieutenant-general. A half-French, half-Annamese committee was set up to help him administer the colony.
3. Miguel Angel Sevilla, 'Duras et le nom des autres,' *Critique*, p. 22.
4. *The Lover*, p. 22.
5. Emile Bonhoure, *L'Indochine*, Editions géographiques, maritimes et coloniales, 1900.
6. C. Mayer, *Des Français en Indochine 1860–1910*, Hachette, 1985.
7. In a 1902 guidebook specifically targeted at those planning to go to the colonies, Louis Saloun rather sententiously pointed out that the French in Indo-China should only take up positions of a particular rank.

'It is not recommended that a minor employee be exported to a country where his poverty would be made worse than in France by a climate that demands considerable creature comforts and a particular quality of life. All things considered, the only menial tasks he could do are carried out just as well, if not better, and certainly more economically, by the native whose everyday life is much improved by the meagre pay he receives, and who is, moreover, quite used to the environment, and, furthermore, docile and devoted.'
(*Indochine*, ed. Saloun.)

8. Ibid.
9. Pierre Brocheux and Daniel Hémery, *Indochine. La colonisation ambiguë (1858–1954)*, La Découverte, 1994.
10. Denise Bouché, *Histoire de la colonisation française*, Fayard, 1991. See also Pierre Bezançon's *Education, colonisation et développement en Indochine: l'adaptation de l'enseignement primaire (1860–1949)*, DEA Université de Paris, 1992–93.
11. From Napoleon III via Jules Ferry, political power in France had always stressed the country's civilizing mission in order to justify expanding in that part of the world. The Tonkin campaign so impassioned the deputies that two camps emerged. The one on the right, led by the Duke of Broglie, attacked the very notion of colonization, rebelled against these far-off expeditions that weakened the French nation and saw the whole principle of colonial expansion as a threat to the stability of France. The left, under the leadership of Jules Ferry, argued in support of the Tonkin expedition in the name of the ideals of the French Revolution, the vitality of the people and economic interests. 'It would be abhorrent, anti-French, to prohibit France from having a colonial policy,' Jules Ferry explained to a stormy chamber. We know what ensued. France did not abandon Indo-China. See G. Hanotaux and A. Martineau, *Histoire des colonies françaises* (especially volume V), and Edmond Chassigneux, *L'Indochine*.
12. 'Les yeux verts', *Les Cahiers du cinéma*, No. 312, June 1980, extended reprint, edited by Serge Darney, *Les Cahiers du cinéma*, 1987, p. 244.
13. *Un barrage contre le Pacifique*, Gallimard, 1950, Biblos reprint, 1990, p. 162.
14. Overseas administrators were bemoaning the lack of publicity on life in the colonies and had suggested to the minister to replace the academic reports, full of facts and figures, which put off the general public, with more attractive leaflets. The poster of a colonial couple dressed in white, rocking sensuously in their rocking chairs in the shade of a banana tree, used by Marguerite Duras to explain her parents' departure for the colony, therefore came later.
15. Pierre Loti (Louis-Marie-Julien Viaud, 1850–1923) drew on his travels as a naval officer to write romances in exotic settings, including the Far East.
16. *Un barrage contre le Pacifique*, pp. 162–3.
17. Stanley Karnov, *Vietnam*, Presses de la Cité, 1983. The cost of acquiring Vietnam was considerable. In 1895, Cochin-China, Annam and Tonkin left huge holes in the colonial budget. Appointed governor general in 1897, Paul Doumer consolidated the administration, centralized power, immediately dissolved the last vestige of Vietnamese sovereignty (the Mandarin cabinet) and developed the country's economy for the sole benefit of France. This he did by breaking up the traditional rural society with a brutal agrarian policy that dispossessed the peasants of the land they had cultivated. Doumer later wrote in his memoirs: 'When France set foot in Indo-China, the Annamese were ripe for subjugation.' Although Doumer was the author of an extraordinary report on education, he was nevertheless responsible for setting up an economic model in Indo-China that would prevail until 1954. Without causing a stir, he transformed Indo-China – on the backs of the Vietnamese – into a country that was economically viable and reduced the anticolonial drift to a handful of eccentric intellectuals. When Doumer was elected president of the Republic in 1931, he was replaced by liberals who, more

NOTES

concerned with the country's culture and identity, found it difficult to handle the financial groups that were blithely and with complete impunity pillaging Indo-China. See also Marc Meuleau, *Histoire de la banque d'Indochine (1875–1975)*, DEA d'histoire, 1994, and P. Morlat, *La répression coloniale au Vietnam (1908-1940)*, L'Harmattan, 1990.

18. Monograph, *La femme de Cochinchine*, Saigon, 1882.

19. A. Maybon, *L'Indochine*, 1934.

20. 'For those seeking the spirit of the colonizer the education issue is probably the more important as well as the most complex, for it probably involves most of the others,' declared in 1931 Albert Sarraut, former governor general of Indo-China, former minister of the interior and future president of the Council. As Denise Bouché stresses, the government took control of education the moment colonization began.

21. A school was built in every village, although it was often no more than a simple hut that gave on to the street. From early childhood, pupils were taught formal and moral rules. From the village school with its one teacher to the imperial college, the mind learned to be embodied in words. Moral integrity and filial piety were held up as cardinal virtues. The Vietnamese teacher was also a teacher of life, taught the art of calligraphy as well as music, poetry as well as geography. The rhythms of traditional education were maintained and corporal punishment non-existent. The masters were treated, esteemed, and responded like older brothers, their role being to guide rather than impose. At the beginning of colonization, the French left education as such in the hands of these traditional schools and of the Catholic missions. In 1906 they attempted to update the system by establishing a so-called 'Franco-native' system. Compared with the extremely effective, popular and well-established Confucian school the first mechanical and vicious drive at frenchification was a catastrophe. At the time, an overwhelming number of Vietnamese were familiar with the Chinese characters used to write Vietnamese. In an attempt to destroy cultural unity, the French banned the use of Chinese characters in schools and had them replaced with French and Quac-ngu, a kind of Romanized alphabet. The general government of Indo-China soon realized that the policy had been a disaster and some officials even openly admitted it had been a mistake. 'Today, it is difficult to see what principle, what mystical conception of Western civilization, drove a Republic, which had secularized state teaching back home, to endeavour to destroy the so-called idols of Indo-China and make a clean slate of the moral doctrines being taught, only to replace them with goodness knows what philosophical orthodoxy, introduced moreover with the same intolerance as religious orthodoxy.' See Louis Saloun, *L'Indochine*, op. cit.

22. As Trinh Van Thao explains so well in his book *L'école française en Indochine*, Karthala, 1995. See also Nguyen Van Ky's *Les Vietnamiens et l'enseignement franco-indigène*, DEA thesis, Inalco, 1983.

23. *The North China Lover*, English version translated by Leigh Hafrey, Flamingo, 1994, p. 32.

24. *La vie matérielle*, P.O.L., 1987, Folio reprint, 1994, p. 62.

25. She wrote in one of her wartime notebooks. IMEC archives.

26. *The Lover*, p. 17.

391

27. *La vie matérielle*, p. 32.
28. See Elisabeth Laffus, 'Mémoire quand tu nous mens,' *Pour la science*, Duche, 1998.
29. *La vie matérielle*, p. 32.
30. Ibid.
31. *The Lover*, p. 35.
32. Even though Marguerite gave her biographers' imagination free rein, it is highly unlikely the mother had a Chinese lover, given her lifestyle and the moral values of the time. However, several of Marguerite's friends who, like her, lived for a long time in Indo-China, are living proof – as are their faces even today – of the physical and sensual influence the country had on their bodies. As for Angelo Morino's *Le Chinois et Marguerite* (Editions Sellezio, Palermo, 1997), the book is a brilliant psychoanalysis and not a biography based on documentary evidence.
33. Told to François Peraldi and quoted by Christine Blot-Labarrère, *Marguerite Duras*, Les contemporains, Seuil, 1992, p. 42.
34. *Le monde extérieur*, P.O.L., 1993, and conversations with the author, 3 March 1990.
35. *The Lover*, p. 50.
36. Author's interview with Marguerite Duras, 18 January 1996.
37. *La vie matérielle*, p. 30.

CHAPTER 2 The Mother

1. At that time no more than 8 per cent of schoolchildren were girls.
2. *The Lover*, p. 89.
3. *Nuit noire Calcutta*, unpublished notes. IMEC archives.
4. *Le Monde*, 29 July 1974.
5. *The North China Lover*, p. 18.
6. *Eden Cinema*, in Marguerite Duras, *Four Plays*, translated by Barbara Bray, p. 76.
7. The right to tender for and own a concession was only granted to registered companies and French nationals approved by the authorities who would decide on the conditions under which the transfer could be made. See A. Maybon, *L'Indochine*, op. cit.
8. National overseas archives, Aix-en-Provence.
9. *The Lover*, pp. 80–81.
10. Ibid., p. 10.
11. *Les lieux de Marguerite Duras*, p. 59.
12. Ibid., p. 56.
13. *Un barrage contre le Pacifique*, p. 234.
14. Unpublished manuscript, IMEC archives.
15. IMEC archives.
16. IMEC archives.
17. IMEC archives.
18. Unpublished manuscript, IMEC archives.

CHAPTER 3 The Lover

1. Unpublished manuscript, notebook containing passages from *The Lover*, *The Sea Wall*, 'Boa'. IMEC archives.
2. 'Boa' in *Whole Days in the Trees*, Gallimard, 1954, reprint Biblos, p. 996.
3. Manuscript of *The Lover*, IMEC archives.
4. *The North China Lover*, p. 50.
5. Author's interview with Denise Augé, 18 March 1995.
6. *The North China Lover*, p. 38.
7. *Un barrage contre le Pacifique*, p. 178.
8. See *Un barrage contre le Pacifique*, where she is only interested in Mr Jo because of his diamond ring, p. 178.
9. IMEC archives.
10. *The Lover*, p. 14.
11. *The North China Lover*, p. 29.
12. IMEC archives.
13. IMEC archives.
14. IMEC archives.
15. IMEC archives.
16. Delly: pen name of Jeanne-Marie and Frédéric Petitjean de La Rosière, who wrote numerous popular romances; *Magali* was published in 1910.
17. IMEC archives.
18. IMEC archives.
19. IMEC archives.
20. IMEC archives.
21. IMEC archives.
22. IMEC archives.
23. Interview with Luce Perrot, IMEC archives.
24. For more on this subject, read *La montée des nationalismes* by Denise Bouché. In 1929–30 the signs of unrest were obvious. On 1 May 1930, the Vietnamese Communist Party organized strikes, marches and the storming of the administrative buildings. In 1931, the administration regained control of the situation and terrible repressive measures were brought in. When the colonial minister Paul Reynaud visited Indo-China, Phom Quynh upheld Vietnamese patriotism on behalf of his people: 'We are a people in search of a homeland and who have not yet found one. This homeland, Minister, will never be France.' Werth's book caused a scandal. The author was accused of being in the pay of the Bolsheviks and even of the intelligence service. Werth's reaction had been that of a politically committed witness to a cruel, perverse and autocratic colonial regime.
25. In this passionate and lyrical text, Malraux attacked the games played by colonial companies and the authorities, and condemned the lack of state laws. Indo-China was far away so people could not hear the screams. The adventurer first visited Indo-China in 1923, having gone there to extricate a few statues. He found the settlers to be violent and their officials corrupt. In 1925 he launched *L'Indochine*, a daily paper, demanding equality. The pressures were many and various, the intimidation constant. There was a general outcry from the colony's elite and the

newspaper was shut down. Malraux continued his struggle in France.
The journalist Andrée Viollis, arriving in Indo-China in 1931, noted that the situation had worsened. The colonial authorities, faced with secret societies and associations of Marxist Annamese students demanding autonomy, responded by increasing repression in rural areas and by imprisoning huge numbers of student protesters in the towns.

26. IMEC archives.
27. Undated interview, IMEC archives.

CHAPTER 4 Rue Saint-Benoît

1. Author's interview with Dionys Mascolo, 4 June 1996.
2. Undated notebooks, IMEC archives.
3. Author's interview with France Brunel, 5 September 1996.
4. Author's interview with France Brunel, 11 July 1996.
5. Extract from transcript of undated radio interview, IMEC archives.
6. Film by Jean Mascolo and Jean-Marc Turine, *Le groupe de la rue Saint-Benoît*. Available from the Paris video library.
7. Author's interview with Georges Beauchamp, 23 April 1996.
8. Author's interview with Edgar Morin, 18 September 1995.
9. Author's interview with Henri Thano, 30 December 1997.
10. As Herbert Lottman explains in *La rive gauche, du Front populaire à la guerre froide*, Seuil, 1981.
11. Pierre Péan, *Une jeunesse française, François Mitterrand (1934–1947)*, Fayard, 1994, p. 61.
12. Author's interview with Jacques Benet, 15 April 1996.
13. Author's interview with François Mitterrand, 7 September 1995.
14. Michel Winock and Jacques Julliard, *Dictionnaire des intellectuels*, Seuil, 1996.
15. Robert Antelme's correspondence. France Brunel's personal archives.
16. *Libres*, 22 June 1945.
17. Author's interviews with Monique Antelme and Georges Beauchamp, March–April 1996.
18. H. Lottman, op. cit., chap. 'Plongeon dans la barbarie'.
19. Bertrand Favreau drew attention to this in his biography, *Georges Mandel ou la passion de la république*, Fayard, 1996. See also Nicolas Sarkozy, *Mandel*, Grasset, 1997.
20. Author's interview with Dionys Mascolo, February, March and April 1996.
21. France Brunel's personal archives.
22. In P. Péan, op. cit., chap. 'Le sergent Mitterrand au front'.
23. *Lettres au Castor et à quelques autres (1940–1963)*, Gallimard, 1983.
24. In B. Favreau, op. cit.
25. IMEC archives.
26. Pierre Assouline, *Gaston Gallimard. Un demi-siècle d'édition française*, Balland, 1984, reprint Points Seuil, 1996.

27. The government looked upon the empire as a human resource. Indifference to the empire seemed to have grown in the 1930s.
28. *L'Empire français.*
29. B. Favreau, op. cit.
30. Author's interview with Jacques Benet, March 1995.
31. Author's interview with Georges Beauchamp, September 1994.
32. From *The Lover*, unpublished IMEC archives.
33. To his son Dominique Fernandez on the publication of *Porfirio et Constance*, Grasset, 1991. (Dominique Fernandez exorcised the memory of his father with two novels, *L'école du Sud* and *Porfirio et Constance*.) 'Your father was discretion itself,' she told him.
34. 'Molière', *NRF*, 1929, and 'André Gide', *NRF*, 1931.
35. Author's interview with Marguerite Duras, April 1990.
36. IMEC archives.
37. P. Assouline, op. cit., p. 319.
38. Dominique Arban, *Je me retournerai souvent. Souvenirs*, Flammarion, 1990.
39. IMEC archives.
40. As Christine Blot-Labarrère points out in her book *Marguerite Duras*, Seuil, 1992.

CHAPTER 5 From Collaboration to Resistance

1. Quoted by P. Fouché, op. cit., t. II.
2. Author's interview with Claude Roy, 3 April 1996.
3. Author's interview with Dionys Mascolo, April 1995.
4. IMEC archives.
5. Marguerite Duras interviewed by Luce Perrot.
6. Author's interview with Dionys Mascolo, 24 March 1996.
7. Author's interview with Dionys Mascolo, 12 March 1996.
8. Author's interview with Dionys Mascolo, 7 May 1996.
9. *Les yeux verts*, p. 148. Editions Cahiers du cinéma, 1987.
10. Author's interview with Dionys Mascolo, 12 September 1996.
11. Author's interview with Jacques Benet, 5 October 1995.
12. Author's interview with Jacques Benet, November 1995.
13. Alain Peyrefitte, *C'était de Gaulle*, De Fallois/Fayard, 1997.
14. In P. Péan, op. cit., chap. 'Le girondisme'.
15. *L'Autre Journal*, 26 February–4 March 1986.
16. Author's interview with François Mitterrand, 8 September 1995.
17. Dionys Mascolo, archives.
18. Dionys Mascolo, archives.
19. Author's interview with Dionys Mascolo, 24 March 1996.
20. Author's interview with Dionys Mascolo, 17 April 1996.
21. Author's interview with Edgar Morin, 4 December 1995.
22. In P. Péan, op. cit., p. 251.
23. A. Peyrefitte, op. cit.
24. Dionys Mascolo, archives.

25. *L'Autre Journal*, 26 February–4 March 1986.
26. *La Douleur*, Flamingo, 1987, translated by Barbara Bray, p. 73.
27. Ibid., p. 74.
28. Ibid., p. 75.
29. In *La Douleur*, in the interview with François Mitterrand for *L'Autre Journal* and in conversation with the author.
30. Author's interview with Georges Beauchamp, 25 November 1996.
31. *La Douleur*, p. 99.
32. Author's interview with Jean Munier, September 1995.
33. *La Douleur*, pp. 90–91.
34. IMEC archives.
35. *La Douleur*, p. 100.
36. *L'Autre Journal*, 26 February–4 March 1986.
37. *La Douleur*, p. 111.
38. *L'Autre Journal*, 26 February–4 March 1986.
39. Author's interview with Nicole Courant, 4 October 1996.

CHAPTER 6 The Road to Liberation

1. A. Peyrefitte, op. cit., II. De Gaulle stated that, following a proposal by Henri Frenay, executive member of the Ministry for Prisoners, Deportees and Refugees, the provisional government agreed in May 1944 that Mitterand be appointed acting secretary general. He was twenty-seven.
2. *L'Homme libre*, 22 August 1944.
3. Author's interview with Georges Beauchamp, September 1995.
4. IMEC archives.
5. Author's interview with Bernard Guillochon, 26 December 1996.
6. Author's interview with Edgar Morin, 3 February 1995.
7. *L'Autre Journal*, 26 February–4 March 1986.
8. Author's interview with Paulette Delval, 13 December 1996.
9. Author's interview with François Mitterrand, March–April 1995.
10. P. Péan, op. cit., chap. 'Marguerite, Edgar, François et les autres'.
11. Author's interview with Paulette Delval, 2 February 1997.
12. Author's interview with François Mitterrand, March–April 1995.
13. Luce Perrot archives.
14. Author's interview with Paulette Delval, January 1996.
15. Delval case files, national archives.
16. Author's interview with Paulette Delval, 8 December 1996, and author's interview with Dionys Mascolo, 26 May 1996.
17. Author's interview with Paulette Delval, January 1996.
18. *La fin d'été* was a provisional title. She said it had taken her two years to write.
19. The idea was even mooted that Gaston Gallimard should retire. Was it Sartre's or Paulhan's influence, the committee's limited powers or the fact that virtually all publishing houses had collaborated? The fact remains that nothing happened. As Pierre Assouline pointed out, 'It's as though the mechanism were functioning in a

vacuum and the powers that be had come to agreement with editors that nothing should happen.'

20. The book was later revived and reprinted in 1972.
21. *Ecrire*, Gallimard, 1993, Folio, p. 36.
22. Editorial in *Libres*, 9 February 1945.
23. IMEC archives.
24. Edgar Morin, Suzie Rousset, Dionys Mascolo.
25. Author's interview with Dionys Mascolo, March–April 1996.
26. IMEC archives.
27. *La Douleur*, pp. 50–51.
28. Author's interview with M. Bugeaud and Jacques Benet, March–April 1995.
29. Author's interview with Georges Beauchamp, September 1995.
30. Author's interview with Dionys Mascolo, March–April 1995.
31. Dionys Mascolo, *Autour d'un effort de mémoire. Sur une lettre de Robert Antelme,* Maurice Nadeau, 1988, p. 56.
32. Author's interview with Dionys Mascolo, March–April 1996.
33. *La Douleur*, p. 56.
34. Author's italics.
35. Dionys Mascolo, archives.
36. *La Douleur*, p. 63.
37. Ibid., pp. 63–4.

CHAPTER 7 The Party

1. IMEC archives.
2. Author's interview with Dionys Mascolo, 4 May 1996.
3. Jean-Pierre Rioux, *La France de la IVe Républic, I, L'ardeur et la nécéssité (1944– 1952)*, Seuil, 1980.
4. Author's interview with Edgar Morin, 12 November 1995.
5. *Outside*, 'Le rêve heureux du crime,' p. 354.
6. Author's interview with Monique Antelme, 14 October 1995.
7. Dionys Mascolo archives.
8. Dionys Mascolo, *Autour d'un effort de mémoire,* op. cit.
9. Diary, Dionys Mascolo archives.
10. Author's interview with Dionys Mascolo, April 1996.
11. Author's interview with Jacques-Francis Rolland, 25 April 1996.
12. This was explained in the afterword to *L'Œillet rouge*, Gallimard, 1950.
13. Author's interview with Dionys Mascolo, 12 April 1996.
14. Claude Roy, *Nous*, Gallimard, 1972.
15. D. Desanti, *Ce que le siècle m'a dit*, Plon, 1997.
16. Author's interview with Edgar Morin, 4 May 1995.
17. IMEC archives.

CHAPTER 8 Motherhood

1. Author's interview with Monique Antelme, 4 October 1995.
2. IMEC archives.
3. Article reproduced in *Robert Antelme, textes inédits sur 'L'espèce humaine'*, op. cit.
4. Ibid.
5. *Jeunesse de l'Eglise*, No. 9, September 148, ibid.
6. Author's interviews with Pierre Daix, 3 March 1997, February 1997.
7. Dionys Mascolo archives.
8. Manuscript of *Les yeux verts*, IMEC archives.
9. Author's interview with Bernard Guillochon, 12 March 1997.
10. Author's interview with Jorge Semprun, 23 February 1998.
11. Author's interview with Jorge Semprun, 12 December 1996.
12. Author's interview with Pierre Daix, 12 December 1996.
13. *Autocritique*, op. cit.
14. IMEC archives.
15. To Benoît Jacquot in an unpublished interview, prologue to *Ecrire*, IMEC archives.
16. Author's interview with Marguerite Duras, 8 April 1994.
17. *Cahiers Renaud-Barrault*, December 1965.
18. Competing for the prize that year were Serge Groussard (*La femme sans passé*), Paul Colin (*Les jeux sauvages*), Michel Zenaffa (*Le salaire de la peur*), Gérard Bourtelleau (*Les ventriloques*) and Jean Hougron (*Tu récolteras la tempête*). Colin won.
19. *Le Nouvel Observateur*, 28 September 1984.
20. Quoted as an epigraph to Chapter 3 of Christine Blot-Labarrère's book, op. cit.
21. *Le Nouvel Observateur*, 28 September 1984.
22. Author's interview with Edgar Morin, 22 September 1996.

CHAPTER 9 How Can Anyone Not Write?

1. Simone de Beauvoir, *Lettres à Nelson Algren (1947–66)*, Gallimard, 1997.
2. Maurice Blanchot, *Le livre à venir*, Gallimard, 1959.
3. Author's interview with Marguerite Duras, 16 March 1994.
4. Interview reproduced in a boxed set by Radio France, edited by Jean-Marc Turine, *Le ravissement de la parole*, 1996.
5. IMEC archives.
6. *Le Figaro littéraire*, 29 November 1953.
7. Luc Estang, *La Croix*, 29 October 1953.
8. *Le Nouvel Observateur*, 14–20 June 1985.
9. Author's interview with Louis-René des Forêts, 18 February 1995.
10. Author's interview with Claude Roy, 3 October 1994.
11. IMEC archives.
12. *Dimanche*, 19 February 1956.
13. Letter from Marguerite Duras to Gaston Gallimard, 2 March 1954, Gallimard archives.
14. *Paris-Normandie*, 6 December 1956.

15. Jean-Jacques Gautier, *Le Figaro*, 3 May 1957.

CHAPTER 10 The Journalist

1. *La vie matérielle*, pp. 105–6.
2. *Les Parleuses*, p. 59.
3. *Le ravissement de la parole*, op. cit.
4. Author's interview with Pierre Assouline, *Lire*, No. 112, June 1985.
5. Author's interview with Alain Robbe-Grillet, 16 June 1996.
6. Author's interview with Alain Robbe-Grillet, 23 June 1996.
7. *Les Parleuses*.
8. Author's interview with Dionys Mascolo, 18 January 1996.
9. After 13 May 1958, in a footnote to an article on Proust in the reputedly Gaullist *NRF*, he insisted on expressing his political opposition: a coup d'etat is a nothingness to be opposed by our own nothingness. He had not taken a political stance for twenty years, since he was pro-fascist.
10. Preface to Dionys Mascolo's book *A la recherche d'un communisme de pensée*, Fourbis, 1993.
11. *France-Observateur*, 24 July 1958.
12. Colette Garrigues, interviewed by Outa and Jean-Marc Turine thirty years later, in the film *L'esprit d'insoumission*.
13. From the foreword to *Outside*. In 1980, on the suggestion of Jean-Luc Hennig, she collected together some of her articles, beginning with 'Les fleurs de l'Algérien', in her eyes one of the most important.
14. *Outside*, p. 8.
15. The British officer Peter Townsend had a romance with Princess Margaret in the 1950s.
16. In 1980 she stated in the preface to *Outside* that she always put herself in the accused's shoes so that she could denounce the inadmissibility of an injustice whatever it was, and whether suffered by a single individual or the whole nation.
17. *France-Observateur*, 8 May 1958.
18. Ibid.
19. *Arts*, 7 May 1958.
20. Jean Dufourd, *Combat*, 7 May 1958.
21. *L'Express*, 8 May 1958.
22. Author's interview with Alain Resnais, 6 December 1997.
23. Author's interview with Alain Resnais, 4 February 1996.
24. Preparation for the film, IMEC Archives.
25. *Image et son*, No. 128.
26. IMEC archives.
27. IMEC archives.
28. 'These nocturnal evidences', IMEC archives.
29. Author's interview with Alain Resnais, 4 February 1996.
30. *Le ravissement de la parole*, op. cit.

CHAPTER 11 Roots and Revolt

1. Author's interview with Madeleine Alleins, 18 September 1995.
2. *Le monde extérieur*, p. 106.
3. Author's interview with Louis-René des Forêts, 18 February 1995.
4. *Outside*, p. 119.
5. *Les yeux verts*, p. 18.
6. *La vie matérielle*, p. 82.
7. *Les lieux de Marguerite Duras*, op. cit., p. 85.
8. *La vie matérielle*, p. 82.
9. Author's interview with Dionys Mascolo, 18 January 1996.
10. Fonds Dionys Mascolo, IMEC archives.
11. *Libération*, 1 October 1985.
12. See *La guerre d'Algérie sous la IVᵉ République*.
13. IMEC archives.
14. IMEC archives.
15. IMEC archives.
16. IMEC archives.
17. *Le ravissement de la parole*, op. cit.
18. IMEC archives.
19. IMEC archives.
20. Author's interview with Alain Resnais, 6 December 1997.
21. *Les parleuses*, pp. 81–2.
22. Author's interview with Anatole Dauman, 4 April 1996. See also Anatole Dauman, *Souvenir écran*, Centre Georges Pompidou, 1996, pp. 105, 111, 117.

CHAPTER 12 In the Dark Room

1. IMEC archives.
2. Conversation with Jean-Louis Barrault, *Cahiers Renaud-Barrault*, No. 91, September 1996.
3. IMEC archives.
4. IMEC archives.
5. *Le ravissement de Lol V. Stein*, Gallimard, 1964, Folio, 1994, p. 48.
6. *Cahiers Renaud-Barrault*, December 1965, special issue reprinted in *Marguerite Duras* by Marguerite Duras, Jacques Lacan, Maurice Blanchot, Dionys Mascolo, Xavière Gauthier, Albatros, 1975.
7. *Arts*, 15–21 April 1964.
8. Quotation also found in *Duras, romans, cinémas, théâtre: un parcours 1943–1993*, Gallimard, Quarto, 1997.
9. Author's interview with Michel Mitrani, 10 September 1997.
10. IMEC archives.
11. 'Rencontre au théâtre', *Cahiers Renaud-Barrault*, No. 91, September 1996.
12. IMEC archives.
13. Quoted by Helen Garey Bishop in the *New York Times*, 17 October 1976.

14. IMEC archives.
15. *Réalités*, March 1963.
16. *Les Lettres nouvelles.*
17. *Ecrire*, pp. 35–51. She spoke on more than one occasion of her difficulties describing the universe of *The Vice-Consul.*
18. Marin Karmitz archives.
19. Marin Karmitz archives. And all subsequent quotations.
20. Author's interview with Marin Karmitz, 18–24 April 1996.
21. *Le ravissement de la parole*, op. cit.
22. Ibid.
23. IMEC archives.
24. IMEC archives.
25. Agreed prior to publication of script, *Théâtre I*, Gallimard, 1965.
26. Author's interview with Marguerite Duras, 18 March 1995.
27. *Les Cahiers du cinéma*, February 1967.
28. *Outside*, p. 254.
29. Author of *Repos du guerrier* (1958), *Petits enfants du siècle* (1961) and *Stances à Sophie* (1963), all published by Grasset.
30. Author's interview with Robert Hossein, 20 March 1996.
31. *Arts*, 27 July and 2 August 1966.
32. Author's interview with Paul Seban, 4 February 1996.
33. Author's interview with Robert Hossein, 11 March 1996.
34. Reprinted in *Outside*, p. 296.
35. *Les Nouvelles littéraires*, 9 December 1967.
36. Unpublished interview with Jeanne Moreau and Marguerite Duras by Jean Daniel, 17 September 1965, IMEC archives.
37. IMEC archives.
38. *Cinéma 66*, December 1966.
39. Henri Chapier, *Combat*, 28 November 1966.
40. In the interview published in the programme note distributed to the audience. IMEC archives.
41. François Novrissier, *Les Nouvelles littéraires*, 23 March 1967.
42. Foreword in the theatre programme. IMEC archives.
43. RTL, 7 May 1967, reprinted in *50 ans de Festival de Cannes*, Cahiers du cinéma, 1997.

CHAPTER 13 The Street and the Camera

1. Henri Chatelain archives.
2. Preparation for the Alain Vircondelet interviews, IMEC archives. See also *Duras*, Julliard, 1991, *Marguerite Duras*, Ecriture, 1994, *Pour Duras*, Calmann-Lévy, 1995, *Marguerite Duras*, Le Chêne, 1996.
3. Ibid.
4. *Le ravissement de la parole*, op. cit.
5. Author's interview with Alain Robbe-Grillet, 16 June 1996.

6. Ibid.
7. Gallimard archives.
8. *La quinzaine littéraire*, 16–30 June 1969.
9. Which she confirmed to Pascal Bonitzer, IMEC archives.
10. Author's interview with Michelle Porte, 21 May 1996.
11. Author's interview with Michael Lonsdale, 4 April 1996.
12. Film notes, IMEC archives.
13. Film notes, IMEC archives.
14. IMEC archives.
15. IMEC archives.
16. Author's interview with Marguerite Duras, 4 March 1995.
17. To Jean-Pierre Ceton, IMEC archives.
18. *Le ravissement de la parole*, op. cit.
19. Ibid. and IMEC archives.
20. Pierre Desproges's sketch 'Les Piles' was part of the show at the théâtre Grévin in October 1986: 'Hiroshima mon amour! There's a strange cry! said Marguerite Yourcenar about this title by Marguerite Duras. Marguerite Duras, so you've heard of her then? Marguerite Duras, the senile apologist of rural infanticide ... Marguerite Duras didn't just write bullshit ... She also filmed it ... A strange cry, indeed: Hiroshima mon amour – why not Auschwitz my pet!'
21. Preliminary interview for special issue of *Les Cahiers du cinéma*, *Les yeux verts*, IMEC archives.
22. Author's interview with Jean-Marc Turine, 16 May 1996.
23. *Les Cahiers du cinéma*, No. 501, April 1996.
24. *Les yeux verts*.
25. In a handwritten note found among the preliminary notes for the film *Jaune le soleil*, IMEC archives.
26. IMEC archives.
27. IMEC archives.
28. Author's interview with Dionys Mascolo, April 1996.
29. *Les parleuses*, pp. 72, 73, 75.
30. *Les Cahiers du cinéma*, No. 501, April 1996.
31. An expression she used in *Les lieux de Marguerite Duras*.
32. *Les Cahiers du cinéma*, No. 501, April 1996.
33. Ibid.
34. Commissioned by Peter Hall, director at the National Theatre, London.
35. *Cahiers Renaud-Barrault*, No. 91, September 1996.
36. *Les parleuses*, p. 171.
37. IMEC archives.
38. IMEC archives.
39. *Les Cahiers du cinéma*, No. 501, April 1996.
40. Unpublished interviews with Dominique Noguez, IMEC archives.
41. *Le ravissement de la parole*, op. cit.
42. Author's interview with Michael Lonsdale, 4 April 1996.
43. Dominique Noguez, *Les films de Marguerite Duras*, produced by the Ministry of Foreign Affairs.

44. *Outside*, p. 328.
45. Gallimard archives.
46. IMEC archives.
47. *Marguerite Duras*, Albatros, op. cit.

CHAPTER 14 The Duras Cult

1. *Les yeux verts*, p. 18.
2. Author's interview with Bruno Nuytten, 8 October 1996.
3. IMEC archives.
4. Author's interview with Marguerite Duras, 8 April 1994.
5. Author's interview with Bruno Nuytten, 8 October 1996.
6. IMEC archives.
7. Author's interview with Claude Régy, 8 October 1995.
8. IMEC archives.
9. *Les Cahiers du cinéma*, No. 501, April 1996.
10. Michelle Porte, *Le camion*, Minuit, 1977, p. 99.
11. D. Noguez, op. cit.
12. Ibid.
13. IMEC archives.
14. Cannes Film Festival, talk given by Marguerite Duras.
15. *La vie matérielle*, p. 23.
16. Ibid., p. 24.
17. IMEC archives.
18. *Le Quotidien de Paris*, 25 October 1977.
19. IMEC archives.
20. *Le Quotidien de Paris*, 25 October 1977.
21. General observations published at the end of *L'Eden Cinema*.
22. In an article published in *Le Monde*, 19 November 1992.
23. *Marguerite Duras à Montréal*, texts and interviews collected by Suzanne Lamy and André Roy, Quebec, Spirale, 1981.
24. Michèle Manceaux, *L'amie*, Albin Michel, 1996.

CHAPTER 15 Yann

1. *Les Parleuses*, p. 240.
2. Ibid., p. 239
3. *Les Nouvelles littéraires*, June 1990.
4. *La vie matérielle*, p. 25.
5. IMEC archives.
6. Author's interview with Henri Chatelain, 25 November 1996.
7. Author's interview with Jean-Pierre Ceton, 14 September 1996.
8. Author's interview with Henri Chatelain, 14 October 1996.

9. *Yann Andréa Steiner*, English version, translated by Barbara Bray, Hodder & Stoughton, 1993, p. 9.
10. Ibid., p. 12.
11. Ibid.
12. *L'été 80*, Minuit, 1980, p. 91.
13. IMEC archives.
14. IMEC archives.
15. To Jean-Pierre Ceton, programme for France Culture, shorthand notes, IMEC archives.
16. IMEC archives.
17. IMEC archives.
18. Unpublished shorthand interview. IMEC archives.
19. Ibid.
20. IMEC archives.
21. Author's interview with Marguerite Duras, 8 March 1995.
22. Author's interview with Luce Perrot, 6 June 1997.
23. *Le ravissement de la parole*, op. cit.
24. *Marguerite Duras à Montréal*, op. cit.
25. Interview with Jean-Jacques Fieschi, IMEC archives.
26. M. Manceaux, op. cit.
27. *L'homme atlantique*, Minuit, 1985, p. 31.
28. *Le monde extérieur*, p. 14.
29. 'A propos de l'Homme Atlantique' in the weekly *Des femmes*, March 1982.
30. Unpublished manuscript for *Ecrire*, IMEC archives.
31. She admitted to Marianne Alphant. *Le bon plaisir*, broadcast on France Culture in September 1984, reproduced in *Le ravissement de la parole*, op. cit. To Michèle Manceaux she said, 'We are tramps' (op. cit., p. 144).
32. Yann Andréa, *M.D.*, Minuit, 1983, pp. 9–13.
33. Author's interview with Marguerite Duras, 18 March 1995.
34. Author's interview with Michelle Porte, 4 November 1996.
35. Yann Andréa, op. cit., p. 118.
36. IMEC archives.
37. Manuscript of *La maladie de la mort*, IMEC archives.
38. M. Manceaux, op. cit., p. 149.
39. *Le Quotidien de Paris*, 30 September 1983.
40. Film by Michelle Porte.
41. M. Manceaux, op. cit., p. 126.
42. *Le monde extérieur*, p. 25.
43. *Libération*, 5 January 1983.
44. IMEC archives.

CHAPTER 16 The Lover

1. Interpretation reproduced and commented on by Alain Robbe-Grillet, interview with the author, 16 June 1996.

2. *The Lover*, p. 12.
3. Repeating theories expressed by Gilles Deleuze in *Logique du sens* (Minuit, 1969) in an interview published in *Caractères*, No. 7, a biannual magazine on literature funding in Lower Normandy (1996).
4. *Libération*, 4 September 1984.
5. Jacques-Pierre Amette in *Le Point*.
6. *Libération*, 13 November 1984.
7. Video edition produced by Jérôme Beaujour and Jean Mascolo, 13 December 1984, Ministry of External Affairs, directed by P. Gallet.
8. Marion Scali, *Libération*, 2 April 1985.
9. Michel Cournot, *Le Monde*.
10. IMEC archives.
11. *Le Monde*, 17 February 1985.
12. *Libération*, 20 May 1985, article in the section 'Déceptions atroces'.
13. His wife Monique remembers his indignation and distress at reading a text where his ex-wife was giving detailed descriptions of the evolution of his faeces. He and Marguerite had actually fallen out ten years before, one memorable evening in the Les Charpentiers restaurant. When Robert told Marguerite that her narcissism and perpetual self-glorification were becoming unbearable, Marguerite got up and left.
14. She told François Mitterrand that if she had waited this long to publish it was also because she had wanted to protect the Rabier-Delval child (*L'Autre Journal*, 26 February–4 March 1986).
15. To Marianne Alphant, *Libération*, 17 April 1985.
16. Author's interview with Paul Otchakovsky-Laurens, 16 June 1996.
17. *La Douleur*, p. 27.
18. 6 December 1985, Jacques Benet archives.
19. Author's interview with François Mitterrand, 8 April 1994.
20. *Les Cahiers du cinéma*, September 1996.
21. The text, from an interview produced by Danièle Blain, was used as the commentary for the film *Les enfants* when the French Film Theatre organized a Duras retrospective.
22. *Le Figaro*, 23 February 1985.
23. Michel Perez, *Le Matin*, 22 February 1985.
24. Gérard Lefort, *Libération*, 22 February 1985.
25. *Les Cahiers du cinéma*, September 1995.
26. Author's interview with François Mitterrand, 8 April 1994.
27. IMEC archives.
28. Author's interview with Michel Butel, 4 October 1996. The article was not published until February 1986, in the first issue of *L'Autre Journal*.
29. Author's interview with Paul Otchakovsky-Laurens, 18 December 1997.
30. *Libération*, 8 May 1986.
31. *Le ravissement de la parole*, op. cit.
32. IMEC archives.
33. *Le Figaro*, 11 February 1986.
34. *La vie matérielle*.

35. *Le bon plaisir,* France Culture, op. cit.
36. *Le ravissement de la parole.*
37. *Libération,* 13 October 1987.
38. TF1, July 1988.
39. IMEC archives.

CHAPTER 17 Eyes Wide Open to Nowhere

1. *Libération,* 11 January 1990.
2. *Le ravissement de la parole,* op. cit.
3. *L'Autre Journal,* No. 3, 12 March 1986.
4. *L'Evénement du jeudi,* 11–17 January 1990.
5. *Le Magazine littéraire,* June 1990.
6. *L'Evénement du jeudi,* 1–7 February 1990. Interview with Jean-Marcel Bourguereau.
7. *Globe,* July–August 1988.
8. *Outside,* pp. 345–6.
9. Author's interview with Jean-Jacques Annaud, 18 September 1995.
10. Author's interview with Claude Berri, 8 October 1996.
11. Author's interview with Jérôme Lindon, 8 June 1996.
12. Author's interview with Marguerite Duras, 8 April 1994.
13. Author's interview with Jérôme Lindon, 8 June 1996.
14. IMEC archives.
15. Author's interview with Marguerite Duras, 8 April 1994.
16. *Libération,* 13 June 1991, interview with Marianne Alphant.
17. Ibid.
18. Author's interview with Jean-Jacques Annaud, 18 September 1995. This was strongly denied by Outa, who claimed Marguerite never saw the film.
19. Play produced by Didier Bezace.
20. IMEC archives.
21. *Le Point,* 27 June 1992.
22. *Yann Andréa Steiner,* p. 57.
23. IMEC archives.
24. IMEC archives.
25. Note on the *Ecrire* manuscript, IMEC archives.
26. Picture, Caroline Champetier. Sound, Michel Vionnel.
27. See Frédérique Lebelley, op. cit.
28. Author's interview with Marguerite Duras, 8 April 1994.
29. In Mondadori, Petite Bibliothèque Oscar, 1995.

THE COMPLETE WORKS OF MARGUERITE DURAS

⌇

Les impudents, 1943, novel, Plon. Reprint, 1992, Gallimard.
La vie tranquille, 1944, novel, Gallimard.
Un barrage contre le Pacifique, 1950, novel, Gallimard.
Le marin de Gibraltar, 1952, novel, Gallimard.
Les petits chevaux de Tarquinia, 1953, novel, Gallimard.
Des journées entières dans les arbres, including 'Le boa', 'Madame Dodin', 'Les chantiers', 1954, short stories, Gallimard.
Le square, 1955, novel, Gallimard.
Moderato cantabile, 1958, novel, Editions de Minuit.
Les viaducs de la Seine-et-Oise, 1959, plays, Gallimard.
Dix heures et demie du soir en été, 1960, novel, Gallimard.
Hiroshima mon amour, 1960, film script and dialogue, Gallimard.
Une aussi longue absence, 1961, film script and dialogues in collaboration with Gérard Jarlot, Gallimard.
L'après-midi de Monsieur Andesmas, 1962, novella, Gallimard.
Le ravissement de Lol V. Stein, 1964, novel, Gallimard.
Théâtre I: Les eaux et les forêts, Le square, La musica, 1965, Gallimard.
Le vice-consul, 1965, Gallimard.
La musica, 1966, film, co-produced with Paul Seban, distr. Associated Artists.
L'amante anglaise, 1967, novel, Gallimard.
L'amante anglaise, 1968, play, Cahiers de Théâtre national populaire.
Théâtre II: Suzanna Andler, Des journées entières dans les arbres, Yes, Peut-être, Le Shaga, Un homme est venu me voir, 1968, Gallimard.
Détruire, dit-elle, 1969, Editions de Minuit.
Détruire, dit-elle, 1969, film, distr. Benoît-Jacob.
Abahn Sabana David, 1970, Gallimard.
L'amour, 1971, Gallimard.
Jaune le soleil, 1971, film, distr. Films Molière.
Nathalie Granger, 1972, film, distr. Films Molière.
India Song, 1973, novel, play, film, Gallimard.
La femme du Gange, 1973, film, distr. Benoît-Jacob.

Nathalie Granger and *La femme du Gange*, 1973, Gallimard.
Les parleuses, 1974, interviews with Xavière Gauthier, Editions de Minuit.
India song, 1975, film, distr. Films Armorial.
Baxter, Vera Baxter, 1976, film, distr. N.E.F. Diffusion.
Son nom de Venise dans Calcutta désert, 1976, film, distr. Benoît-Jacob.
Des journées entières dans les arbres, 1976, film, distr. Benoît-Jacob.
Le camion, 1977, film, distr. D.D. Prod.
Le camion and *Entretien avec Michelle Porte*, 1977, Editions de Minuit.
Les lieux de Marguerite Duras, 1977, in collaboration with Michelle Porte, Editions de Minuit.
L'Eden Cinéma, 1977, play, Mercure de France.
Le navire night, 1978, film, Films du Losange.
Le navire night, followed by 'Césarée, 'Les mains négatives', 'Aurélia Steiner', 'Aurélia Steiner', 'Aurélia Steiner', 1979, short stories, Mercure de France.
Césarée, 1979, film, Films du Losange.
Les mains négatives, 1979, film, Films du Losange.
Aurélia Steiner, dit Aurélia Melbourne, 1979, film, Film Paris-Audiovisuels.
Aurélia Steiner, dit Aurélia Vancouver, 1979, film, Films du Losange.
Vera Baxter ou les plages de l'Atlantique, 1980, Albatros.
L'homme assis dans le couloir, 1980, novella, Editions de Minuit.
L'été 80, 1980, Editions de Minuit.
Les yeux verts, 1980, Cahiers du Cinema.
Agatha, 1981, Editions de Minuit.
Agatha ou les lectures illimitées, 1981, film, prod. Berthemont.
Outside, 1981, essays, Albin Michel, reprint, P.O.L. 1984.
La jeune fille et l'enfant, 1981, cassette, Des femmes ed. Adapted from *L'été 80* by Yann Andréa, read by Marguerite Duras.
Dialoque de Rome, 1982, film, prod. Coop. Longa Gittata. Rome.
L'homme atlantique, 1981, film, prod. Berthemont.
L'homme atlantique, 1982, novella, Editions de Minuit.
Savannah Bay, 1st edn, 1982, 2nd edn extended version, 1983, Editions de Minuit.
La maladie de la mort, 1982, novella, Editions de Minuit.
Théâtre III: La bête dans la jungle after Henry James's 'The Beast in the Jungle', adapted by James Lord and Marguerite Duras; *Les papiers d'Aspern*, after Henry James's *The Aspern Papers*, adapted by Marguerite Duras and Robert Antelme; *La danse de mort*, after August Strindberg's *The Dance of Death*, adapted by Marguerite Duras, 1984, Gallimard.

L'amant, 1984, Editions de Minuit.
La douleur, 1985, P.O.L.
La musica deuxième, 1985, Gallimard.
La mouette de Tchekhov, 1985, Gallimard.
Les enfants, with Jean Mascolo and Jean-Marc Turine, 1985, film.
Yeux bleus cheveux noirs, 1986, novel, Editions de Minuit.
La pute de la côte normande, 1986, Editions de Minuit.
La vie matérielle, 1987, P.O.L.
Emily L., 1987, novel, Editions de Minuit.
La pluie d'été, 1990, novel, P.O.L.
L'amant de la Chine du nord, 1991, novel, Gallimard.
Yann Andréa Steiner, 1992, novel, P.O.L.
Ecrire, 1993, Gallimard.
C'est tout, 1995, P.O.L.
Romans, Cinéma, Théâtre, Un parcours 1943–1993. 1997, Gallimard, Quarto series.

WORK IN ENGLISH TRANSLATION

L'amant du Chine du nord/The North China Lover, HarperCollins, London, 1994; New Press, New York, 1992.
L'amante anglaise/L'Amante Anglaise, Hamish Hamilton, London, 1968; Grove, New York, 1968; Pantheon, New York, 1987.
La musica, Suzanna Andler, L'amante anglaise/La Musica, Suzanna Andler, L'Amante Anglaise, Calder, London, 1975.
L'apres-midi de Monsieur Andesmas, Le square, Dix heures et demie du soir en été, Moderato Cantabile/Four Novels, Grove Press, New York, 1990.
L'après-midi de Monsieur Andesmas, Les eaux et forêts/The Afternoon of Mr Andesmas, The Rivers and the Forests, Calder, London, 1964.
Un barrage contre le Pacifique/The Sea Wall, Farrar, Strauss & Giroux, New York, 1967, 1985; Perennial Library, New York, 1986.
Un barrage contre le Pacifique/A Sea of Troubles, Methuen, London, 1953; Penguin, London, 1969; Faber, 1986.
L'apres-midi de Monsieur Andesmas, Le square, Dix heures et demie du soir en été/A Marguerite Duras Trilogy: The Afternoon of Mr Andesmas, The Square, Ten-Thirty on a Summer Night, Calder, London, 1977.
Des journées entières dans les arbres, Whole Days in the Trees and other stories, Calder, London, 1984.

La musica deuxième, L'Eden Cinéma, Savannah Bay, India Song/Four Plays: La Musica, Eden Cinema, Savannah Bay, India Song, Oberon, 1992.

Le square, Des journées entières dans les arbres, Les viaducs de Seine-et-Oise/Three Plays, Calder, London.

Dix heures et demie du soir en été/Ten-Thirty on a Summer Night, Calder, London, 1962; Grove Press, New York, 1963.

Hiroshima mon amour, Une aussi longue absence/Hiroshima mon amour, Une aussi longue absence, Calder, 1966.

Hiroshima mon amour/Hiroshima mon amour, Grove Press, New York, 1961.

India song/India Song, Grove Press, New York, 1976.

Le marin de Gibraltar/The Sailor from Gibraltar, Calder, London, 1966; Grove Press, New York, 1967; Pantheon, New York, 1986.

La musica in *Traverse Plays* (8 plays, one of which *La Musica*), Penguin, UK, 1966.

Les petits chevaux de Tarquinia/The Little Horses of Tarquinia, Calder, London, 1960, 1980.

Le Ravissement de Lol V. Stein/The Rapture of Lol V. Stein, Hamish Hamilton, London, 1967.

Le Ravissement de Lol V. Stein/The Ravishing of Lol V. Stein, Grove Press, New York, 1964, 1979; Pantheon, New York, 1986.

Le square/The Square, Calder, London, 1959, 1965; Grove Press, New York, 1959.

Le vice-consul/The Vice-Consul, Hamish Hamilton, London, 1968; Flamingo, London, 1990; Pantheon, New York, 1987.

La douleur/La Douleur, Flamingo, 1987.

ACKNOWLEDGEMENTS

~

My warmest thanks to Monique Antelme, Dionys Mascolo, Jean Mascolo and Edgar Morin, without whose help and support this book would not have been possible.

This study is the product of many interviews undertaken over a number of years. All those who agreed to be interviewed went back in time in order to impart their memories. I should like to thank each and every one of them for their patience and generosity.

Madeleine Alleins, Yann Andréa, Jean-Jacques Annaud, Denise Auge, Nicole Bauchard, Georges Beauchamp, Jérôme Beaujour, Jacques Benet, Pierre Benichou, Max Bergier, Claude Berri, Maurice Blanchot, Nicole Bouchard, France Brunel, Michel Butel, Jean-Pierre Ceton, Henri Chatelain, Henri Colpi, Michel Cournot, Pierre Daix, Jean Daniel, Anatole Dauman, Paulette Delval, Louis-René des Forêts, Dominique Desanti, Geneviève Dufour, Roland Dumas, Dominique Fernandez, Robert Gallimard, Xavière Gauthier, Marcel Haedrich, Robert Hossein, Jean-Louis Jacquet, Benoît Jacquot, Eva Jarlot, Marin Karmitz, Odette Laigle, Claude Lanzmann, Antoine Lefebure, Bernard le Guillochon, Jérôme Lindon, Michael Lonsdale, James Lord, Michel Mitrani, François Mitterrand, Patrick Modiano, Jeanne Moreau, Jean Munier, Maurice Nadeau, Violette Naville, Bruno Nuytten, Bulle Ogier, Paul Otchakovsky-Laurens, Robert Pansand-Besson, Pierre Péan, Luce Perrot, Michel Piccoli, Michelle Porte, France Queyrel, Claude Régy, Alain Reynais, Alain Robbe-Grillet, Jacques-Francis Rolland, Claude Roy, Paul Seban, Jorge Semprun, Jacques Tronel, Jean-Marc Turine, Yvette.

Lily Phan and Alban Cerisier from Gallimard archives were ever patient and considerate all the time I was carrying out my research.

Albert Dichy, Olivier Corpet and François Laurent from the Institut de la Mémoire de l'édition contemporaine (IMEC) were always pleasant and helpful when it came to helping me understand the Marguerite Duras collection.

Without Jean Mascolo's confidence in me, I should not have been granted access to the archives.

The friendly assistance of the editors Isabelle Gallimard, Teresa Cremisi and Georges Liébert proved invaluable when it came to the publication stage.

Alain Veinstein, Anne-Julie Bémont and Christine Lhérault for being there and for all their help and encouragement along the way.

INDEX

≈

414

417

Mangano, Silvano 216, 218
Mann, Thomas 385
Mannoni, Eugéne 173, 174
Marcelle (class-mate of MD's) 52
Marianne, André 136
Marie-France 317
Marin, Robert 154, 273
Marivaux, Pierre de 305
Marker, Chris 218
Marmande 14, 15, 20, 21
Marseille 20, 21, 26, 28, 31, 38, 67, 74
Martin, Claude 201
Marx, Karl 154, 158, 161
Marxism 160, 162, 274, 309
Marxist Study Group *see* Groupe d'études marxistes
Mascolo, Dionys 120–1, 123, 164, 170, 201, 233, 235
on MD's marriage to Robert 86; Queneau becomes a mentor 97; love at first sight for MD 103; appearance 103; takes Gratien as a pseudonym 108; joins the Resistance 109; meets Mitterrand 111; friendship with Robert 112, 147, 166; MD wants a child by him 113–14, 149; risk-taking 114; edits *Libres* 128; military operations 129–30; arrests Delval 131; liaison and child with Paulette Delval 135–6, 156, 164, 199; Robert brought out of Dachau 142–3; and MD's communism 157–8; and the Groupe d'études marxistes 161; expelled from the PCF 173; unfaithfulness accusations 184; employment at Gallimard 193; co-founds *Le 14 Juillet* 211; and the popular revolt 273, 274; in MD's films 284, 286, 296; last sees MD 386
Mascolo, Jean ('Outa'; MD's son) 285, 289, 291, 306, 343, 370
birth (30 June 1947) 166–7, 191; childhood 168, 171, 172, 174, 182, 183, 195; MD's love for 199; education 203; love of the cinema 264; contributes to MD's films 284, 286, 356, 357; *Duras filme* (with Beaujour) 332
Mascolo, Mme 162–3
Mascolo, Solange (née Leprince) 272, 287, 299
Matin, Le 357
Matta 212–13
Mauriac, François 197
Maurras, Charles 138
Mekong River 9, 18, 39, 58
Mercouri, Melina 240, 268
Mercure de France 318
Merleau-Ponty, Maurice 155, 158, 161, 184
Mery, Jacques: *Laissez passer mon peuple* 153
Messageries Maritimes 17, 74
Meunier, Jean 314, 318
Mézin 14
Michaux, Henri 271
Un certain Plume 271
Michelet, Jules 158
Milan 173
Miller, Henry 161

Ministry of Defence 83, 92
Ministry of Information 101, 120
Ministry of the Interior 91–2, 101
Ministry of Justice 153–4
Ministry of prisoners 129
Miou-Miou 351
Mirande, Pyrenees 88
Mitrani, Michel 204, 229, 242, 243
Mitterrand, François 80, 122, 130, 167, 192, 296, 349, 374
on military service 82–3, 87; former Vichy connections 109, 114; organizes a Resistance movement 109; meets Beauchamp 109; commits first act of public resistance 110; a leader of ex-POWs 111; MD and Mascolo meet 111; leaves for London, then Algiers 115–16; reputation for being late 117–18; warns MD 119; feels responsible for Robert's arrest 120; asks MD to leave the Resistance 121; Dionys warns 124; and *Libres* 128, 153; interrogates Delval 131–2; and Robert's return from Dachau 141, 142, 144, 145; criticizes Camus 151; and Algeria 198; MD on 333, 352; elected president 333; delegation to the USA 333, 334; and *La Douleur* 354; and the Villemin affair 360; *L'Autre Journal* interviews 361–2, 382
MNPGD *see* Mouvement National des Prisonniers de Guerre et Déportés (MNPGD; National Movement for Prisoners of War and Deportees
Moby Dick (Melville) 271
Moderato Cantabile (film) 211, 219, 226
Molière 66, 95
Monde, Le 352, 381
Mondor, Henri 347
Monteton 30
Montherlant, Henry de 138
Montivier, Monique 278
Montparnasse, Paris 75, 81, 108
Montreal 332
Moravia, Alberto 235
Moreau, Jeanne 238, 242, 255, 268, 287, 288
Morin, Edgar 115, 129, 130, 131, 152, 153, 155, 161–4, 170, 171, 173, 178–9, 197, 199, 212, 296
Autocritique 150, 161
Morin, Violette 162, 163
Moukhine, Tatiana 248, 356
Moulin-Rouge, Paris 217
Mouvement National des Prisonniers de Guerre et Déportés (MNPGD; National Movement for Prisoners of War and Deportees) 114–15, 117, 121, 124–5, 129, 130–1, 135, 136, 141, 142, 145, 153
Munich agreement 83
Munier, Jean (alias Rodin) 115, 117, 118, 119, 121, 122–3, 128
Museum of Man, Paris 94
Musica, La (film) 264–7, 351